THE LEGACY OF SHINGWAUKONSE
A Century of Native Leadership

This book examines the careers of the Ojibwa chief Shingwaukonse, also known as Little Pine, and of two of his sons, Ogista and Buhkwujjenene, at Garden River near Sault Ste Marie. Theirs was a period in which the Great Lakes Ojibwa faced formidable challenges from entrepreneurs, missionaries, and bureaucrats, as well as from new policies set by the Canadian state. Shingwaukonse sought to establish links with the new government agencies, to preserve an environment in which Native cultural values and organizational structures could survive, and to devise strategies to enable the formation of band governments capable of assuming a degree of proprietorship over the resources on Native land.

Using an impressive array of evidence from a huge range of government, church, manuscript, and oral sources, Chute reconstructs a period of energetic and sometimes effective Aboriginal resistance to pressures visited on the community. She demonstrates that Shingwaukonse and his sons were vigilant in their attempts to maximize the autonomy and security of the Garden River Ojibwa even while many other parties insisted on their assimilation.

The Legacy of Shingwaukonse contributes greatly to anthropological debates about Ojibwa leadership and to a historical understanding of the relationship between Native people and newcomers throughout the nineteenth century.

JANET E. CHUTE, PhD, has taught Native studies, anthropology, and sociology at Dalhousie University and has been involved in numerous Aboriginal claims cases. Since 1996 she has been a research associate with Dalhousie's School of Resource and Environmental Studies.

D1604317

THE LEGACY OF
SHINGWAUKONSE

A Century of Native Leadership

Janet E. Chute

UNIVERSITY OF TORONTO PRESS
Toronto Buffalo London

© University of Toronto Press Incorporated 1998
Toronto Buffalo London

Printed in Canada

ISBN 0–8020–4273–2 (cloth)
ISBN 0–8020–8108–8 (paper)

Printed on acid-free paper

Canadian Cataloguing in Publication Data

Chute, Janet Elizabeth
The legacy of Shingwaukonse : a century of native leadership

Includes bibliographical references and index.
ISBN 0-8020-4273-2 (bound)   ISBN 0-8020-8108-8 (pbk.)

1. Shingwaukonse, 1773–1854.   2. Ojibwa Indians – Politics and
government.   3. Ojibwa Indians – Government relations.   4. Ojibwa
Indians – Social life and customs.   5. Indian leadership – Canada – History.
6. Ojibwa Indians – Biography.   I. Title.

E99.C6C48 1998   971′.004973′00922   C97-932778-4

Frontispiece: Shingwaukonse used this *dodem*, the Plover, on one of his petitions
from the 1840s.

This book has been published with the help of a grant from the Humanities
and Social Sciences Federation of Canada, using funds provided by the Social
Sciences and Humanities Research Council of Canada.

University of Toronto Press acknowledges the financial assistance to its publishing program of the Canada Council for the Arts and the Ontario Arts Council.

Dedicated to my father, Walter John Chute,
a chemist who loved history

The Great Spirit in his beneficence, foreseeing that this time would come when the subsistence which the forests and lakes afforded would fail, placed these mines in our lands, so that the coming generation ... might find thereby the means of subsistence. Assist us, then, to reap that benefit intended for us ... Enable us to do this, and our hearts will be great within, for we will feel that we are again a nation.

Shingwaukonse, or Little Pine

And before him shall be gathered all nations: And he shall separate them one from another ... Then shall the King say unto them on his right hand, Come, ye blessed of my Father, inherit the kingdom prepared for you from the foundation of the world.

Matthew 25: 32, 34

Contents

Preface

In 1980, Edward S. Rogers of the Ethnology Department of the Royal Ontario Museum and the Anthropology Department of McMaster University mentioned to me that the Council of the Garden River First Nation, an Ojibwa community near Sault Ste Marie, Ontario, was looking for a graduate student to write about one of their most noted chiefs, Shingwaukonse, or Little Pine. Would I consider the offer? Of course! I leapt at the chance. How often does a doctoral student receive an *invitation* to acquire data on a subject in which she has had an interest for many years? It seemed like a dream come true.

After having my project proposal approved by the Garden River Band Council, I began fieldwork in the summer of 1982 under the combined supervision of my doctoral supervisor, David Damas, of the Anthropology Department of McMaster University, and Edward Rogers. To both men I owe an enormous debt of gratitude. David Damas proved an organized and inspiring mentor, while Ed Rogers always remained thought-provoking and extremely fair. I am also grateful to Ed's' wife, Mary Black-Rogers, whose insightful analyses of power relations in Ojibwa society provided the key to my understanding of the nature of the reciprocal ties between Little Pine and his followers.

The kindnesses I experienced while interviewing residents of the Garden River and Batchewana* communities left an indelible impression on my mind, and testify to the pride which Little Pine's legacy evoked in those who shared their memories of this remarkable man. In particular, I want to thank Ronald Boissoneau, who was chief in 1982, George Agawa,

---

* 'Batchawana' is the present-day spelling, but during the period covered by this study the spelling was 'Batchewana.' The earlier spelling has been used throughout the text.

Charles Andrews, John Biron, Irene Boissoneau, Joseph Boissoneau, Sr, Angeline Clark, Betty Graubarger, Ernest Jones, Norman Jones, Eva Kabaosa, 'Abe' Lesage, Oliver Lesage, Lawrence McCoy, Daniel Erskine Pine, Sr, Mark Erskine Pine, Richard Pine, Sr, Jackie Rickard, Bertha Sayers, and Jerome Syrette, all of whom helped to make my repeated visits to Garden River memorable ones. Ex-councillor Frederick Erskine Pine, Sr, a man then in his eighties whose energy and enthusiasm often shamed many a much younger person – including myself – joined wholeheartedly in the research and travelled with me in 1983 to L'Anse in Michigan to collect historical material.

Of the numerous other individuals who over the years have shared insights and ideas, Harvey Feit, John Webster Grant, Stanley Heaps, Donald Jackson, the Reverend Alan Knight, Donald Macleod, David McNab, David Nock, Richard Preston, Richard Slobodin, Donald B. Smith, and James G.E. Smith come immediately to mind. I also owe thanks to the staff of St Peter's Cathedral Archives, Marquette, Michigan, and to Mrs Elizabeth Nock, for making the materials in the Anglican Heritage Collection available for perusal, and for hospitality which made the Anglican Bishop of Algoma's residence at Bishophurst, Sault Ste Marie, a home away from home.

The Reverend Frank Coyle, Father Frank Lynch, SJ, and Father Joseph Lawless, SJ, shared experiences drawn from their long associations with the Garden River community. Sister Irene Howell and the Reverend John Henry similarly enlivened the history of the Assinins and Zeba missions in Michigan with their personal reminiscences.

Special thanks are owing to Laurie Connon of Hamilton, for her friendship while I was a graduate student at McMaster University, and to my parents, Walter John Chute and Betty Chute, for their loving concern.

Fieldwork for this study was funded from special grants from McMaster University, the Canadian Ethnology Service of the National Museum of Canada – the predecessor of the Museum of Civilization – and the Wenner-Gren Foundation, New York. Postdoctoral grants from the Social Sciences and Humanities Research Council of Canada assisted in the final stages of preparation.

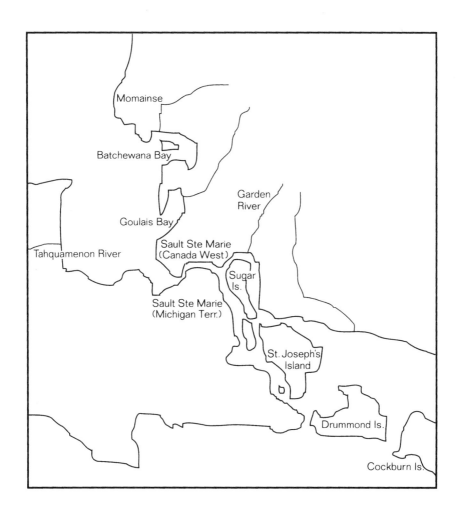

MAP A   Map of Sault area, including Garden River

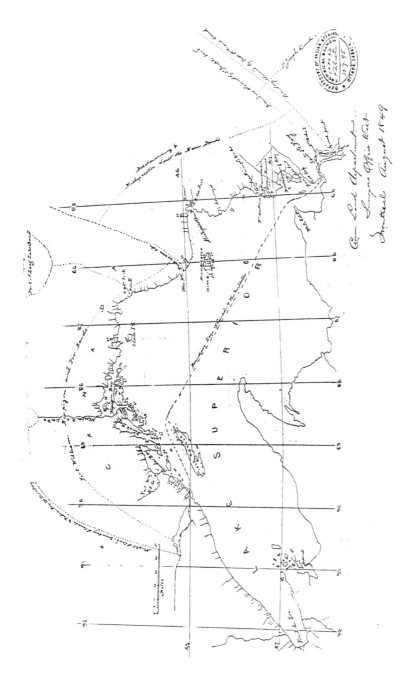

MAP B   Vidal and Anderson's map of band hunting ranges of Lake Superior, 1849.

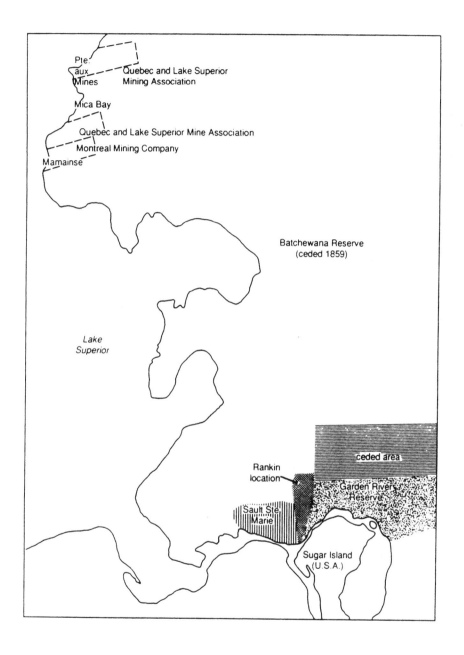

Within the image (labels):

Pte. aux Mines

Quebec and Lake Superior
Mining Association

Mica Bay

Quebec and Lake Superior Mine Association

Montreal Mining Company

Mamainse

Batchewana Reserve
(ceded 1859)

Lake
Superior

Rankin
location

ceded area

Garden River
Reserve

Sault Ste.
Marie

Sugar Island
(U.S.A.)

MAP C   Map showing Garden River and mining locations in the vicinity of Mica Bay

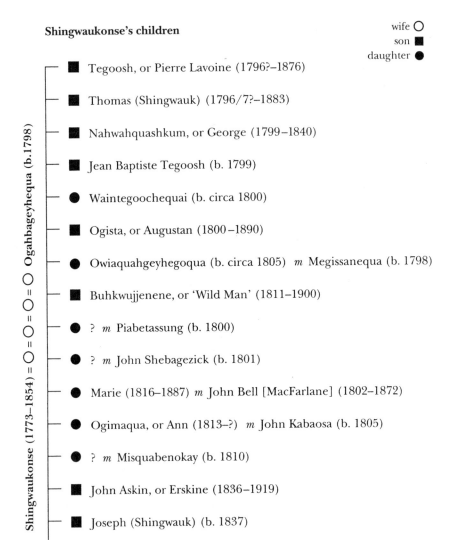

Shingwaukonse's children

wife ○
son ■
daughter ●

Shingwaukonse (1773–1854) = ○ = ○ = ○ = ○ Ogahbageyhequa (b.1798)

Ogahbageyhequa (b.1798)

■ Tegoosh, or Pierre Lavoine (1796?–1876)

■ Thomas (Shingwauk) (1796/7?–1883)

■ Nahwahquashkum, or George (1799–1840)

■ Jean Baptiste Tegoosh (b. 1799)

● Waintegoochequai (b. circa 1800)

■ Ogista, or Augustan (1800–1890)

● Owiaquahgeyhegoqua (b. circa 1805) *m* Megissanequa (b. 1798)

■ Buhkwujjenene, or 'Wild Man' (1811–1900)

● ? *m* Piabetassung (b. 1800)

● ? *m* John Shebagezick (b. 1801)

● Marie (1816–1887) *m* John Bell [MacFarlane] (1802–1872)

● Ogimaqua, or Ann (1813–?) *m* John Kabaosa (b. 1805)

● ? *m* Misquabenokay (b. 1810)

■ John Askin, or Erskine (1836–1919)

■ Joseph (Shingwauk) (b. 1837)

■ George Menissino (Pine) (1838–1923)

■ Louis (Shingwauk) (1839–1899)

THE LEGACY OF SHINGWAUKONSE

Introduction

The speeches of Shingwaukonse, or Little Pine, furnish some of the most explicit testimonials to the principle of Native rights to be expressed in the United Canadas during the nineteenth century. Little Pine's ideas and actions exerted a profound influence on the future course of Indian policy in Canada. This chief defined three major goals for Ojibwa peoples: first, to establish linkages with the government agencies that were just beginning to exercise jurisdiction in the Upper Great Lakes region; second, to preserve an environment in which Native cultural values and organizational structures could survive; and finally, to devise new strategies that would promote the formation of band governments capable of assuming a degree of proprietorship over resources on First Nations lands.

Little Pine rooted his proposals in historical precedents familiar to him. As early as 1760, British colonial administrators had formally recognized the existence of Native territorial prerogatives in the vicinity of Sault Ste Marie. By this time, head chiefs had assumed complex roles as policy makers and political negotiators. Many were wealthy, in terms of their potential to accumulate material assets, and during the War of 1812 gained additional prestige by acting as allies of the British Crown.

The years following the close of the war constitute a significant era for the study of traditional modes of Ojibwa decision making, since the Native peoples of the Upper Great Lakes region still lay beyond the westward thrust of agricultural settlement and industrialized resource development. Despite the uncertainties caused by the decline of the fur trade, bands could maintain a degree of economic autonomy by continuing an uninterrupted round of seasonal activities such as hunting and fishing, limited horticulture, berry gathering, and maple sugar production. Yet times were changing, and certain Ojibwa leaders, among them Little Pine, sought to devise strategies for preserving what to them had become a cherished way of life.

Little Pine was an engaging character. Noted for his fighting ability during the War of 1812 as well as for his forceful oratory, he was more than sixty years old when he reached his political prime. Born in 1773, he did not emerge as a head chief until the mid-1830s, and his career as a prominent political negotiator spanned another twenty years. After 1836, he and his followers settled permanently at Kitigaun Seebee, or Garden River, in what was then Canada West. His community remained relatively unaffected by the events that transformed the fur trade and mission station at Sault Ste Marie, ten kilometres to the west, into a bustling industrial centre; however, the influence of Little Pine's ideas and policies, coupled with this semi-isolation, facilitated the growth of a strong sense of group identity at Garden River.

Leaders identified themselves by *dodem*, an Ojibwa word denoting an individual's personal designating mark and usually rendered as 'totem' in the English language. Totemic symbols, derived from the natural world, acquired meaning in the colonial transactional forum from a syncretistic blend of indigenous religious and European heraldic symbolism. Head chiefs exercised regulatory and protective jurisdiction over lands flanking the water routes into the interior and used as hunting and fishing grounds. With the growth of territorialism, fostered by the availability of firearms and more efficient technology for local resource exploitation, it became essential for the chiefs to establish a balance of power in the Upper Great Lakes area. Elaborate systems of alliance and exchange developed. Bands, integrated internally, as well as allied laterally over time with neighbouring groups by marriage and *dodemic* affiliation, developed into significant political entities under the influence of indirect colonialism and the fur trade.

When the era of intercolonial rivalries drew to a close, and conceptions of laissez-faire liberalism bred new commercial policies, the old transactional system collapsed. The War of 1812 temporarily revived the Native people's value to the British as military allies, and somewhat delayed the erosion of colonial institutions and their concomitant relational practices on the frontier. Many western Ojibwa leaders, foreseeing the major threat to their independence inherent in the historical process, briefly supported a movement which encouraged violent resistance to the encroaching powers, and then subsequently adopted an attitude of passive defiance towards both British and American authority.

Little Pine, by contrast, listened attentively to views on Native rights and the potential role of Aboriginal peoples within the developing nation state, as expressed by the independent traders, officials, and missionaries whom he encountered on his widespread travels throughout Michigan and the Canadas. After much careful thought and preparation, in 1846 he devised a plan which he believed might grant the Ojibwa a measure of control over their future in a rapidly changing world. His efforts were frustrated, however, when, during negotiations over Native rights to minerals north of Lake Superior in 1849, Alexander Vidal, a young and inexperienced Indian commissioner, drew on vague American precedents to relegate Aboriginal peoples to the status of mere occupiers of lands. Resource developers quickly exploited this concept to suit their own purposes: on the basis of the young commissioner's proposals, the government henceforth denied the Native population rights to resources other than fur.

This position on Native status, although ultimately legally encoded, was riddled with ambiguities. The anomalies and contradictions were attacked by Ojibwa leaders intent on breaking legal barriers and establishing Native rights over land and resources. Determined to succeed, Little Pine's successors made some headway and, despite government policy, won the respect of local missionaries, merchants, and government agents, several of whom actively supported Native goals. Their careers are relatively easy to trace. Extensive documentation exists in both Canadian and American archives on the activities of four of Little Pine's sons: Ogista, or 'Augustan' (1800–90); Buhkwujjenene, or 'Wild Man' (1811–1900); John Askin (1836–1919); and George Menissino (1838–1923).

In addressing the subject of Ojibwa leadership from the theoretical standpoint, this study employs information derived from an ethnohistorical analysis of Little Pine's career to assess the prevailing view that self- interested action came to characterize leadership among south-western Ojibwa bands by the mid-nineteenth century. It is argued, however, that this position is appropriate mainly to western groups defiantly resisting U.S. Indian policy, which many had come to regard as hostile and authoritarian.

By contrast, Ojibwa head chiefs in the north-eastern sector of the Upper Great Lakes region actively sought creative policies which might enable bands to preserve the reciprocity of interest and intention that traditionally characterized relations between leader and group. From this viewpoint, self-interested action may be seen as a temporary anomaly, fostered by stressful circumstances. To support this proposition, the present study examines the nature of the checks and balances which were in

place and which rendered Ojibwa leadership accountable to group interests. The investigations of Mary Black-Rogers demonstrate that Ojibwa
views on power and power relationships differ substantially from modern
western conceptions of competitive self-interest. Little Pine had some
leeway to structure, according to Ojibwa values, the domains of power in
which he acted; yet he also operated in a frontier setting that was subject
to external processes and agencies and shot through with indeterminacy.
Black-Rogers's findings, thus, provide a convenient point of departure for
investigating Little Pine's leadership career, and the political, social, and
economic developments which were a legacy of this chief's actions and
policies.

Oral traditions constituted a major source for this study. During the
initial stages of my fieldwork, a number of those I interviewed were reti-
cent and, seemingly, suspicious both of me as an investigator and of the
project. While reticence has been identified as a characteristic of the
north-eastern Algonquian personality structure, I withheld judgment and
continued my efforts. I received a clue to the wariness I was encountering
from Dan Pine, Sr, Shingwaukonse's grandson, during a conversation in
August 1982. According to Dan, the affection one individual holds for
another, or for the group, makes that relation vulnerable to interference
from undesirable external influences. Ties of special significance are thus
often kept secret from outsiders, or else so great a field of ambiguity is
maintained about the relationship that the true nature of the tie is never
made known to the outsider.

To the Ojibwa, relationships are not static but evolve and change. Circumstances also strongly affect relationships. On my travels around Lakes
Huron, Michigan, and Superior, I had many opportunities for observing
meetings between elders of different bands. In the traditional forum the
aim of each elder is often to determine the extent of the other's 'power,'
while at the same time weighing his or her own and deciding how best to
influence the outcome. These meetings frequently take place in partial
isolation from other family members. Much information is non-verbal in
nature: careful hand and eye movements and a generally poised and dignified demeanour characterize such exchanges. While travelling with me
in 1982, Fred Pine, Sr, Shingwaukonse's great-grandson, noted that such
unspoken messages constituted the Ojibwa's main way, in the absence
of other protections, of preserving what they most value. 'Ants,' he
explained, 'run carrying their eggs from one hole to another when danger comes. That's like us. We go back and forth so you never see what or
where it is.' What surprised me was the degree to which the Ojibwa have

internalized this trait. It constitutes a cultural strategy, handed down from generation to generation. Leaders, in particular, are judged for their competence in using such indirect communication in transactions with others.

Chapter 1 looks at theoretical considerations concerning the Ojibwa belief system and sets the stage for an examination of Little Pine's later activities. It also provides an analysis of social and cultural changes among the Ojibwa during the late eighteenth and early nineteenth centuries. Shingwaukonse passed through three distinct phases in his career as a head chief, each of which is dealt with in a separate chapter (chapters 2, 3, and 4). During the first phase, from 1827 to 1845, the chief concentrated on appealing for government and missionary aid for a projected Native settlement. When such assistance failed to materialize, he briefly divested himself of leadership status. The beginning of mineral exploration north of Lakes Huron and Superior meanwhile increased government interest in Native issues, but for far different reasons from those operating during the period of intercolonial rivalries.

In 1846, drawing on a syncretistic blend of Native and Christian beliefs, traditional Ojibwa prerogatives, and western legal principles, Little Pine began a movement to found a homeland for U.S. Ojibwa bands threatened by Washington's intention to move them west of the Mississippi River. His bid for Native control of mineral and timber resources, although peaceful and accommodational in intent, aroused government resistance, and in 1849 Aboriginal peoples were divested of specific resource rights. Chapters 5 through 8 investigate his successors' struggle to regain some measure of self-determination over affairs within their communities, in keeping with Little Pine's original goals.

Finally, chapter 9 raises the question whether Little Pine acted according to a consistent plan, or merely reacted to a series of crises. This study holds that the chief acted in accordance with a scheme which embodied specific values and goals. In so doing he exhibited a degree of power-control which his sons, given a rapidly changing social, economic, and political milieu, had difficulty in emulating. His descendants nevertheless continued to exhibit a special sense of purpose derived from Little Pine's vision, the development of which underlay and shaped their actions and provided a rallying point for other groups.

Chapter One

Little Pine: Man, Leader, and Legend

A Shrewd and Politic Chief

In August 1822, Henry Rowe Schoolcraft, Indian agent at Sault Ste Marie, Michigan, received an unexpected office visit from Shingwaukonse, a person 'of some consequence among the Indians.' His caller stood just under six feet tall, sported a tuft of beard on his chin, wore a hat, and displayed other traits in his dress and gear which 'smacked of civilization.' Appraising his visitor patronizingly at first, Schoolcraft quickly reversed this attitude on the basis of the man's impressive demeanour and keen powers of observation and analysis. Presenting a 'shrewd and grave countenance,' Little Pine broached the subject of American motives in erecting and garrisoning Fort Brady so near the straits of the St Mary's River, making the agent wonder if his visitor was seeking information about the possibility of a distribution of presents to the Ojibwa later in the season. Schoolcraft prevented his suspicions from guiding his conduct, however. He knew that Little Pine was influential as 'a counsellor, a war chief, and an orator or speaker,' a *djiskui*, or practitioner of the shaking-tent rite, and a member of two important Great Lakes medicine societies, the *Midéwiwin* and the *Wabano*.[1] In the interests of political expediency, the agent avoided any remark which might be construed as an insult from a representative of Washington's Indian Department and welcomed his guest cordially.[2]

Schoolcraft had been encountering difficulties in persuading the Great Lakes bands to support his attempts at intertribal peacemaking; yet he shrewdly surmised that, although British influence was a problem, it was not the main cause of Ojibwa defiance. Rather, he believed the Aboriginal people themselves were taking a unified political stand against radical social, economic, and religious changes that were threatening their way of life. Instead of responding positively to U.S. attempts to check their wars, the western Ojibwa had intensified hostilities against the Dakota, their traditional enemies, by making warfare a route to interband solidarity. Furthermore, they upbraided Ojibwa outside the arena of war for their lack of courage in not adopting a similar course. While Schoolcraft argued for segregation of the Aboriginal population and the white settlers on the Upper Great Lakes frontier, he feared that a massive gathering of discontented and war-prone nations might result in a major uprising. For this reason he would later in his career strongly oppose Washington's proposal to transport all the Ojibwa to lands west of the Mississippi.

The agent offered few solutions for the problems he identified, apart from advising the American government to secure as much Native land as possible and to guard against the formation of unruly band aggregations. His perspectives on Indian policy cannot be considered apart from his ideology in general. He placed chiefs he met into two broad categories: those he favoured, he felt would welcome state intervention in their people's affairs; those he distrusted, he saw as potentially disruptive to Native–government relations. Yet Schoolcraft also found certain leaders more difficult to understand – and thus to classify – than others. These chiefs could be haughty and were, the agent believed, primarily self-interested. Some, like Little Pine, seemed to demonstrate a Machiavellian flair for political diplomacy which won Schoolcraft's grudging respect. Each time this particular Ojibwa leader made an appearance, the agent attempted to obtain his help in keeping order. When he failed to do so, he was thankful for his proximity to the garrison at the rapids, since he knew his own personal control over the western tribes was minimal. In the meantime, by manipulating a few material and symbolic inducements – medals, flags, and sundry small presents, such as shells and metal ornaments – he maintained a tenuous hold over chiefs such as Shingwaukonse, whom he hoped wielded a measure of influence over the essentially independent activities of the indigenous population.[3]

Shingwaukonse and the Cranes

The agent's next line of action was to analyse and eventually try to control leadership succession among the Ojibwa residing closest to his agency. Once he felt he had mastered some basic guidelines, he appointed chiefs with alacrity, despite Ojibwa protests, and demoted oth-

ers if they met with his disapproval. From talking to fur-trading families at
Sault Ste Marie, and through his observation of Native council meetings,
he understood that most of the chiefs traced their genealogy from an api-
cal ancestor, Gitcheojeedebun, or Great Crane, who had been the Sault
head chief at the time of the British Conquest.[4] All of Great Crane's
descendants in the male line identified themselves by the mark, or
dodem,[5] of the Crane. The *dodem* acted as a device for delimiting the
parameters of an exogamous – or out-marrying – unit, and for laterally
extending the range of kin obligations to non-kin. Those who possessed
the same *dodem* treated each other as siblings. Holders of the Crane *dodem*
further referred to themselves as belonging to the *Bo.wating.inini.wug*, or
'people of the rapids,' which constituted an Ojibwa group recorded at
Sault Ste Marie as early as 1640.[6] From it derives the term 'Batchewana,'
which designates one of two First Nations currently residing near Sault
Ste Marie, Ontario. The Batchewana band took shape in the late 1830s
under the auspices of Nebenagoching, a chief of the Crane *dodem*. It also
has been posited that *Outchibous*, denoting a named group encountered
by French missionaries in the early seventeenth century, may be related
to the Ojibwa term *Otchitchak* or 'Crane.'[7]

The fact that the chief who represented Sault Ste Marie at peace negotiations in Montreal in 1701 drew a Crane symbol as his or his village's
identifying mark on the French document[8] suggests that the succession
of chiefs *may* have followed a lineal pattern by this time, although conclusive evidence for lineality is lacking. Certainly the group always retained a
veto power in matters of succession. In his initial years as an administrator, Schoolcraft assumed that the *dodem* of the Crane encapsulated the
identity and composition of the entire Sault 'home band,' and frequently
referred to this hypothetically homogeneous patrilineal social and political unit as the 'Cranes.' Little Pine, he held, 'traces his lineage from the
old Crane band here.'[9]

In this last assumption he was mistaken. Little Pine's affiliation with the
'old Crane band' stemmed from his mother, who was said to have possessed
the Crane *dodem*. Later, the chief had married a Crane woman by the name
of Ogimaqua, or 'Chief Woman,' who, in turn, had been a granddaughter
of Tuhgwahna, probably a brother of Great Crane.[10] By reckoning his
descent through both his mother and his wife's maternal grandfather, Little Pine could claim membership in the Crane unit, as well as rights to residence and resources at the rapids.[11] His *dodem*, however, was the Plover,
which elders at Garden River stated he obtained in a vision fast.[12]

In the early 1820s, the Cranes occupied a village on a hill overlooking the rapids on the American side of the St Mary's River. A narrow strip of level land lying just below the hill and along the banks of the St Mary's channel served as the site on which visiting bands erected their hemispherical huts and larger pole and bark structures for ceremonial and trade purposes. The Cranes remained economically autonomous from their hundred or so Métis neighbours, who owned wooden bark-roofed family dwellings on both sides of the rapids. Although both the Métis and the Ojibwa fished together at the rapids, the Ojibwa showed a far more detailed knowledge of the local environment. The spring and fall fish runs were the only times of the year when, for several weeks, the Native population congregated in large numbers at the Sault. The rivers flowing from watersheds north of Lakes Huron and Superior and cascading over a fall zone lying not many kilometres back from the coast also offered good locations for the use of lines and lures, leister spears, shallow seines, and stone and brush weirs. Maple sugar production began in April. Families planted corn and, during the historic period, potatoes and other root crops in the sugar bush. Autumn once again brought the fish, after which families proceeded inland to harvest the crops they had planted in the spring, and then farther inland by bark canoe to their winter hunting grounds. The head man of each extended family maintained a hunting territory, several hundred square kilometres in area, for the exclusive use of himself and his immediate kin unit. The band chief often exercised a regulating influence over the hunting-territory system, and might intervene if disputes over boundaries arose.[13]

Crane band members pursued moose and woodland caribou, both non-migratory species, throughout the year for their meat and hides. Bears could also be plentiful, as was the case during the 'bear year' of 1811.[14] Before their numbers declined from overhunting by white sportsmen as well as Ojibwa hunters, beaver and migratory wildfowl constituted important food sources. The Native people grew corn, but harvested it green, trapped and snared rabbits and smaller fur-bearing animals, collected berries, and may have gathered some wild rice, although the latter was not an important resource in this region. Virginia deer, though present on the Upper Peninsula of Michigan, were late migrants to the Canadian shore of the St Mary's channel, arriving only after the disappearance of caribou in the late nineteenth century, and so likely did not constitute important prey for Ojibwa hunters north of Lakes Huron and Superior. Each segment of the Ojibwa economic cycle provided a surplus to tide a family group over part of the next phase. Meat and fish could be dried or smoked, and berries, corn, and maple sugar preserved.

Changes in environmental conditions and trade patterns compelled the Ojibwa to set a premium on mobility, flexibility in social structure, and resilience. Edward S. Rogers and James G.E. Smith have proposed the term 'range' to describe a territorial tract over which any one band hunted, fished, and gathered throughout most of the year.[15] Most bands retained considerable political and economic autonomy during the seventeenth and eighteenth centuries by exploiting a wide range of seasonally available resources within large, roughly defined ranges over which they had hunted for many generations. Within each hunting range, emphasis was on efficiency of movement; the light, birchbark canoe, toboggan sled, bark wigwam, and hemispherical hut were essential to this peripatetic settlement pattern. With their well-developed technology for river transportation, the Sault band had access to many different locales. Should resources fail in one region, they could readily move to another, although if a district were under the jurisdiction of a head chief, permission would first have to be asked from the resident leader. Fish could be taken near Whitefish Point west of the American Sault, and, during the winter, through the ice on the numerous bays which indented the northeastern coast of the St Mary's channel. Encampment sites existed at Garden River, Sugar Island, Thessalon, and St Joseph Island. Since lakes north of Sault Ste Marie fed river systems which flow both south-east into Lake Huron and south-west into Lake Superior, bands whose winter grounds spanned those watersheds could choose which coastal trading posts to visit each spring.

The fur trade was not the only Native commercial enterprise in the area. Maple sugar was traded, and the French, interested in founding a Native fishery to provision their military and trading posts, introduced the Ojibwa to the use of deep-water gill nets and encouraged them to bring dried and smoked fish to Michilimackinac to trade. This pattern of exchange, according to Bacqueville de la Potherie in 1671, superseded an all-Native trade system which had already been operating in that area.[16] Yet the French experienced mixed success in persuading the Native people to supply their establishments with fish, as bands proved reluctant to be drawn into any unilaterally controlled commercial nexus which might impinge on their political autonomy. It appears that colonial agencies promoted an increase in productivity in certain areas of the Native economy, but without effecting any radical changes in either traditional attitudes or values. Head chiefs exercised a strong sense of responsibility with regard to land and resources.[17] All adult males were expected to participate with their leader in defending their land. Several elders whom I interviewed in the 1980s placed more emphasis on a band's ability to defend its range than on its economic assets. All group territories had an offshore island which was used for burial and ceremonial occasions, usually a high bluff as a lookout station, numerous entrances into the interior for dispersal of population, and sufficient diversity of inland resources to allow a group to withstand a siege of its coast. Ojibwa thinking on these matters was strategically oriented to a high degree and exhibited marked attention to geographical and topographical detail.

Depending on the time of year, the Sault band at the rapids could range in size from one hundred to three hundred individuals, and until 1828 was led by an elderly head chief, or *ogima*, named Shingabaw'osin, 'The Image Stone.'[18] This man was the son of Maidosagee, a noted leader during the early years of the British colonial administration in the Great Lakes area. Like all Ojibwa bands, this group's structure was flexible, based on the existence of a bilateral 'nodal core,' formed of Shingabaw'osin's kindred, which derived its cohesiveness mainly from male sibling solidarity. This unit served as a gravitational core for larger groups formed through both consanguineous and affinal kinship ties. Given a pattern of cross-cousin marriage in a bilateral kinship universe, such groups under stable conditions could resolve themselves into two categories: one formed wholly of consanguineous or parallel kin who shared the same *dodem*, and another composed of cross-kin or cognatic kin with whom one might marry.[19] Leadership of groups larger than the nodal core tended to be diffuse, and fission readily occurred, with small units splitting off under new leaders when resources were scarce, or because of internal disputes.

An *ogima* or head chief, such as Shingabaw'osin, usually had to prove himself as a 'war chief' before assuming his higher status as a civil leader. *Ogima.sug* exercised their traditional powers, which granted them far more prestige than the trappings of genealogy, with assistance from a number of specialized aides. From nineteenth-century ethnographic accounts, it appears that many other leadership roles existed, that of civil chief being only the most prominent. Such roles, almost all achieved rather than ascribed, included that of *kekedowenine*, an advocate who acted whenever disputes arose within the band,[20] *tebahkoonegawenene*, a judge in such disputes, and the *ani.ke.ogima*, a 'step-below chief,' or subchief.[21] Other ranked statuses existed within the medicine societies, particularly the Grand Medicine Society or *Midéwiwin*, a forum for expressing power in ways which conferred considerable prestige within the Upper Great Lakes Native community. *Midéwiwin* rituals centred on the revitalization of the individual as well as the cosmos. The *oskabewis* was a speaker and messenger; the *mishinowa* was an 'economic aide to the chief' and had the responsibility for the distribution of presents and other goods.[22] It is interesting to note that the roles both of *mishinowa* and *oskabewis* derived from those of functionaries within conjuring and medicine societies. Famed for their courage in war and for their medicine powers, important chiefs arose in the vicinity of French military and trading establishments, and their leadership prerogatives usually remained unchallenged until their death. Because these men provided vital links between their bands and the colonial authorities, they were referred to in European narratives and their groups received special benefits and trading privileges. The rise of young men as warriors, brigade leaders, and spokesmen on behalf of bands brought them to the attention of the French. Where the French early on had favoured a family designated by a certain mark, members of this family throughout the Upper Great Lakes region might well have expected to receive similar recognition from the colonial authorities. Yet it is doubtful if the Native peoples viewed the attainment of these advantages as the consequence of a chief's interaction with colonial authority. A leader might consider himself to have been approached by the authorities because he had a special power and control over events, the same power which delivered his enemies to him in war and enabled him to contact the spirit agencies of the animals which gave their lives to him in the hunt. The nature of the relationship varied from leader to leader, but the idea that benefits accrued because of the possession of power and control remained a constant.

Ambitious young men chose to press westward into lands historically occupied by the Menomini, Sauk, Fox, and Sioux. As time passed, the groups they led, numbering anywhere from twenty to two hundred, carved out niches for themselves along the upper reaches of watercourses flowing into western Lake Superior and the headwaters of the Mississippi. In their westward expansion, they fought against hostile nations, aided and abetted by traders who, owing to exigencies of trade, had come to oppose colonial policy.[23] The leaders among the coastal bands acted as middlemen and heads of brigades, but their tenure was usually shorter and less strictly focused on economics than that of the inland 'captains' and their retinues who travelled the river routes between Lake Superior and Hudson Bay well into the late eighteenth century.[24] This westward migration of young war leaders from regions where 'upward mobility' sometimes proved a challenge was undoubtedly responsible for the predominance throughout the Lake Superior region of individuals and groups bearing the Crane mark.

Within the Sault band each extended family also recognized a head man, known as *ani.ke.ogima* or a 'step-below chief,' who might temporarily act as a 'spokesman' or 'war chief,' as circumstances dictated. Little Pine's activities in the 1820s suggest that it was difficult for an ambitious, middle-aged man like himself – even one with visionary power, membership in the *Midéwiwin*, and a notable war record – to rise above the rank of *ani.ke.ogima* to become a head chief, or *ogima*, within what appeared to be a solidly based leadership hierarchy, however covertly expressed. Recognition of gradations in power-control made factional strife over any one issue a rarity. Disputes arose primarily over succession following the death of a leader, when close kin of the deceased temporarily strove for the highest position in the band. In later years, the frequency of such conflicts may have been associated with the breakdown, under external pressures, of internal group mechanisms governing succession. Head chiefs acted as protectors and leading negotiators on behalf of their bands. The exigencies of such politics often demanded radical measures. In accord with their role as protectors, these leaders often threatened supernatural retaliation if they were angered or felt insulted. They also were expected to help maintain a balance of power among the leading chiefs representing groups within the Upper Great Lakes region.[25]

Shingwaukonse as an adult proved an able and willing spokesman for the Cranes, although in his youth he had been more closely associated with the Grand Island band, which resided near present-day Munising, Michigan. Grand Island may have been the place of origin of at least one of his wives, of whom he had four by 1820, and of two of his sons-in-law, Piabetassung and Misquabenokay. Before 1800, Little Pine had acted as a spokesman for the Grand Island head chief, Shawanapenasse, or South Bird.[26] An ambitious individual, Little Pine evidently acted in the capacity of an orator with several groups before leading a following in his own right.

In many ways the pattern of leadership displayed by Little Pine later in the century would parallel that exhibited by Ojibwa leadership a generation earlier, but with one important difference. Certain results of decisions made by Native representatives contending with policies which were essentially alien to them became standards by which later leaders could weigh the pros and cons of similar responses to such external schemes. The old transactional universe, the 'the middle ground' of cultural understandings which once had existed between colonial administrators and Native leaders in the Great Lakes region, was passing away.[27] In this climate of social change, instead of rejecting traditional values, leaders could use their newly developed funds of knowledge to make future decisions whose consequences would be more compatible with the values they wished to preserve.

The Concept of 'Power-Control'

Elders whom I interviewed in the early to mid-1980s at Sault Ste Marie and Garden River added some important insights to data derived from historical sources, and laid much of the foundation for the choice of theoretical perspective adopted in this study. They stressed that economic and political self-determination constituted as important a goal during the period of indirect colonialism as it does today within modern state society. Head chiefs, they continued, exercised a strong sense of responsibility with regard to land and resources.[28] In her analyses of Ojibwa beliefs regarding power, anthropologist Mary Black-Rogers likewise proposes that a concept of individual 'power-control' exists which is inseparable from the notion of personal responsibility.[29] She emphasizes that the individual is not only a power-holder but, in certain instances, also a provider of services, especially in the religious sphere, whose legitimacy is based on his acting ethically towards 'those he is responsible for.' Black-Rogers's work is of crucial importance to the theoretical and methodological orientation of this study, and for this reason I have given her premises special consideration. Black-Rogers directs her work on Ojibwa leadership towards the testing of premises advanced a number of years earlier by A. Irving Hallowell. In an article entitled 'Ojibwa Ontology, Behaviour and World View,' Hallowell argues for the presence in Ojibwa thought of a categorical domain, *bema.diziw.d*, or 'living things,' within which he could define no clear natural-supernatural boundary.[30] Black-Rogers finds she is able to support Hallowell's assertions that the Ojibwa belief system tolerates considerable ambiguity regarding the taxonomic boundaries of the 'persons' classes, which form components of the broader domain *bema.diziw.d*. The Ojibwa view certain living creatures, human as well as non-human, as able to undergo metamorphosis, an attribute which temporarily enables these 'persons' to be placed in categories other than that in which they usually reside. Black-Rogers recorded regularities in the behaviour of the Ojibwa men and women during interviews when discussion focused on certain classes of 'persons,' such as the *adiso.'ka.nag*. *Adiso.'ka.nag* are immortal beings, known to possess abilities that humans often lack, whose activities are recounted in legends, which are also termed *akdiso.'ka.nag*.

Black-Rogers proposes that the respondents' behavioural manifestations, usually denotative of an underlying sense of respect towards the subject, were related to a complex system of beliefs concerning power-control which she views as 'central and integrating' within the sphere of Ojibwa thought and action. Like earlier investigators of the Ojibwa culture, Black-Rogers finds one definition of 'power' to be that of a personalized possession, a 'gift' or 'blessing' bestowed on human beings by spirit guardians. 'Power' is also dependent on hierarchical structure: it stands as a 'dimension along which each class in the domain of living things shows a characteristic or relative value.' She suggests that a distinction may be drawn between particularized power, *'gas ki?ewiziwin*, and power as a gradient, *manido*, by which power-holders may be ranked in a manner similar to that which she recorded from her study of distributional meaning. The primary criterion informing such semantic structuring, she contends, is the Ojibwa's equation of 'power' with autonomy and self-sufficiency. Power-holders rarely publicize their capabilities. Ojibwa individuals possess a wide range of behavioural modes and devices, with many of the latter falling into the category of 'protective medicine.' These allow them to retain autonomy in situations where their independence may be threatened. Another behavioural strategy is deliberately to refrain 'from forcing a definition of the situation, to underline ... [one's] own relative powerlessness.'[31] In such instances, the link between 'power' and 'control' becomes clear, since individuals may seek to manipulate the relation by compelling the other to decide on the definition of the situation.

Individuals in Ojibwa communities also have acknowledged capabilities which are not so ambiguous, however. Among these are humans who share attributes with spirits in that they actively use their powers to help or harm. While Black-Rogers maintains that Ojibwa leaders, in particular, provide exceptions to the usual powerless stance, she embeds the indigenous concept of leadership deeply within the operation of the power-belief system itself. Each individual is expected to be self-sufficient, but those with great powers are charged with special responsibility to use their gifts to aid others in becoming self-sufficient also. This sharing relationship does not always develop; gifts may be misused for selfish ends. However, the sharing role is socially sanctioned, and leaders must conform to it if they wish to maintain their status within the group:

> An Ojibwa root, *debenima-*, has been variously translated as 'boss,' 'master,' 'the one in charge,' or 'the one in control.' But the favoured translation of a sensitive bilingual was 'those I am responsible for.' The idea of bossing is generally rejected, as is the idea of competition, yet both must occur at

times. It can be seen that the areas of social control, of leadership and political structure, of the various cooperating social units necessary to kinship
organization and to subsistence activities – all these must be balanced some-
how to accord with the rules of the system about power.[32]

This stress on the idea of reciprocal responsibility, rather than on authoritative action, parallels in many respects a 'paradox' which certain anthropologists have encountered in their studies of the north-eastern
Algonquian winter hunting group.[33] In such instances, the range of a
leader's decision-making powers over allocation of material resources
and land use varies as a function of the self-sufficiency and productivity,
not just of the leader, but of the group as a whole. Although a leader's
'gifts' remain covertly expressed except in certain ritualized settings,
demonstration of their working to the benefit of the band in the economic, political, and religious spheres assures others of the consistency
with which such powers are used to further the welfare of the group.

Since to the Ojibwa political power was not separated from the idea of
spiritual blessing, the leader had no need for a lengthy genealogy to con-
firm his status. A man blessed with a vision might boast an unending legacy of power, as his spirit helpers were immortal. An aspirant's claim to
power resided in his progressive ability to share in – and eventually to
reflect – the vision of older and wiser mentors. At the same time, the
youth elaborated on earlier versions of the story by drawing on symbolic
representations from his own experience. The individual thus came to
draw upon the power encapsulated in vision-legend. While Native ideology stressed that the transmission of such power was through vision experience alone, a father's selective telling of specific stories to his offspring
tended to ensure that the political and spiritual pre-eminence of an elder
would remain for several generations in his family.[34]

Such a view of Ojibwa leadership differs greatly from that held by
Schoolcraft. Since, however, the vast majority of the agent's encounters
with chiefs occurred in an official capacity, it is not surprising that his outlook should have been coloured by the aims of nineteenth-century U.S.
Indian policy. When chiefs did not conform to his wishes he tended to
see them as devious or fickle, and their bands as faction-ridden and politically unstable. Yet most Native leaders, naturally, were wary of government policies which threatened to deprive them of access to lands and
resources.

Scholars studying modern-day Ojibwa band factionalism, which often
results from the limited options open to the groups, sometimes seem

reluctant to ask whether the chiefs, given more diverse opportunities, might not work together harmoniously to develop the resources at their disposal. It seems likely that, if given the opportunity to establish permanent linkages with external agencies capable of helping the band to secure a sustained yield from its assets, a leader would be strongly motivated to pursue policies that would further group goals. In such circumstances, a leader who focused solely on attaining short-term returns might be thought to be motivated more by personal gain than group interest, and might eventually be rejected as a liability by his band. This approach – the one taken in this study – views the maintenance of sufficient good, rather than constant adaptation to limited good, as the goal sought by Little Pine within the emerging Canadian nation state, and suggests that intractable external factors were responsible for the failure to develop unifying policies.

According to Ojibwa elders interviewed at Garden River, personal achievement, coupled with a responsibility for others, has always constituted the primary gauge of competent leadership among the Ojibwa. There could be no doubt that the body of legends in which Little Pine figured prominently fell into the category of *adiso.'ka.nag*, *'gitchi.adiso. 'ka.nag*, 'great sacred stories,' as they were specifically designated by those telling them. References to Little Pine often drew responses similar to those which Hallowell and Black-Rogers found associated with discussions of certain 'other than human beings.' With regard to terms accorded the leader, for example, at least three of Little Pine's descendants consistently referred to him as 'my grandfather' – an expression of respect – although in only one instance, that of Dan Pine, Sr, was Little Pine actually a grandfather according to kinship reckoning.[35]

Another indication that Little Pine, had passed from human status to that of a spirit is that he was considered a source not only of spiritual blessings, but also of their manifestations in the form of necessary skills and material resources for his community. In a manner reminiscent of the culture hero Nanabush, the chief provided knowledge to cope with contingencies in ways beneficial to all *anicinabek* (Aboriginal people). Unlike Nanabush, however, who was credited with the invention of many Aboriginal technologies, such as how to weave nets (which he discovered by watching a spider spin a web), Little Pine, through a combination of vision and personal observation, discovered the mechanical principles underlying the workings of tools, weapons, and other instruments associated with Western culture.

In one story, the chief constructed a musket from a suitably shaped piece of wood by extracting the pith core and blocking one end. All the musket's components were obtained locally, except for the gunpowder, which was pilfered from a ship. Lumps of lead cut from exposures at Garden River provided ammunition, while a substance prepared from a wasp's nest, found with the help of Woodpecker, served as wadding. Thus, Little Pine's ingenuity rendered the Ojibwa independent of reliance on European traders. Since self-determination constitutes a primary value, Little Pine's mythical abilities in this regard not only approximate a collective ideal, but also serve as inducement for the extension of competence, defined according to cultural standards, into modern settings.[36]

On one level, in these stories Little Pine acts to preserve a valued way of life by working within and gradually extending, through parallel and independent invention, the parameters of Ojibwa culture until the latter can hold its own against the tide of intrusive Western knowledge and technology. This capacity may be transmitted to others in vision experiences, and several elders stated that 'their grandfather' had appeared to them in this manner to offer guidance. To these people, Little Pine demonstrated his status as one of the *adiso.'ka.nag* by remaining a potential source of cultural knowledge.

His ability to expand the range of Ojibwa technical skills is only one of the many dimensions of the chief's legendary character. A second and far more striking characteristic was the key to understanding certain references in historic sources to this leader's activities. It first came to my attention when Fred Pine, Sr, remarked that his great-grandfather 'Shingwaukonse was looking for a home for his people, the Ojibwa nation.'[37] He mentioned this while discussing the chief's prodigious capacity for lengthy fasting, the vision sanctions he obtained to use medicine powers, and the continuous guidance and sense of purpose he derived from the 'other than human persons' with whom he formed close association. Through his newfound abilities the chief focused his energies on the search for a homeland where Ojibwa could live with sufficient resources for a secure economic future and enjoy a fair degree of political autonomy.

'You were put in for a purpose.' That's what Shingwaukonse said. 'If you run into any trouble, you're the cause of it. You can bring disturbance ... You can make a good thing or a bad thing of yourself.' He was really smart, just like a minister.

He told the others ... 'You be proud of the gift. Don't make fun of anything, don't waste anything. The sun will help you. It's not for sale. If you throw it away ... if you do, I'll live naked.'

Shingwaukonse's career rose coterminously with new policies, of both the American and the British governments, designed to manipulate trade relations in order to exercise social control on the frontier. The U.S. government took the first step to act by establishing a system of bonding and licensing traders, situated at trading houses, and imposing duties on goods imported across the international border. The relatively light restrictions on commerce of the Trade and Intercourse Acts of 1796, 1799, and 1802 gave way to new measures[38] which restricted group movements to specific geographical areas and interfered directly in bands' internal regulatory mechanisms.[39] Thus, after 1790, the area within which a chief could exercise his traditional range of powers progressively shrank. The process was a gradual one, however, and traditional modes of leadership adapted remarkably well, given the accumulating hardships.

Oral Traditions Regarding Little Pine's Ancestry

Although biologically of Métis ancestry, Little Pine hailed from an exclusively Ojibwa cultural background. Even though many of his close allies, such as the Crane chief Nebenagoching,[40] were fluent in both the French and Ojibwa languages, Little Pine could not speak French. More is known about his mother, who was a member of the Sault Crane band, than about his father, a white man. When his father settled at Detroit – while Little Pine was still an infant – his mother separated from her consort and joined a man of the Grand Island band. The vagueness surrounding the identity of Little Pine's natural father has given rise to speculation. According to one legend, recounted by Dan Pine, Sr, the chief had a claim to the nobility of Europe, for he was no less than the son of Napoleon Bonaparte:

> He [Shingwaukonse] came on a ship across the Atlantic. Why did he come? See ... that's part of the mystery. When his father Bonaparte found he was gone he was broken hearted. He [Bonaparte] came over on a ship and landed somewhere on the coast. When he found his son he was glad. He tried to get him to go back, but Shingwaukonse wanted to stay.[41]

Another story, recorded by J.G. Kohl during the 1850s, described Little Pine as the son of a British officer who presented the young boy with an opportunity to become 'white,' an offer Little Pine declined.[42] Both Kohl's account and the legend, passed down from generation to generation within the Pine family, make the same point: Little Pine's identity was the product of choice. That he once had the opportunity to be raised as a 'white' remained secondary, and served only to heighten the importance of the chief's decision to remain an Ojibwa.

According to present-day oral traditions, Little Pine set out early to learn as much as possible about his people's beliefs and their bearing on power relationships in the Upper Great Lakes area. He spent much of his youth fasting, often leaving to go to a solitary place for several days. Dan Pine, Sr, said that his father, John Askin, one of Shingwaukonse's sons, had told him that prior to marriage Little Pine had fasted nine times, for ten days at a time – a superhuman task.[43] Traditionally, Ojibwa men married in their late twenties, after they had secured a sense of purpose from their dreams. Little Pine was said to have been twenty-nine when he completed his series of fasts. Dan Pine also explained that Shingwaukonse's loyalties to Ojibwa culture emerged from his visions, never merely from political motives or self-interest.

Kohl provided a detailed account of one of Shingwaukonse's youthful visions, gleaned from information he gathered during a brief stay at Garden River:

[The boy] lay, half naked and sleepless, trembling with cold and hunger, on his hard bed. He whimpered for a long time, but at length fell into a state of half dreaming and half waking. Then he fancied that a gentle voice said, 'Thou, poor Shinquakongse, thou are wretched; come to me!' He looked around him but he could see nothing. But he perceived a path hovering in the air, which gleamed in the darkness, and which, commencing at his bed, ran upwards through the doorway of his cabin. He comprehended that it was a way on which he must walk. He went upon it, and kept on rising higher and higher into heaven. There he found a house, from which a man came out to meet him, wrapped from head to foot in white garments, like a priest. 'I called thee, O Shinquakongse, to me, to show thee something glorious. Look thou thither, towards the rising sun.' When he looked, Shinquakongse perceived the entire field full of tents and groups, among them the great tents of the kings and chiefs, and a multitude of braves, warriors, and leaders, sitting together at the war-council. His eyes were, as it were, blinded by the dazzling brilliancy, and he felt a longing to be among them. The white-robed man proceeded, 'I give thee this picture, thou art still young, and thou are at the same time poor, wretched and persecuted. But hereafter thou wilt be as grand as those thou seest there in the field, and will become, thyself, a mighty hero. I will always think of thee, if thou doest the same by me, and give thee this symbol in remembrance of this moment.'

With these words he handed little Shinquakongse a gay fluttering pennant, and with this in hand, he again descended his hovering path. The path, too, was decorated on either side with fluttering pennants, through which he marched in triumph. The flags in the glistening path extended down to his hut, and the last of them stood by his bed. When the rough winter's wind again blew right coldly through the hut, he started and woke up, and lo! all had suddenly disappeared. But the glorious reminiscence remained to him, and the lad firmly believed from that moment that he would once become a great chieftain of his people. And the dream was really fulfilled. He became the greatest 'general' of his race, and was known and celebrated everywhere among the Ojibbeways on the entire lake of Mitchigaming [Lake Michigan] and Kitchi-Gami [Lake Superior].

   After that dream he also changed his name of Shinguacongse which ... had the very trivial meaning of 'The Little Pine.' He called himself from that time forth Sagadjive-Osse, which means almost identically 'When the sun rises.' 'It was amusing,' my narrator added, 'how highly he adored the sun from that time forth; and when he dreamed of it, he ever saw it before him, like a person walking before him and conversing.'[44]

This story contains many of the symbolic elements borrowed from both Ojibwa and colonial traditions, together with a stress on height and luminosity which is intrinsically Native.[45] Elders at Garden River volunteered information regarding Little Pine's relationship with the sun. His most powerful name, *Sa.ujeu.a.say*, or 'The One Who Rises over the Hill,' refers to the position of the sun in the morning.[46] It became evident during these discussions that a spirit's physical appearance, because it was regarded as so mutable, constituted only a minor facet of the identity of the guardian being, *Waube.che.chaug*, the 'White Soul,' or as one elder referred to it with considerable reverence, 'the Great White Stirring Soul.'[47] It was also maintained that Little Pine, whose power was considered to have increased as he grew older, could at times assume the character of *Waube.che.chaug*: 'The priest said to him, "Do you believe in the soul?" And Shingwaukonse said, "I must believe, I am the soul."'[48]

   It would not have been a major step for Little Pine, following his conversion to Christianity after 1833, to endow his essentially traditional vision of the sun with traits of the Christian God. Schoolcraft, recalling the chief's statements to him about the sun, wrote: "The sun is depicted, in several places, to represent the Great Spirit.'[49] According to elders at Garden River, the luminescent spirit gave power to see deeply into things and represented the idea of spiritual renewal in the form of a being with whom one could communicate as one would with a friend. Kohl's use of the word 'longing' to describe the impetus which drove Little Pine to make his vision an actuality is probably not accidental. Residing in the Great Soul's 'blessing' lay an embryonic purpose which the chief sought to bring to fruition, an endeavour that also fostered the development of his own competencies and sense of self-worth. The correspondences between the oral testimony and Kohl's description of Little Pine's vision experience suggest that the German visitor presented a reasonably accurate account of what he had been told concerning this chief's concept of the permanent source of his 'power' as a leader.

Historical Documentation Relating to Little Pine's Parentage

Little additional oral data could be secured regarding Shingwaukonse's parentage. According to documentary sources, John Askin, an influential trader and commissary officer stationed at Mackinac from 1764 to 1780, fitted Kohl's description of Little Pine's father as a Scotsman associated with the British military. Askin moved to Detroit at the turn of the nineteenth century. Interesting but far from conclusive evidence may also be found in the journal of Charles Gaultier, storekeeper at Mackinac. During February 1791, Gaultier distributed provisions both to 'Chinwak, Chief Saulteaur,' and 'La Vieille Askin, pauvre infirme.'[50] It is possible that this 'Vieille Askin' residing in the neighbourhood of Sault Ste Marie was one of Askin's Indian consorts, and Little Pine's mother.[51] Yet perhaps even stronger argument may be made for an alternative paternity.

On 19 March 1778, Jean Baptiste Barthe, a trader at Sault Ste Marie, noted in his account book, 'Donnez à La Mère de l'enfant de Lavoine.'[52] The phrase 'de l'enfant de Lavoine' suggests that Barthe had been providing supplies for the Indian mother of a child named 'Lavoine.' It also implies that not only was the youth called 'Lavoine,' but also that he was the son of a man bearing the name 'Lavoine.' This is significant for two reasons. First, Little Pine and one of his sons, Tegoosh, on occasion both adopted 'Lavoine' as a synonymous name.[53] Second, it implies that the trader exhibited a special paternalistic concern for the Métis child, which suggests that Little Pine may well have been the son of Lavoine Barthe, a trader at Sault Ste Marie and Mackinac.

In 1778, Jean Baptiste Barthe employed an individual by the name of Lavoine Barthe at an annual wage of 1000 livres.[54] Although the precise relationship remains uncertain, it is possible that Lavoine was Jean Baptiste's brother, which would also make him brother-in-law to John Askin, Sr, who married Jean Baptiste's sister. The marriage of John Askin, Sr, to Archange Barthe cemented the close social, political, and business relationship which had developed between the Askin and Barthe families after the Seven Years' War. Both families were militaristic in attitude, oriented commercially towards Montreal, and loyal to Britain. It would have been natural, given the willingness to aid one another displayed by members of these families, for both Jean Baptiste Barthe and John Askin, Sr, to have felt a degree of concern for the welfare of a 'country-born' son, one of their close kin.

A third and more remote possibility was that Little Pine was the son of Jean Baptiste Chevalier and his wife, Frances Alavoine, 'Lavoine,' or 'Manon.' Some support for this idea comes from Dan Pine, Sr, who remembers the chief as being descended from a 'chevalier.'[55] Other assertions that Little Pine's father was called 'Lavoine Pat,' however, suggest that Lavoine Barthe was the more likely paternal candidate, since the name 'Barthe' would be rendered 'Pat' or 'Bart' in the Ojibwa dialect. Little Pine also was known to have affixed the name 'Augustin Bart' to a treaty made between the Sault Ste Marie 'home band' and the American government in 1820.[56] In this instance, 'Bart' could mean 'Barthe,' but it could just as easily reflect a desire on Little Pine's part to associate his name with the British aristocracy by employing the titular designation for 'Baronet.' The weight of evidence nevertheless suggests that the chief may have been related to both the Barthes and the Askins of Detroit.

Census and church records provide additional information. A census taken at Garden River in 1867 recorded that Little Pine's eldest son, Tegoosh (1796?–1876), had been born at Portage Lake on the Keweenaw Peninsula near Hancock, Michigan. The same census gave 'British Lake Superior' as the birthplace of two of his other sons, Ogista (1800–90) and Buhkwujjenene (1811–1900). No birth information could be obtained for Thomas (1796/7?–1883) or for Little Pine's daughters Owiaquahgeyhegoqua (c. 1805–?), Ogimaqua (1813–?), Marie (1816–87), and Waintegoochequai (c. 1800–?). Marie may have been raised at Michipicoten. Jean Baptiste Buhkwujjenene, an independent trader living in the vicinity of Fort William, may have been yet another son. Younger sons included John Askin or 'Erskine' (1836–1919), Joseph (1837–?), George Menissino (1838–1923), and Louis (1839–99), all born at Garden River.[57] Ambiguity surrounding the birthplaces of other children implies that, as Fred Pine, Sr, asserted, before he arrived at Sault Ste Marie, Little Pine acted 'a bit like a lone ranger.'[58]

Little Pine and the War of 1812

British and Ojibwa interests tended to complement one another during the 1780s and early 1790s, since British policy supported the recognition of the Ohio River as the boundary between U.S. and Native territory. Partly in view of the advantages to trade, but mainly in response to the threat of French and Spanish incursions from the south, Governor Simcoe of Upper Canada argued that Britain should attempt to maintain a neutral Native buffer zone in the Ohio region.[59] Simcoe received backing for his plan from the Mohawk chief Joseph Brant, who attempted to convince the Ojibwa, Ottawa, Shawnee, and Miami to resist any further land sales in the western district.[60] In association with several leading officials of the British Indian Department, Brant forged the Ojibwa, Wyandot, Delaware, Shawnee, Miami, Mingoe, Potawatomi, Mississauga, and Munsey into a loose military confederation, with each member 'nation' taking a particular identifying symbol. The Ojibwa, possibly because of their associations with Maidosagee, civil chief at the Sault, bore the mark of the Crane.[61]

This government-sponsored confederacy collapsed within a few years. General Anthony Wayne's victory over the Shawnee and their allies at Fallen Timbers in 1794, and the signing the following year of the Treaty of Greenville by which the Native people surrendered most of their lands in Ohio, diminished the appeal for the Ojibwa of Brant and his league. There was also a growing distrust of the British, who had failed to come to the aid of the western nations after promising to do so.[62] Under the terms of the Jay Treaty of 1796, the British relinquished occupation of the oldest forts in the Northwest, making it clear to the Native people that Britain's western hegemony had declined.[63] The Ojibwa, particularly, were affected since their population now fell under two separate jurisdictions. After 1796 they were increasingly drawn into the militant activities of more southerly nations, for without the support of British power, their strength depended on unity as American settlement pressed further into the Northwest.

In 1807–8, a full-fledged Native resistance movement sprang into life. Known as the 'Shawnee uprising,' it was nourished by the dualistic ideology of the Shawnee prophet Tenskwatawa, Tecumseh's brother. Tenskwatawa portrayed whites as evil serpents to be forced back into the sea, and defectors as witches who must be expunged from a new emerging order.[64] Many south-western Ojibwa chiefs, among them well-known leaders such as Besheke at La Pointe and Eschekebugecoshe at Leech Lake,[65] contributed their personal skills in war and negotiation to this collective effort, although their support for resistance waned when Ojibwa fell ill while residing with the Prophet in Ohio during the winter of 1808–9.[66] It has been argued that dependence on the fur trade militated against the Ojibwa's support of the Shawnee uprising.[67] It may also be, however, that leaders like Maidosagee knew the strategic value of their geographic position between rival powers and, when conditions favoured negotiation and compromise over resistance, simply abandoned the Prophet and his erratic views.

After 1808, the Ojibwa at Sault Ste Marie, with Shingwaukonse as their spokesman, once again supported the British government's original scheme of preventing American expansion west of the Ohio River. This sudden reversal in Native policy is reflected in oral traditions which survive to the present day at Garden River. Somewhere along the way there had been a political imbalance, on a cosmological scale. 'Ojibwa was once too powerful,' Fred Pine, Sr, explained. 'He tried to kill the Snake. But that was wrong because old Snake had young ones coming along.'[68] The Sault band had not joined in the Shawnee resistance, but had continued with their trading activities as usual. Shingwaukonse, who according to oral tradition had been trading at Fort William, near present-day Thunder Bay, Ontario, when the British summons came to join in war with the United States, hastily returned to the rapids and prepared for combat under the direction of John Askin, Jr.

If John Askin, Jr, the son of the Mackinac merchant, knew of any genealogical relationship between Shingwaukonse and his own family he never acknowledged it publicly, although he regarded Little Pine as an influential Ojibwa war leader. Each spring, Lake Superior chiefs sent messengers with wampum to bands residing on Lakes Huron and Michigan calling for assistance in their conflicts with the Dakota. In response, parties of men joined contingents of warriors as they passed the different Native villages on their way west. In May 1810, John Askin, Jr, wrote to William Claus, deputy superintendent of Indian affairs, that Little Pine was among those soliciting assistance for a foray into 'Nataway' (or Dakota Sioux) country.[69]

Little Pine had to attain the rank of leader through his own achievements. An aspiring man had to secure recognition from the British authorities to complement his rising status within the Native community, and in this Shingwaukonse was fortunate, since John Askin, Jr, readily accepted him as a figure of note. In turn, Little Pine evidently admired Askin, and he may have shared Askin's father's viewpoint that Aboriginal rights on lands unceded to the state would be respected at all times.[70] Mutual respect and possibly more personal ties between the Native leader and the Askin family strengthened Little Pine's resolve to join the British cause should war erupt between Britain and the United States. Richard

Pine, Sr, and Fred Pine, Sr, both argued that, at St Joseph Island, before 1812, Little Pine received a number of medals and other honours to distribute to Native leaders throughout the Great Lakes region in order to encourage loyalty to the Crown.[71]

According to Fred Pine, Sr, the chief shared Brant's and Tecumseh's view that the British would assist the Native people to prevent American settlement west of the Ohio. This accords with a tradition recorded in 1910 by Dr Oronhyatekha, a Mohawk medical doctor who helped found the Independent Order of Foresters, that the Ojibwa held a council in 1808 on Mackinac Island to decide whether or not to join the British in the event of war with the Americans. The gathering found itself divided in its allegiances, and a wampum belt was made to commemorate the split. Little Pine became the belt's recognized keeper, and it remained in the Pine family until Dr Oronhyatekha acquired it in the early twentieth century.[72]

Little Pine would have been among equals in 1808, since the influential Crane chiefs at the Sault also decided to fight for the British. In June 1812, Shingwaukonse joined approximately 230 other Ojibwa and Ottawa warriors under the command of John Askin, Jr, in a decisive attack on the Americans at Mackinac.[73] Askin then directed the Indians to Amherstburg to join General Isaac Brock in the siege of Detroit in August. General Brock saw clearly the value of his Native allies.[74] '[No] effort of mine shall be wanting to keep them attached to our cause,' he proclaimed; 'if the condition of this people could be considered in any future negotiation for peace it would attach them to us for ever.'[75]

It is not known whether Little Pine participated in the abortive attempt to capture Fort Miami in September after many of the Mackinac deserted owing to British indecisiveness over the feasibility of the attack.[76] Yet his own statements clearly indicate that he joined Brock at Queenston Heights in October:

In the summer [of 1812] I was on my lands in the centre of Lake Superior, now the Long Knives' land, whence I was called to the Great Fall with my men, there I fought and there much of Ojibway blood was shed, some of my young men lay on the ground and some reddened the soil with their blood. Yes it was red with Indian blood. All the summer I was on this war party with my young men and it was only when the winter snow whitened the ground that I returned to my place. They are still with me, three of my people, now old men who were with me there at the Great Fall. Three different days I led the attack on the Long Knives, and much Long Knife blood was shed on these occasions, for I conquered on the two first occasions and on the third was not worsened by the Nahtahwas [Americans] who were opposed to us though I suffered much and was myself wounded yet I beat them back. We rushed too far in pursuit and many perished – only two of us returned alive. This my Father is the account of my conduct when I helped you when you fought for your territory. All the Indians of different tribes helped you and we helped you, we who are called Indians, to retain possession of your lands, therefore you retained it Father.[77]

The following summer Little Pine fought in engagements around Lake Erie. John Askin, Jr, retained control over the dispatching of Native warriors to assist in these various campaigns. Acting under orders from Askin, in July 1814 Shingwaukonse may well have participated in the taking of Fort McKay, near Prairie du Chien, and in the Battle of Lundy's Lane later the same summer. Schoolcraft maintained that Little Pine himself 'conducted the last war party from the village in 1814.'[78] It may have been due to the close attachment Shingwaukonse felt for the Askin family that he persevered in fighting with such fervour until the end of the war, even after the deaths of Brock and Tecumseh. More than thirty years later, Little Pine would refer to his association with John Askin, Jr, as the source from which he first derived official sanction to exercise territorial prerogatives on the north shore of the St Mary's straits:

> When the war was over the [British] chiefs spoke to me through my friend the late Mr Askin and said, thank you Shinguaconce, many thanks to you, you will never be badly off, even your children will be looked after by the English. You have lost your land in the bargain, made between us and the whites. Choose for yourself land in the neighbourhood of the Sault on the British side. Have nothing to do with the Long Knives [Americans], you will soon find that you will be visited by good days which will not end as long as the world exists.[79]

It appears that after the war Little Pine tried to stay near his 'friend' Askin, who in 1816 was posted to Amherstburg. The 'Shingwalk' and 'Shingwalk jun' whose names appear on an American treaty concluded at Saginaw on 24 September 1819 probably refer to Little Pine and his son Ogista.[80] Shingwaukonse's presence at these negotiations would not have been particularly remarkable. Ojibwa from the Sault Ste Marie area regularly travelled back and forth to the Saginaw region. Little Pine sojourned at Saginaw for four years. When, in January 1820, Askin suddenly died, it appears that Shingwaukonse no longer had reason to reside in Lower

Michigan, and by July of the same year he was encamped at the St Mary's rapids.[81]

The British resumed distributing presents to the Upper Great Lakes bands in 1816, in response to Washington's garrisoning of Mackinac and American plans to build a second fort at Sault Ste Marie. At the same time, the colonial authorities were more concerned to ensure amicable neutrality among the western bands than to encourage active demonstrations of loyalty. Following the signing of the Treaty of Ghent, the British took care not to press issues which might prove offensive to the United States. Brock's recommendation, made at the war's height, that Native interests should be considered in any forthcoming peace agreement was no longer thought appropriate. As Lt-Col. Robert McDouall, commander at Drummond Island, commented, peace favoured expediency:

> Through me, the Western Indians were taught to cherish brighter hopes, to look forward to happier days – to repose with confidence in the sacred pledge of British honors – to anticipate the time when they would be restored to the abodes of their ancestors! How have such prospects been realized? – they are abandoned at their utmost need, and [are] about to be immolated on the altar of American vengeance. Can I be otherwise as the author of these gay delusive hopes – than the object of their bitterest reproaches or can their hapless fate fail to touch me nearly and awaken every sentiment of pity and compassion? Nevertheless in this emergency, I have, with the utmost cautious circumspection, abstained from any act which might give just cause of offense to the American government.[82]

Chiefs who had distinguished themselves in battle may even have been deliberately passed over during the distribution of special honours after 1816. In 1819 the British Indian Department vested Nebenagoching, the eight-year-old son of the Crane chief Waubejechauk, with the head chieftainship at the rapids.[83] From the mid-1830s until 1858, Nebenagoching,[84] also known as 'Joseph Sayer,' lived a Métis lifestyle near his Métis relations at the British Sault, engaging in the fur trade, exploring for minerals, and planting near his wooden house. Oral traditions at Garden River, where Nebenagoching resided for most of his later life, claim that the British appointment arose from a need to reconcile conflicting claims to the honour by rival head men.[85] Within the broader historical context, however, one may also argue that British policy following the war favoured selection of a figurehead who would ensure diffuse attachment to the Crown rather than overt loyalty.

American versus 'Crane' Sovereignty at Sault Ste Marie: An Analysis
of an Episode in the American Drama of 'How the West Was Won'

British fears of Native aggression against the United States were not without foundation, for during 1815 and 1816 the Ojibwa population at the Sault adopted a cohesive stance against the imposition of American sovereignty over their lands at the rapids. This Native enmity acquired form and focus under the direction of a Crane subchief by the name of Sassaba. The actual degree of Sassaba's participation in two brief attacks on American military expeditions in the St Mary's channel area is unknown, although Schoolcraft viewed this war leader as the principal perpetrator.[86] On both occasions, Native hostility curtailed efforts by American military personnel to penetrate the Lake Superior region by way of the straits.[87]

The third and final demonstration of Ojibwa animosity towards the American exercise of authority over Ojibwa territory occurred on 16 July 1820, during negotiations between the Crane band and U.S. officials led by Gen. Lewis Cass. The negotiations concerned the surrender of acreage for the military post of Fort Brady. No annuities were offered, since the American government maintained that it already possessed title to the land under the terms of the French seigniorial grant made in 1750 and the Treaty of Greenville of 1795. These were questionable arguments, especially since Washington in later years disallowed land claims submitted by heirs of the early French estate.[88] Yet these events cannot be divorced from their historic context. The securing of a site at the rapids was an issue of grave national significance to the Americans. A failure in negotiations would have been publicly construed as a demonstration of the inability of the United States to resist the growth of British influence along the international border.

Success, on the other hand, would constitute a moral as well as territorial victory for an emerging international power, and sides were drawn even before the contest began. Not surprisingly, therefore, contemporary American accounts of the event depicted a conflict between rationally planned American expansion and an 'archaic' fur trade, with Britain encouraging Indian atrocities in defence of the Northwest commerce – a view in vogue in the United States since the American Revolution.[89] White signatories to the treaty of 1820 lauded the document as heralding a new age of settlement and resource development. Dualities allegedly present in the event were heightened by emphasizing the contrast between what was seen as General Cass's straightforward and decisive conduct and the disorderly behaviour of the numerically and strategically superior Native bands. It was stressed that Cass's expedition consisted of 'eleven soldiers, twelve Canadian voyageurs, nine friendly Indians, suite of eight, and a small escort ... of twenty-nine soldiers.'[90] George Johnston, who portrayed himself as a leading actor in this drama, contended that the resident Native population had been swelled by the presence of visiting bands and could easily have raised a formidable force:

> The Indian village [was] situated on an elevated bank, and at this season of the year was well populated by the Indians who had arrived from the different regions of the country from their winter hunting excursions; ... and this annual assemblage of Indians were now encamped on either side of the river, dotting the shores with their wigwams, the probable assemblage of Indians at this time could not have been less than fifteen hundred men capable of bearing arms.[91]

In actuality, the odds against the American party were much less. Schoolcraft maintained that the number of Native people likely to become involved should trouble occur amounted to 'forty or fifty lodges, or two hundred Chippewas, fifty or sixty of whom were warriors,' whereas the Americans had thirty-four manned muskets 'in addition to which, each of the savans, or Governor's mess, were armed with a short rifle.' Fifteen or twenty houses, standing 'in the midst of picketed lots,' belonged to Métis families, who would remain neutral.[92]

Accounts of what happened at the treaty negotiations on 15 and 16 July differ in details, but agree on the general order of events. The Cranes initially had welcomed General Cass's military and scientific expedition. As Schoolcraft, a member of Cass's retinue, noted: 'Long before reaching the place, a large throng of Indians had collected on the beach, who as we put in towards the shore, fired a salute, and stood ready to greet us with their customary bosho [welcome].' It was only when the government interpreter was directed in council by General Cass to remind the Native people 'that their ancestors had formerly conceded the occupancy of the place to the French, to whose national rights and prerogatives the Americans had succeeded' that the Native audience registered alarm. Schoolcraft divided the Ojibwa response into two camps, the 'moderates' and the 'hostiles.'[93] Other accounts ignored this distinction, preferring instead to portray the event as a dynamic drama from which only villains and heroes could emerge.

Sassaba arose as the leading villain in the scenario. On hearing the interpreters' words, he refused to smoke the tobacco proffered by the Americans and tried to persuade others of the band to follow his lead. A 'tall, martial-looking man, [he] ... stuck his war lance furiously in the ground before him' and began haranguing the assembly. The malcontent then 'wheeled around ... and walked off towards the [Ojibwa] village and hoisted the British colors ... while the chiefs and all were amazed ...'[94]

General Cass emerged as the hero of this event. Unarmed, and accompanied solely by his interpreter, the General went to the Native encampment, hauled down the British flag and declared to the Native people that 'as sure as the sun that was then rising would set, so sure would there be an American garrison sent to that place, whether they renewed the grant or not.'[95] Cass declared that two flags could not fly over the same territory, and thus stood his ground as the intrepid defender of American sovereignty. In response, the band contacted Susan Johnston, the Ojibwa wife of a local British trader, John Johnston. Her husband being absent in Europe, Mrs Johnston instructed her son George to call the chiefs together and commanded the assembled chiefs to suppress Sassaba's follies.[96]

Replying to Mrs Johnston's appeal, the band selected Shingwaukonse – perhaps because he was an outsider, divorced from the social and emotional bonds of close kin ties and obligations to the Crane group – to lead a delegation to prevent Sassaba from inflicting injury on the American camp. George Johnston acted as the sole chronicler of this secondary confrontation, in which Little Pine persuaded Sassaba to lay down his arms:

[The group met] Sassaba, who, having divested himself of his regimentals ... [emerged] painted and in war accoutrements, leading a party of warriors, prepared and determined for a desperate encounter with Gen. Cass. Shingwaukonse, on meeting Sassaba, and addressing the party with him, said to them: 'My friends and relatives, I am authorized by our chiefs and elders to stop your proceedings.' Sassaba, instantly replying said to Shingwaukonse, 'You was [sic] a war leader when my brother fell in battle; he was killed by the Americans, and how dare you come to put a stop to my proceedings?' and raising his war-club, struck at Shingwaukonse and grazed his left shoulder and Shingwaukonse, undismayed, still kept up his oration and with his eloquence and the power vested in him by the chiefs, he prevailed on the party to return quietly to their respective lodges, then situated at the head of the portage and along the shore of the falls.[97]

The treaty was signed soon afterwards in George Johnston's office. Under its terms, the Native leaders surrendered an area sixteen miles square, and received confirmation of perpetual rights to fish at the rapids. Shingabaw'osin had his name placed first on the document. Shingwaukonse waited until all the others had made their mark, before requesting his name be affixed as 'Augustin Bart.' Sassaba refused to sign.

The attitude expressed by the Ojibwa during these proceedings has never been thoroughly examined. Most accounts assume that the Native population were simply acting in conformity with 'insidious counsels' given by British authorities and traders upon whose presents and goods they had become dependent.[98] This view depicts the Native people merely as extensions of British and military commercial policy along the northern frontier. Yet Schoolcraft's distinction between 'moderates' and 'hostiles' at the negotiations suggests that there were different degrees of animosity expressed towards the American presence, of which Sassaba's violent disapproval constituted the extreme. The most interesting interplay was that between Shingwaukonse and Sassaba, since both men were war leaders and both had been attached to the British. Although the fact that Sassaba had lost his brother Waubejechauk in the War of 1812 was raised as the primary explanation for his deep resentment of the Americans, other brothers of the deceased had been present at the negotiations and had not acted similarly. For this reason it seems that a more plausible clue to Sassaba's behaviour might be found in his age and status relative to his brothers. The war leader was portrayed as young, perhaps not much older than thirty, and would not have reached an age when he would be respected for possessing the experience and power-control to deal competently with issues effecting the welfare of the entire band. By contrast, the older and more experienced Shingwaukonse, even though he had a disposition to side with the hostiles, was expected to subordinate personal self-interest to band considerations in accord with the status he had attained.

Moreover, Shingwaukonse, unlike Sassaba, was not a leading member of the Crane unit. If a rank order existed within this group, then Sassaba might have been trying to enhance his relative status by gauging it against an external measure – that of a British military commander. Sassaba persisted in conforming to this model, even when other Ojibwa recognized its inappropriateness in their transactions with the Americans.

After Sassaba's denunciations of the Americans won no response from his band, he became an outsider. The former war leader adopted a culturally structured mode of behaviour by which he could retain possession of power, but of a kind recognized by the Ojibwa as unpredictable and potentially dangerous. Having been rejected by the group in his adopted status as a 'British officer,' Sassaba began to clothe himself in little else than a wolf skin, with the tail of the animal trailing behind him. Those who were not immediate kin removed themselves from his presence as his behaviour grew increasingly antisocial. He drank heavily and, just over a month after the collective denial of his former identity, he drowned in the rapids when his canoe overturned.[99]

Two anthropological interpretations have been presented to account for incidences of such behaviour among the Ojibwa. The first, presented by L. Marano,[100] would view the fate of the central figure, Sassaba, as the result of a form of 'witch hunt' in which he played the victim; the second would argue that Sassaba's own rash and precipitate actions led to his downfall. These interpretations were discussed with Richard Pine, Sr, and Fred Pine, Sr, at Garden River. Both concluded that Sassaba's fate had been the result of his 'unbalanced use' of power. Richard Pine, Sr,, when told of the incident, repudiated the first explanation, arguing instead that Sassaba's behaviour showed all the signs of an individual who was intent on increasing his power.[101] The fact that Sassaba had placed himself in a vulnerable position while intoxicated meant he was trying to appeal to the spirits of the rapids. It was noted by the two Ojibwa elders that Sassaba had been overtly favouring the British over the American government without first consulting the wishes of his group. This behaviour – unleaderlike, according to Ojibwa standards – designated him as 'unpredictable' as far as group perceptions of his power were concerned. An interpretation of a group behaviour which saw Sassaba as a victim might have helped in explaining events surrounding Sassaba's activities had the Cranes in 1820 perceived the young chief's actions as entirely uncontrollable and potentially injurious to their welfare. The fact is that the Sault band so successfully exercised its decision-making powers to effect a compromise between the contending parties that the group did not need to seek Sassaba's destruction. Shingabaw'osin and his subchiefs made it clear to all concerned that their band would no longer resist the American presence at the rapids. Shingwaukonse's success in thwarting Sassaba's conspiracy against Cass's party had lasting consequences for his career. From 1820 onward, Little Pine could assert that, with the backing of his group, he had been instrumental in containing a potentially volatile situation on the western frontier. This would carry considerable weight with Schoolcraft for years to come.[102]

Schoolcraft, for his part, firmly believed that Little Pine's actions paved the way towards a permanent and stable accommodation between the Ojibwa and the American government. He hoped in this calm atmosphere to discover as much as possible about the Ojibwa's religious beliefs, and to this end set out to cultivate a 'good understanding with this powerful and hitherto hostile tribe.'[103] Although he found the Ojibwa reluctant to discuss such matters with him, he was able, 'by suitable attention and presents,' to persuade Shingwaukonse to teach him two sets of songs, with their corresponding mnemonic devices cut into wood tablets, relating to the *Midéwiwin* and the *Wabano*.[104] He also obtained information from the chief relating to various Native artifacts, items of archaeological interest, and Ojibwa pictographs on a rock face at Agawa Canyon, on the northeastern coast of Lake Superior.[105]

Yet even though Schoolcraft treated Little Pine with special respect, the chief still remained *par inter pares* among his own people. He did not have a following large enough to separate from the 'home band.' Almost nothing is recorded of his activities between 1820 and 1826, although oral traditions suggest that he travelled extensively during these years. That Shingwaukonse acted as a fur-trade middleman for either the Johnston family or the North West Company would explain why he had contacts ranging as far west as the Red River by 1827.[106]

Little Pine Emerges as a Major Power-Holder

While Little Pine, in conformity with the 'policy' adopted by the Sault Ste Marie band after 1820, did not express his attachment openly to the British government, it is nevertheless evident that he was very much engaged in strengthening alignments with representatives of the British Crown. Schoolcraft attributed the rise in anti-American feeling at La Pointe after 1826 to the agitations of Mezai, or the Catfish, a brother to Keche Besheke who was chief of the Loon *dodemic* group at Chequamegon. Mezai's activities, the agent felt, could be traced to the influence of British traders at Sault Ste Marie and Drummond Island. Yet George Johnston, subagent at La Pointe between 1826 and 1829, saw Little Pine and another man, Kawgodaheway, as the principal impetus behind the contest. (This Kawgodaheway was either Peter Marksman, who eventually became a Methodist missionary in the Lake Superior region during the 1830s,[107] or another Ojibwa by the same name.) In May 1827, Johnston notified Schoolcraft of the following information he had received from Tugwaugaunay, a chief from south-western Lake Superior:

Kaw go dah e way and Shing wah konce ... told Missi if you do not listen and come to your English father ... he is determined to fire four shots, and there will not be left, one single man, woman or child living on the south shore of Lake Superior and throughout the interior country, within the limits of the United States, the power of his shots will be great inasmuch that he will not leave a tree standing.[108]

Johnston's words imply that Little Pine may have been involved in a minor stress-induced revitalization cult. The affair had undoubtedly been prompted by Britain's decision to vacate Drummond Island, until then a major power centre in the Upper Great Lakes. That political rather than economic factors underlay the disturbances is indicated by the fact that Kawgodaheway, Little Pine, and Mezai were political spokesmen for, respectively, the head chiefs at Mackinac, Sault Ste Marie, and Chequamegon. Once these three principal power-holders had readjusted their alignments to compensate for the radical political change, tensions subsided. Following Britain's establishment of a new centre for distributing Indian presents at Penetanguishene, Little Pine set out to repair relations with the American agent. It was important to restore balance to the complex fabric of Native political interactions on the frontier, given that the Native community was caught between two state powers. In this Little Pine was almost immediately successful. By 1828, the chief's relationship with Schoolcraft was such that the Native leader could anticipate as warm a reception from the American official at Sault Ste Marie as he could expect from the British at Penetanguishene.

In delivering a speech to Schoolcraft in the fall of 1826, Little Pine formally 'recapitulated his good offices and exertions towards the Americans' and ended by expressing a hope that the Ojibwa would continue to enjoy the protection of the American government.[109] Thus he demonstrated that he had made a firm choice to remain in the Sault area, a stance to which he held firm even in the face of British pressure for his band's removal to Penetanguishene on the eastern shore of Lake Huron a few years later. As later events were to prove, however, his words to Schoolcraft, contrary to the agent's assumptions at the time, did not necessarily reflect allegiance to American sovereignty. It constituted mainly a personal demand for aid and protection for his band.

Little Pine's bid for protection suggests that the chief could no longer be considered a 'lone ranger,' merely acting as orator to the different bands as the occasion arose. Rather, he had become a leader in his own right, exhibiting responsibility for his followers. He demonstrated his power-control in forming advantageous linkages while surrendering as little political or economic autonomy as possible. It was a position he strove to maintain, despite changing political and economic conditions, for the next twenty-five years.

Chapter Two

For the King and the King's Church

The Ojibwa Peace Advocate

While George Johnston's pronouncements in 1827 had represented Little Pine as hostile to American Indian policy, these assertions lost credibility for lack of further evidence. Shingwaukonse's subsequent activities brought him into increasing favour with Schoolcraft. The Ojibwa's seeming vacillation regarding their national loyalties also attracted attention at Penetanguishene; Superintendent Anderson sent the chief a wampum belt, upbraiding him and his followers for having 'two hearts' and encouraging them to reaffirm their ties to the Crown.[1] During a council held on St Joseph Island in 1829, Little Pine admitted that he had formerly believed that the British, in choosing to close their western post in response to American demands, had abandoned his people; but, he added, if the British proved faithful to their Native allies and continued to supply presents, he and his band would consider moving permanently to the Canadian shore.[2] Pleased with his reply, the British agent promised to build houses for his band in the vicinity of the rapids.[3]

Little Pine may well have used strong words against the United States in response to speeches delivered at annual present distributions by authorities such as Thomas G. Anderson, or when faced with the anti-American sentiments expressed by independent British traders. The commercial ventures of men such as Charles Oakes Ermatinger depended on keeping the Ojibwa loyal to the Crown in order to draw the western fur trade north of the border. Schoolcraft sourly observed the detrimental influence of Ermatinger's invective on Native individuals who had once been neutral, or even friendly to the Americans. One man, Bisconaosh, he stated, 'has been taken advantage of by Mr E., a trader on the opposite shore, who told him the Americans would cause him to be whipped, with other idle stuff of that sort, if he came over.' Not surprisingly, Bisconaosh gave the American agency a wide berth, and hesitated even to encamp on the American side, although 'he was anxious to return to the seat of his forefathers.'[4]

The Sault social sphere was charged with ambiguities. The divisive, bellicose rhetoric which so often characterized formal speech-making and commercial transactions did not affect everyday relations. Despite their different political and economic affiliations, Schoolcraft and Ermatinger exchanged visits. The agent stayed more than once in the trader's home, enjoying his host's generous hospitality and the lively, convivial atmosphere. Little Pine, moreover, could declare in council with the British that if a Native child were ever to break a mere pane of glass on the American side, he would be 'flogged for it,'[5] while at the same time remaining on cordial terms with Schoolcraft. Within this social milieu it remains unlikely, despite George Johnston's allegations in 1827, that Little Pine would ever have advocated open opposition to the United States.

Schoolcraft must have sensed this, for when told that Shingwaukonse had discouraged his people from participating in 1832 in the Black Hawk War, he immediately lauded the chief as a peace advocate. The news dispelled all the agent's former suspicions. Since Schoolcraft knew that Little Pine's example carried weight among all the Lake Superior bands, this disclosure eased the agent's anxieties regarding the likelihood that the Ojibwa west of the Sault would join in any hostilities.[6] In 1827, the Winnebago's resistance to the American takeover of their lead mines in southern Wisconsin had involved the Dakota, the Ojibwa's traditional enemies, and so had not threatened a widespread outbreak of violence. But now in 1832 the situation looked more serious. Little Pine, the agent realized, had once supported Brant's and Tecumseh's stand against the alienation to the United States of Native lands west of the Ohio. Now, given Shingwaukonse's disinclination to espouse war, it appeared that Brant's old 'western confederacy' had finally succumbed to internal political rifts, with the Ojibwa both in Canada and the United States generally reluctant to take up arms in land disputes.

In September 1833, Shingwaukonse explained to Francis Audrain, the subagent who took over at Sault Ste Marie after Schoolcraft's removal to an agency at Mackinac, how critical the Ojibwa's decision not to fight had been to subsequent Potawatomi activities in 1832. The Sauks and Foxes under Black Hawk were not the only ones intent on going to war. Little Pine stated that Shawanapenasse, a chief of the Grand Island band, kept

him abreast of events occurring west of the Bay de Noc region of Upper
Michigan. Although, according to Audrain, the chief at this time referred
to Shawanapenasse as his 'son,' this terminology likely denoted neither
close consanguinity nor even a major difference in ages between the two
men.[7] Shingwaukonse regarded those for whom he bore a special responsibility as his 'sons' and 'daughters,' especially when referring to Ojibwa
leaders whose interests he had promised to represent to government
authorities at the Sault.

> He [Shingwaukonse] said that wampum was sent from Penetanguishene in
> the spring of 1832 by some person in his name to the Potawatomi, he dis-
> claimed having any knowledge of it, and said it was unauthorized by him,
> that he was much surprised this last spring when his son Oshawwunne-
> benace visited him at Nibish [Nebish] rapids in the vicinity of the Sault to
> find he had in his possession the wampum which I now hand you, purport-
> ing to be a reply to the one above mentioned, that this was the first intima-
> tion he had of the wampum being sent to them in his name from
> Penetanguishene, he said he would like to find out who sent it, he thought it
> was some of the Ottawa and requested Mr Johnston to try to find out at
> Mackinac who had used his name.
>
> The purport of the message he received was that the Potawatomi were dis-
> satisfied, that they had drawn their war clubs from behind their backs and
> now held them in their hands ready to strike at any time, that they had one
> year to listen and observe the movements of their brothers the Chippewas.
>
> He said that two years ago he visited his son at Bay de Nock and men-
> tioned to the Indians there his intention of remaining quiet and adopting
> the religion of the white man.
>
> He said he had always listened to his Father Mr Schoolcraft's counsels and
> would do so still and would remain quiet.
>
> He said that the wampum, pipe and war hatchet ... given to him in the
> spring of 1832 ... [were] intended by the Sauks to be an invitation to go to
> war against the Americans, that it was sent through a Potawatomi living near
> Chicago who had altered the words of the speech and informed him it was to
> go against the Sioux.[8]

Schoolcraft increasingly became familiar with several members of the
chief's family, especially Buhkwujjenene, whom he invited in June of 1832
to join him on a journey to the sources of the Mississippi River. The
agent's aims in conducting the expedition, in addition to ascertaining the
degree of support for the Black Hawk War among the western bands,

included geographical and mineralogical exploration and the vaccination of the Native people against smallpox. Buhkwujjenene left in company with Schoolcraft, with Dr Douglas Houghton acting as surgeon and naturalist, George Johnston as interpreter, Lt James Allen of the United States Fifth Infantry as head of a ten-man military escort, and about twenty *engagés*. Buhkwujjenene, however, may not have travelled with the others beyond La Pointe, for Boutwell noted in his journal for 21 June that 'Poquochenini remains with Mr. Hall, who is alone, Mr. W[arren] being on his journey to Mackinac.'[9] Buhkwujjenene's association with the Reverend William Boutwell, who had been sent by the American Mission Board to the band at Leech Lake, and the Reverend Sherman Hall, an Episcopal missionary stationed at La Pointe since 1831, suggests that Little Pine's son, a youth of twenty-one years of age at the time, became fairly well acquainted with the teachings of Christianity before he returned from his travels in August. He had travelled to La Pointe and points west many times with his father as a boy, and knew his father's contacts, particularly the Cadottes. Within five years, these new relationships led him to marry Marguerite Cadotte from La Pointe, who willingly acquiesced, since two of her brothers previously had decided to remain permanently at Garden River.[10] Buhkwujjenene's growing knowledge of this subject nevertheless paralleled, rather than fostered, his father's interest in the Christian faith, since by the summer of 1832, Shingwaukonse had already begun his own investigations into the nature of the Christian god.

By his own admission the chief had gained his first insights into Christianity through the Roman Catholic Church.[11] His initial contacts with this faith could have occurred between 1815 and 1827 when priests from Quebec sporadically held summer services at Drummond Island *en route* to and from their main mission field at Red River. Since questions surrounding his conversion were intriguing, I developed several interview sessions with elders from Garden River to discussing what might have led Little Pine to seek an understanding of Christianity. The following section draws on the explanations provided by these elders.

The Preservation of Potentiality in the Ojibwa Universe

Traditional Ojibwa belief required a leader to form an intimate, long-term relationship with spirit persons, to whom he appealed both for material help and for the preservation of a workable balance among powers in the Ojibwa universe. Such a balance was viewed as necessary for man's security and survival. Invocations to these beings included the plea that the reciprocity implicit in the relationship might never fail.[12]

The 'blessings' of white technology and skills would similarly issue from assuming respectful behaviour towards the white man's god. It was therefore important to choose the religious affiliation and mode of conduct which would best establish a beneficial relationship with that god. For this reason Little Pine was willing to listen to the often-conflicting religious arguments offered by the different denominations of missionaries whom he encountered from 1828 onward. By subtle forms of questioning, he rapidly distinguished the main ideological differences among them. Discussions between Shingwaukonse and representatives of the Methodist, Anglican, Baptist, and Roman Catholic religions have been preserved and offer valuable insights into the attitude which the Native leader held towards these denominations as potential sources of blessings. Although the chief exclusively espoused the Anglican faith between 1833 and 1838, he relaxed his commitment somewhat when Anglicanism failed to bring the expected reciprocal results. In later years, he remarked that his initial problem in trying to learn about Christianity stemmed not from lack of available sources of instruction, but from the danger of confusion bred through encountering such a variety of religious views and opinions.[13]

Little Pine evidently retained a sense of balance and perspective within this sea of ideological diversity by retaining much of his faith in his traditional beliefs, while gradually adding aspects of Christian belief to the range of his religious knowledge. This constituted a syncretistic process, involving little polarization of meaning in symbolic terms. The locus of this integration lay with the individual, although such was the nature of Shingwaukonse's influence within his band that elements of his modified belief system have become a cultural legacy, maintained by his descendants. Otherwise, Native thought and its expression remained little changed in structure and content. The traditional world view continued to inform most activities. Little Pine apparently continued participating in the *Midéwiwin*, *Wabano*, and conjuring ceremonies. He also retained his religious paraphernalia. According to Ogista, 'his father destroyed all his papers and birch-barks, and painted dreams, dances, and songs, shortly before his death.'[14]

Elders contacted at Garden River argued that Shingwaukonse would have accorded high priority to the need for maintaining balance in the affairs of men, although such matters remained subordinate to relationships maintained with the spiritual realm, the source of all power. White people were there to stay. Aggression no longer posed a viable alternative for Native peoples residing in the Upper Great Lakes region, and Little Pine counselled others to preserve peace. At the same time, he sought to have his territorial rights as a Native leader recognized by the British and

Americans, not only for the sake of his own band but also on behalf of Ojibwa who wished to escape the pressures of white settlement and resource exploitation south of Lake Superior. This extension of a refuge was not necessarily an appeal for the permanent settlement of all who might respond to his call, but an offer which would hold until a measure of stability returned to the sphere of Native–white relations. For an enlarged population to reside even temporarily on these lands would require instruction in the white man's skills. Since, in keeping with the Native perspective, such blessings would come only after a period of adequate preparation, one had to choose a course of action appropriate to the nature of the gift desired. In consequence, Shingwaukonse set out to learn as much as he could about the white man's god.

Opportunities, but with a Price

Opportunities for religious instruction and training in practical skills arose in conjunction with a government-sponsored program for Native agricultural settlements on a plan devised by the Methodists. British Indian policy had been undergoing revision for more than a decade. In 1828, Maj. Gen. H.C. Darling, soon to assume the office of chief superintendent of Indian affairs, submitted a number of proposals to the colonial secretary, Sir George Murray. These would form the basis for a new perspective on the administration of the Native population in the two Canadas, in keeping with the dominant philosophy of the era, philanthropic liberalism. This ideology engendered humanitarian and evangelical missionary movements which perceived political, social, and moral reform as the leading causes to be upheld in the colonies, as well as in Britain. Darling's proposals developed into policy measures under the direction of Sir James Kempt, administrator of Lower Canada, and Sir John Colborne, lieutenant-governor of Upper Canada. The idea was to concentrate Native people in villages with only enough land to encourage the cultivation of family farms, and to assist in the development of these communities by providing tools and training in agriculture and animal husbandry.[15] Education and religious instruction, Colborne suggested, might be supported by a fund financed by the sale or lease of Native lands. The civilization scheme was expected to attain two important goals; it would render the Native population self-sufficient, and it would make the system, once in place, economical for the government. The Indian Department's transfer in 1830 from military to civil control brought its budget under the annual scrutiny of the Imperial Parliament, which ensured emphasis on retrenchment during the experimental phases of the policy's implementation.[16]

One of the first actions of the British government under the new policy was to collect three groups of south-eastern Ojibwa, as well as a band from Drummond Island, into two settlements at Coldwater and the Narrows just north of Lake Simcoe, and to furnish them with agents, missionaries, teachers, farmers, blacksmiths, and mechanics. Although the Sault Ste Marie band was invited to join, it refused to leave the St Mary's straits area. The reason for declining seems to have arisen from the band's wish to distance itself from British and American control, which, although dispensing benefits, also threatened to interfere directly in band affairs. By remaining at the Sault, Shingwaukonse and his band could enjoy advantages, such as the services of a blacksmith, extended by the American government, while preserving the autonomy necessary for observing and weighing the outcomes of following either British or U.S. policy. Little Pine's band was well aware of its strategic position *vis-à-vis* the British and American Indian agencies on the north-western frontier in the early decades of the nineteenth century. And the group was careful to preserve a range of options.

To attain Western technical knowledge remained a foremost aim, since such knowledge could be adapted to expand the range of economic possibilities open to Native people. But the process would be gradual, not imposed. Shingwaukonse concentrated on adding to traditional skills, rather than replacing major aspects of a valued way of life. He focused on further developing a technical and social organizational base already in existence. By contrast, migration to Penetanguishene and an exclusive reliance on farming would mean relinquishing a large body of proven traditional practices developed in response to a familiar environment.

In the early 1830s, Shingwaukonse was progressing towards achieving three goals. All would ensure long-term continuance of much-needed 'blessings.' The first two were economic: they were to obtain external aid for developing the range of Native technical skills; and to devise new ways of protecting the band's resource base. The third and perhaps most important task involved establishing new linkages with what he perceived to be both the spiritual and political sources of the white man's strength. Little Pine and his band set out to develop an approach which might rapidly secure their goals. If missionary endeavours at the rapids tended in following years to be strongly influenced by Native interests, it was because the chief and his people had a strategy for attaining their goals in which the resident missionary, even before his arrival, had already been cast in a key role.

The Influence of Protestant Missions on Ojibwa Leadership at the Rapids

Little Pine had no need to leave the rapids area to seek religious instruction, since missionaries were close at hand. While the Church of England did not send a denominational representative to the Canadian side until 1830, American Episcopal missionaries had been sporadic visitors to the area since the 1820s. The Society of Jesus resumed active work after 1834, and in 1846 the Roman Catholic mission at the American Sault became a Jesuit charge under Father Jean Baptiste Menet, SJ.[17] Father Frederick Baraga, after his labours at L'Anse and prior to his consecration as bishop in 1853, erected a church on Sugar Island, where he held services for approximately three years.[18] Meanwhile, the Native population between Thessalon and Batchewana Bay on the Canadian shore drew the attention of both Catholic and Episcopal itinerant missionaries.

When a fund reserved under the terms of the 1826 Fond du Lac treaty provided for the erection and maintenance of Native mission schools in the vicinity, the Sault became the special focus for missionary exertions. In 1828, the Baptists under the Reverend Abel Bingham established the first of these institutions behind Fort Brady. Three years later, Methodists entered the field, petitioning Schoolcraft's agency for a grant of land and funds to begin their own school on Sugar Island.

This venture was part of a larger scheme, developed by the exhorter John Sunday, to induce Ojibwa from Grape Island, Bay of Quinte, to form an agricultural settlement on Sugar Island. The scheme attracted considerable notice at the rapids. In September 1831, several head men signed a document surrendering a rectangular tract of land on Sugar Island, extending along the shore from a point opposite Garden River. Although Little Pine was not party to this treaty, he was well known to the Methodists. George Copway, a Methodist exhorter who was at the Sault in 1831, described him as commanding in appearance: 'a chief of much celebrity – noted for his bravery, activity, and perseverance.'[19]

The Sugar Island settlement floundered owing to opposition from both Native traditionalists and Roman Catholics, and cholera forced the mission congregation to disperse by the spring of 1832.[20] Yet these setbacks failed to discourage Methodist missionary activity. In June 1833, the Sault band substituted land at Little Rapids, approximately three kilometres below Fort Brady and closer to the main fishing grounds, for their former grant to John Sunday on Sugar Island. From this base, the Methodists soon extended their activities along the south shore of Lake Superior. In 1832, John Sunday and the Reverend John Clarke began a mission on Keweenaw Bay which developed into the Native community of Pequaming near L'Anse, Michigan.

Methodist missionaries often found the established head chiefs reluctant to embrace the new beliefs. These leaders preferred to retain their traditional regulatory powers over their groups' social, economic, and political activities. The missionaries' desire 'to improve' or 'to elevate' could develop into actual control over Native groups, and some chiefs saw this as a very real threat to their leadership.[21] By contrast, bands whose political and economic autonomy had been severely undermined by the decline of the fur trade and white usurpation of their lands saw attaching themselves to the missions as a way of alleviating their difficulties.

During the 1830s many of the most notable Methodist preachers of Ojibwa extraction laboured in the Upper Great Lakes region; among them, Peter Jones, John Sunday, George Copway, and Peter Marksman gained widespread attention by promoting the idea of Native 'homelands' set apart from the pressures of frontier society, where Native people could seek spiritual solace, Christian fellowship, and material assistance in the development of their communities. This vision of refuge areas promoted and protected by Christian missionary endeavours greatly influenced Little Pine's own scheme for a settlement north-east of the rapids.

Seeking the Great Spirit of Peace

Following the distribution of presents at Penetanguishene in 1832, Little Pine continued his search for religious knowledge by attending a Methodist council at the Narrows, near Lake Simcoe. He evidently had been invited by John Sunday and represented one of six 'pagan' chiefs from localities 'scattered abroad between that place and the Rocky Mountains.'[22] No whites attended, although, according to Charles Elliot, a Wesleyan Methodist visiting from England who received the account indirectly from an Ojibwa missionary by the name of Peter Jacobs, Shingwaukonse's appeal for instruction in Christianity and the benefits of civilization stemmed from a wish to espouse peace. The chief's speech, in which he told of his failing faith in traditional spiritual agencies and his desire to learn of Christianity, was one of the highlights of the occasion:

I ... began to think, 'What shall I do without a God? I remembered John Sunday speaking about a great God; and I thought that I would come to this country, to see who knew about John Sunday's God. I have heard of many stars shining over my head' [meaning the different denominations of Christians]. 'I wish very much that some of you would give me information which is the true star. Just before I left home, I received a string of black and white wampum, and a tomahawk, the blade of which was painted red. When I considered that although my arms were very long, and my body very large, should I enter into this war, I should be the means of spilling much blood, I determined to decline it, and therefore made this answer: – "I am now unable to render you any assistance in this warfare, having just commenced to seek after a Great Spirit [Keche Munnetoo], and feeling very poor in my heart."'[23]

In reply, the Christian missionaries and chiefs acknowledged that they had received many material benefits from adopting Methodism. Joseph Sawyer, an especially staunch Methodist from the vicinity of present-day Mississauga, Ontario, stated that if Little Pine could 'visit our village at the Credit River ... [he] would see a great many good houses, a chapel, a school house, a work shop, a saw mill, and many other improvements.'[24] Shingwaukonse thus heard about the sort of material advantages one might expect from adhering to Christianity. But he also had a deep faith in the ability of Christianity to help the Ojibwa gain a secure place within the changing society of the Upper Great Lakes region. To this end he proved willing, between 1832 and 1838, to forward letters and wampum belts carrying promises of peace and brotherhood from the Lake Simcoe Methodist head chief, Mesquahkeence, or Yellowhead,[25] to the leaders Quezezhanshish and Nezhepenasse on the Keweenaw Peninsula. Little Pine was in regular communication with both men.[26]

Scholars are now beginning to examine the manner in which Native leaders expressed their receptivity to Christian instruction and its concomitant rewards.[27] In the past, however, it was generally supposed that missionaries themselves provided the initiative for change, with Native people either accepting or rejecting the teaching set before them. Missionaries have been viewed as major catalytic agents in easing the transition of Native society from relative political and economic autonomy to dependence on government policy. They have also been regarded as heady idealists, determined to establish a form of heaven on earth among the 'benighted heathen' – a role which made them unsympathetic to government interference in affairs pertaining to their special mission. The role of the missionary has been seen as an extensive one 'which contains many differing roles in itself [with] ... particular facets being defined by the context or situation in which the role is played ...'[28] The principal limitations on the scope of missionary endeavours, it has been argued, stemmed from government interference, particularly competition from government agents for power and prestige. At the Sault, however, the missionary would find his own goals subordinated to plans already set forth by the Native community. Native expectations would cast him in a role he was far from anticipating.

Choosing a Denomination

Shingwaukonse remained uncommitted to any Christian denomination throughout 1832. Instead, he engaged in numerous private conversations with missionaries, trying to find one man on whom he could rely to help him achieve his goals. In December, for instance, he informed the Baptist missionary, Bingham, not only that he intended to become Christian, but also that he was encouraging Native people living far to the west to come to the Sault and embrace the white man's religion. Bingham, who concentrated almost entirely on eliciting signs of 'grace' as a prelude to personal salvation, was taken aback. Faced with such a grand scheme, put forward by an individual he knew to be a medicine man, he treated the suggestions lightly:

> In a conference I had with him [Shingwaukonse] about a year ago, in which I compared the two religions [Christianity and the *Midéwiwin*], he acknowledged that the meta religion looked like the religion of the Devil. Today he acknowledges his belief in the truth of the Xtian religion and expresses his desire that all the Inds. should embrace it. He says he has the past summer taken it upon him to visit several distant clans of Inds. in the Chippewa country to recommend to them unitedly to embrace the Christian religion, yet he acknowledges his neglect of the concerns of his own soul, and pleads his misfortune which has disabled him from meeting the demands of his Trader.[29]

Bingham's response was to direct Little Pine to meditate on the condition of his soul and to refrain from drinking. The chief's desultory reply to the last admonition particularly concerned the missionary: 'He acknowledges the advice was good,' Bingham reflected, 'but whether he will adopt it is another question.'[30]

Shingwaukonse, it turned out, had little patience with emotional evangelism. About a month later, two of the chief's daughters and two of his sons-in-law – the first a son of the Crane Nawgichigomee, and the second named Megissanequa – arrived at the Baptist mission, and Bingham organized a conference. All had been members of the Baptist congregation. Both daughters admitted to 'backsliding'; one had twice joined in the *Midéwiwin*. As he had with their father, Bingham spared no pains in pointing out the evils of following the traditional religion. Not surprisingly, both became very frightened, especially as they had recently experienced a death in the family.[31]

Two days afterward, Bingham and his interpreter, John Tanner,[32] went to visit Shingwaukonse and other members of the Garden River band to arrange a similar testimony meeting. This time the chief controlled the conversation, curbing the missionary's inclination to expound on individual 'failings.' The chief impressed on the missionary the seriousness of the situation among the western Ojibwa and their need for a peaceful reconciliation with the whites. 'Was informed by him that most of the Ojibwa country was about upon the point of rising against the Americans,' Bingham recorded. 'If one man was foolish enough to strike, the whole would follow.'[33] Shingwaukonse's answer to the crisis involved settling the western bands on the British side and instructing them in the Gospel. Yet it was quite obvious that he could expect little help from the Baptist missionary in developing his own plan. Bingham evinced little or no interest. Assistance would have to come from elsewhere.

The King's Church at the Canadian Rapids

As far as the Anglican church was concerned, the British Sault presented a virgin field, unspoiled by interference from government agencies and rival denominations apart from those on the American side. With the support of Lt-Gov. Sir John Colborne and James Stewart, Bishop of Quebec, the Society for Converting and Civilizing the Indians of Upper Canada was founded at York on 30 October 1830, with the Bishop as president and Colborne as patron. The society described its purpose in grand terms by attributing the success of Britain's imperial designs in part to the special mission of the established church: 'The sacred use to which Great Britain, at this day, puts the enlargement of her empire in remote parts, is to impart to them the religious faith to which she owes her superiority: – and it is before her influence, thus exercised, more than any other nation, that superstition and ignorance are fast disappearing from the globe.'[34] Financial backing for the society failed to match these grand expectations, and it was only with the promised aid of the Indian Department that the society could make plans for the development of a model agricultural community at the Sault.

During the summer of 1830, the Reverend George Archbold visited the Lake Huron district to examine possible sites for a Native mission. Archbold recommended several locations, and in the fall of 1830 James D. Cameron, Jr, the son of the Hudson's Bay Company factor by the same name, set out with a schoolteacher to begin his labours at La Cloche and Sault Ste Marie.[35] The reception he received from the Ojibwa at La Cloche differed radically from the response he encountered at the Sault. Despite his initial zealousness, young Cameron had failed to win any adherents at all during his brief stay at the La Cloche post. According to factor John McBean, the missionary departed for the Sault in June of 1831 leaving the La Cloche band in exactly 'the state in which he found them.'[36]

Cameron's experiences with Little Pine's people, by contrast, led him to entertain grand hopes for the Sault mission. In January 1832 he placed the number of converts at fifty-two souls and the number of children attending the school at between eighteen and twenty. He was encouraged by the interest taken in learning the Ten Commandments, which he had translated into the Ojibwa language, and prayer meetings, he reported, 'are generally numerously and punctually attended.'[37] Little else is known of the fledgling Anglican mission. In the spring of 1831 the society removed him from his position, since he had joined the Reverend Abel Bingham and become an itinerant Baptist preacher. After marrying one of Shingabaw'osin's daughters in 1835, he retired to the locality of the Tahquamenon River, west of the American Sault, while still sporadically acting as an interpreter for his successor at the Anglican mission, William McMurray.[38]

McMurray, who arrived on the north shore in the fall of 1832, received as enthusiastic a welcome from Shingwaukonse's band as had Cameron. With the abandonment of the La Cloche mission, the Anglicans focused their energies on the British Sault. But this did not necessarily mean that the Church of England was well prepared for the task ahead of it. McMurray embarked on his labours with little knowledge of the Ojibwa people and even less about the locality to which he had been appointed by Lieutenant-Governor Colborne. He carried with him an introductory address from the Society for Converting and Civilizing the Indians which, in a paternalistic tone, stated, 'If you listen to the teacher ... and hear all that he will tell you out of the Great Spirit's book ... the Great Spirit will forgive your former bad deeds, and will make you his Friends.'[39]

Shingwaukonse ignored the patronizing tone of the address and demanded to know if the missionary had been sent by the lieutenant-governor. McMurray handed him his credentials, with the provincial seal attached. Only 'after comparing this with the medal which had been given him for his services to the King, the Chief was satisfied that he was duly accredited.'[40] In a set speech, Little Pine then demanded to know why the houses had not been built according to promises made him between 1829 and 1832: 'We have heard for the last four years that houses were to be built for us, but we do not even see them begun; but we have ears to hear with, and hearts to understand. If we should see the buildings up, it would satisfy us, together with our young men, and then we would attend to the pursuits of agriculture and settle upon our lands.'[41]

The houses would stand as a token of the government's desire to help the Ojibwa develop their economic base, he continued, but they would not be ends in themselves. The Anglicans should be made aware of the nature of the grave relationship they were about to assume, for the lands were poor. Without long-term aid, even if 'we were to settle upon them and endeavour to follow the pursuits of agriculture, they would not yield a sufficiency to support us.'[42] Little Pine implied a preference for the hunting way of life, but admitted that game had grown scarce.

The chief next admonished the missionary not to blame or belittle the Ojibwa because they sometimes drank: 'I suppose our Father thinks we are like children; always sitting and warming ourselves at the fire, and also thinks we are such, as regards rum; but it is not so with us, for during the winter we live upon meat and fish, and any other game we may chance to get in the woods: but when we see the white people in the spring, they offer us a glass and we take it.'[43] He charged the missionary to care for several widows who could no longer help themselves. Finally, he declared that his people would prefer to have the distribution of their presents take place at Sault Ste Marie rather than at Penetanguishene.

Shingwaukonse's speech evidenced power-control by merging the power-of-the-powerless approach with a strategy gauged to warn the missionary not to take his words lightly, especially his challenging of the white stereotype of the 'drunken Indian.' In this manner the chief forced the new missionary ultimately to define the situation using terms outlined by Shingwaukonse himself. The chief continued to wield the same degree of control over McMurray's endeavours for the next six years. But it would not be all one way. The Ojibwa also would prove willing to accede to many changes which, their chief persuaded them, would be for their eventual good.

Reciprocity and Compromise – A Two-Sided Venture

The range of meanings brought to a transaction by each party taking part in it need not necessarily be congruent in order for a relationship to function well.[44] Neither is the expressed intention of the most dynamic party always the one which most influences the eventual nature and outcome of the transaction. The relationship which gradually came to be established between McMurray and Shingwaukonse evolved out of a series of minor compromises and adjustments made on both sides. When it was finally terminated in 1838, it left precedents which served to shape the expectations of the Ojibwa regarding the role of future Anglican missionaries. McMurray, on a salary of £120 per annum,[45] lacked the means to effect any radical changes in the Ojibwa's way of life. Instead, his primary goal was to spread the Gospel and induce his flock to behave like a Christian congregation. He wished to wean the Ojibwa away from drinking and towards raising enough agricultural produce to make them self-sufficient. He did not expect great advances in the way of schooling during these early years, and made no secret of the fact that he thought missionaries highly overrated the need for and benefits of education.[46] Primary attention, he argued, should be given to helping the parents of the children assume settled habits, and then better attendance at a school would in all probability follow.

In this respect, McMurray differed greatly from the Low Church evangelicals who would succeed him. Prior to his appointment to the Sault, he had been enrolled as a divinity student in a school run at York by the High Church archdeacon John Strachan, and had served as catechist at St James Church, York, of which Strachan was rector. McMurray did not view himself as God's special appointee to radically reform and enlighten the Native people. If anything, his religious credentials were rather humble. He did not receive his deacon's orders until August 1833. Before this time he could preach but not conduct full-scale services. As a deacon, he was not permitted to administer the Eucharist – the prerogative of a priest. His main authority resided in a special commission, bestowed on him by the lieutenant-governor, which enabled him to swear in the Hudson's Bay Company factors William Nourse, Angus Bethune, and John Swanson as the first magistrates on the north shore of the straits, and which vested him with the responsibilities of an Indian agent. Young, inexperienced, and occupying the lower echelons of the Established Church, McMurray adapted to the Sault milieu more rapidly than it responded, in turn, to his teachings. During the first winter he resided at the Hudson's Bay post and at the Johnston home. He was readily accepted into the Johnston family. They, in turn, were familiar with Shingwaukonse's reputation as a medicine man and leader, and doubtless enabled McMurray to form a far more intimate and favourable impression of the chief than he would otherwise have gained on his own. In the fall of 1833 he cemented his relationship with the Johnstons by marrying Charlotte Johnston, or Ogenebugoquay – 'The Woman of the Wild Rose.'[47] By this time McMurray had ceased to live up to his name, Nazhekawahwahsung – 'The Lone Lightning' – bestowed on him by Little Pine's band. Charlotte, who had formerly aided Bingham in his work, now joined James Cameron in acting as an interpreter at the Anglican mission.[48]

Soliciting McMurray's Aid in Defending Band Resources

Little Pine immediately endeavoured to gain McMurray's assistance in protecting the 'home band's' prerogatives to land and resources on both sides of the St Mary's River. The American Fur Company's entry into commercial fishing in 1832 provided employment for the resident Métis; but for the chief, who sought to further the interests of the group as well as of individual residents, the need for a degree of economic independence from major monopolistic enterprises remained paramount. The American Fur Company's endeavours to attain exclusive privileges to several fishery locations on northern Lake Michigan led to confrontations with Native users of these grounds. By June 1833, Little Pine was representing Ojibwa leaders in a similar dispute with the American government regarding usurpation by non-Natives of the rapids fishery secured by treaty in 1820. The Anglican missionary agreed to help when Shingwaukonse informed him that his people might have to quit the south shore of the rapids altogether, since the American government proved unwilling to interfere.[49]

Little Pine approached the subject of resource use from the Ojibwa standpoint: individual initiative had to be reconciled with a moral premise that one should not harm a fellow group member's ability to make a living. He extended Ojibwa regulatory powers to new commercial resources such as timber, which was now becoming important to the Ojibwa economy. Fishing and logging would provide revenue for the band under a primarily Native-controlled extractive system.

He soon had mustered a local lobby group, which included the Anglican missionary and Kaygayosh – the third-eldest son of Maidosagee. In addition, a local medical doctor and a merchant lent their support. If

Francis Audrain failed to respond sympathetically, he threatened, his band would move permanently to the Canadian side. Completely taken aback by this forthrightness, Audrain cast around for possible non-Native perpetrators to blame for this sudden turn of events:

> Shingwauk & Kawguash [Kaygayosh] with about twenty-five or thirty follow-ers, principally of the Home band visited the office, accompanied by the Revd. McMurray, Dr. Hoyt and Levake – The visit was an unexpected one to me. Kawguash and Shingwauk made speeches, the tenor of which were com-plaints against the white people for building Houses and fishing on the res-ervation above the garrison, & destroying their timber on Sugar Island. The foregoing appeared to me as a mere pretext for their visit – & to my astonish-ment they concluded by saying, that the Indians were all going to the Can-ada side to encamp ... I told them I thought if they went over & made a permanent abode on the Canada shore that you would shut the door of this office. Several of them said they would not go over, & I believe few if any will cross.[50]

The timing of events none the less suggests that the primary impetus behind this migration to the Canadian side came from Little Pine, not the missionary. For years before McMurray's arrival, Shingwaukonse had been encouraging the Ojibwa to settle at Garden River and on Sugar Island. In addition to securing protection for the timber and fishery, the chief also directed the missionary to ensure that, in terms of government assistance and protection, the Ojibwa of Sault Ste Marie would be placed 'upon the same footing as those of the River Credit.'[51] There was no doubt that by 1832 the chief had an array of tasks ready and waiting for McMurray to perform.

The chief had been priming Native leaders throughout the Upper Great Lakes area for years to expect a missionary-sponsored community on the north shore of the St Mary's channel; he now proclaimed the time to have arrived. In consequence, McMurray received numerous applica-tions from head chiefs residing between L'Anse and Fond du Lac who wanted to join the mission community. Keche Besheke, a La Pointe leader, personally visited the missionary in March. 'Waishkey,' another prominent individual from La Pointe and a relative of the Johnston fam-ily, also 'seemed to be desirous of settling on our side, provided he had a house to settle in.'[52]

Shingwaukonse considered that, at last, his powers were equal to the task of revitalizing the Native community. He had expended a small fortune in skins in acquiring his knowledge of power-control from medicine people willing to impart their knowledge at a high price, and he evidently felt confident that his power alignments would work. Yet, throughout the summer of 1833, he still refused to commit himself to one particular Christian denomination, although he stated that his band regarded McMurray as their main Christian guide. He may have been reluctant to commit because of his close attachment to Kaygayosh, who had assumed the head chieftainship of the Crane band following Shingabaw'osin's death in December 1828.

A well-known medicine man, Kaygayosh had been Little Pine's mentor in the *Midéwiwin*, and doubtless remained a confidant in other matters as well. The price of Kaygayosh's esoteric knowledge of medicine had been high. Little Pine had expended 'at least forty packs of beaver skins,' with each pack containing 'one hundred pounds of beaver skins.' Since beaver at the time was worth from 'eight to ten dollars a pound,' the cost of forty packs would have been in the range of 'thirty thousand dollars.'[53] Kaygayosh, meanwhile, viewed his own political power as issuing from his prominent position within the Crane group, rather than from his wealth as a *Midéwiwin* practitioner or from any attachment to a mission establishment.

Little Pine Accepts the Anglican Faith

While he continued to work with traditional leaders such as Kaygayosh, Little Pine eventually saw his way clear to requesting baptism from McMurray in the summer of 1833, following the missionary's expedition to the Eastern Townships to receive orders as a deacon. Buhkwujjenene had suffered from a severe nasal haemorrhage, and during a prayer session held by the Anglican mission for the youth's recovery, the father suddenly 'threw down his pipe, arose and proclaimed: "Why should not I also offer up a prayer to the Great Spirit on behalf of my son?"'[54] Buhkwujjenene's recovery soon afterwards reinforced Little Pine's confidence that he was following the correct course. On 6 October he requested baptism for himself, and in November assumed the appearance of monogamy by marrying his youngest wife, Ogahbageyhequa, in an Anglican ceremony, although at least two of his former wives remained with the band after this date. Buhkwujjenene; Ogista and his wife Pewaundahgahsenequa; Kabaosa and his wife Ogimaqua; and Megissanequa and his wife Owiaquahgeybegoqua formed the initial core of Anglican converts at the Sault.[55]

Then in March 1834, McMurray baptised Mezai, who had come from La Pointe to join the settlement, Mezai's brother Ahnahgeah, and Mezai's wife. A week later, a woman by the name of Ojanganuse, either one of Little Pine's daughters or one of his former wives, and a youth of fifteen, who was likely her son, named Apequash, accepted baptism. James Robertson known as Odahbit, the sole survivor of the tragedy which had claimed Sassaba's life more than a decade before, was also among this number.[56] Robertson had been interpreter at the Hudson's Bay Company's Michipicoten post, but had resigned his position on being employed as a catechist by McMurray at the Sault.

By June, Piabetassung and his wife Obahbahmejewenoqua had also accepted baptism, along with the sixty-five-year-old Isabella Sayers and the fifty-five-year-old Omenahkumigoqua or 'Susan Askin,' who may have been Shingwaukonse's sister. Piabetassung's entire family took the surname 'Askin,' likely at the head chief's insistence. Shingwaukonse himself assumed the missionary's name of 'William McMurray,' but rarely used it except in correspondence with McMurray himself. Ogista became 'Thomas McMurray' and Buhkwujjenene, 'Henry McMurray.' Nahwahquashkum, Shingwaukonse's eldest son, finally baptized in June in spite of opposition from his in-laws, accepted the name 'George McMurray.'

The missionary kept his promise about arranging an interview with the lieutenant-governor and accompanied the chief, two of Little Pine's sons, and two of his sons-in-law to York (Toronto), on snowshoes during the winter of 1833–4. One can only imagine the difficulty of negotiating icy coastal trails along the north shore of Lake Huron, but the party arrived safely and the chief, on meeting the lieutenant-governor, presented a wampum belt.[57] Colborne granted Little Pine authority to protect timber and fisheries near the Sault and stated that houses would be built in accordance with earlier governmental promises. According to McMurray, 'His Excellency gave a gracious reception and ultimately answered by ordering one hundred and fifty pounds to be appropriated for the foundation of a village, which will be commenced in the ensuing spring.'[58]

With the expectation that a farming community would be established, the years 1833 and 1834 proved rewarding ones for McMurray. The Ojibwa, dressed in a tasteful blend of Native and European clothing, attended worship regularly and were orderly in conduct and polite and helpful in disposition. During the winter, families travelled from their hunting grounds, more than twenty kilometres distant in many instances, to listen to McMurray preach, and deposit their children at the mission school, which opened in November 1833. The numbers grew week by week:

On the 14th November, sixteen days after his arrival, Mr McMurray ...

preached to an assembly of thirty persons, chiefly Indians. On the 25th, a considerable increase was visible in the attendance; and on Sunday, 10th January, fifty persons assembled for divine worship ... on the next Sabbath, eighty persons united in the service of the church.[59]

Most abandoned drinking. The chief, on being approached by whisky sellers, was quoted as replying, 'When I wanted it, you would not give it to me. Now I do not want it, you try to force it upon me. Drink it yourselves!'[60] Such statements, quoted over and over in missionary reports, created a lasting, but erroneous impression of Little Pine as having remained a teetotaller for the rest of his life.

While McMurray diligently accorded credit for such changes to the intervention of God and the church, he at times felt swept along by a momentum he did not fully understand. Little Pine and his sons expected the clergyman to expand the scope of his missionary endeavours along Lake Superior's north shore long before McMurray was ready to take such a step. As early as December 1833, Ogista asked for supplies so that he and a companion might travel to Michipicoten and the Pic to preach the Gospel. McMurray hesitated – the society disapproved of persons not properly qualified acting on behalf of the church. Yet still, when Ogista repeated the offer, the deacon thought he could justify the undertaking:

> As I considered the objections of the Committee [regarding unauthorized preaching] to apply only to the permanent engagement of such services, I acquiesced in their proposal, and furnished them with provisions to and from Michipicoten, at the expense of 6 dollars. I trust the sanction of the Committee will not be withheld [with regard] to this step, which I considered it my duty to take.[61]

Not long afterwards, McMurray heartily proclaimed, quoting the Bible, that, indeed, 'all things worked together for good,' since George Keith, the Hudson's Bay Company factor at Michipicoten, provided transportation for Ogista's party free of charge.[62] At the same time Keith spoke highly of McMurray's work, as evidenced 'per Augustus [Ogista] and his companions': 'I am really amazed at the knowledge they have acquired of Christianity. They have behaved in every respect with the greatest propriety, and I am persuaded the seeds they have sown will bring forth fruit to repentance and reformation.'[63]

By this time McMurray felt that no dynamic, other than the divine will, could be operating to sponsor such willing attention to the Gospel on the part of Native peoples in the Upper Great Lakes area. Chiefs at Michipicoten and the Pic invited missionaries to reside permanently with their bands. In the spring of 1834, Ojibwa from west of Lake Superior began congregating far in advance of the time they usually assembled at the Sault *en route* to the distribution of presents. 'The number of Indians ... during the summer has been very unusual, chiefly from the head waters of Lake Superior, Leech and Sandy Lakes,' McMurray noted. His work load grew dramatically because of these newcomers. He increased his services on Sunday to three, and the weekly services to two, with the number attending varying from 150 to 200 persons. And still the crowds continued to grow:

> Many more are thinking seriously and incline to follow the example of their brethren, all of whom remain steadfast in the Faith, in no instance, whatever, reverting to their former practices. They hold religious meetings among themselves, on such days as they do not attend to me. As might be expected from the nature of our holy religion, the new convert soon becomes warmly interested for his benighted brethren, and his anxiety on this account will be no matter of surprise to those whose birth and education have been Christian.[64]

By the fall of 1834, McMurray had assisted the chief in a major way by helping him gain a special status for his territorial claim through Colborne's commission of 1833. McMurray may have appreciated Shingwaukonse's determination to protect resources on behalf of the Sault Band, since the chief also forbade work on Sundays in keeping with his newly acquired Christian beliefs. By September 1834, Little Pine also expected the Métis to comply with these new instructions: 'The Indian Chief [Shingwaukonse] held a Council with the Canadian & half-breed inhabitants to put a stop to the cutting of wood on the British side for sale to the Americans, and to prevent anyone from scooping at the rapids on the Sabbath day.'[65]

The Hudson's Bay Company raised no objections either, since the chief, by demanding that his permission be obtained before any commercial outfit could set seines along the coast between Thessalon and Batchewana Bay, helped reduce competition in the fishing industry. George Johnston, who entered the Mackinac fish trade with Ogista as his assistant, secured Little Pine's permission to establish an outpost at Batchewana Bay. Others failed to respect Shingwaukonse's prerogatives and were penalized. For instance, when one American merchant, Samuel Ashman, established a commercial fishery at Goulais Bay, Little Pine asked to William Nourse, the local Hudson's Bay factor, to investigate the illicit enterprise:

> During the winter a party of Americans have been carrying on an extensive traffic with smuggled property at Goulais Bay. The Indian Chief [Shingwaukonse] under an authority from the lieutenant governor, gave them warning to quit the 6th January, but they paid no attention to it. I apprised Captain [James] Anderson, the Collector of Customs [at Michipicoten]. The abuse had become too great – I therefore procured an authority to act.[66]

By March of 1835 Norse had put a stop to the illegal venture: '[We were met by Mr Laronde, the Hudson's Bay Company agent] at the place where the smugglers were encamped and there made the seizure – distributing the Fish, etc. to the Indians to whom they of right belonged ... & destroying the remainder.'[67]

With the assistance of the local magistracy, Little Pine continued to oppose commercial interests operating without his permission on the northern side of the home band's traditional hunting and fishing range. The missionary's cherished goal, by contrast, was the establishment of a model farming community. Two years before, owing to scarcity of funds, it had seemed like an impossible dream. The Hudson's Bay Company, moreover, had ridiculed the idea. To Sir George Simpson, the company's governor, embarking on such a project would prove to be a fruitless proposition unless at least £300 could be procured, which Simpson felt to be an unlikely prospect.[68] Yet by the spring of 1834 everything had changed. Colborne had promised funds to build twenty Native houses and provide a farming instructor, a schoolteacher, and a carpenter. Shingwaukonse's band seemed so enthusiastic that McMurray felt the Ojibwa shared his hopes for the future. His goal now seemingly within range, the missionary wrote to the society concerning his charge: 'For myself I felt lastingly attached to them and have reason to believe that the attachment is reciprocal. Our prospects brighten daily, and justify my belief, that with the continuance of the Divine blessing, the success of the mission is now placed beyond all doubt.'[69]

Foxes in the Vineyard – Power Struggles at the Rapids

McMurray's role as intermediary between the Ojibwa and the lieutentantgovernor had not been taxing; indeed, there is reason to believe that the missionary enjoyed the status it conferred upon him in the eyes of his Native congregation. When Thomas G. Anderson suggested that he let his temporal duties as Indian agent fall to his catechist and interpreter, James Robertson, McMurray rejected the idea. The missionary also hedged when the society suggested that Robertson should run the school. The Ojibwa, McMurray contended, would never listen to a schoolmaster who was 'an Indian like themselves.'[70] The missionary saw no future in altering his role as the sole dispenser of government benefits and relief. To permit Robertson a degree of authority would undermine the personal understanding he felt existed between Shingwaukonse and himself. He and Little Pine were the head people responsible for the success of the mission; all others of the congregation would be mere recipients of the fruits of their labour.

As long as the chief and the missionary shared understandings about the projected settlement, McMurray held, everything went smoothly. Yet it was Shingwaukonse, acting in concert with Kaygayosh, rather than McMurray, who wielded the greatest influence within the home band. Under the leadership of the two chiefs, the Ojibwa community remained cohesive. Since the Anglican mission in the long run proved more a divisive than a unifying influence, Little Pine eventually had to overrule the missionary and himself direct the course of the settlement towards new goals.

Conflict within the community erupted in the spring of 1835, beginning with a clash between McMurray and Little Pine over the location of the mission establishment. Shingwaukonse and his band wanted to plant their gardens at Kitigaun Sebee, or Garden River. With the sanction of Kaygayosh at the rapids, Little Pine had arisen as leader of one of the most prominent Ojibwa villages along the north shore of the St Mary's channel. The east bank of the Garden River had been seasonally occupied by Native people since the eighteenth century as a supply station for fur brigades passing up the north channel *en route* to Lake Superior.[71] Before 1812, its proximity to the British post on St Joseph Island and accessibility from the eastern end of Sugar Island had enhanced its position. Following the 1827 relocation of the British station to Penetanguishene, the merger in 1821 of the North West and Hudson's Bay companies, and the resulting termination of the east-west brigades, the locus of trade activity had shifted to Sugar Island. A number of merchants resided on the island, foremost among them being Michael G. Payment and Malcolm McKerchie, who maintained market connections in Michigan, Ohio, and Upper Canada. These men traded with the seasonal Ojibwa population at Garden River for fish, preserves, timber, handicrafts, vegetables, firewood for steamer fuel, and probably copper ore as well.

McMurray rejected Little Pine's repeated proposals that the mission settlement be established at the mouth of the Garden River, near the trading establishments on Sugar Island. In the spring of 1834, the missionary had been able to rent the Ermatinger estate, which not only furnished the missionary's family with comfortable lodgings, but also offered an expanse of cleared, surveyed land for farming purposes. McMurray contended that the Ojibwa could raise hay, potatoes, and other vegetables on the slope behind the mansion.

In June, Indian superintendent Thomas G. Anderson arrived at the Sault in company with the Reverend Adam Elliot, former Anglican missionary to the Home District. Anderson and Elliot had been interviewing band leaders north of Lake Huron to determine the feasibility of establishing a government-funded Anglican mission at Manitowaning, on Manitoulin Island. As an extension of Anderson's duties, Lieutenant-Governor Colborne had requested the agent to look into affairs between McMurray and the Ojibwa, since news had reached Colborne that the mission's proximity to approximately forty Roman Catholic French and Métis families had become a contentious issue. Colborne proposed that the rapids area be reserved exclusively for the Anglican Church and that the French and Métis be removed from Sault Ste Marie.[72]

Shingwaukonse arranged a viewing of the Garden River area on 2 July, and attempted to persuade Anderson to agree to the site. In this the chief was unsuccessful. Anderson considered the soil to be pure sand, and supported McMurray's preference for Sault Ste Marie. While concerned about the nearness of the mission to Fort Brady on the opposite shore, Anderson felt that economy justified the renting of the Ermatinger estate. The 'state of the funds and the very low price for which Mr Ermatinger's property is offered' overruled Ojibwa opposition.[73] Government and missionary priorities prevailed against Shingwaukonse's wishes. Anderson expected the Native population to comply unquestionably with his decision. The Ojibwa were dismayed by this state of affairs. Years later they would recount to Anderson's son, Gustavus:

When the first Blackcoat [Mr McMurray] came here, he found us encamped at the Sault, and asked us where we proposed settling. We told him that as our fields were at Garden River, and our fathers before us planted their potatoes there, we hoped, if a mission was to be established, that our Father in Toronto [Sir John Colborne] would allow us to have it where the land was good.

In about two years after this, our Blackcoat said that he had received a letter from our Father, who said that he thought the Sault the best place for a mission. Accordingly a commencement was made by building the church [actually the schoolhouse]. We did not like this, but we said our Father at Toronto knows what will be for us his children's good; let us then obey him and willingly agree to settle where the church is.[74]

Besides choosing a site, Anderson's responsibilities included settling the dispute between McMurray and the Métis. McMurray had complained to Colborne that most of the Métis engaged in smuggling whisky and other goods, an allegation Colborne instructed the Indian Department to investigate. This task eventually fell to the Hudson's Bay Company. Bethune, the chief factor at Michipicoten, argued, in his company's interest, that free traders' grog shops constituted a nuisance to the peace and order of the community. Nourse, the factor at the Sault, also supported Colborne's proposal that the Métis be removed. He had long opposed the company's employment of this 'class,' and forwarded a plan which, he maintained, would improve financial prospects: '[We] are under a state of thraldom as things are now [the factor complained], the Freemen here knowing we cannot do without them are often very saucy, to keep them in humour credits are often given to them – and money often lost: were we able to do without them no such risks would be incurred, and some saving might be effected.'[75]

Nourse's solution to the labour problem was simple: dispense with the 'habitants' and employ Ojibwa on a wage system. Native labour, the factor argued, could readily be hired and as easily dismissed, since they had traditional hunting occupations to which they could readily return. Those who had already been employed proved reliable workers. Men like Buhkwujjenene and Mezai knew the routes well, and so could act as mail carriers and canoemen.[76] The mission's goals thus offered the Hudson's Bay Company a moral justification for removing its main competition. Whether or not the Métis actually posed a threat to the public peace, however, was another question.

Confronted by the combined forces of the Established Church and a commercial monopoly, the Roman Catholic Native people and Métis not surprisingly felt both threatened and angered, and accused Little Pine of siding with agents of discord. Although Anderson depicted the affair as a contest between 'Indians' and 'Half Breeds,' the primary cause of the unrest stemmed from McMurray's assumption of control over resources and land in the interests of the Anglican Church. Little Pine had tried to stem the growth of conflict by proposing to have the mission based at Garden River. This would allow the Métis and the Ojibwa under Nebenagoching, who depended principally on the rapids fishery, to reside in the vicinity of the rapids free from external interference. In response, the population at the Sault would respect the territorial prerogatives vested in Little Pine. There is no evidence that, before Anderson's arrival, bad feeling existed towards the chief. Until 1835 the community had remained socially cohesive, in spite of outside intervention designed to drive a wedge between Roman Catholics and Protestants. For instance, in a petition to Colborne, numerous signatories, among them 'Pierre L'avoine ... Chief's son' (Tegoosh) and 'Joseph Ne.pa.nin.toting' (Nebenagoching), argued that they had been prohibited by McMurray from cutting wood to construct a Roman Catholic chapel even though they had 'previously obtained the consent of the principal chief, for so doing.'[77]

With Anderson's and Elliot's appearance, the situation radically changed. Anderson made no secret of the fact that Protestants would be favoured over Roman Catholics, and that 'Indians' would be recognized, while 'Métis' were to be ignored. The 216 'Protestants' received presents at the Sault mission, while all others were forced to travel to Penetanguishene. The same policy governed the distribution of agricultural assistance and relief. Anderson also stressed that the only valid channel to the Indian Department henceforth lay through the Anglican missionary. It may have made good financial sense to streamline expenditures and administration by centralizing power in the hands of the missionary at the rapids, but it split the band 'owning' the land, and by late June Little Pine's followers found themselves embroiled in a series of local disputes, some of which may have involved the use of witchcraft.[78]

Anderson's desire to integrate all controlling agencies on the frontier also led to his manipulation of prevailing power alignments within the 'home band' to suit government interests. On the grounds that the Roman Catholic Crane chief had participated in smuggling operations, the agent exercised the considerable powers conferred upon him by the Indian Department by divesting Nebenagoching of the chieftainship he had held by British consent since 1819. In Nebenagoching's stead, Anderson announced, 'Shing-gua-conce ... [would be] Grand Chief and all the tribes coming to this place must be obedient to him.'[79]

Shingwaukonse was not long in making use of his favoured position. He presented Anderson with a map of the coast from Thessalon to Goulais Bay, with his 'jurisdiction' clearly marked. When pressed, Anderson promised to uphold the territorial prerogatives of this 'Protestant' Native leader.[80] By obtaining a commitment from Anderson to recognize Native territorial rights, Little Pine had thrown into question the nature of the mission's land tenure at the rapids. McMurray paid a fixed annual rent to Ermatinger who, since no formal surrender of the property to the Crown had ever been made, was just as much a 'squatter' as the French and Métis. Anderson also failed in his endeavours to persuade the French and Métis to move to St Joseph Island. The French had requested upwards of £1800 for their strip lots fronting on the channel, a sum which dealt a severe setback to Anderson's plans and, ultimately, left the settlement at the rapids unaltered.[81]

The Influence of Indian Department Policy on Native Political Alliances

Between 1832 and 1835, McMurray had won the approbation and respect of his Native congregation. Yet this state of affairs did not necessarily derive from forceful, authoritative directives on the part of the missionary. The Ojibwa were receptive because the structure of the relationship was shaped at least as much by Native expectations as by doctrinaire Christian beliefs. It was a reciprocal relationship which worked. Anderson's determination to control the frontier bands through a program of systematic settlement nevertheless tended to undermine the status of the missionary, who became little more than a puppet of the Indian Department. Without notifying McMurray, Superintendent Anderson placed James Robertson in charge of certain administrative responsibilities and dismissed James D. Cameron, Jr, as interpreter. Anderson felt it his duty to impress on the Ojibwa the idea that government priorities took precedence over those of the missionary, and that both official and mission goals were opposed to those of free trade.

Government policy on Native matters had become, first and foremost, a tool of international diplomacy. Well aware of American fears concerning the influence British independent traders might exert over the Native population of the north-western frontier, Anderson had been instructing the western bands for more than a decade to leave their often lucrative commercial pursuits and settle permanently near the British military posts.[82] The idea of encouraging missions to run farming communities emerged as an afterthought – inspired by Methodist endeavours at New Credit – and was promoted because it promised to be the most inexpensive way of dealing with Britain's former Native allies.

What this policy failed to consider, however, was that broad lateral political networks already existed among head chiefs. When exacerbated by the Indian Department's policy of favouring members of the Established Church over adherents of other denominations, rivalries between Native leaders eroded old power structures, while alliances, partly based on religious commonality, bred new political alignments. This process had divided the three principal head chiefs at Coldwater and led to a dispersal of the settlement's inhabitants.[83] Government attempts to exercise control over the movement of peoples by encouraging attachment to government goals produced results the opposite of what was intended.

In order to protect the integrity of their leadership, head chiefs sought to entrench their groups more securely both within the Upper Great Lakes Native community and in the favour of the British government. Jean Baptiste Assiginack, an Ottawa chief from L'Arbre Croche in Michigan, who frequently acted as agent to the western bands on behalf of the Indian Department, saw his valued status falling into jeopardy because of his preference for Roman Catholicism. To counter this possibility, Assiginack built up a strong power base at Pentanguishene, including within his retinue the prominent Ojibwa chief John Aisance, whom he persuaded to convert from Methodism to Roman Catholicism, and Jean Baptiste Tagwaninini, an Ojibwa originally from Saginaw, Michigan. Tagwaninini had temporarily joined Aisance's band, but later moved to Wikwemikong on Manitoulin Island. The fourth member of this group, John MacFarlane, also known as 'John Bell,' was a Métis from Nipigon whose father had ensured that he learned to read and write English and speak French. This background led Bell to become an interpreter for both Anderson and the trader Andrew Mitchell at Penetanguishene.

It did not take Anderson long to discover that Assiginack, Aisance, Tagwaninini, and Bell had been in frequent contact with the Roman Catholics at the Sault who opposed the Anglican mission.[84] The superintendent's elevation of Shingwaukonse to the status of head chief and his demotion of Nebenagoching had partly been a ploy to break up this seemingly religious-based alliance. Both Anderson and the Reverend Adam Elliot, meanwhile, proclaimed Shingwaukonse to be a model Anglican convert, while attempting to sever the chief's allegiances to the broader Upper Great Lakes Native community by encouraging his dependency on government patronage. In this last aim, they were totally unsuccessful. Shingwaukonse had sought government favour in the first place on behalf of his Ojibwa and Ottawa allies and his own followers. For the chief to have renounced his alliances would have deprived his actions with respect to the government authorities of their essential meaning.

An Appeal for New Allies

The Ojibwa had been distrustful of American policy ever since 1833, when Washington refused to protect their fishery locations. Successive events increased their concern. Blacksmith services to Native people at the Mackinac agency were suddenly withdrawn in 1834.[85] The following year, the American garrison disregarded the existence of a Native burial ground, reserved under the terms of the 1820 treaty, in adding an extension to Fort Brady. In answer to these grievances, Shingwaukonse offered a simple solution: move to the Canadian side. Despite Anderson's and McMurray's choice of the Ermatinger estate as the main mission site, Little Pine continued to exercise authority over the much wider territory extending from east of Garden River to Batchewana Bay.

Little Pine still retained associations with the Cranes through his relationship with Kaygayosh, and encouraged the elder Crane leader to become a 'British chief.' Shingwaukonse had already publicly stated his own stand on the matter of national loyalties. During negotiations at Mackinac in March 1836 concerning a major land cession in northern Michigan, he had declared his independence from the American government. The decisive tone of his speech had won Schoolcraft's admiration, though its content did not. 'Attention was perfectly arrested by the force, comprehensiveness and striking oratorical turns' of the speech, the agent noted approvingly.[86]

Owing to his privileged position with regard to the British government, Shingwaukonse could afford to exercise autonomy apart from the Crane band. Kaygayosh, his loyalties in 1836 divided between his responsibilities to his group and his dislike of American Native policy, faced a far more difficult decision. Schoolcraft had selected Native delegates whom he knew to be amenable to the government's terms to travel to Washington for preliminary negotiations regarding the forthcoming treaty. The agent neglected to inform those who leaned towards the British interest until the delegates had already departed. Schoolcraft deliberately excluded the Crane head chief from the proceedings on the grounds that the views of dissenting leaders should automatically be overruled in the interest of the state. For Kaygayosh, however, striving to retain his band's unity, things appeared in a different light. Why, for instance, Kaygayosh complained, should Waubojeeg, who was Schoolcraft's uncle by marriage and a head of the Caribou *dodem* from La Pointe, be made 'at his own will ... the representative of the ancient red men whose totem is the lofty Crane?'[87]

Although Schoolcraft eventually permitted Kaygayosh to participate as a 'first-class' chief in the treaty, this was more a concession to Kaygayosh personally than a recognition that the Crane band still existed as a functioning political entity. Not long after, Kaygayosh, his younger brother Muckedayoquot, and Muckedayoquot's two sons, John Kabaosa and Waubmama, joined Shingwaukonse's group on the Canadian side.[88] When Kaygayosh died in the fall of 1836, Schoolcraft attempted to gain control over the Sault band, in order to divide it into three geographic divisions, by personally appointing Kebay Nodin, Shingabaw'osin's son, to the head chieftainship.[89] The new incumbent, the agent hoped, would not exhibit Kaygayosh's penchant for following Shingwaukonse in supporting the British interest. Schoolcraft's actions failed to achieve their purposes, however, since the main Native council at the Sault, while willing to recognize Kebay Nodin as an *anike.ogima*, immediately elevated Oshawano to the head position of the American sector of their group,[90] while Shingwaukonse himself assumed Kaygayosh's former pre-eminence as a *Midéwiwin* leader. The youthful Nebenagoching – now in his early thirties – who had remained firm in his attachment to the British despite Anderson's attempts to demote him, also continued to act as a prominent Crane chief.

Head men from Mackinac and St Ignace entered into alliances with Little Pine as well, although still retaining their names on the American band lists in order to share in annuity payments. To these leaders, linkages with Little Pine constituted a form of insurance that would permit their bands to move to the Canadian shore if the U.S. government tried to make them leave Michigan. The 1837 annuity distribution had already brought an unwelcome surprise. The treaty of March 1836 had been modified by Washington, without the Ojibwa's knowledge, prior to its ratification in May. The original agreement had maintained that removal would take place only when the Ojibwa desired it. In its amended form, it restricted Native occupancy at the rapids to 'five years ... and no longer' and made 'lands south-west of the Missouri' – outside the Ojibwa's familiar mixed-woodland habitat – the place of destination.[91] Social tensions escalated among the south-western Ojibwa as the United States sought to compel bands to relocate, with long-term unfortunate results.[92] With the likelihood of a major removal in the near future, Shingwaukonse's plan for the establishment of a refuge for bands throughout the Lake Superior district rapidly gained widespread appeal.

At the same time, Little Pine had to protect his own power base at Garden River. Anderson's recognition of Shingwaukonse's territorial prerogatives north of the St Mary's channel had been a minor victory for the chief, but the Superintendent was still contemplating drawing all bands along the north shore of Lake Huron to Manitowaning on Manitoulin Island. Little Pine strongly disapproved of the idea. The Roman Catholic settlement at Wikwemikong, composed of Ottawa migrants from L'Arbre Croche, had become a new focus of operations for Assiginack, Tagwaninini, and Bell, and Shingwaukonse felt no inclination to confront his rivals.

The faction led by Assiginack had been developing a political ideology which would enable its formerly disparate elements to work together harmoniously. Historical precedents were sought to validate the political unification of the Ojibwa, Ottawa, and Potawatomi within the Lake Huron district. The answer lay in the Ottawa tradition of the Three Fires. In one version, it was maintained, the Ottawa leader Sagimah, in the mid-seventeenth century, had led the Ottawa, Ojibwa, and Potawatomi to victory against the Iroquois. The legend 'worked' because the Saginaw Ojibwa. Ottawa could identify with it, especially since seventeenth-century French historical accounts located at least one Ottawa band on Manitoulin Island. Yet the same legend meant far less to the Lake Superior Ojibwa. If their ancestors and had participated in this drive against the Iroquois – and many had not – they had returned to their traditional lands in the Upper Great Lakes region and felt no need to justify their rights to territory by tales of conquest.[93]

Subsequent events sharpened rivalries between the Sault Ste Marie and Manitoulin factions. In the fall of 1835, Sir Francis Bond Head succeeded Sir John Colborne as lieutenant-governor. After a tour of Indian missions in Upper Canada, Bond Head declared the idea of establishing yet another government-supported settlement a costly and probably fruitless endeavour, and suggested removing as many bands as possible to Manitoulin Island to obtain more land for settlement. In order to further his removal plan, in 1836 Bond Head secured a surrender of Manitoulin Island from the Aboriginal inhabitants. The Ottawa at Wikwemikong felt their pre-eminence on the island to be unquestioned at this point, and Father Proulx, the priest at Wikwemikong, even went so far as to ask Anderson on behalf of the Roman Catholic mission for permission to occupy the houses and outbuildings which had been erected the preceding year at Manitowaning in readiness for the projected Anglican mission settlement.

While the Ottawa on Manitoulin Island may have had reason to be pleased, Protestant Upper Canada was horrified. The British organization the Aborigines Protection Society, founded in 1836, retaliated with the statement, quoted repeatedly in the Protestant press, that the Canadian government had exchanged three million acres of good farmland for 23,000 barren, rocky islands.[94] Although Bond Head's project assumed priority throughout 1837, Shingwaukonse continued to press for assistance for his people near Sault Ste Marie. His attempts to secure support from head chiefs residing on Lake Huron in 1837 drew comment from the Reverend Charles Elliot, who viewed Shingwaukonse as valiantly upholding the banner of Anglicanism in the north, regardless of reversals in government policy: 'Chinguacounse assembled his brother chiefs of the Chippewa nation who are not Christians, but have often assured me that they would become members of the Church, and when he reminded them of their promises, they each made speeches in turn and renewed their assurances that they would adopt the Established religion.'[95] There could be no doubt by this time, however, that McMurray's presumption of control over unceded property at Sault Ste Marie had long been overruled by Shingwaukonse's strong assertion of his own proprietary right to the land. Over the next several years, Little Pine hoped to retain his control over territory which, according to Ojibwa custom, he considered to be under his management and protection by pressing the government for the construction of the houses promised by Colborne. These houses soon became political counters in an intense power game between Little Pine's band and the government, since the building of the houses would constitute firm recognition of a strong Ojibwa presence at the rapids. On the other hand, Shingwaukonse's failure could threaten the band's survival as an autonomous political entity and its capacity to determine its own social and economic future.

Given the direction of Bond Head's Native policy, the Anglican missionary could no longer fulfil the expectations of Little Pine's band, and in 1837 he left the Sault. McMurray cited the government's failure to honour its promises to the Native people as the reason behind his decision:

> This reflected sorely upon me as their missionary. I made the promises to the Native people on the strength of those made to them by Sir John Colborne; but as they were not carried out by his successor my position was seriously altered, for the Native people began to think that I had no authority for making the promises referred to, thus casting doubt upon my veracity. This induced me to resign my mission, not because I did not love the work ...[96]

The precedent set by the reciprocal relationship existing between the missionary and the Ojibwa informed the positive attitude the band expressed towards those who would succeed McMurray in the Anglican mission field at the Sault. McMurray's labours, while they had produced no long-lasting material changes within the Native community, had been invaluable to Little Pine in securing direct lines of communication both to the Crown's representatives and to heads of the Established Church. These linkages raised Shingwaukonse materially in the sight of the Indian Department and, at the distribution of presents in 1838, the chief was formally recognized as spokesman for the western bands. He quickly turned his new status into a public platform for discussing his own views on the responsibility of the Crown to the western bands – ideas that were at variance with the prevailing attitude of assembled officials and clergy, who supported revival of the fledgling Anglican mission on Manitoulin Island. While retaining connections with the government and the Anglican Church, Little Pine also set out to harness other dynamic agencies, legal and commercial, which might assist his people in achieving their goals.

On becoming a head chief, Shingwaukonse exercised control over his group's membership and the use of resources within the scope of his territorial jurisdiction. He also maintained the choice of whether or not to speak or act, when invited to do so, on behalf of other leaders and their bands. In 1837, however, he was approached to represent a new group, the Métis at Sault Ste Marie. To this Shingwaukonse agreed, not only because many Métis had become bona fide members of his band through intermarriage, but also because he had come to recognize that the Métis could help him realize his plans for the Native community.

Chapter Three

Years of Testing and Trial

By 1837, Shingwaukonse had secured backing for his plans from the Métis at the Sault, and for a while both parties found the new alliance mutually beneficial. The Métis population found it necessary to have an 'Indian' represent their interests, since the government refused to recognize them politically as a group. At the same time, Little Pine appreciated the skills and experience that Métis individuals contributed to the realization of his scheme for his Native community.[1] The Sault region yielded valuable resources, particularly pine timber, which local Métis knew how to market to advantage. Indigenous economic aims differed so radically from metropolitan society's views of the roles Native peoples might occupy on the frontier that only a strong united stand would enable them to prevent future economic marginalization. Yet because the Ottawa on Manitoulin Island were developing a community of their own which would rival that of Garden River in the government's estimation, Little Pine and his new allies soon encountered formidable problems.

While often the target of unmerited non-Native prejudice, Ojibwa society at Sault Ste Marie continued to exhibit a high degree of organizational stability. The core of Shingwaukonse's band consisted of three generations of his family, including his wives, many sons and daughters, his sons-in-law Kabaosa, Misquabenokay, Piabetassung, Megissanequa, Shebagezick, and John Bell (the son of a trader named MacFarlane originally from Nipigon, but who lived many years at La Cloche), and his grandchildren. This core group maintained wider alliances with the Abatossaway family of Manitoulin Island, the Gegwetosse family of Sugar Island, and the Missegan family at L'Anse. Marriages also occurred between Little Pine's band and that of Nebenagoching, whose family members – many of whom were Métis – resided in cabins scattered along the north shore of the St Mary's straits. In 1834 Nebenagoching himself purchased rights at the British Sault to two and one-half acres of enclosed land on which he and his family constructed a small house and outbuildings. Like his Métis and French neighbours, he claimed a narrow frontage on the St Mary's River, of only three chains' width.[2] Since only persons like Nebenagoching who were legally vested with Aboriginal status could justify their continued residence at the rapids, Métis descendants of one-time trading personnel often emphasized whatever consanguineous and affinal ties they could trace to the local Native community over and above their French or British ancestry. With the consent of the head chief and subchiefs, dyadic linkages between siblings, where one of the pair already was married to a member of a band's nodal core unit, were frequently exercised to gain entry. Some of these chain-like connections could be intricate. Xavier Biron's wife's sister, a daughter of Michael Cadotte at La Pointe, married Francis LaRose, whose brother Charles LaRose later wed one of Little Pine's granddaughters. Charles LaRose's link to the Garden River core group thus enabled Xavier Biron's two sons, Francis and Charles, to enter the Garden River band. And Francis Biron's marriage to Isabell Boissoneau from Red River later allowed other Boissoneau family members to join the Garden River community.[3] These Métis incomers formed a stable periphery around the core, and eventually came to share equal privileges with other group members. With time they dropped their former individualized form of property holding and accommodated to the Ojibwa's flexible band organization. All spoke either French or a specialized language which, while structurally French, had an extremely strong Ojibwa content.[4]

Major Economic Changes

Since the traditional subsistence economy was well adapted to draw on the strengths and cope with the deficiencies of the local environment, it remained relatively stable until well into the nineteenth century. The major change resulted from the need to prevent resources under Native jurisdiction from being appropriated by American business interests. The reduction in the numbers of fur-bearing animals led to a greater emphasis than before on the Mackinac fish trade to finance the purchase of provisions and goods. Native users of fisheries soon came to compete with white commercial fishermen, who after 1830 claimed the same areas.

Following American expansion westward into Illinois, fish prices soared to five dollars a barrel as demand from white settlers grew. Fur companies moved into this new area of commerce, driving Native persons not attached to their organizations from the fishing grounds. Since the Native fishers could be violently assaulted on their locations near Manitoulin Island, Cockburn Island, and Thessalon, the issue became politically volatile by 1849, when Native peoples sent delegations to the Canadian and American governments to obtain the exclusive use of their traditional sites. Both the Canadian civil secretary and Washington refused to protect Native fishing rights, since protectionism in the prevailing *laissez-faire* atmosphere was likely to provoke a public outcry against what might be conceived as a revival of aristocratic privilege.[5] Native leaders nevertheless continued their campaign, since the sale of fish provided trappers with the funds to secure their winter staples of salt pork, flour, cornmeal, tobacco, and tea.

Trapping continued from fall until spring, as long as furs could be obtained and commanded a good price. The animals hunted included beaver (although after 1840 beaver numbers declined drastically), mink, marten, fisher, muskrat, and especially foxes, which brought the highest return. Trappers employed a number of dead-fall, spring mechanism, and baiting techniques which remained unchanged by French and British contact. Steel traps, gill nets, guns, and ammunition could be obtained by trade. Hunting was done with muskets and, later, rifles, although older ways persisted. A local Anglican missionary, Frederick Frost, noted that certain elderly individuals as late as 1900 eschewed the 'new' hunting technology and preferred the bow and arrow to all other means.[6]

In the mid-1830s, as in the 1820s, heads of nodal core groups 'owned' individual hunting territories. Bush camps were established near a body of water where trout could be taken in nets. Men travelled the trails in search of beaver and large game, while women snared rabbits, trapped, hunted, and fished near the camp. Large game was distributed within the hunting group, although individuals usually retained the proceeds of their own fur catches. While sons shared in the territorial prerogatives of their fathers, affinal and friendship ties could also be activated to gain admission to family hunting grounds, provided the 'owner's' decision met with the approval of the band as a whole. In such instances, a share of the furs taken by a hunter would be offered in payment to the owner of the hunting limits in return for the latter's willingness to 'lend' his territory.

Following the return from the interior, each family group planted corn, pumpkin, squash, and root vegetables in proximity to their maple-sugaring operations. Residents sold their surpluses of potatoes and other vegetables to merchants on Sugar Island and St Joseph Island. The uncertainties of the climate and the scarcity of fertile soil prevented the growth of large, strongly nucleated village settlements in the rapids area, even at the height of the fur trade. Horticulture along the St Mary's channel remained a risky venture because of the frequent rains during the harvest season as the cold waters of Lake Superior met the warmer waters of Lake Huron.

It was not until the mid-1830s that agriculture came to be practised under the supervision of missionaries intent on establishing a new social order on the frontier. The Ojibwa acquired horses and cattle from traders and raised oats as fodder for these animals as early as 1830, if not earlier. However, a declining local economy following the signing of the Robinson Treaties made it difficult for Native families to keep animals and, in consequence, many continued to rely on hunting and trapping for food. Farming at Garden River depended on the Ojibwa's being able to engage in logging and mining to acquire funds to purchase seed, animals, and farming equipment.

Boat building, guiding, mining exploration, and lumbering became important occupations by the late 1840s. A continuity may thus be traced with the fur trade in the Native people's continued participation in activities associated with large-scale resource exploitation. Not surprisingly, the Ojibwa in 1846 considered their occupations as contributing to the growth of the national economy, and initially proved optimistic when it became clear that new resource industries would supplant the failing fur trade. Their knowledge of the locations of ore deposits, their familiarity with the land and river routes, and their willingness to share their expertise made the Ojibwa an integral part of the history of early resource development north of Lakes Huron and Superior.

From 1840 to 1846, Canadian developmental policies ran directly counter to Ojibwa and Métis plans for the establishment of 'homelands,' on the frontier as places of refuge for self-determining bands. Only after 1846, when timber was sought by a new class of Canadian entrepreneurs, were Little Pine's appeals for protection and aid finally heard by the governor general. Until that time, official attitudes focused primarily on ways of diplomatically soothing American fears about the Ojibwa presence rather than on responding to Native desires and grievances.

Little Pine as Spokesman for the Western Bands

There appeared to be an especially pressing need in 1837 for the Canadian government to draw Ojibwa away from the American frontier. George Johnston warned that the Native bands, angered by the State of

Michigan's intention to construct a canal through their fishery preserve and influenced by anti-American sentiment triggered during the rebellions in the Canadas, might attack Fort Brady. Although relations between the commander of the fort and the Sault 'home band' grew more cordial after the military stepped in to prevent the canal project from being undertaken, American concern over the possibility of further Native unrest lingered on for years. Washington tinkered with the idea of moving the Ojibwa to lands along the Missouri River.

Removal constituted only one of a number of challenging issues facing the Native peoples on the American side. Scarcity of game and a financial depression in the United States, lasting from 1837 to 1844, dampened prospects in the fur and fish trade and made the thought of joining government-sponsored settlements tempting. Yet, to be compelled to take up residence west of the mixed woodland zone, in country which had no sugar maples or other resources integral to the Ojibwa way of life was less inviting. 'The Sault chiefs,' wrote James Ord, subagent at the Sault, to Schoolcraft's brother James, 'are not adverse to going to land between Lake Superior and the Mississippi, but are not aware of any obligation to go west of the Mississippi River.'[7]

Little Pine, well aware of the mounting tension south of the border, used his influence and relatively undiminished political autonomy as a leading British chief to impress Schoolcraft with the extent of Native opposition to the Americans' proposed Native policy. Returning from the British distribution of presents on Manitoulin Island in 1837, he informed the agent that a Potawatomi chief had told him about the circulation of a large wampum belt, stressing that 'fourteen different tribes, to the west and north, had acknowledged and received it, binding themselves to support one another.'[8] In response, Schoolcraft suggested to the American commissioner of Indian affairs, C.A. Harris, that a small military force, or at least a special agent, might be placed on Drummond Island to prevent the north-western Native peoples from visiting Manitoulin Island in the future.[9]

This was another blow. At the distribution of presents Little Pine had already launched an unsuccessful attack on British plans to control the movements of the western Ojibwa. In the future, he declared, the annual gift giving should be transferred to St Joseph Island, since it would be more accessible to visiting Lake Superior bands. 'Many of your children live at a great distance from this Island,' the chief proclaimed to the assembly on Manitoulin, 'and there is a high hill [the American Indian agency] between which prevents their seeing the fire which burns or the flag which floats from the staff erected at this place. But,' he continued, 'I can see all the Natives belonging to our tribe. I can see as far as the Red River, or even to this place.'[10] By these words, Shingwaukonse not only offered the British government an option for retaining the loyalties of autonomous bands from as far west as the Upper Mississippi, but also set himself up as the main spokesman for the Lake Superior Ojibwa 'nation' – a political entity forged from Native alliances existing since at least the 1760s.

Formidable opposition immediately arose from two influential chiefs, Mocomanish and Ottanwish. Although Little Pine claimed to speak on behalf of the Potawatomi and Ottawa, as well as the Ojibwa, Ottanwish branded the Ojibwa chief a presumptuous upstart. 'The chiefs who live at the Bay to the west [on Manitoulin Island] have not before heard that your red brethren desire the flag to be removed from this place to St Joseph's,' Ottanwish charged.[11]

Nor was the government sympathetic to Little Pine's appeal. The Indian Department favoured the Ottawa's sedentary village mode of life, based on corn horticulture and fishing rather than on hunting, trapping, and trade. When the time came to bestow a flag on an Native band, the honour fell to the Ottawa residents of Wikwemikong. Little Pine and the western Ojibwa whom he represented found themselves regarded on all sides as unwelcome aliens. Anna Jameson, a British writer present at the 1837 ceremonies, observed that the Red River Ojibwa bands particularly aroused much 'wonder and curiosity' among the Ottawa contingent, who saw them as 'cannibals ... the title being ... quite gratuitous and merely expressive of the disgust they excited.'[12]

Little Pine thus temporarily found himself outmanoeuvred. His first suggestion, that a British fort be established on St Joseph's Island, was rejected out of hand by the British Indian Department, mainly for practical reasons. The original military and trade establishment had been a concession to Britain's Native allies prior to the War of 1812, but in 1837 the government showed little interest in the site since it lacked a good harbour, had no lime and stone for construction purposes, and would be hard to defend from attack by water. Second, Little Pine's pleas for government assistance went directly counter to Bond Head's stress on fiscal restraint. Anna Jameson, who sympathized with this viewpoint, thought the chief's proposals showed an outmoded reliance on the beneficence of British colonialism. Reflecting on an address which she had read, sent by the chief to Sir Francis Bond Head in January 1837, about the government's failure to provide houses at the Sault, Jameson concluded that the chief lacked both foresight and cultural flexibility. 'The Indians have no comprehension of a change of governors being a change of principles,' she observed. In an era of self-help and emerging responsible government in the Canadas, it seemed only proper for the Ojibwa to construct the houses themselves. Yet, she unfairly maintained, owing to their cultural 'backwardness' such work would be 'absolutely inimical to their habits.' 'It requires,' she claimed, 'more strength than the women possess; and for the men to fell wood and logs [was] an unheard of degradation.'[13] Jameson failed to consider that there might be another reason for Shingwaukonse's position.

It upset Little Pine that the Bond Head had not bothered to visit the Anglican Ojibwa settlement at the rapids during his recent tour of Native missions in the province, but the Lieutenant-Governor's interest extended only as far as the Native people on Manitoulin Island.[14] In 1837, Sault Ste Marie fell geographically into what one historian has termed the 'undistributed middle' – too far south to be under the jurisdiction of the Hudson's Bay Company charter, too far west to be of much concern to Upper Canadian legislators.[15] For many years the Native community at the rapids would remain principally an out-station of the government-sponsored mission establishment at Manitowaning on Manitoulin Island.

Washington registered even less concern for Native interests than its apathetic northern neighbour. The discovery of untapped mineral wealth and virgin pine forests south-west of Lake Superior gave rise to public pressure for further land surrenders. Disagreements arising among the head chiefs about the signing of a treaty in July 1837 between the United States and the western bands at St Peter's on the St Croix River, Minnesota, left the Upper Great Lakes peoples deeply divided. This state of affairs suited Washington, since it reduced the likelihood of Native uprisings along the frontier. When informed that the British Parliament sought the eventual elimination of its annual grant for presents to the western bands Washington and other related expenditures, cancelled plans to build a post on Drummond Island. American annuity payments, meanwhile, were timed to conflict with the British distributions.

Despite these problems, Little Pine remained determined to provide a place of refuge for Ojibwa from the United States. More than houses or presents were at stake. Cloth, blankets, needles, combs, awls, kettles, guns, ammunition, and other practical articles received at Manitoulin Island remained welcome items, especially as monopoly prices at American trading posts had risen steeply for all categories of goods. More important, however, was the need to establish a secure, long-term relationship with a government power which would allow the Native people to establish and develop a place that would sustain them in what had suddenly become a very threatening world.

A Model Chief

At the distribution of presents in August 1838, Little Pine subordinated his grievances about Canada's failure to honour its promises to build houses, and concentrated instead on praising the religion of his 'Great Father, the Red Coat,'[16] His words were timely. The opposition of Britain's Protestant missionary societies to Bond Head's Manitoulin Island scheme had led to a return to the former civilization program initiated by Sir John Colborne. Shingwaukonse shrewdly strengthened his political position by stating that his decision to embrace Christianity derived from advice offered him by Colborne six years earlier. The chief declared that he had remained faithful to the trust Colborne vested in him; he prayed regularly and had not taken alcohol in six years. His lodge emerged as a centre for Anglican prayer meetings. To officials who wished to commence an Anglican mission establishment at Manitowaning, Little Pine appeared a 'model Indian' – a status formally bestowed on the chief at a special ceremony held on Sunday, 12 August.

The Canadian Indian Department, by favouring the chief in this manner, could not fail to annoy the Roman Catholics and Methodists who were present at the occasion. One Methodist minister, James Evans, was particularly upset, since Shingwaukonse had only recently approached him to request that a Methodist missionary be sent to the Sault. There had even been discussion of establishing a Methodist schoolhouse and an agricultural and fishing community at Batchewana Bay, north of the Sault. On 7 August, Evans recorded in his diary that the Methodist contingent had been willing to 'proceed no further than the Sault until this chief decided on a matter which must govern our future movements.'[17] In spite of their generous overtures, however, the Methodists came off second best. Once Little Pine learned of arrangements for an Anglican missionary to proceed to the rapids that fall, he declined the Methodists' offer, although Evans noted that, if the arrangement with the Anglican church were to fall through, the chief would rescind his former position and 'consider us as his nearest relations.'[18] In the circumstances, it is hardly surprising that Evans considered Shingwaukonse to be susceptible to government manipulation.

Even though Evans might consider Shingwaukonse 'much abused and deceived by false promises' of the Anglican church,[19] it is probable that the chief's choice of Anglicanism over other denominations was as much political as it was religious. Rather than passively going along with government schemes, Little Pine decided to test the political capacities of his new, government-bestowed status. To Shingwaukonse, the time seemed auspicious to press for an extension of presents to the Red River Ojibwa and the Métis whom he wished to include in his Native community.[20] The unique political climate that emerged after the 1837 Rebellions in the Canadas had caused the Upper Canadian authorities to reverse decisions made the previous year to stop the distribution of presents to Native people. In the spring of 1838, Anderson had Assiginack carry a wampum parole as far west as the headwaters of the Mississippi, inviting bands to aid the British cause and partake in the queen's bounty. Assuming a radically different identity from the one with which the Indian Department had so recently vested him, Shingwaukonse first requested that the Métis be treated the same as the Ojibwa, since both peoples had demonstrated a similar loyalty to the Crown during the War of 1812. The chief had been travelling in the interior south-west of Lake Superior, to the Vermillion Lake–Rainy Lake area of Minnesota, and to points even farther westward.[21] 'I went last year to the Head Waters of Lake Superior to a friend (a half-breed, like myself), to inform him how good our Great Father was,' he continued. Little Pine then spoke before an audience of more than three thousand gathered at Manitowaning about the necessity for a road to be cut to Red River so that many more 'poor people who drip in rabbit skins may come ... and partake of these presents.'[22]

It must have been an awkward moment for Anderson, who had been freely extending invitations all spring to western Ojibwa leaders. The superintendent hedged at first; nevertheless, after warning the chief that he should not be overly optimistic about the government's response, he promised to relay the contents of the speech to the lieutenant-governor.

When there was no reply, the chief repeated his desires at Manitowaning the following summer, with several significant additions. The Ojibwa needed a blacksmith, he declared, while he himself required 'money to be able to pay someone to protect the timber of his lands.'[23] By this time he had put his plan to develop a logging industry at Sault Ste Marie into action. As an initial step, he had asked the government to purchase some necessary equipment, and Bond Head's successor, Sir George Arthur, had promised to supply 'axes and other tools.'[24] The chief's next goal was to secure use of the sawmill on the Ermatinger estate which had stood vacant since McMurray's departure from the mission. Shingwaukonse discussed the subject with Thomas G. Anderson, now Indian superintendent at Manitowaning, who informed his superiors of the increasing complexity of the chief's scheme:

> On the 7th inst. Shin-gwa-konce from St Mary's came down ... [to the Manitowaning agency] with a part of his tribe to enquire whether the halfbreeds would be clothed as mentioned last year, but I could not enlighten his understanding on the subject. He at the same time requested me to say to you, he was going to work at present and wished to get a yoke of oxen to draw logs and a carpenter & blacksmith and to have the wind mill repaired![25]

As Little Pine explained to Anderson, the goal was to establish at the Sault a thoroughly loyal, hard-working Native community espousing the ideals of self-sufficiency valued not only by the Indian Department but also in Ojibwa tradition. Natives and Métis would help one another, both groups working to preserve the spirit of reciprocity which traditionally characterized relations within Ojibwa bands. After 1838, the chief no longer urged his followers to act in accordance with external behavioural guidelines, as laid down by either the missionaries or the government. From now on, his primary emphasis was on the values of his group, since political strength would come only from creating a large, unified community at the rapids.

Though Shingwaukonse understood that the concept of the Christian God could not be confined within one denomination's creed, he remained personally loyal to the Church of England. He also expected the missionary of the Established Church to act as an intermediary between the Ojibwa and the state authorities. Since the chief viewed himself as equal in rank to the Anglican missionary, he considered a transaction between himself and the priest to be as binding as a formal agreement between two Native power-holders. For this reason, government failure in the future to uphold promises made to the Ojibwa would be regarded by the chief and his band as a serious breach of trust.

Little Pine's Resistance to the Manitowaning Settlement

Little Pine was careful not to endorse official plans for settling bands on Manitoulin Island. Instead, he requested that an Anglican missionary be sent to Sault Ste Marie to replace McMurray. Although the chief continued to press for 'advantages of civilization' to be extended to the Native people, he disapproved of the government's scheme, resurrected in 1838, of isolating Native people from the kind of commercial influences which had formerly characterized the fur trade.

Anderson, by contrast, viewed the isolationist policy as potentially effective both in drawing bands away from the international border and in protecting them from unsavoury white frontier influences. The scheme would also provide education and allow the transmission of social, agricultural, and mechanical skills which would facilitate Native assimilation into mainstream society.[26] The agent sought to lessen the Ojibwa's resistance to the plan by assuring Shingwaukonse and other leaders that their territorial prerogatives over lands on the north shores of Lakes Huron and Superior would be protected by the Crown should they move to Manitoulin. Yet retention by the state of all decision-making powers relative to the assimilation process made it possible for government administrators to turn a deaf ear to the head chiefs' views on removal. For Anderson, trying to align the reality of Native demands with the state's stereotype of the politically impotent 'Indian' involved a delicate juggling act. It usually proved much simpler to ignore Little Pine's statements whenever they appeared inconsistent with government policy.[27]

Anderson further overlooked the fact that, because of rivalries between head chiefs, bands did not always locate themselves where official plans governing the laying out of missionary settlements decreed. At first, for example, the agent had sought to lessen religious rivalries by allocating a specific locale on Manitoulin Island to each denomination. Assiginack, however, owing to his official status as Anderson's Roman Catholic interpreter, resided at Manitowaning, where his house rapidly became the centre of a Roman Catholic following within the Church of England settlement. Anderson had to admit that Assiginack's activities often contradicted government expectations and, during the winter of 1838, he found himself engaged in a minor power struggle with the interpreter. 'Assiginack is a clever man and designing enough to obtain, indirectly, influence sufficient to make himself appear the author of the Native willingness to fight the Queen's enemies & and thus draw them from the Department and accomplish the object he would have in view, the destruction of the Establishment.'[28] Yet Assiginack's influence with the Wikwemikong Ottawa made him indispensable to the government. Shingwaukonse had no corresponding status with the Indian Department. Regardless of his attachment to the Established Church, Little Pine mainly provided token 'proof' that a combined church-state mission establishment could work. By remaining at the Sault, however, the chief avoided direct competition with Assiginack and the Wikwemikong leaders, and so preserved his power base intact.

In 1839, Little Pine's most difficult task was to keep the western Ojibwa chiefs residing south of the international border loyal to his vision of a perpetual reciprocal relationship with the Crown. The previous year, which saw the first distribution of annuities under the terms of the American treaty signed on the St Croix, not one western band had travelled to Manitowaning for the distribution of presents. In response, Little Pine sent a communication to La Pointe upbraiding the head chief, Keche Besheke, for surrendering his political autonomy for a pittance in money and goods. Keche Besheke proved apologetic, and promised to ask Eschekebugecoshe from farther west at Leech Lake, among others, to come down with him to Manitowaning the following summer.[29] Little Pine thus remained the central figure promoting annual visitations by the western Ojibwa to Manitoulin Island. At the same time, the chief concentrated on furthering his own policy for Sault Ste Marie and its environs. Should bands from west of Lake Superior wish to join his settlement he would endeavour to have everything in readiness to receive them.

One Remove from the Missionary

The Reverend Frederick Augustus O'Meara arrived at the Sault in the fall of 1838, and took up residence on the Ermatinger estate. Unlike McMurray before him, O'Meara espoused Low Church views. He came to the north with a feeling of deep personal responsibility, as an ambassador of Christ, to spread the Gospel as effectively as possible over a wide geographical area. The thought of souls cut off from Christ's influence depressed him, yet he was unwilling to administer the redemptive sacrament of baptism before he felt participants were adequately prepared for the rite. The Roman Catholics and especially the Methodists, he held, were far too lenient in bestowing the privilege. O'Meara was quickly caught up in the task of saving souls, to the exclusion of the temporal concerns raised by the Natives. He deeply resented the intrusion of matters outside his pastoral duties, and quickly let this be known among his Native congregation.

During his first winter at the mission, O'Meara found the Ojibwa encouragingly responsive to his preaching. Although he was aided by George Johnston, who acted as interpreter, and James Robertson, a catechist, as well as by an assistant by the name of Sanson, O'Meara preferred to think of himself as a lone and independent servant of Christ. He was possessive about his flock, and upbraided any pastor who 'trespassed' on his territory. Not surprisingly, this regularly led him into disputes with the Roman Catholics, Methodists, and Baptists. Still, his devotion to duty made him willing to undergo considerable hardships to reach Ojibwa at Goulais Bay several times during the first winter. On being met by a group of Native people from Batchewana Bay who had been baptized by McMurray, O'Meara decided to include occasional visits to this band. The long, arduous journeys did not blunt his zeal. By June 1839, he decided to dispense with his interpreter, asking Shingwaukonse to teach him the Ojibwa language so he could communicate directly with his Native congregation.

During one of these teaching sessions, Little Pine showed O'Meara letters from Keche Besheke and several other head chiefs from the La Pointe region. The chief already had cast O'Meara in the role he had formerly assigned to McMurray – that of an intermediary between the band and the British authorities. The missionary had no idea of the identity of the Lake Superior and interior chiefs who sent these communications to Little Pine or of the purport of the wampum messages. Yet he missed no opportunity of impressing on the chief the importance of using his influence – which, the minister proclaimed to his superior, Bishop Strachan, 'appears to be considerable' – to keep the Natives attentive to religion.[30] One of O'Meara's duties was to convey two large wampum belts, sent to him by chiefs in the interior, to the chief superintendent of Indian affairs. And wampum was not the only mnemonic instrument in circulation. O'Meara also was expected to relay to the government messages 'formed of pieces of eagles' claws strung on deer skin or silk ribbon which are according to their arrangement ... made to speak the mind of the person sending them.'[31]

Little Pine wanted to establish his settlement at Garden River rather than at the rapids, and in late May 1839 persuaded O'Meara and the Reverend Crosbie Brough, who had come on a visit from Manitowaning, to view the lands and soil at the location east of Sault Ste Marie. Although neither O'Meara nor Brough regarded finances as the salient factor in their decision to veto the chief's proposal, as Anderson had done earlier, they considered Garden River to be unsuitable. It was necessary, both argued, for the Native people to gather at some permanent, central location during certain seasons of the year, and the rapids fishery seemed to provide them with the most stable form of subsistence, apart from agriculture. Regardless of the Ojibwa's views, the missionaries had the backing of the government, which maintained that the Sault Ojibwa devoted their time almost exclusively to fishing, while hunting served only as a secondary occupation. A government-directed change from a fishing economy to a mainly agricultural one seemed more feasible to the policy makers than a transition from hunting to agriculture, since the farmer merely required the modification of an already largely sedentary subsistence pattern.

Though temporarily frustrated in his plans to move the mission to Garden River, Little Pine did not neglect his other responsibilities. He was determined to have the western head chiefs ready to express an active allegiance to the British Crown. By late May, a large assembly had collected at the Sault. O'Meara, surprised by the great influx of interior Ojibwa who wanted to be baptized, frequently found it necessary to explain that he reserved baptism for what he termed 'proven candidates.' In early June, the crowd at the rapids was augmented by some other 'strange Indians from the north shore of Lake Superior.'[32] The Leech Lake band arrived soon afterward from Minnesota, and all stated their readiness to accept an Anglican missionary. Though the Episcopal missionary, the Reverend Boutwell, had decided to terminate his mission to Eschekebugecoshe's Leech Lake band in 1838 owing to its defiant attitude towards Christianity, O'Meara naïvely regarded the members of this band as 'interesting sons of the forest' who had not yet heard the word of the Gospel.[33]

O'Meara at first saw the requests for baptism as the seeking of the 'natural man' for God's truth. To support this view, he argued that Little Pine had even prepared questions, to which the priest had responded before a large attentive audience:

> In the course of my visiting among the Lodges today I met a good many Natives in the chief's wigwam when some questions that the old man put to me led me to explain the second Commandment pointing out the gross impropriety of which Roman Catholics have been guilty of leaving out of their catechisms [a] portion of God's word and I also took occasion in the hearing of those who were by and who I was anxious should derive some benefit to enlarge on other truths of Christianity to which all listened with apparent interest.[34]

It soon became evident that O'Meara was not the man to further a Native settlement based on either agriculture or commercial fishing. He lacked both an interest in such goals and the aptitude to promote them. His main concern remained with 'souls' – their preparation for the next world and the dangers posed by heathenism and the 'erroneous doctrines' of rival denominations. Though his religious colleagues praised him for zealousness, they also saw that there was a rash and precipitate side to his character.[35] This rashness must also have struck Shingwaukonse, whose technique in 'testing' people lay in subjecting them to careful questioning for long periods of time,[36] at least until he could assess their fundamental personality traits.

For his part, O'Meara considered Little Pine more dignified and rea-soned in his judgment than the rest of his band. 'Reason' constituted a trait the missionary valued highly, since he felt it was only through the rational faculty that man could gain insight into Christian truth. At the same time, he continued to hold a romantic view of Native people as nature's 'children,' a view which blinded him to the problems they faced in trying to adapt successfully to the changes around them. O'Meara undoubtedly felt personal pride in being associated with an influential British chief. In August he wrote with almost proprietary admiration about the arrival of the Sault Ojibwa at Manitowaning in 'a fleet of about seventy canoes, which as they sailed before a strong wind with the chief at their head in a large batteau with two British flags displayed, had a very pretty appearance.'[37]

The Ojibwa's willingness to listen to O'Meara's teachings lasted a year, and then ended. This was not a personal rejection of the missionary, but involved a gradual withdrawal prompted by a series of events, including the refusal of the government, once again, to fulfil its promise to con-struct houses. O'Meara's attitude did not improve matters. Little Pine made clear his wish to have the promise honoured, and the priest agreed to take a pipe to the lieutenant-governor as a reminder of the trust estab-lished between the band and the queen's representative six years before. Yet, once in Toronto, O'Meara made no effort to promote the settlement Little Pine desired. In his own account of his meeting with the lieutenant-governor in the fall of 1839, O'Meara stated:

> During the ensuing week I had several interviews with his Excellency the Lieutenant Governor on the subject of the Natives and the surest mode of advancing their best interests. It is pleasing to see how deep an interest he takes in everything that concerns them and instead of falling into the same error that many have done supposing that their civilization must precede their conversion, His Excellency is of opinion that the only way of civilizing them is to endeavour to have that change effected in their hearts and motives which will be sure completely to soften down their savage manners and habits ... [38]

O'Meara described the results of these sessions to the Ojibwa soon after his arrival back at the Sault. Although disappointed, they continued to attend religious meetings, and obeyed the missionary's directives not to join with the Métis population in the usual New Year's drinking spree. Little Pine nevertheless found himself in an increasingly difficult position because of the way O'Meara responded to the illness of his son Nah-wahquashkum. According to O'Meara, Nahwahquashkum had suffered an internal injury while lifting a heavy object at Mackinac Island during the summer. Suspecting witchcraft to be the cause of the injury, the chief asked the missionary to try to reconcile Nahwahquashkum's wife and in-laws to Christianity, since he evidently suspected that they were the perpetrators of the problem.

O'Meara's account of his response to Little Pine's appeal evidenced a dogmatic and unsympathetic attitude, prompted not only by emotional evangelicalism, but also by strict adherence to the tenets of prevailing government policy:

> The chief applied to me to interfere in the matter, and to speak to his daughter-in-law on the sinfulness of her conduct in neglecting the vow of love in sickness and in health that she had made to her husband when they were united after the form of our Church ... Having had information from more than one individual that the old man himself had on one occasion been betrayed into the sin of drunkenness, I took this opportunity to speak to him on the awful consequences of ... falling into his old practices and warning him of the certain destruction from the presence of the Lord that awaits on drunkards.[39]

The missionary felt Nahwahquashkum's ailment to be of a minor character, and railed against the use of Native medicines to effect a cure. Nevertheless, the chief's son rapidly declined in health, and in early March of 1840 proved too delirious to listen to the missionary. It angered O'Meara that the family had not sent for him before the man had lost his reason, since it was then too late to establish the state of the dying man's soul. 'Seeing that it would be useless to remain ...' O'Meara wrote to J.J. Grasett, secretary of the Society for Converting and Civilizing the Indians, 'I took my leave to return home the same evening, leaving directions that should his reason return they would immediately send for me.'[40]

O'Meara's attitudes differed so radically from those of the traditional shaman healer that his refusal even to try to cure the malady must have seemed to the Ojibwa like an amazing admission of weakness. They never asked for his help again, and from then on, O'Meara found a change in the attitudes of the whole Native population from Garden River to Batchewana Bay. News travelled fast. Where before he had been eagerly received, now he often had to pry the Ojibwa out of their lodges. Reflecting on one cool reception he had received at Goulais Bay, he confessed that, when the 'message is received with ... apathy ... this breaks the spirit and saddens the heart of the ambassador of Christ ...'[41] O'Meara lacked the experience and understanding to heal the breach. Had he sought the assistance of others familiar with Native culture, such as George Johnston or Mrs McMurray, both of whom had proved of inestimable help to Rev. William McMurray, the gap might have been bridged. But he did not. The Ojibwa had not assumed an overtly hostile stance, but simply one of lack of interest.

O'Meara's pride would not allow him to admit failure, and he cast about for an explanation which would absolve him of blame for losing command of the Native congregation. This he found in the context of Nahwahquashkum's funeral. During the preparations for the burial, O'Meara expressed annoyance at being asked to contribute food or money on behalf of the church and the government to the traditional funeral feast. It was a minor request, but it was transformed in O'Meara's mind into evidence of 'flaws' in the Ojibwa character. The Native population was by nature worldly minded, he maintained, concerned only with gaining material benefits. Shingwaukonse and his band viewed missionaries simply as a source of government advantages, and only for this reason had converted to Christianity.[42]

Little Pine grew increasingly reluctant to respond to O'Meara's requests as he found his band unwilling to heed the missionary's instructions. When O'Meara demanded that he use his authority to persuade his people to make their children attend school regularly, Little Pine gave a noncommittal reply. But O'Meara could be unreasonable as well as callous, as Shingwaukonse had discovered the previous fall when, in response to a near failure of the rapids fishery, the Ojibwa had stayed out long hours on the water trying to take whatever fish they could catch before leaving for their hunting grounds. Having fished all Saturday night, many grew tired during the Sunday service. O'Meara showed no mercy. 'I told them thro' their Chief that they were not only to abstain from work on the Sabbath itself, but also from such extra labour on the Saturday night as would render them incapable of putting the day to the purpose for which it was intended,' he informed the Upper Canada Clergy Society.[43] Shingwaukonse was placed in a difficult position by the unpopular missionary's behaviour. As well, because of his return to heavy drinking, he had to endure the missionary's scolding. O'Meara's warnings about the danger to his soul made little impression, however. From September 1840 onward, Little Pine and several others became involved in drinking sprees on the American side. These incidents grew so frequent that during the New Year celebrations of 1841, the chief had to be carried to a hut, lent by O'Meara to the Ojibwa, where the missionary discovered him in a drunken, disorderly state.[44]

The winters of 1839–40 and 1840–1 were exceedingly harsh. Fish were scarce owing to unusually high water levels, and the band's residence at the Sault favoured neither farming nor the storing of agricultural produce. Conditions for hunting remained poor. Little Pine's earlier plans to begin a logging industry with the help of the Métis had fallen through. O'Meara had antagonized the Roman Catholic Métis, thus making impossible the Native–Métis cooperation that was essential to the scheme. Refusing to consider any of the chief's proposals seriously, Anderson pressed for the Ojibwa's removal to Manitoulin Island, citing the unfavourable climate and poor soil at the Sault as suitable reasons.[45] To avoid such hardship in the future, Shingwaukonse held a council with his people late in the spring of 1841 and afterwards relayed to O'Meara that his band would no longer remain at the rapids.

Unable to see the broader picture, O'Meara despondently informed Strachan that his mission had fallen victim to government intransigence:

The reason of this change in the place of encampment during the summer seems to be that in former years they looked forward to having houses built for them by Government at the Sault, but now having waited so long in vain they have ceased to expect them, and therefore each family continues [to encamp] in the summer in or about their sugar bush which is usually contiguous to the spot on which they make their gardens, near which it is much more convenient for them to remain than at the Sault, and thus they are likely in future to be as much scattered in summer as they are in winter, and indeed more so, as the necessity of fishing makes them collect more in one place during the winter, but in summer wherever each family chooses to pitch their tent they can generally obtain subsistence ... [46]

O'Meara now expected the worst. Little Pine's band would become extinct, he maintained, for without missionary guidance a 'propensity for intoxicating drink' would undoubtedly destroy the current generation of Ojibwa 'both in soul and body.'[47] The only hope for preserving a remnant, he argued, lay in insulating a number of children from all contact with their parents. To this end O'Meara initiated an experiment, keeping six children under instruction at the mission house during the winter of 1840–1. On 9 March 1841, however, Mezai removed most of the children because, O'Meara stated, 'their poor foolish parents, believing some most ridiculous stories invented by the malice of the Canadians here, sent for them ...'[48] O'Meara's earlier interest in following the Ojibwa on their seasonal round of activities disappeared; he devoted his time instead to Ojibwa translations of the Collects, Epistles, and Gospels, with the aid of a Native interpreter from the Credit mission. Ojibwa from away no longer visited the Sault, and O'Meara no longer felt pleasure in travelling long distances. The Indian Department's plan for removing the Ojibwa to Manitowaning looked more and more inviting. Souls must be saved, but such could be done better in milieu in which the Ojibwa were more under the control of the missionary.

Little Pine Seeks Semi-seclusion

The missionary's presence had not in any way lessened the band's political autonomy. By scattering their lodges, they avoided his scrutiny over their affairs, and often it seemed that their absences and bouts of intoxication coincided rather neatly with O'Meara's arrival with news from Anderson which needed an immediate reply. The government's plan to form a settlement on Manitoulin Island, by contrast, posed a considerable threat. During February and March of 1841, Anderson and Little Pine engaged in a heated exchange of views regarding the band's removal. The superintendent pressed vigorously for residence at the Anglican 'Establishment,' as it came to be called. Shingwaukonse, for his part, informed both Anderson and the governor general that he refused to 'sit like a gull' on the barren rocky terrain near Manitowaning when he could raise adequate agricultural produce at Garden River. What kind of markets, the chief asked, existed on the island? And more important, if he left, what would happen to his lands at the Sault?[49] Anderson responded by declaring all the arguments to be out of line with government policy, and exhorted Little Pine to consider the benefits instead. For the Ojibwa to be away from the influence of the Métis traders and their 'whiskey traffic' would save their souls from destruction, the agent explained. 'Now would it not be better to die like a gull, and your soul to go to heaven,' the agent inquired in the same moralistic vein, 'than to die like a king and your soul be cast into hell?'[50]

Anderson also quickly produced some simple statistics to undermine Little Pine's determination to pursue agriculture at Garden River. On Manitoulin Island, he chided, single families 'raised more produce than you say all your tribe have raised.'[51] Anderson lacked an argument to counter the chief's reluctance to give up the fur trade, however, since the mission project concentrated on the insulation and regulation of Native labour, not on the creation of commercial enterprises. Trade might be carried out at La Cloche or Penetanguishene, he responded, although it would be better for the Native people to engage in wage labour than in trading activities. To Anderson, the traders' system of taking credit kept the Ojibwa trappers 'weighed down' so that they could not call the products of their labour their own. Finally, while Anderson's answer to Shingwaukonse's inquiries regarding Native prerogatives to lands in the vicinity of the Sault proved both elliptical and abstruse, his words *seemingly* indicated that the government would recognize the chief's rights:

> As regards your Lands: suppose you were on your bed of sickness, you could not take these lands with you – your Heirs would inherit them; and so on, until your tribe sold them. By coming here, you only leave them, as it were, for a time; you used to leave them when you went to hunt for skins. You leave them now for better motives – to seek a better inheritance; you neither give nor sell them, they remain yours until you die; no-one has a right to deprive you of them; therefore you need not be uneasy on that head.[52]

Anderson's statements branded the Ojibwa as both politically and economically weak. Shingwaukonse now knew that there would be little scope for independent enterprise at Manitowaning. At Sault Ste Marie, by contrast, he could negotiate for favourable terms for the sale of his band's products among a number of competing merchants. His critique of the system of isolating Native people from commercial intercourse with whites was one of the first and most cogent stands made against the government establishment at Manitowaning by either a Native or a white person in the early 1840s. Within twenty years this viewpoint would constitute accepted policy.[53] But in 1840 and 1841, Shingwaukonse and his band had to confront the threat to their political and economic autonomy by relying on their own resources and initiative.

Little Pine gained time through vacillation. He rejected the idea of removal in November 1840, agreed tentatively to it in January 1841, and finally, in May, conceded that he would go. O'Meara held a service at Garden River for the largest congregation he had met with in months, since many Ojibwa had assembled to bid farewell to their chief. On 15 May, Shingwaukonse and John Bell, who acted as the chief's interpreter, left for Manitowaning.[54]

The Garden River band members meanwhile continued their usual activities, undeterred by Little Pine's absence. Ogista was now in charge, with his brother-in-law, Piabetassung, as a minor chief in his own right on

Sugar Island. The Baptist missionary, Abel Bingham, found Ogista, Kabaosa, Megissanequa, Wabanosa, Shebagezick, and their families, as well as Buhkwujjenene – who was still unmarried at the time – camped at Garden River. Most listened willingly to the Baptist and informed Bingham that although they had previously joined the Anglican Church at the urging of their chief, they had grown disillusioned and wandered from their Christian faith. But they also maintained contact with Little Pine, for Bingham's journal entry for 14 November 1841 tells of a meeting the missionary held with Little Pine and his wife at Garden River, during the very period when O'Meara and the Indian Department assumed the chief to be residing on Manitoulin Island.[55]

The chief must have slipped away to visit his band during the season when most of the Manitoulin Island residents were at their fishing grounds, so that his absence would not be noticed by either O'Meara or Anderson. The fall was also the time when bands traditionally met near the rapids fishery to conduct ceremonies and exchange information. Shingwaukonse, while he had evidently transferred the weight of responsibility for his own band's affairs to his son Ogista, refused to isolate himself from the large general councils which would have been held at the Sault during this season. These meetings provided him with news of events within the Upper Great Lakes Native community and food for reflection in the winter months ahead.

Little Pine's Agreement to Remove: Bluff, Sincere Consideration, or Blind Concurrence?

Shingwaukonse left his band in the spring of 1841 and lived separately from it, except for short return visits, until the following spring. In so doing, the chief relinquished all traces of his former high status. Apart from John Bell, who had become his son-in-law, none of his immediate family joined him. The strain of Anderson's repeated probings into the nature of Ojibwa land tenure at the Sault was beginning to tell on the old chief. During the winter, Little Pine was plagued by feelings of confusion and emotional fatigue, and occasionally sought release in bouts of drunkenness. Finally, in June 1841, he explained to O'Meara that he had decided to depart for, as things were, he could no longer cope. His condition would merely worsen if he remained, 'so he must go immediately even should no one wish to follow him.'[56]

O'Meara believed that Shingwaukonse was feeling remorse about his drinking and was seeking escape from the temptations of the whisky traders. O'Meara further assumed that Little Pine had been abandoned by his band for failing them as a leader. Yet the boisterous farewell the departing chief received at Garden River suggests that any disagreements between Shingwaukonse and his followers had been resolved. Moreover, by temporarily relinquishing his leadership status, Little Pine shed the roles of 'model convert' and 'government intermediary' imposed on him by the Indian superintendent and the Anglican missionary. Freed from these constraints, he could now weigh the available options. At the same time, by relying on the Indian Department for his subsistence and accommodation, the chief represented himself to the government as politically and economically powerless. It seems that Shingwaukonse, with the full comprehension and compliance of his band, assumed a liminal role as a prelude to taking more focused action on behalf of his people.

In line with a three-stage sequence outlined by Arnold Van Gennep in his seminal discussion of a rite of passage,[57] Shingwaukonse's stance during the fall and winter of 1841–2 exhibited none of the traits of his past or future state. Nor did it hint, in the initial stages, at the result of the transition which would emerge by the following spring. In the formal ritual context, the range of outcomes of the liminal state are strongly structured by traditional expectations. But because the cultural milieu in which Shingwaukonse acted derived its formal aspects from interrelations among dynamic personalized cosmological concepts, a considerable degree of indeterminacy affected the process. It might be assumed that limitations imposed by external agencies on the chief's conduct would have prevented him from engaging in activities in keeping with an internally consistent thought system. However, because the Ojibwa power-belief system advocated ritualized 'powerlessness' as an important avenue to spiritual 'blessings.' A behaviour pattern stressing indeterminacy would be compatible with the absence of individual initiative during the liminal state, and would automatically protect the chief from government and missionary manipulation.

Little Pine reached his decision to leave Garden River during the spring season, a time of spiritual and physical renewal to the Ojibwa. The timing of his decision thus suggests that his departure may have been viewed by his people as an act of semi-ritual importance. The chief's absence from his band, furthermore, would be felt in more ways than one. Perhaps most significantly, he had persuaded John Bell, the resident trader and outfitter for his band's winter hunts, to accompany him to Manitoulin Island. But Shingwaukonse evidently had no intention of putting economic or political pressure on his followers to move to Manitowaning. That he had abdicated as intermediary is clear from the fact that several members of the Garden River band now approached Anderson directly to ask for houses to be built, rather than calling on the chief to speak for them. Meanwhile, with the assistance of his interpreter, Bell, who spoke English, French, and the Native tongue, Little Pine was well positioned to gather information about the government's plans for the Upper Great Lakes area. (Shingwaukonse's influence over Bell in 1841 must have been considerable, since Bell renounced his earlier Roman Catholicism and joined the Ojibwa leader in profession Anglicanism.)

Somewhat naïvely, Anderson viewed the chief's willingness to reside at Manitowaning as a sign of future success for government policy, hailing Shingwaukonse's capitulation as a victory for the Anglican mission. On receiving news from O'Meara of the chief's decision to leave Garden River, Anderson wrote to Jarvis, 'And now that an opportunity offers itself to prove that the experiment of trying to civilize the Natives is not in vain I trust the object may be carried to its full accomplishment.'[58] So certain was the superintendent that Little Pine would persuade his band to resettle that he immediately ordered twenty-five houses to be built at Manitowaning. By September, Anderson had raised this number to forty houses.

Anderson had recognized Shingwaukonse's territorial prerogatives to the Sault area merely as a preliminary to a major land surrender which the agent expected to follow as a matter of course after the settlement of Little Pine's band on Manitowaning Island. Seen from this perspective, the chief's liminal state also doubled as a clever defensive strategy. Shingwaukonse's arrival on the island with a meagre retinue seriously disrupted the superintendent's long-range plans. When Anderson attempted to secure Little Pine's agreement to a land surrender at the Sault and Garden River, the chief stated that he was powerless to act independently of his band. By this reply, Shingwaukonse protected Métis as well as Ojibwa territorial claims, as the agent evidently intended to force the Métis to vacate their holdings by ceding the land out from under them. But when Little Pine instead demanded compensation in rent or specie for any land ceded, including at least the money for the sale of the Ermatinger property, should it occur, Anderson found himself in a difficult position. The agent could not compel a surrender from a chief who refused to act as a representative for his people. Since Little Pine had rendered himself almost totally invulnerable to pressure, he could bargain freely, without fear of consequences. He ceased using the government's promise to build houses at the Sault as a counter in the power game. During the winter he would simply collect information. In this way he would acquire the rudiments for new and possibly more workable strategies to employ on behalf of his people.

But strategies were not enough. There would have to be a revision of goals. Little Pine had spent a decade trying to secure government assistance for his Native settlement, but so far his attempts had failed. He also knew that the Native people on the south shore of Lake Superior would be approached by the American government to cede their land during the summer of 1842. To Keche Besheke, among others, he had denounced the idea of relinquishing land to the Americans, since loss of autonomy usually followed. Yet the question remained: did the Native people on the British side have better alternatives than those on the U.S. side? Did they necessarily have to sell all their lands at once, or might they keep control over the timing of the sale of the amount of land to be ceded? What choices did they have? Shingwaukonse's struggle to understand the cultural variables implicit in the white man's view must have been a frustrating one, but he clearly felt that he had a duty to make the effort. In early June, when both O'Meara and Father J.B. Proulx, the Roman Catholic missionary from Wikwemikong, happened to visit his house, Little Pine began his usual questioning, proceeding from Native premises. A single theme permeated his inquiries, all of which concerned intergroup relations. What, from the white person's standpoint, he asked, was the cause of war? Were human beings 'related to all animal and immaterial things and also to the Heavenly Bodies?' Finally, which would be better: Presents? Or money given in payment for one's lands? Neither O'Meara's nor Proulx's responses proved very enlightening, other than to show the chief the degree to which interdenominational rivalries promoted hostility. Proulx's attempts to answer the first question by reference to Joan of Arc and certain French and continental conflicts only irritated the volatile British patriot O'Meara. O'Meara passed over Little Pine's second question with a few perfunctory remarks, although Proulx was willing to give the question at least some consideration. In answering the chief's questions regarding the surrender of land, the two missionaries expressed diametrically opposed points of view. O'Meara favoured land surrender and removal to the Establishment, while Proulx remained decidedly hostile to this option, encouraging the chief to protest the termination of presents.

After some consideration, Proulx admitted that he could see no reason why the Ojibwa would wish to come to the Establishment. This touched off a rejoinder from Shingwaukonse, who apparently could not resist poking fun at discrepancies between what he viewed as white-sponsored agricultural utopias and the harsh realities of life in the north:

Mr P. said, You old man, what are [*sic*] you come for? I have always heard your lands were very good. Yes, said the Pine, everything grows well on them. Wheat grows as high as a man. Mr O'Meara said I never saw it. How could you, you came so seldom the Pine said. I never wanted for anything at the Sault, plenty of food last winter. We killed 20 Reindeer – but here not one.[59]

Shingwaukonse found it difficult to sustain his sense of humour, however, when the discussion turned to the Canadian government's policy of discontinuing presents to Aboriginal groups living in the United States. Little Pine introduced the topic himself in response to what he evidently felt was the parochial tendency of the priests, whom he called 'Blackcoats,' to focus on affairs relating solely to Manitoulin Island. The chief's concerns, by contrast, embraced the whole of the Lake Superior region and lands far to the west. Not surprisingly, he cast his description of the territory in Ojibwa terms, with Lake Superior – the lake of the Ojibwas – constituting the geographic centre of the 'Great Island' of North America. He told the missionaries of his struggles to understand how, when all living things possessed some degree of power, the entire 'island' of North America now fell under just two powers. Where were the other forces which might have counterbalanced these two powers and their arrogance in dividing, to their own advantage, his people's lands? Why had the many religious denominations not interfered? After all, 'Me me-nik ke-puk-ka-e-ne-nim?' ['How many preaching men are there?'] he asked. And were these Blackcoats truly concerned about the fate of his people in this increasingly dualistic universe in which Natives seemed to have no place?

You are two Black Coats, now I want to know if our Saviour marked in the Bible, that the whites would journey towards the setting sun until they found a large Island in which there were many Indians living in a rich country – that they should rob the natives of their animals, furs and land, after which the English and Americans should draw a line, from one to the other end of the Island and each take his share and do what he pleases with the Natives, I ask if that's written in the Bible?[60]

A fourth party to the discussion, George Wilson, the newly appointed collector of customs at Sault Ste Marie, interjected regarding the position of the American Indians: '[It's] their own fault, why don't they come here?' Annoyed by the remark, Little Pine retorted, 'How is it their fault? [T]hey remain there to receive payments for their lands.'[61] To Shingwaukonse, the whites had shown a distinct lack of concern for group territorial prerogatives. As a Native leader he knew he could encourage bands to migrate to Canada, but could not force them to do so.

According to oral traditions at Garden River, the problem lay at a deeper level. From Shingwaukonse's shamanistic standpoint, the 'disruptions' among his people were cosmological, not merely geopolitical, in scope. It would require a brave man to confront the hidden powers which threatened to displace, even annihilate, the Ojibwa. But, as one legend maintained, 'He could not turn back. He had a purpose, a gift. "And then what kind of man would I be?" he said. "You cannot leave the path ... You wouldn't be remembered."'[62]

Shingwaukonse meanwhile kept his 'allies' abreast of his findings during the winter of 1841-2. While he maintained a low profile at the Establishment, he was doubtless active in sending and receiving messages through the far-reaching Native communication networks. It would probably be fair to see his encouragement as instrumental in bringing an 'unusual number of Indians from the Upper Lakes' to the Sault in July, from whence they proceeded to Manitowaning to join an even larger assemblage of about six thousand for the distribution of presents.[63]

The response from the western bands heralded the chief's reintegration into Native society. Little Pine re-emerged fully into the mainstream of his group's activities in late July, his period of semi-ritual separation ended. He had dwelt for a year in the 'wilderness' of strange ideologies and ideas, and now he returned to his familiar rivers, lakes, and woods, with their inhabitants, human, animal, and spiritual. The Garden River band by late July also had decided independently of their chief against settling at the Manitowaning Establishment. On 15 August, Shingwaukonse told O'Meara of this decision, to which the missionary could only react with chagrin that the chief and his followers had once again slipped from his control.[64]

The band's decision coincided with the chief's own departure for Garden River, which suggests that a reciprocal relationship between leader and group had reasserted itself. Several band members' earlier tentative receptiveness to the idea of removal may well have arisen from their fears that Little Pine would fail to find an alternative by the spring of 1842. In that case, residence at the Establishment might be the safest option during a time of rapid change, for the government at least would supply basic necessities. In this case, the band's vacillations about resettlement was neither blind concurrence nor mere bluff. The burden of responsibility for the group's reply to the government lay on Little Pine's shoulders. After giving the subject much consideration, he had decided at last that it might still be possible to establish a strong, self-determining Native community at Garden River. There would thus be no land surrender. He would retain his power base intact. The territory, instead, would be logged, farmed, and fished by the Native population. Commercial prospects, moreover, had improved by 1843. A return to better economic times in the United States encouraged a rise in fish prices, followed in turn by a resurgence of commercial fishing at the rapids and elsewhere along the coast. After the demise of the American Fur Company in 1842, trade competition increased, but there was also a choice of buyers. As well, Philetus Swift Church, a merchant on Sugar Island, began hiring band members to cut wood for sale as fuel to passing steamers during the winter of 1845.[65]

The rising power of the two developing nation states which threatened the economic and political autonomy of the western bands would have to confront an indigenous movement at the Sault led by Little Pine. But Shingwaukonse and his allies, Ojibwa and Métis, would not negotiate with these expanding state entities without special external assistance. The chief intended to ask for assistance from the leaders of as many Christian denominations as he could contact.

Calling on the Churches for Aid

Shingwaukonse immediately began his search for representatives of Christian denominations who might be sympathetic to his plans. On 3 August 1842, he approached the Anglican bishop, John Strachan, and his companion, Lord Morpeth, who had attended the distribution of presents, to ask for an Anglican missionary to be sent to Garden River. Little Pine's appeal impressed Strachan, who argued that there had been 'a good deal of art and management in his arrangement & mode of introducing it.'[66] In reply, Strachan promised to visit Garden River during the summer, although he confided to the chief justice, Sir John Beverley Robinson, that he basically disapproved of the chief's suggestion, since Little Pine's band 'were too few & will be much better off [at Manitowaning].'[67] Viewing the site did not change Strachan's opinion.

Shingwaukonse next approached Michael Power, the Roman Catholic Bishop of Toronto. Power responded sympathetically to Little Pine's appeal to send a clergyman, but would make no firm commitments. Whenever Baptist and Methodist missionaries visited Garden River, their assistance was also requested. The Baptists' expectations regarding Christian duty proved rather too stringent for Little Pine's liking, however.

Whenever Bingham stressed the need for temperance, the chief proclaimed that 'Ogista was now ... their chief & he wished him to lead & them to follow him in the path of sobriety.'[68]

Shingwaukonse's scepticism regarding emotional evangelism may also have arisen in the context of an 'experiment' he conducted to test the validity of the Millerite beliefs described by an itinerant Baptist preacher. William Miller was one of a number of American millenarians who proclaimed that the biblical prophecy of Revelation would be fulfilled in the United States during the mid-nineteenth century. The Baptist preacher whom Little Pine encountered had set the Day of Reckoning at 30 April 1842. After keeping note of the date, carefully watching for signs in the sky, and recording the passage of time by making notches in his pipestem, the chief eventually concluded that the prophecy was a hoax.[69]

Little Pine indicated by this that he could not be easily swayed either by religious fanaticism or political polemics. Different manifestations of Christian belief had evidently come to exhibit different degrees of 'power,' according to Shingwaukonse's own cultural yardstick for assessing such matters. Denominations which sought through emotional appeals to make a man into an idealized creature, indifferent to the cares and obligations of day-to-day existence, ranked low. According to Bingham, Little Pine had scant interest in conforming to specific church creeds. 'By the remarks made by the old chief who spake for the whole of them,' he concluded, 'I think they have not much notion of listening very attentively to our instructions any farther than suits their own conscience.'[70] It would be Ogista's task to maintain relations with the more emotionally inclined of the denominations, while his father would concentrate on strengthening linkages with the Established Church. But no potential source of aid would be overlooked.

A Second Appeal to the Anglican Church

Since the Anglican missionary provided Little Pine with his most direct link to the queen's representatives, Little Pine prevailed on O'Meara in August 1842 to draft a petition to the governor general requesting that the land belonging to the Ermatinger estate revert to the Ojibwa. For several years there had been a minor power struggle going on over land between the Garden River chief and the sons of Charles Oakes Ermatinger, accompanied by their Ojibwa relatives from Sandy Lake and Fond du Lac, in present-day Minnesota. Charles Oakes Ermatinger had married Charlotte, the daughter of Katawabidai, the Sandy Lake head chief of the Loon *dodem*, who after the War of 1812 had acted as one of the most prominent spokesmen for the western bands in their dealings with the British.[71] William Ermatinger in particular proved a strong contestant, and brought along his brother-in-law, Mang'osid of Fond du Lac, to support his claims. Charles Oakes Ermatinger's retirement to Montreal in 1828 had undermined the economic security of the Sandy Lake and Fond du Lac Loon chiefs and thrown them into conflict with Shingwaukonse, who had usurped their prominent place with the local Sault independent trading establishment.[72] Knowing he had formidable competition from the Loons, and receiving no response to his petition about this matter, Little Pine travelled to Montreal for an interview with the governor general in 1843. When assistance was still not forthcoming, he set out in the spring of 1844 to ask the resident missionary to forward a message to McMurray, who was now the rector of St James Church in Dundas, near Hamilton, and whom he knew O'Meara would be seeing in the near future. Little Pine had already made three attempts to contact McMurray, but McMurray had apparently not received the letters, since he had not replied. In each letter, Little Pine assured McMurray that interest in Christianity was on the rise in his band. Members attended religious meetings, conducted by Ogista, Bukhwujjenene, and Piabetassung, twice weekly. The chief's fourth letter was a particularly eloquent plea to the rector as a 'brother' and 'friend' to use his influence to have a minister reside permanently at Garden River. 'My brother William,' Shingwaukonse appealed, 'I call on you for the goodness and love of God, I call on your brother Minister who is listening to me, that you both help with me [*sic*], that we may again have a Minister ... you will be strong, you that are Ministers, and with all your might help with me.'[73]

Shingwaukonse was worried that the Ermatinger contingent would succeed in gaining recognition for their claims to Sault property on the basis of Aboriginal right, particularly through their kinship associations with Katawabidai of Sandy Lake, their maternal grandfather, and Mang'osid of Fond du Lac, their maternal uncle. On 21 October 1844 he hailed Joseph Wilson, who the previous year had been appointed collector of customs, and interviewed him for three hours straight 'concerning Native rights to the lands.'[74] The chief then dictated a three-page letter to the governor general, setting out his and his allies' proprietary rights. He felt he had to act quickly in order to stem the growing tide of opposition to his own Native campaign.

Oral traditions at Garden River indicate that the years 1844 to 1846 proved particularly arduous for Shingwaukonse. He had not yet entered into the final phase of his career in which he would jeopardize his links with government and church to secure his goals. At the same time, he suffered major disappointments and illness. In his letter to McMurray, he reported that his daughter, Owiaquahgeyhegoqua, Megissanequa's wife, had died. During the summer of 1845 he had also cut his foot with an axe, which 'for some time threatened to prove fatal.'[75] Worse still, he had failed to secure the help of the Anglican Church.

The appeal to McMurray initially aroused the interest of the Reverend James Beaven, a High Church man and personal friend of McMurray. Beaven even considered raising funds in England for the revival of the Sault mission. In August 1845, he set out for the Sault with the sole purpose of determining the viability of the mission project at first hand. On his arrival at the rapids, he found about forty houses occupied by French and Métis, but no Ojibwa. When he found that the Garden River community he had come so far to see consisted of only 'six or eight Native huts and a log house or two under construction for the chief,'[76] his enthusiasm waned markedly. While acknowledging the strategic importance of the Sault in attracting Native peoples from around Lake Superior, the minister felt that it would take a considerable sum to establish a mission or industrial school, and the smallness of the bands, their scattered distribution along the coast, and competition from equally valid appeals for monetary aid from groups residing nearer to the seat of the Episcopal See in Toronto argued against such an expenditure.

Meanwhile Little Pine's responsibilities to his Native allies had increased. In 1845, many prominent Ojibwa leaders in the United States, under pressure from the American government to cede their territory, opted for annuities without a struggle. They did so not out of self-interest, but because there no longer seemed to be any alternatives. Following the La Pointe treaties of 1842 and 1845, serious political rifts divided bands. Some leaders thought that migration to Canada, in accordance with Shingwaukonse's plan, offered a more secure future for their families than remaining crowded onto American reserve lands. Leaders who had been forceful in opposing the surrenders at La Pointe, moreover, found themselves hounded by both American authorities and members of their own bands. As a result of internal band strife, breakaway family groups joined together in making a representation to the Crown through the collector of customs at the Canadian Sault in June 1845. 'I have to inform you,' wrote George Wilson to Thomas G. Anderson, 'that two Chippeway Indian chiefs, Muckedaypenasse and Neokema, from La Point, Lake Superior, have called upon me requesting me to inform them whether the Government would permit them to come and make their home in Canada.'[77] A number of closely related families, totalling five hundred individuals, had asked Muckedaypenasse to make the appeal on their behalf. It would be the first step towards the migration which Shingwaukonse had been anticipating for many years.

The Unretreating Frontier

Shingwaukonse by 1846 had made a firm commitment to remain on his lands and to try to develop their economic potential. The merchant Church had already suggested selling wood to passing steamers as a way of enhancing the local economy. Shingwaukonse hoped, given the protection of this industry by the Crown and the links he had carefully fostered with religious organizations, that his plans for a settlement would bear fruit within a year. Then, in the spring of 1846, his scheme suffered another setback. Joseph Wilson, a son of George Wilson, who in 1845 had been appointed Crown Lands agent, suddenly confiscated wood cut by Native people on Squirrel Island, not far from the main Ojibwa village. According to Wilson, Church and the Ojibwa had disregarded the international tariff on timber and taken the resource without a licence. Writing to the commissioner of Crown Lands, the agent described Church as 'an American adventurer that has enriched himself by defrauding [the government of] revenue on both sides of the Frontier.'[78] Church nevertheless had local connections, and on 18 March Wilson was arrested in the American Sault and sent to jail. To the Sault community, divorced from strong metropolitan controls, Wilson constituted a meddlesome nuisance, and when he refused to sign a document granting permission for the continuation of timber cutting, he remained confined for two days.[79]

On 20 February 1846, Shingwaukonse sent a petition to George Ironside, Anderson's successor as Indian superintendent at Manitowaning, setting forth his own position on the matter. He explained that his territorial prerogatives from Batchewana Bay to Thessalon had been recognized by Colborne in 1833 and that his band derived much-needed revenue from the timber on the lands. '[When] Mr Wilson sells our wood & acts with us as he does, I feel as if he entered into my house and took without my leave what he might find therein,' he asserted.[80]

Shingwaukonse continually anticipated a recognition of the reciprocal relationship existing between the Ojibwa and the Crown, as previously dictated by an attenuated form of feudal custom since the French era. For this reason, he swore to uphold the promises made by his people in the past to defend their sovereign in return for protection on their lands: 'Tell him my people are ready if necessary to go to war,' he stressed,'[for] it is only because we are poor, naked & shivering that we complain.'[81] He concluded his appeal by begging for 'pity,' a traditional way of approaching a protector.

Unfortunately for the chief, the times did not favour his appeal. On 10 October 1845, the Legislative Assembly, with the approval of the governor general and Executive Council, had passed legislation extending the jurisdiction of the United Provinces of Canada East and Canada West over the lands at the Sault. The sympathies of the naval commander, Lieutenant Harper, who had been dispatched by the Crown Lands Department to report on land tenure at the rapids, lay with the Métis population. Harper's decision to recognize an individualized system of land tenure as already existing at the rapids negated all prior claims of the Ojibwa based on Aboriginal right. '[Not] one individual on the British side (with the exception of the Hudson's Bay Company) own one foot of soil or land – their Houses are built and their little gardens planted under the fear that they may be ordered off at any moment and lose all – no title deed can be got as the Natives here claim the land ...'[82]

Harper suggested that the Métis lacked incentive to farm intensively because of the precariousness of their land tenure. When he contended that the Métis constituted a loyal population and recommended that their lots be surveyed and title extended to each resident, Little Pine's territorial prerogatives were threatened as never before. An ideological clash had arisen on the western frontier between the fading political forms associated with feudalism and indirect colonialism, on the one hand, and 'Little Englandism,' a rising new philosophy which espoused colonial self-rule, on the other.

The imperial government had been gradually reducing its burden of expenditures for Native presents and missionary settlements. From now on, the emphasis would be on retrenchment. New policy measures, based on the findings of a major investigation into Native affairs begun in 1842 under Governor General Sir Charles Bagot, still retained Native people as charges of the Crown rather than of the province. But a major problem remained in frontier areas where Native people had not yet ceded lands, and so did not live on reserves. Revenue to further the process of 'civilizing' Native people would, in the future, come in great part from the sale or lease of surrendered territories.

This placed Shingwaukonse and his band in a classic double bind: their appeals to the government for assistance in protecting and developing their territory in its unsurrendered state undercut the principles on which the whole system operated. With this new threat on the horizon, Shingwaukonse's relations with the government moved into a new phase. He had proven conscientious, determined, and shrewd in seeking a Native settlement, and had always shown respect for the Crown and its representatives. From 1846 onward, however, he would add direct confrontation to his strategies for maintaining the integrity of his original policy. On the morning of 27 April 1846, Alexander Vidal, a provincial land surveyor working in the vicinity of the Sault, found himself faced by a small delegation of Ojibwa headed by Shingwaukonse and Nebenagoching. The chiefs expressed indignation at the surveyor's presence on lands they claimed as their own. Vidal, concerned by the determined manner in which they defended their claims, promised not to proceed with the survey until he had contacted his superiors at the Crown Lands office. In response, the land commissioner, D.B. Papineau, instructed Vidal to ignore Native complaints, assuring the surveyor that he could proceed safely since 'should [the bands] offer any kind of resistance ... we will of course suppress the same at once.'[83]

Most likely it was the Ojibwa's determination to retain their land base intact, which, in 1846, prompted Anderson to reverse his official position of six years before and to undermine any legal grounds on which the Ojibwa might obtain recognition from the Crown for their rights to resources and territory.[84] It may also have been owing to Anderson's stand on the Aboriginal rights issue that, on 11 May 1846, Ironside at Manitowaning received a letter from the civil secretary's office instructing him to inform Shingwaukonse that 'the lands on which he resides and the timber are claimed by the Province.' The chief could expect no assistance, the communication continued, 'unless he and his band will remove to Manitoulin Island, where they might enjoy the same advantages that others who already reside there have so much profited by.'[85] The ideological battle lines had been drawn. The Ojibwa would defend their rights to land in opposition to a policy which, ironically, had been proclaimed to aid in protecting the rights of Aboriginal peoples.[86] Little Pine would act far differently from the government's stereotyped image of the politically defenceless 'Indian.' By drawing allies from many sides, he won the notice of the press, and within three years his Aboriginal claim had become an international issue.[87]

Aspects of this contest have defied easy historical analysis. Historians dealing with the subject have come to different conclusions about the forces that shaped events.[88] Moreover, uncritical acceptance of the highly sensational reports in the metropolitan press about the activities of Little Pine and his allies in the fall of 1849 has distorted some historical accounts: at no time did the Objibwa ever resort to force to achieve their goals. All scholars have agreed, however, thet the contest arose as frontier resistance to metropolitan control. And yet, the protest bore none of the marks of such flamboyant, tumultuous cult-induced movements as the Shawnee uprising of 1808 or the Northwest Rebellion of 1885. Rather, it was a principled show of opposition, basically moderate and non-violent. This study argues that the forces motivating this Native movement have eluded simple historical description because they drew upon and complemented, rather than challenged, mid-nineteenth-century Western aspirations and goals.

Chapter Four

Pursuing the Great Spirit's Power

Revitalizing a Failing World System

Native leaders gradually accepted the fact that their pursuit of a peaceful land of refuge, inspired by Methodist teachings in the 1830s, would never succeed as long as they lacked rights to land or resources. As the political and economic foundations of British colonialism crumbled away, the Methodist mission movement had provided a brief reprieve for Native hopes. By the mid-1840s, however, Ojibwa plans began to assume a far more distinctly indigenous character. Little Pine no longer spoke to the bands west of Sault Ste Marie about his hopes for a mission-sponsored, or even exclusively Christian, Native 'homeland.' Faced by the pressing threat of removal, the south-western Ojibwa found no conflict in plans for the distant future. The situation demanded immediate help.

The chief realized the futility of direct confrontation with the encroaching powers who refused to grant his people a place in their new order. Resistance would have to be of an ideological nature, in order to produce a political and economic solution. While historians have realized that Little Pine could be a clever political negotiator,[1] his role as a coordinator of incipient dynamisms on the frontier has not been adequately acknowledged. The Ojibwa had their own solutions and found means of expressing them in ideological forms.

Shingwaukonse the Prophet

Little Pine withdrew for a time from regular contact with the colonial authorities. Then, in 1846 he re-emerged at the head of a movement, espousing a syncretistic blend of Native and Christian belief – a movement he believed might enable his people to secure the kind of 'homeland' he had pursued for so many years. According to Fred and Richard Pine, Sr, Shingwaukonse called upon the spirit of the Thunder for assistance. 'Blessed' with a vision from this source, he appealed for aid to other Native leaders and Métis who shared his religious outlook.[2] Those, like his son Ogista, who chose to adhere openly to Methodism, which disparaged attachment to the Aboriginal religious system, rejected the chief's call. But older leaders, like Keokonse and Nowquagabo of Thessalon, who still believed in the traditional conceptual framework, responded at once.

Little Pine set out to reinvigorate existing Native beliefs. Viewed from the traditional religious standpoint, the cosmological system needed bolstering, since many formerly responsible spirit guardians had vacated their 'posts,' and so allowed alien forces to disturb the world balance. Working within this thought system, the chief began mustering his 'powers' to stop the erosion of the broader whole. As a prophet capable of discerning relationships among dynamic agencies, Little Pine, so elders at Garden River maintained, used his diagnostic skills in an attempt to alleviate the cosmological 'disruption' he saw arising from rapid political and economic change. In this role he assumed responsibility for reviving the weakened cosmological system, and so obtaining for his people a future share in the benefits of a 'restored' world. For this reason his focus would be more on group rights and responsibilities than on material factors. Once such were secured, the resource base would constitute the raw ground from which an enterprising leader might extract future benefits for his people through development and judicious regulation.

He also had access to another tradition, that of Alexander Henry the Elder's copper mining exploits north of the Sault in the late 1760s and early 1770s. Although the collapse of the French imperial design in North America in 1760 had temporarily halted commerce, Henry found that it had not seriously harmed the underlying mercantile organization of the Montreal traders. In partnership with Jean Baptiste Cadotte, a tenant on the French seigniory at Sault Ste Marie, he had based his own fur trade ventures on Native–French contacts already in existence, employing experienced voyageurs. Henry's interest in mining copper on both shores of Lake Superior, at Michipicoten, and in the Ontonagon River region thus drew on French precedents. Unfortunately, problems in obtaining sufficient manpower, provisions, and equipment, and the difficulties of transporting ore to London markets, plagued Henry's mining ventures, until in 1773 the mines were abandoned. The venture was remembered in the Cadotte family, however, possibly through fireside tales passed down through the generations. Then, in the 1830s, Jean Baptiste's granddaughter Marguerite Cadotte married Shingwaukonse's son Buhkwujjenene, and Louis, Marguerite's brother, moved to Garden River to become the chief's personal interpreter. In 1903, Charles Cadotte, another descendant of Jean Baptiste Cadotte, would become a chief of the Garden River band.

More than seventy years after Henry's ventures, a revival of mining on the north shore of Lake Superior led miners, traders, French, and Ojibwa in the region to join forces. Little Pine's open concern with Native proprietorship over mineral resources was radically different from the attitude of other Aboriginal leaders, most of whom kept the location of outcroppings a closely guarded secret. Elders emphasized that copper had once been associated with dangerous spirits, among them the giant water lynx, Mishibesheu. Even as late as 1929, one Ojibwa recalled his grandfather's description of the 'gathering on the Canadian shore, and of the ceremonies, the dance and the appeal to the Spirits, that were deemed necessary before the trip [to Isle Royale in western Lake Superior where copper can be found] could be made.'[3] A similar attitude was held towards Michipicoten Island, north of Sault Ste Marie.

In devising a plan of action, Shingwaukonse also drew upon Christian teachings which emphasized the integrity of peoples and nations who loved God. Fundamentally peaceful in intent, his appeal to the Canadian government called for laws to be passed that would protect Aboriginal territorial prerogatives and establish permanent linkages between Native groups and the developing nation state. His faith in the efficacy of Christianity led the leader to regard missionaries as potential friends, and he was not disappointed in this respect. James D. Cameron, Jr, the Baptist preacher, willingly responded to the chief's requests for aid in communicating Native demands and grievances to government agencies and religious organizations.

Shingwaukonse and the Mining Interests

Shingwaukonse regarded as allies two mining explorers, both of whom promised to support Native aims in return for the chief's assistance in their prospecting ventures. Evidently, memories of the workable relationship which had existed in the mid-1700s between the Native peoples and the independent trading establishments aroused his hope that something similar might develop between the Ojibwa and the mining companies during the nineteenth century. Continuities with the past certainly existed. The two explorers, Allan Macdonell and John William Keating, spoke the Ojibwa language fluently and were familiar with Native beliefs and customs. Allan Macdonell's father, Alexander Macdonell of Collachie (1762–1842), had been assistant secretary in the Indian Department between 1816 and 1822. Alexander Macdonell's uncle, John Macdonell, furthermore, had acted as John Askin's forwarding agent at Mackinac before joining the North West Company.[4] Allan Macdonell, who was a lawyer as well as an entrepreneur, was also known to the Roman Catholic Métis, since Bishop Alexander Macdonell had been related to him. Keating had seen active service in the War of 1812 and, until the mid-1840s, had been Indian agent at Amherstburg.[5] Macdonell and Keating both responded to Little Pine's appeals for help, since, under the chief's direction, the Garden River, Sault Ste Marie, Michipicoten, and Fort William bands had agreed to guide the prospectors to copper, iron, silver, and gold exposures on their lands. In return, Macdonell and Keating pledged to see that the Ojibwa's claims to proprietorship over the mineral deposits would be recognized in law and that a system of leases and royalties would be implemented to ensure the Native peoples a share in potential mining returns. The Ojibwa predicted that their future would be enhanced by a system of special protections, new entrepreneurial contacts, and improved linkages to government.

Shingwaukonse informed his western Ojibwa allies that times were auspicious for their migration to the new 'homeland' in the Sault Ste Marie area. He stressed that the area's mining, lumbering, trapping, and fishing potential could support an incoming population of at least two thousand individuals from Michigan west to the Red River District. At the same time, Macdonell, Keating, and the local merchant, Church, agreed to help with the establishment of sawmills, mining operations, and markets for agricultural produce. Aboriginal leaders from Red River, Rainy Lake, and Lake of the Woods proved impatient by the spring of 1846 for the Canadian government to grant leave for their move to the projected Ojibwa settlement.

Meanwhile the miners' dependence on their Native guides obliged them to recognize prior Native rights to mineral resources. In response to a request from Shingwaukonse, in June 1846, Keating drafted a petition to J.M. Higginson, the civil secretary, to be directed to the governor general. To avoid taking sides, Keating explained in an accompanying letter that his own actions stemmed from personal necessity rather than advocacy of Shingwaukonse's views. 'As I depend much upon them for assistance in exploring,' he stressed, 'I could not refuse to give them my aid in addressing His Excellency.'[6] Shingwaukonse, for his part, admitted that he 'had no certain knowledge' regarding the authority which had sanctioned the miners' activities north of Lakes Huron and Superior, and he requested the governor general, Sir Charles Metcalfe, to meet with him in Montreal to discuss arrangements relating to proprietorship, royalties, and dues. 'I want always to live and plant at Garden River,' Little Pine concluded, and so expect 'a share of what is found on my lands.'[7]

The idea that Native willingness to assist in mining explorations might grant Ojibwa a secure and valued place in Canadian society also influenced bands east of Sault Ste Marie. In September 1846, a number of Native people from the vicinity of Manitowaning, Manitoulin Island, approached Indian Superintendent Ironside with specimens of copper. The agent, in turn, informed his superiors that the petitioners desired all future operations on Native territory to be subject to government regulation: 'The Indians have a very high idea of the value of these things, and have requested me to beg of His Excellency that any mines which may be discovered shall not be subject to the enterprise of private individuals, but that the matter be taken into the hands of the Government and that they, the Indians, may receive whatever portion His Excellency may be pleased to award to them.'[8]

As long as mining prospects appeared encouraging, the Ojibwa could rely on Ironside and Keating to convey their wishes to the provincial authorities. Keating, in particular, was generally trusted because of his connections to the Native community through his Ojibwa wife from Walpole Island and his past associations with government and the military. His activities, however, soon showed that such confidence was mostly unwarranted. Reorganization of the Indian Department in 1845 had cast Keating adrift. Dismissal from his post at Amherstburg in the name of government retrenchment had led him first into trading with Native people and then into prospecting. However, he became increasingly undependable as an ally to the Native people in a competitive world where, to Keating, the ends increasingly came to justify the means.[9]

Once having secured Native aid in his mining explorations, Keating joined politician and entrepreneur Arthur Rankin, and also James Cuthbertson and Robert Stuart Woods, in forming the Huron and Sault Ste Marie Mining Company, which sank a shaft at Bruce Mines in 1846. Then Rankin, with Allan Macdonell and others, set about organizing the Quebec and Lake Superior Mining Association, which began operations at Mica Bay on the north-eastern coast of Lake Superior.[10] Financial difficulties dimmed Keating and Rankin's initial optimism, however, and they suddenly severed ties with both the Ojibwa and Macdonell. Macdonell continued to honour his promises to the Native people. By 1849, Keating had publicly renounced all obligations of himself or his associates to recognize Native rights to minerals or timber. Owing to the costs of exploration, he argued, it was impossible to regard the Native people as more than a convenient source of labour.

Finally compelled to restrict the scope of their enterprise, Keating, Rankin, Cuthbertson, and Woods sold their workings both at Bruce Mines and Mica Bay to the Montreal Mining Company.[11] The trustees of this second organization – among them Sir George Simpson, the Honourable Peter Moffatt, the Honourable Peter McGill, and William Collis Meredith – represented some of the most prominent financiers and political figures of the day. Their company's promotional campaign depended to a great extent on parading the virtues of advanced technology in meeting the challenges which had defeated Alexander Henry's mining operations at Point aux Pins during the eighteenth century.[12] They did not wish to be party to a bid for recognition of Aboriginal rights, as put forward before 1821 by supporters of the North West Company. They felt that the old political and economic order should make way for the new. It was thought best to ignore the Native claims issue, hoping it would disappear.

Yet Native pressure continued. Under the influence of the mining companies, the Indian Department finally ordered Ironside in June 1847 to instruct Shingwaukonse and his people to move to Manitoulin Island, as the governor general did not want them to remain near the Sault. The chief was further directed not to come to Montreal 'as all communications can be made in writing ...'[13] Undaunted, Shingwaukonse, Nebenagoching, Nowquagabo, Kabaosa, Keokonse, Piabetassung, Megissanequa, Ogista, and Buhkwujjenene sought out O'Meara and requested that he prepare a petition declaring their commitment to remain at Garden River. The Great Spirit had given them the land, and no temporal government could deprive them of that which God himself had granted:

Already has the white man licked clean up from our lands the whole means of our subsistence, and now they commence to make us worse off. They take everything away from us, Father. Now my Father, you are too high to help those people who take from us, you who sit on high place at Montreal are he who helps those who are wronged, as those who have lately come to work as wishing to wrong us. I call God to witness in the beginning and do so now again and say that it was false that the land is not ours, it is ours.[14]

This letter received no reply. By November the Executive Council had authorized the sale of approximately thirty large mining locations along the north shore of Lakes Huron and Superior in keeping with the terms of an Order-in-Council passed earlier in May.[15] Each location had to conform in size to 6,400 acres to accord with a government standard set to discourage speculation and prevent minor entrepreneurial interests from competing with the Montreal-controlled mining companies. Applicants had to pay £150 down and were given two years to submit the balance at a rate of forty shillings an acre, after which time the sites would be forfeit to the Crown.

Four locations fitting this description had been staked and surveyed adjacent to one another in the vicinity of Garden River. The westernmost boundary of the series ran due north from a point west of Partridge Point on Little Lake George. Each of the surveyed areas was a rough rectangle approximately two miles wide along the St Mary's channel, and extending five miles due north. The interior boundary, common to all, roughly paralleled the indentations of the coastline. Rankin and Cuthbertson held the major interest in the two western locations, applied for under the names of F.C. Clark and John F. Elliot. Farther to the east, the Benjamin H. Lemoine and John Simpson locations fell under the control of the Garden River Mining Company, with George Desbarats, the queen's printer, as agent. A fifth location, registered in the name of John Wilson, lay north of Echo Bay.

The Lemoine location took in the whole area of the Native village and extended a good way up the Garden River. Since the chief had never negotiated in any way with Desbarats or any member of his company, Little Pine took offence and, in early May 1847, Desbarats reported that his exploring party had been driven off by the Ojibwa. The agent also noted that no form of land surrender had been conducted with the Native population. Any delay in so doing, he continued, would 'increase the cupidity of the interests and with it, also the difficulty of compromise.'[16] Desbarats knew that any direct conflict between the parties would place the mining companies in an ambivalent legal position. Prompt government action, Desbarats argued, was necessary to rectify the situation, especially since Captain William Ermatinger, a lawyer and the son of Charles Oakes Ermatinger and Charlotte Katawabidai, intended to uphold the concept of Aboriginal right in order to lay claim to his father's estate at Sault Ste Marie.[17]

In yet another petition drafted by O'Meara and dated 5 July 1847, Shingwaukonse, with Nebenagoching, Piabetassung, and Kabaosa as witnesses, stated that he had fought in the War of 1812, had been wounded, and so considered himself a deserving ally of the British. Shingwaukonse repeated his claim that John Askin, Jr, had recognized his people's right to locate themselves at Garden River, although they had originally migrated from the United States. He had granted his band the choice whether or not to treat with the United States. In reply, they had retained their sovereignty over the soil on the Canadian side by refusing American offers of money, although they had been taunted for it by American officials. He also repudiated the charges that his people had driven away explorers by force. According to Little Pine, he and his principal men had 'waited upon the leader of it [Desbarats's party] in his tent and requested that he would desist as this was their land ...'[18] The chief emphasized that he would continue to protect his territory against trespass even though Ironside had written to him stating that 'it was the wish of the government that these persons should occupy our land.'[19]

Again, no reply followed. In August a disgruntled Shingwaukonse complained to Ironside that the government's delay had placed him in an embarrassing position, as the other leaders whom he represented 'were daily calling on him for information.'[20] Little Pine also laid a grievance before Samuel Peters Jarvis, the superintendent general of Indian affairs. All Native applications for redress directed to the local magistrate, William Nourse of the Hudson's Bay Company, against the illegal removal of timber and minerals from Native land had been futile, the chief explained, even though the Ojibwa had on occasion experienced ill usage from the trespassers. Jarvis, in response, communicated Shingwaukonse's grievance to the Reverend William McMurray and appealed to the clergyman to look into the case. Soon afterwards Little Pine himself left for Toronto where he spoke with McMurray and the Reverend James Beaven, to whom he presented an ornate pipe as proof of the sincerity of his desire for another Anglican missionary to be sent to Garden River.[21]

Noting that no cession of Native title to lands along the north shores of Lakes Huron and Superior had ever occurred, the Committee of the Executive Council argued that the Ojibwa applicants were merely immigrants, who had no claim as 'Aboriginal Inhabitants of the Country.' They should be compelled, the committee recommended, to move to 'some other place sufficiently distant to render it probable that they might not again be called upon to give place either to Agriculturalists or Miners.'[22] A final decision on the matter was suspended, however, pending a report from D.P. Papineau, the commissioner of Crown Lands.

Papineau did not submit his report until November. In the interim the Native community at the Sault directed another petition to the Indian Department. This time the Ojibwa took another tack. Although their summer villages had been on the south shore of Lake Superior, they felt they still held claim to the territory extending north to the height of land lying between the Upper Great Lakes and Hudson's Bay 'from time immemorial,' since this region had always been used by them for hunting. They were now willing to surrender the whole area, provided they retained certain specified tracts of land under their own control.[23]

Papineau could not easily ignore their claim. He nevertheless felt he could repudiate it, and supported his decidedly negative views on the issue by reference to conveniently available, if mostly erroneous, ethnographic opinion. He had a popular, high-profile source as well. In 1846, William Logan, the provincial geologist and a noted scientist, accompanied by John W. McNaughton, a provincial deputy surveyor, had conducted mineralogical investigations along the north shore of Lake Superior. On his return, McNaughton, whose reputation undoubtedly benefited from association with Logan, made some demographic predictions and historical judgments concerning the Ojibwa which, in the light of modern ethnographic knowledge, were little more than irresponsible ramblings evidently predicated on poorly digested material from the *Jesuit Relations* and Native oral testimonies of fairly recent date collected while he was in the field. The surveyor declared that the Ojibwa population north of Lake Superior numbered about seven thousand and seemed to be increasing; a not-unreasonable observation. He further contended, however, that their ancestral origins lay along the banks of the Mississippi River, from which region they had been 'expelled by the Sioux.' By ascending the Chippewa River, they temporarily came to reside on the south-west shore of Lake Superior and later emigrated to Green Bay, Wisconsin, remaining there for 'some time under the French Dominion.' During this period they came to Michilimackinac to trade and settled on the south shore of Lake Superior from whence 'they came to the North Shore as they state.'[24]

Regarding the initial Aboriginal occupants of the north shores of Lakes Huron and Superior, McNaughton asserted that their origins were 'of the Algonkin Nation.' Large numbers of these 'Algonkin' had lived along the Ottawa River where they 'were totally destroyed by the Iroquois a few years before the arrival of the French at Montreal.' The remainder were held to have been attacked by smallpox 'to such an extent they ceased to exist as a Nation.' A small and, in McNaughton's eyes, unnoteworthy survivor group could still be found in Quebec at Lake of Two Mountains. Armed with such an astonishing mix of fact and fiction, Papineau boldly dispensed with the claims issue by stating in 1847 that future dealings with mere remnants of Native nations should involve only the extension 'upon the faith of the British government' of a small cash annuity to promote 'civilization.'[25]

On both sides of the international border this callous disregard of local Aboriginal interests aroused Native bitterness – a sorry state of affairs which prompted the Baptist preacher James D. Cameron, Jr, to offer his services to the Crown Lands Department as an intermediary between the Province of Canada and the Ojibwa in the event of unrest.[26] Yet while Native anger continued to simmer, most Ojibwa leaders sought peaceful solutions. Owing in 1848 to the survey for a ship canal through the American rapids, the American head chief, Oshawano, led a delegation to Washington to have his people's title to the local rapids fishery recognized under the treaties of 1820 and 1836.[27] Meanwhile, on the Canadian side, just east of Garden River, Keokonse and Nowquagabo persuaded Alexander Murray, a government geologist, to relay a message to the government that they wished to retain six miles of Lake Huron shoreline on either side of the Thessalon River for their own use, and to have their fishing grounds in front of this tract legally protected.[28]

The atmosphere of heightened tension and potential discord lasted less than a year. Elections in the Canadas during the spring of 1848 ushered in a Reform government with a large majority in the Assembly. Demonstrating a more positive attitude towards settling the matter than his predecessor, the newly appointed Crown Lands commissioner, John H. Price, set out to review Papineau's earlier report, maintaining that in the spirit of fairness, the Ojibwa's grievances should at least be investigated. When Alexander Vidal informed the commissioner in February that the Lemoine location included the entire Garden River settlement, Price immediately asserted that 'the justice or at least expediency of dispossessing [the band] is well deserving of consideration before the land is given to others.' The Ojibwa had exercised considerable choice in fighting for the British cause in the War of 1812, Price continued, and British officers at Mackinac apparently had guaranteed Little Pine territory on the British side. He also noted that, along the Grand River, the Six Nations Loyalists had been granted land under similar terms. It therefore seemed proper to suspend the location assigned to B.H. Lemoine until a well-informed decision could be reached.[29]

Tired of waiting for a firm reply to his earlier appeals, Shingwaukonse organized a delegation of his band, with Louis Cadotte as their interpreter, and journeyed to Montreal in the spring of 1848 to hold an audience with Metcalfe's successor as governor general, Lord Elgin. About the same time, O'Meara began publicly contravening McNaughton's assessment, presenting an almost diametrically opposite picture of the state of the Ojibwa peoples of Lake Superior. To the Anglican missionary, the bands were poverty-stricken, ridden with disease, drastically declining in numbers and faced with the threat of extinction.[30] While O'Meara's stance was gauged mainly to elicit aid for the Ojibwa within the Anglican Church, it also evidently was tinged with a fear that, should the bands present too strong a challenge to provincial policies, the position of the Native peoples might become grave indeed. Far better that they be presented as objects of pity.

The interview in Montreal must have exhibited an incongruous side, especially given O'Meara's public pleading for recognition of the Ojibwa's inability to defend themselves. Shingwaukonse directed a barrage of complaints at Elgin regarding the mining companies' trespass on his territory. The miners, Little Pine emphasized, set fires which had burned for miles, driving away game. Blasting of the rock likewise made hunting almost impossible. At the same time, agents of the mining companies prevented the Native people from cutting timber and firewood, even though no conditions of sale had been fulfilled.[31] To ascertain the validity of these complaints, Elgin sent Thomas G. Anderson, then residing in Cobourg, as visiting superintendent of Indian affairs, to investigate the matter.

Anderson arrived at Sault Ste Marie in early August following the distribution of presents at Manitowaning. Bishop Strachan, Revs McMurray and O'Meara, and a number of other Anglican delegates also attended, anxious to protect what they viewed as an important mission preserve. During his address to the Ojibwa on Friday, 18 August, Anderson must have been aware that before him sat the very same chief who had continuously opposed his scheme for a missionary establishment on Manitoulin Island. In the years following the close of the War of 1812, Anderson had represented a new order which demanded that Native people beat spears into plowshares at a safe distance from the international boundary. The Native peoples had not participated in his vision of developing the wilderness into a pastoral paradise of hardy independent farmers, however, and Anderson's views had become redundant. It had become clear that his mixing of national diplomacy with the affairs of Christianity had deluded no one, especially not the Ojibwa. The English missionaries, moreover, had indicated by their presence at the Sault that they preferred the Ojibwa to be Christianized and civilized on lands chosen by the Native people themselves.

Local entrepreneurial interests were also represented at the assembly. Joseph Wilson, collector of customs and local lands agent, supported the rights of the miners. Allan Macdonell, at the time regarded as 'a licence holder in the Quebec Mining Company,' attended, as did George Johnston from the American Sault. According to Anderson's account, these individuals participated mainly as spectators, while he and Shingwaukonse dominated the discussions.

Anderson first directed Little Pine to explain in what manner the miners had destroyed the Ojibwa's hunting territories and occupied their village. To this the chief responded merely by repeating the message he had relayed earlier to Lord Elgin in Montreal. Yet, when Anderson further challenged the chief to state 'by what authority' he claimed the lands, Shingwaukonse was visibly taken aback. The British had always negotiated treaties with Native people, the chief contended, and as far as he knew no such cession had ever taken place on the Canadian side of the rapids.[32]

The following day, Anderson held a similar discussion with Peau de Chat, a visiting chief and ally of Little Pine from Fort William. Peau de Chat was succinct in his presentation of his band's claim. All men, he stated, once spoke the same language and so understood each other. Since that era, 'a change has taken place, and we speak different languages.' In time fur and goods took the place of words between groups in the Upper Great Lakes region, but no land had ever been surrendered. During the late war the Ojibwa fought for the British. Leaders such as Shingwaukonse had been wounded and so fought 'in much misery.' As Loyalists, the Ojibwa now wished to settle and form villages, but the fur companies and the miners made it difficult, as both pressured bands to act at variance with what the indigenous people believed was now in their best interests. Most important, Peau de Chat stressed, not only the soil, but also the minerals on Indian land should be surrendered for 'good pay.' The Native people would then be free to develop their own territories in their own way: 'The white man, the miner and trader could do what he liked with the land, and so could the Indian on that part which we would like to reserve, when we give our land up, we will reserve a piece for ourselves and we, with our families will live happily on it, we will do what we please with it.'[33] The chief concluded by stating that he wanted a fair evaluation of his land's worth, an offer to be made by the government for his mining locations, and arrears payments for the loss of minerals. Like Shingwaukonse, Peau de Chat spoke as the representative of an independent people, willing to bargain but not to submit to external pressures: 'Tell the Governor at Montreal to send a letter and let us know what he will do, and what our land is worth, in the meantime I will converse with my tribe on the subject, when I am going to sell my land, I will speak again and settle matters. A great deal of our mineral has been taken away, I must have something for it. I reflect upon it, as well as upon that which still remains.'[34]

Anderson's report, written on 26 August at Sault Ste Marie, proclaimed that 'there does not appear a doubt but that the present race are the proprietors of the vast mineral beds and unceded forests, from Grande Bateure [Grand Batture] near Missisangeeny River on Lake Huron, to the Boundary Line at Pigeon River on Lake Superior, throughout which region numerous locations have been granted.' No power by right of conquest or sale had ever deprived them of their proprietorship. Not having any personal interest in mining, Anderson was also disposed to be generous where Shingwaukonse's band was concerned, and recommended the cancellation of all four mining locations at Garden River. He also indicated that he had been advised to make these statements by 'Gentlemen of the Quebec Mining Company' who corroborated Little Pine's statements regarding injuries to the Native people occasioned by blasting and burning of the bush. Among these would have been Allan Macdonell. Anderson concluded his views on the claims issue by maintaining that while the Ojibwa were 'incapable of opposing the forced occupation,' there could be little doubt that they would 'give serious annoyance' until their rights were extinguished. Overall, the agent felt that the care and explicitness with which the chiefs had prepared and expressed their desires and grievances deserved serious consideration. Once the Native people stipulated which tracts they wished, all territory north of Lakes Huron and Superior should be surrendered, 'following the height of land to the Honbl. Hudson's Bay Company Boundary line north of Lakes Huron until it strikes the Frontier line between Lac Le [La] Pluie and the mouth of the Pigeon River.'[35]

Anderson in 1848 expressed a cautious optimism because the Ojibwa seemed to him to be using their own initiative to make something, after all, of the government's earlier drive to encourage settlement. For this reason he placed special emphasis on the fact that the Garden River population, numbering about one hundred individuals, had forty acres planted with potatoes, corn, and other crops, and fifteen houses built. Should lands be secured on which the Native peoples had already begun improvements, then the frontier wilderness might indeed blossom under a new system of promoting geographically dispersed villages. The Oregon dispute had been settled; the international boundary now ran clear to the Pacific. No longer was it mandatory for Native policy to be devised with an eye to the possibly adverse reactions of Canada's powerful southern neighbour. Anderson's perspective also departed from his earlier reliance on missionary assistance in the promotion of 'civilization,' which to him meant agricultural pursuits. Shingwaukonse and Peau de Chat indicated that the Native people were willing, if given suitable conditions, to undertake much of this task on their own. In this spirit, Anderson instructed his son, Gustavus, who had been appointed Anglican missionary at Garden River, not to become dismayed should his efforts not meet with immediate success. The disposition of the Ojibwa was towards independence of spirit and action. Patient channelling in a 'proper direction,' however, might well bring permanent beneficial results.[36]

Yet Anderson's continued stress on relegating a predominantly autonomous people to a narrow economic niche proved the fatal flaw in his scheme. Neither Shingwaukonse nor Peau de Chat had narrowed their demands to emphasize simply promotion of farming. Agriculture constituted only one facet of a number of economically oriented demands. Native arguments focused on the preservation of Native rights, among them the freedom to develop, under the protection of the Crown, a way of life which the Ojibwa believed was naturally adapted to both their present and their historical environment.

In less than a month Anderson received a double shock. Soon after leaving the Sault he had written to his son at Garden River that he had not heard anything from Elgin or others in Montreal about when treaty negotiations might commence. In reply Gustavus stated that Shingwaukonse's impatience had grown to the point where he had engaged a lawyer, who had warned the mining companies against cutting any more timber on the band property.[37] The American press, moreover, had acquired a transcript from Louis Cadotte of Shingwaukonse's speech, presented on 18 August. This account differed substantially in content and emphasis from Anderson's own rendition of Little Pine's delivery. While this disclosure challenged the validity of his earlier report, what particularly piqued the agent was the defiant tone of the speech set out in the American press. Rather than acting in docile conformity with Anderson's wishes, the Ojibwa demanded implementation of a system granting them the right to compensation for all injuries to a resource base which they unquestionably saw as being under their own proprietorship and protection:

> The Great Spirit, we think, placed these rich mines on our lands, for the benefit of his red children, so that their rising generation might get support from them when the animals of the woods should have grown too scarce for our subsistence. We will carry out, therefore, the good object of our Father,

the Great Spirit. We will sell you lands, if you will give us what is right and at the same time, we want pay for every pound of mineral that has been taken off our lands, as well as for that which may hereafter be carried away.[38]

The stress on the Great Spirit as the *primum mobile* behind the Native claim struck Anderson as almost heretical, considering his own firm belief in mid-Victorian concepts of the social order and its proper structure and operation. Raymond Firth in a discussion in *Symbols, Public and Private* of the substance behind symbolic forms, argues that 'God ... can be regarded in many ways, from a very real Supreme Being and controller of the universe to an imaginative human construct of ideal values.'[39] In Anderson's view, God as a ruling power could not be invoked in a manner which seemed to have, as a primary goal, material gain without such intermediary conditions as enterprise, risk, and toil. According to Anderson, the Ojibwa had adopted an instrumental and thus wholly untenable attitude towards the deity. For Anderson the question was not one of rights, Aboriginal or otherwise, but of right and wrong. As his concept of moral right was derived from a hierarchical view of the social order, the Ojibwa's demand that the government should be strictly accountable for all minerals taken from Indian land exemplified to him a moral flaw in reasoning, at variance with the social, political, and economic status of the Native people as he saw it.

Gustavus, meanwhile, found he could wield little influence within the Garden River community. For one thing, the missionary lacked skills in farming, and the Native residents expected him to do all his own chopping of wood, cooking, and other maintenance work. His lack of competence in even such simple matters had quickly become apparent to the band. His mission originally had been planned for Sault Ste Marie, but Little Pine had made it clear in his welcoming speech to Gustavus that his band had no intention of moving back to the rapids, and that he expected the missionary to reside with them at Garden River.[40] Although the missionary stated to his superiors that he felt it his duty to remain at the Native settlement, the Ojibwa having built him a house, the priest still spent much of his time at Sault Ste Marie, living with Joseph Wilson or at the Hudson's Bay Company post.[41] It was mainly Gustavus's inability, as a single man, to maintain himself adequately while attending to his religious duties that compelled him to leave Garden River for long periods during the winter months.

For the residents of the Ojibwa community, life was charged with a sense of expectation regarding the impending treaty. There were several major celebrations, among them weddings for both Piabetassung's daughter and Tegoosh's daughter on Sugar Island, a house raising for which 'all turned out to cut logs,' and festivities for a week following the New Year, during which time Ogista made his appearances around the village 'in grand style.'

To curb what he viewed as the excesses and exuberances of Native activities at Garden River, Gustavus grew stern, threatened to leave, and sought to impose his own sense of order on the dynamic milieu, but to no avail. Against this background of often-boisterous social events a steady stream of visitors appeared; traders, miners, visiting chiefs and their bands, Paul Kane, the artist, missionaries from many denominations, and mining men from Bruce Mines, including William B. Robinson, the mine manager. Shingwaukonse presided over each affair in turn. On one occasion he held a council with the Batchewana people about the right of outsiders to produce maple sugar on Garden River territory. On another he met with certain Métis who wished to reside at Garden River in the event that a treaty was signed. Little Pine granted the appeal of the latter group, as Gustavus Anderson noted in his diary on 23 January 1849: 'Chief Shingwaukonse gave them [the Métis] leave to settle here.'[42]

Gustavus Anderson's diary leaves no doubt about the extensive powers Little Pine could exercise with regard to access rights to territory and resources at Garden River. But while the priest was often present at councils and expressed sympathy for the Native claim, he was not made party to the central scheme taking shape under Little Pine's direction. Gustavus learned indirectly what was happening from Macdonell, who he believed took 'a real interest in [the Ojibwa's] affairs.'[43] In June 1849 Macdonell assisted in drafting a deed conveying two hundred acres, granted by the chief to the Anglican mission the previous January, lying on the west side of the Garden River.[44] By this time, Gustavus felt himself dependent upon, and even an appendage of, Little Pine's own plans for the Garden River community.

Allan Macdonell's much closer relationship with the Ojibwa and the Métis, by contrast, may have been modelled on the kind of responsibility that his relative, Bishop Alexander Macdonell, had exhibited while still a priest in Scotland when the Highland clearances forced Macdonell clansmen to seek employment in the Glasgow factories. The future bishop had not only seen to his people's economic welfare, but had also fashioned the clan into a noted regimental organization under its chief, before finally accompanying the group to North America. Allan Macdonell may have viewed the Ojibwa band as similar to his own Glengarry community, for kin ties, both consanguineous and affinal, still wielded a strong influence on Glengarry politics during the 1840s.[45] Possibly a desire to emulate his worthy relative accounted for Macdonell's loyalty to Little Pine's group, whom he designated as 'his people.' Even his own economic ventures seemed temporarily to have taken second place to his conviction that he had a duty to fulfil towards 'his band' in return for the trust they had vested in him.[46]

When there was still no sign of treaty negotiations by May 1849, Little Pine, along with Nebenagoching, Ogista, Kabaosa, and several others, prepared once again to set out for Montreal. There can be no doubt that their tempers were running high at the seeming betrayal of promises made by Anderson the previous autumn. The arrival at Michipicoten of leaders and bands from western Lake Superior threatening to stop mining operations alarmed employees of the Quebec and Lake Superior Mining Association, although Chief Factor MacTavish at Sault Ste Marie nevertheless tried to appear unperturbed. By this time, Allan Macdonell, at Shingwaukonse's invitation, had accompanied the Garden River delegation to Montreal.

In Montreal, Macdonell and Shingwaukonse together explored effective ways of presenting the Native claim to the governor general. Macdonell's assistance likely extended to tailoring some of the chief's turns of phrase, so that in translation they would make a strong impact on the mind of the reading public. The speech finally delivered by Little Pine before Lord Elgin began with the following declaration:

> Why ask by what right we claim these lands? These lands where our fathers and their fathers' fathers lie buried, you must know it as every Red Skin does know it, that long before your White Children crossed the waters of the rising sun to visit us, the Great Spirit, the Red Man's God, had formed this land and placed us here, giving it to his Red Children as their inheritance.[47]

Undoubtedly owing to Macdonell's influence, Little Pine's address at times resembled that of the North West Company in its contest with Lord Selkirk at Red River three decades earlier. Yet Shingwaukonse espoused violence only as a last resort. Even the most cowardly of animals, 'though they feel destruction sure, will turn upon the hunter,' he warned.[48] The chief's delivery did not threaten Native defiance, for it had not been born out of the matrix of colonial or commercial rivalry. It instead embodied an appeal directed not only to the governor general, but also to the Canadian public at large, to assist the Ojibwa in gaining what had already been ordained by the Great Spirit:

The Great Spirit in his beneficence, foreseeing that this time would arrive when the subsistence which the forests and lakes afforded would fail, placed these mines in our lands, so that the coming generations of His Red Children might find thereby the means of subsistence. Assist us, then, to reap that benefit intended for us ... Enable us to do this, and our hearts will be great within, for we will feel that we are again a nation.[49]

On 7 July 1849, Little Pine's speech appeared in the Montreal *Gazette*, and received sympathetic attention in several other newspapers. His oratorical skills and commanding presence soon attracted the attention of some of the prominent members of the Montreal artistic community. He and Nebenagoching sat while Cornelius Krieghoff made watercolour sketches of their likenesses.[50] And a more pathetic portrait emerged from the pen of Charles Sangster, who in his poem 'Lament of Shingwaukonse' portrayed the Ojibwa leader as longing for a land of freedom on the western frontier for his people, who eventually must flee westward beyond the pale of white civilization.[51]

The publicity alarmed the Montreal-based mining interests, who, not surprisingly, feared that a treaty recognizing Native demands would endanger their title to locations on Lakes Huron and Superior. While Little Pine learned of this 'row at Montreal' from Gustavus Anderson,[52] the chief unfortunately remained ignorant of the fact that his primary adversary lay closer at hand and was a man he trusted, John William Keating. Concerned over his mine holdings, Keating lashed out in the press at the chief, branding the Native leader a mere rabble-rouser. Shingwaukonse, Keating proclaimed in a letter to the *Chatham Chronicle*, 'is a half-breed from the extremity of Lake Superior, shrewd and intelligent, and who has worked himself up to a prominent place, by means of the traders and missionaries, and what is vulgarly called the "gift of the gab."' To separate Little Pine in the public eye from those the chief represented, Keating asserted that only Cranes such as Nebenagoching and older chiefs such as Keokonse and Nowquagabo had any just claim to land at the Canadian Sault.[53]

Most Ojibwa bands, Keating continued, had fallen under the control of the Hudson's Bay Company, whose policy was 'to keep them as much as possible in the interior.' On the other hand, bands living along the coast subsisted wholly on fish, so that mines would be of no use to them, he stated, bending the truth more than a little to suit his own desires. It was far better that these people farm and fish and exchange their produce with the mining towns. This would benefit them far more, Keating held, than 'the empty honour of barren possessions.'[54] It was evident that any competing interest, white or Native, which threatened the hegemony of the Montreal mining interests would face strong opposition. The greatest check to Little Pine's project came from representatives of this clique in the Sault vicinity, and a number of others with minor business concerns, Keating among them, who sheltered under the umbrella of this near monopoly.

Not all officials or Hudson's Bay Company employees in the Sault area shared Keating's perspective, however. Factor William MacTavish viewed his boss Sir George Simpson's mining speculations with a detached eye. His letters also made it clear that the Hudson's Bay Company had not half the influence over the Ojibwa in 1849 that Simpson would have liked.[55] Because of his independent-mindedness, and the fact that he regarded the Native population in the Sault vicinity as a vital semi-autonomous community, MacTavish's correspondence presents valuable insights into events following Little Pine's return to Garden River in July.

Preliminary Negotiations

Macdonell remained in Montreal with Lord Elgin after Shingwaukonse left for the Sault. When Elgin informed the lawyer that commissioners prepared to hold treaty negotiations would be present at the rapids within a month, Macdonell told Little Pine and the chief notified his Native allies. Forty canoes from west of Lake Superior immediately set out *en route* for Sault Ste Marie.[56]

By 10 August a large assemblage of Indians had gathered at Michipicoten.[57] But with news that cholera had broken out within the Sault community, fear spread through the ranks of the would-be visitants, and eventually only two of the Lake Superior families dared venture past the rapids to attend the distribution of presents at Manitowaning.[58] By the second week of September there were still no signs that a treaty would be made. Tempers rose, and suspicions were fuelled by rumours that powder and ammunition had mysteriously started to disappear from mining company stores at Echo Bay, behind the village of Garden River.[59]

When Superintendent Anderson arrived at Manitowaning on 13 September, he presented Shingwaukonse and Tagwaninini with medals for services rendered during the War of 1812,[60] but admitted he lacked the wherewithal to open negotiations. This authority, he knew, already had been delegated to another. Alexander Vidal, the newly installed commissioner designated to carry out investigations into the claim's feasibility, had been keeping a low profile at the rapids since his arrival on 6 September. Times were changing, and Anderson, now over seventy years of age, must have realized that his longstanding role in relations with the Sault and Garden River bands had been usurped by the younger man. Vidal's ability to decide the terms upon which all future negotiations with the Ojibwa would take place underlined the importance of his participation in the commissioners' 1849 expedition. As had happened after the War of 1812, a new order was wrenching power from the old. In 1814, Thomas G. Anderson was one of the officials who had aided the political decline of men such as John Askin, Jr. Now his own power was waning, and he resented it deeply. Even MacTavish was aware that Anderson had been superseded.[61] Shingwaukonse would no longer find himself matching wits with a government official of his own approximate age and depth of experience. Although a talented mathematician and a surveyor with a flair for legal affairs, Vidal was only thirty years old and knew very little of the culture and values of the people with whom he would conduct business during the following days.

In preparation for his task, Vidal spent three days transcribing information from books and documents pertaining to U.S. Indian policy.[62] He also recorded ethnological data – acquired from George Johnston, who had been recommended to him as an informant – regarding Ojibwa leadership. According to Johnston, transmission of leadership status followed principles of 'hereditary right' only if the selection of the successor was 'acquiesced in by all others.' Such democratic principles also governed group responses to matters which dealt with broad political issues affecting the entire Upper Great Lakes Ojibwa community. While lesser leaders usually heeded an influential head chief's summons, the whole decision-making process actually conformed to a more consensual pattern, with chiefs of all ranks generally abiding by expressions of public opinion given at a 'smoking council.' A 'sense of tribe' found expression at these councils, and decisions were almost always unanimous.[63]

This presented a real problem for Vidal, since it was evident from speaking to Johnston that fairly strong and internally coherent political entities existed in the Upper Great Lakes region. For Vidal, the answer lay in discovering the political system's vulnerable points. On page eight of a private notebook in which he jotted down his thoughts, Vidal touched on what he thought might be one such weakness: 'In the [American] treaty negotiations for the surrender of the territory south west of Lake Superior the principal chief (the Buffalo [Ketche Besheke] I think) ... at first refused to sign, not regarding the conditions as sufficiently favourable, and it was not till many of the younger and inferior chiefs had attached their names or totems that he would yield – but he did so at last.' To underline this last point, the commissioner jotted in the margin, 'principal chief can be coerced by inferiors.'[64] Vidal had found his weapon.

While shrewd in his analysis, Vidal nevertheless lacked the power to enter into any negotiations with the Ojibwa on the basis of his findings. Since June the Tories had been taunting the Reform government about its inaction on the claims issue. Rumours that a heated exchange had taken place between Ogista and Lord Elgin in Montreal had only provided additional political ammunition. Ogista apparently had demanded that Elgin state the exact amount the government already had received for mining locations in the unceded district, to which Elgin had replied that he had no certain knowledge but thought that no money had yet been collected. Knowing differently, Ogista had hurled a torrent of verbal abuse at the Governor General. As one newspaper put it, 'the ready tact of the Interpreter to explain in . ... more courteous language' was then required.[65] Following the airing of this incident in the press, the Tories gleefully assailed the Reformers for keeping the Crown's representative ignorant of occurrences in the province.

By the time Anderson arrived back at the rapids after the distribution of presents on Manitoulin Island, Vidal had already devised a policy which the surveyor felt was based on well-defined legal principles and would prove easy to administer in practice. From extracts from reports which he selected from the *Journals of the House of Assembly*, and what at the time were ambiguous American legal precedents, Vidal concluded that the Ojibwa could in no wise hold title to territory or resources. No Native leader, he argued in substantiation of his case, had ever exercised authority to transmit land to a sovereign Western power. 'I perceive *one view* of the original title of the various Indian tribes to have been taken and *one principle* acted upon in all cases,' he continued. '[The treaty] transaction was not considered as a purchase or surrender of territory but as a purchase of the right of hunting in and occupation [of territory].'[66] Productive mineral workings at Bruce Mines and Mica Bay not far from the Sault, and at Princess Bay near Fort William, had further increased the worth of the mining locations so that any dispute with the Ojibwa regarding actual land values would prove embarrassing to the government. For this reason, Vidal also sought to prevent Native participation in any decisions concerning the amount of compensation the Aboriginal people might receive for their 'right of occupancy.'

Vidal's second goal proved difficult to achieve, since the Ojibwa were well aware of the value of their land. What was more, Shingwaukonse defiantly regarded the claims issue as a testing ground for the validity of Aboriginal right.[67] With Macdonell's assistance he had invoked principles of natural law in defining the right of small nations to be recognized as possessing special status; a right which Macdonell averred could be modified or eliminated only through negotiation or conquest. On these grounds, Native leaders were seeking to establish a *modus vivendi* by which bands might abide by their own system of resource management. According to the Native value system, once a head chief became an 'owner' of territory on behalf of a group, he was within his rights to demand return for any loss incurred by removal of resources from his lands. In requesting that the government set royalty standards, if mineral discoveries on their territories proved worth mining, the Ojibwa hoped to establish a long-term source of capital for their bands. Head chiefs also expected help from the Indian Department in surveying the boundaries of the tracts on which their traditional prerogatives would continue to operate.

Little Pine and Nebenagoching meanwhile agreed to lease a mining location to Macdonell and his successors for 999 years, with a royalty of 2 per cent per annum accruing to the Ojibwa. This site, located north of Sault Ste Marie, was one which Macdonell himself had originally explored and surveyed in 1845. The agreement contained one major stipulation; if the mine were not worked within five years after the issue of the lease the location would be forfeit to the band.[68] Although Vidal knew of this transaction, his operational premises so thoroughly negated the Ojibwa's ability to sanction leases or receive royalties that he believed there was no need to consider the proposition seriously. He felt confident that his systematic plan of action would so structure and control future negotiations that any official meetings between the government and the Ojibwa would be mere formalities. Regardless of the Ojibwa's own wishes, henceforth they would receive a perpetual annuity capitalized from a fund controlled by the Executive Council – a system, moreover, which could be dispensed with when necessary.[69] The scheme granted the Ojibwa little decision-making power and no rights to major merchantable resources. To Vidal, to be an 'Indian' and to be the recipient of a share in the compensation fund were, for administrative purposes, functionally synonymous. So, not surprisingly, once the system was implemented, the terms 'Indian' and 'annuitant' often appeared interchangeably in government reports.[70]

The only task left for Vidal and Anderson following the distribution of presents was to determine what amount of compensation might be needed to settle the claim. For this purpose the two Indian commissioners, along with a Mr Sommerville from the *Illustrated London News* and nine men from Garden River, travelled by steamer to Fort William and then toured east along the coast by canoe, visiting Native villages *en route*.[71] Vidal and Anderson lost no time in making their views known. For instance, when Father Fremiot, SJ, of the Fort William Roman Catholic mission supported Peau de Chat's bid for a return on minerals, both commissioners severely reprimanded the priest for interfering in affairs which, they held, did not concern him.[72]

At a council held at Fort William on 25 September, Anderson directed his attention towards L'Illinois, an elderly head man. In his younger years, L'Illinois had been appointed a trading captain by the Hudson's Bay Company and still annually received a regimental uniform from the fur-trading institution as a token of his status, which earned him the name Miskouakkonaye, or 'Red Coat.' For this meeting, L'Illinois wore his full regalia, presented the commissioners with a pipe to smoke, and commenced ceremonies with an extremely lengthy speech in which, an impatient Father Fremiot commented sourly to his superiors, 'he traced his origins back to the flood, I believe, or perhaps earlier.'[73] Meanwhile Vidal, seeking out Peau de Chat as his primary adversary, set out to thwart the younger leader at every turn. Both commissioners described this chief as shrewd, intelligent, and self-interested. 'I think selfishness is the mainspring of his efforts to bring all the Indians to one place, as he would then exercise authority over a large number,' Vidal surmised.[74] Yet in his replies to questions addressed to him, Peau de Chat revealed that he spoke not for himself but for the interests of his group. According to Fremiot, attainment of government recognition for his people's territorial prerogatives constituted Peau de Chat's primary concern. As his band resided on territory that straddled the international border, the chief wished to know if the commissioners approved of his band's receiving compensation from both the United States and the Province of Canada: '"Would it be a crime for the Americans to give me money? Would it be a crime for the English to pay me?" questioned the chief. "Of course not" [replied the commissioners], "it is our duty to pay you. Your question is trifling." "But" [stated Peau de Chat] "is it not my land that is in question in this deal?"'[75] The Native leader thus gradually came to realize that the main point at issue was neither land nor resources but the implementation of a new government-prescribed social order for him and his people.

The commissioners failed to meet any Ojibwa individuals on their return voyage from Fort William to Sault Ste Marie. This they attributed to the lateness of the season and the fact that bands had left for their hunting grounds, although it later became clear that at least some bands had deliberately avoided meeting the government party.[76] With the assistance of

Hudson's Bay Company employees from the Pic and the Sault and what little information Anderson could extract from a crew member, Peter Bell, Anderson and Vidal drafted a rough map of the hunting grounds claimed by the bands.[77] At this time Bell depicted the Nipigon Ojibwa as troublesome, perhaps because certain of them were 'inlanders' and not party to a close alliance with Little Pine and the Fort William head chiefs. Shingwaukonse held that his influence extended only as far as the Puckasaw River, on the Nipigon band's eastern boundary.[78] While the two commissioners could determine geographical features marking band boundaries along the lakeshore, they had little idea of the actual size of the tracts or even the direction in which they extended into the interior. In the majority of cases they simply drew lines on either side of the frontages claimed by each band and then extended these lines northward to intercept the southern boundary of the territory included under the original Hudson's Bay Company charter. On the basis of this understanding, they expected head chiefs to ask for roughly the same amount, in the form of lump sums, as compensation for their groups' 'occupancy rights.'

Those Native leaders who met the officials with the anticipation that the government would make the first offer were both dismayed and confused. They were being asked to define a situation in terms unfamiliar to them and for which they were not adequately prepared. Prevented from consulting among themselves beforehand, chiefs began to diverge radically from one another as to what they expected in terms of compensation. Shingwaukonse demanded ten dollars annually per head in perpetuity, Peau de Chat thirty dollars per head, while other band leaders requested even more. Vidal interpreted these responses not as the shows of defiance they may actually have been, but as the results of 'counsels of designing whites.' Unfortunately, this misconception not only led the commissioner to regard the Native leaders as ignorant and incompetent, but also induced him to stress the importance of imposing the 'ultimatum of the government' upon their activities.[79]

Owing to the rigidity of Vidal's stance, councils held with Little Pine and his followers inside the Hudson's Bay Company's Sault post proved short and stormy. Even MacTavish grew concerned. The commissioner's position undermined the legality of the Cranes' 1789 grant to the North West Company – a transaction which had entitled the Hudson's Bay Company to land rights at the rapids ever since the unification of the North West and Hudson's Bay companies in 1821[80] – as well as the legality of Macdonell's leases. To make matters worse for the factor, Macdonell refused to press the issue, maintaining that his concern for the economic future of the Ojibwa motivated his petition for rights to the mining locations more than self-interest. 'McD[onell] himself,' wrote MacTavish to Simpson, 'distinctly says that if the Indians can obtain better terms from others, he will have great pleasure in giving them [the claims] up, so stands the matter at present.'[81]

In any event, neither MacTavish nor Macdonell had much time to debate their respective views on the matter. For on 15 October, when Vidal demanded that Shingwaukonse place an evaluation on his band's 'occupancy rights,' Little Pine abruptly terminated the discussion by pleading his unfamiliarity with the terms before him. He would have to consult with his people before answering. At this point Superintendent Anderson adjourned the meeting until the following day.

When the council again assembled, Shingwaukonse immediately raised the subject of the Hudson's Bay Company's and Macdonell's claims. In response, Vidal declared that the government owned the land base and that all tracts allotted by the Ojibwa in the past were 'of no value to their holders.'[82] At this remark, Macdonell rose and challenged the government to defend its position in the courts. He knew Native people could not be considered 'minors in law' and he had 'good legal advice on the subject.' The Ojibwa's right to the soil would be vindicated, he would personally see to it. Shingwaukonse, on being asked whether he joined with Macdonell in espousing such views, calmly replied 'Hear him for us – you do not understand what we say, you understand one another; we will not make replies – talk to Mcdonell [sic].' When the commissioners continued to ignore the lawyer and to try to force the chief's hand, Little Pine charged that the government would cast the Ojibwa aside if they disregarded Macdonell, for the latter acted as the spokesman for Native views, not his own. The chief then turned to Macdonell and urged, 'Come, my friend, get up and speak.'[83]

Vidal still would have nothing to do with the lawyer. The meeting was not a court of law, he contended. There was no judge present. His denial of Aboriginal right and Little Pine's support of the opposite position only made a prolonged clash of perspectives inevitable. The prospect of being engaged in an argument in which the Ojibwa might be shown to have grounds for a legal case must have been anathema to him. Rising, Vidal departed, leaving Anderson to listen to one final speech from Macdonell and then close the council.

The Mica Bay Affair

Vidal continued to malign Macdonell, claiming both political and moral justification for doing so. To him, Macdonell constituted nothing less than an agent of intrigue and subterfuge. In a letter to his father dated 17 October 1849, the commissioner bemoaned that fact that, through Macdonell, public opposition to the government 'had been ... made to extend far and wide.'[84] On the local scene, meanwhile, fearing that a secret compact existed among the head chiefs, he focused on isolating Shingwaukonse from his allies by negotiating separately with each Native leader in turn. Advocacy of Little Pine's words and actions, Vidal began to warn each head man, could jeopardize entirely the Ojibwa's opportunities to reach an agreement with the government. Either bands would have to comply with the government's wishes or they would be cast into a state of political limbo without even token monetary recompense for their losses, territorial or otherwise. On 23 October, the commissioner informed his family that his plan of dividing and conquering was working, and even described an example of his technique in action:

As soon as McD. had learnt at our council that in the event Shinquakonse (the Sault Ste Marie chief) proving refractory that we would treat independently with the others who had delegated their authority to him, messages were dispatched up and down to encourage them to remain firm in their adherence to Shinquakonse, and having some doubt about Ke-wa-konse, a special boat was sent to bring him up to Garden River on some excuse, that when we reached his place we might not find him ... [On] arrival [we] found he was in Shinquakonse's in close council ... we sent for him, explained fully the old man's position and succeeded in breaking up the council ... so our cunning opponent outwitted himself nicely and afforded us an opportunity of explaining in [the] presence of Shinquakonse and his subs, and talking at them with great effect, a much better thing than simply seeing Kewakonse alone at his camp, and to crown it all we took him back to his wigwam the next day in our canoe.[85]

From an examination of ensuing events it seems that neither Little Pine nor Macdonell deliberately sought to widen the breach between the opposing sides or to foment serious unrest on the frontier. Shingwaukonse steadfastly pursued his course of reconciling his people's needs for the future with opportunities potentially available within the broader power structure. And as the fall of 1849 approached, his strategy did not change.

MacTavish at the Hudson's Bay Company fort verified Vidal's observation that Little Pine indeed had sent messengers to bands on Lake Huron to 'prevent the Commissioners seeing them.'[86] Yet it does not seem that the factor bothered to inform Vidal – or any other government official, for that matter – of another rumour that had been circulating within the

Sault Ste Marie community since May 1849 to the effect that certain Native leaders planned to take over the operations of the Quebec and Lake Superior Mining Association at Mica Bay before the end of the year if their claims were not met. On 11 November, MacTavish wrote to a friend in a rather jaunty vein to say that a party composed of Ojibwa, Métis, Allan Macdonell, Macdonell's brother Angus, who also was a lawyer, and Wharton Metcalfe from Montreal had started out for Mica Bay. MacTavish knew that Macdonell strongly disagreed with a decision made by the mining company directors in 1848 to treat mining on Lake Superior as a speculative enterprise, rather than a long-term venture that would foster social as well as economic development. The gregarious lawyer had taken to expressing his views on this subject publicly, so that MacTavish not illogically assumed that the expedition constituted a demonstration of protest against company policies. News of the Mica Bay expedition did not even particularly surprise him. 'It is said here Mr. Bonner expected this visitation all fall,' the factor wrote, '[and until] the day before, people thought they intended going to Michipicoten Island ...'[87]

MacTavish expected no violence. Instead, he almost seemed to be enjoying the excitement caused by the affair, since in his prevailing state of being 'bone idle,' as he called it, he spent most of his time hoping for a transfer to York Factory.[88] On 12 November, he informed Sir George Simpson that fifteen American Ojibwa had joined the expedition. The factor also recounted that, on the evening of 13 November, Joseph Wilson had arrived at the mine manager's office at Mica Bay with a deposition warning of the impending takeover and requesting that measures be taken to receive the Native party.[89] MacTavish's ability to keep account of group composition and movements in this way indicated that the various parties made little effort to conceal their undertakings.

John Bonner, the mine manager, took no defensive countermeasures, although Wilson stressed that the expedition was already at Goulais Bay. At four A.M. on 14 November, Bonner was aroused by a loud knocking and opened his door to find Little Pine, Nebenagoching, the two Macdonells, Wharton Metcalfe, and about thirty other Ojibwa and Métis 'in their war dresses, each armed with a gun, and some with Bowie knives.'[90] At daybreak, Bonner gave orders to evacuate the mine, and two days later 160 men, women, and children left for the Sault by schooner. Bonner explained for the benefit of his company's shareholders that he gave the orders because he could not expose the mine workers and their families to possible danger.

Bonner continued to affirm that the Native people had been cajoled into taking part in the Mica Bay expedition by the Macdonells. '[The] friendly language and amiable demeanour of the Indians towards us,' he stated, 'were such as to induce us to consider the intimations of their English allies as mere idle threats, arising from a ... desire of private gain, and not the redress of Indian wrongs.'[91] The mine manager argued that Allan Macdonell desired to use his position as intermediary with the Ojibwa to secure leases which would only be profitable to himself.

Macdonell had plied the Ojibwa with whisky to gain their support for his plan, he declared, maintaining that on Mamainse Island, not far from the mine, he had found 'part of a barrel of whiskey, a loaded musket, and some clothing ... left after their carouse preparatory to the attack.' Although no violence had been committed, he stressed that the party had been heavily armed. They had even removed a small cannon belonging to the Hudson's Bay Company, which had formerly been left in front of Joseph Wilson's house. If violence had not been anticipated, Bonner asked, why were the Native participants supplied with muskets, knives, and ammunition, and even a small cannon?[92]

O'Meara shared Bonner's suspicions that Macdonell was the leading figure behind the mine takeover. Soon after the incident the missionary interviewed an Ojibwa fishing party near Thessalon, one of whom, a daughter of Little Pine, would only say that 'the elder McDonell had taken ... [Shingwaukonse] with him' but did not specify where. The priest, perhaps to shield the Anglican Ojibwa congregation from blame in the government's eyes, then emphasized that no Ojibwa from the Garden River mission had taken part in the expedition, except Little Pine and an 'old heathen Indian named Nahwahquakahbo.'[93]

Unlike MacTavish, neither O'Meara nor the resident priest, Gustavus Anderson, knew prior to the actual event that the mine takeover had even been contemplated.[94] What seemed to him the very suddenness of the affair convinced O'Meara that subversive interests had been at work within the Native population. Maybe Macdonell was a secret annexationist. On 22 October a group of Montreal merchants had published an 'Annexation Manifesto' in the Montreal *Gazette* calling for the union of the Canadas with the United States. Annexation, the manifesto had declared, would bring about a return to favourable market conditions formerly secured by imperial preference. O'Meara argued that the Mica Bay incident, Macdonell, and the annexation issue might be related. The priest could furnish evidence for his hypothesis since Macdonell's weakness for subscribing to grandiose schemes had led him to sign the Annexation Manifesto.[95] Subsequent events in Macdonell's career, however, indicate that this act constituted only a temporary political aberration on his part, since his long-term political interests eventually led him into the Canadian expansionist movement.[96] It is highly doubtful that protagonists of the annexationist cause systematically solicited Native support on the frontier. And while several of Macdonell's family had been associated with the Montreal-based North West Company fur trade, Macdonell himself repeatedly denounced the shift in emphasis towards monopoly control by Montreal commercial interests north of Lakes Huron and Superior. After 1849, Macdonell aligned himself with the rising Toronto business community, which opposed the annexationism of the Montreal merchants.

O'Meara nevertheless wrote outlining his suspicions to the superintendent general of the Indian Department, who passed the communication along to Lord Elgin. In December, after conducting a brief investigation into the allegations, Elgin contacted the British colonial secretary, Earl Grey, with news that almost no supporting evidence could be found, except that one Métis missionary on the U.S. side had received 'communications from persons in Canada who were desirous to render the American Indians on ... [the] frontier troublesome in connexion with the annexation movement.'[97] Yet an educated man such as the Métis Baptist missionary James D. Cameron, Jr, would most certainly have known of the manifesto and been able to speak at some length of its effects on thinking persons on the frontier.

Governor General Elgin refused to give O'Meara's fears much serious consideration. For his own part, he suspected that Bonner's reluctance to repulse the aggressors in November sprang from the mine manager's intention to use the incident to collect substantial damages from the province.[98] And it was unlikely that Bonner had acted alone. So when T.G. Anderson warned that if the government did not act quickly, the Ojibwa would think Macdonell had 'overawed the government,' Elgin dispatched a detachment of the Rifle Brigade, under the command of Capt. Ashley Cooper, to repossess the Mica Bay mine. Joseph Wilson, George Ironside, and William MacTavish accepted appointments as special constables.[99] Ironside, accompanied by the Ojibwa head chief Mishiquongai from French River, and Joseph Wilson joined the troops, but owing to inclement weather, the entire party had to give up hope of reaching the mines by boat before spring.[100] On orders from Sir George Simpson, the Rifles quartered at the Hudson's Bay Company's buildings, much to MacTavish's distaste, and an uneventful winter season closed in at Sault Ste Marie.

Little Pine, Macdonell, and their allies remained in peaceful possession of the mine throughout the late fall and winter. Yet in contrast to the tranquil state of affairs north of the Sault, comment in the metropolitan press regarding the Mica Bay incident had stimulated lively debate. In November the *Patriot*, a Toronto Tory newspaper, took an almost macabre pleasure in reporting, albeit erroneously, that owing to government mismanagement of the claims issue, Indians had attacked miners on Lake Superior, 'killing 150 persons and taking 80 persons into the interior.'[101] Such articles echoed a certain smugness in Tory circles on learning of the Reform government's acute embarrassment concerning the claims affair.

On the other hand, the newspaper also cautioned that the rumours of 'killings and abductions' were probably greatly exaggerated.[102] Bonner, stung by allegations that he had vacated the mine solely in order to be able to claim compensation, wrote an article in the *Pilot* attacking Macdonell for leading the mine takeover.[103] In the lawyer's defence, the Montreal *Gazette* portrayed Macdonell as no less than a champion of Native rights, while placing the blame for events at the mine on Lord Elgin, who was charged with 'duplicity' in his treatment of the Ojibwa and their valid claims.[104] Meanwhile Macdonell expressed a reluctance to declare his stand publicly on the issue until a trial date could be set, when 'in the witness box the truth [would] be elicited.'[105]

By mid-December, however, Macdonell could no longer remain silent in the face of Bonner's accusations. Bonner charged that Macdonell had threatened to raise 'two thousand Indians' to subdue the mining interests by violence and had unscrupulously manipulated his Native allies. According to Bonner, Little Pine himself had admitted to being so drunk before the expedition that he had been 'wheeled over the [Sault] portage' in a cart and shipped to the mine 'in a state of insensibility.'[106] Macdonell immediately fired off a rejoinder in the *Patriot* that it had been Shingwaukonse, and not he, who had declared that there 'would be 1500 or perhaps 2000 in the spring, determined to maintain their rights.'[107] As to the charges that he harboured violent intentions against the mining company, the lawyer reminded his adversary that in the spring he had still been in Montreal with Little Pine when Native leaders, and particularly Peau de Chat, arrived at Mica Bay and warned Bonner that the miners must cease operations until a settlement could be made with the government. Responding to Bonner's accusations that he, as a lawyer, sought only his own interests, Macdonell maintained that he had acted, and continued to act, solely as Shingwaukonse's agent. Recalling a conversation between himself and Bonner on the morning after the takeover, Macdonell stated that he and his group actually had tried to save the mine workers from having to vacate the site by trying to gain a lease for the company from the Ojibwa and thus solve the Native claims issue on the spot: 'I said a lease might be taken from the Chiefs, thereby acknowledging the Indian right. I told ... [Bonner], however, that I could promise nothing until I saw the Chiefs. I went over to them and made the proposal. They authorized me to agree to anything which would not be a means of depriving them of the position they then held.'[108] Finally, Macdonell denied all allegations that he had given Little Pine whisky in order to compel the chief to join the expedition: 'I will defy any one throughout the whole extent of the country, to fix upon me the crime of making an Indian drunk. I was in the boat that carried Shingwakonce and the other Chiefs, and there was not a drop of spirituous liquor of any kind in it. Upon the following day we did fall in with a boat in which there was liquor, and I induced one of the Chiefs to order it to be thrown away, which was instantly done.'[109]

On December 3, Bonner declared publicly before George Ironside that the Mica Bay operations had been 'violently dispossessed' – a statement to which Allan Macdonell objected, since the mine manager had not been an eyewitness to the event.[110] Canadian and American newspapers which picked up on this incident singled out Macdonell as the main perpetrator of the Mica Bay affair, although they later qualified their views as events unfolded.[111] The day following Bonner's accusations, Allan and Angus Macdonell, Shingwaukonse, Nebenagoching, Nowquagabo, Pierre Lesage, Pierre's brother Eustace, and Charles Boyer voluntarily surrendered themselves to the justices of the peace at Sault Ste Marie. The small group of 'miscreants' was refused bail and left almost immediately by steamer for Penetanguishene, and then Toronto. In Toronto they underwent about an hour's questioning, were committed to gaol for a few days, and finally were released by the chief justice, Sir John Beverley Robinson, a relative by marriage of Macdonell.[112] Robinson held that the party had been arrested illegally.[113]

The government had not been interested in the petty squabbles which had erupted in the press between Allan Macdonell and Bonner during the early winter. Yet the arrival of the Native party in the metropolis had caused considerable excitement, and the fact that Shingwaukonse had fought in the War of 1812 as a British ally and was now on trial by the Canadian government was mentioned in American as well as Canadian newspapers.[114] When, suddenly, in January 1850, the issue shifted to considerations of the validity of Aboriginal right, the government seriously began to search for an approach that would settle the claims question once and for all.

Shingwaukonse, circa 1849

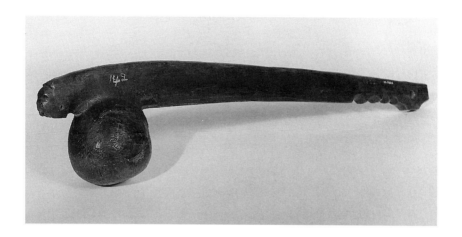

Shingwaukonse's war club

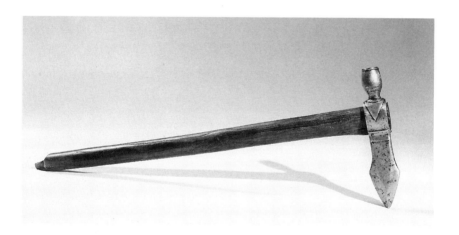

Shingwaukonse's tomahawk pipe

Shingabaw'osin, 'the Image Stone.' Crane head chief on the American side of the
Sault rapids until his death in 1828, Shingabaw'osin was the father of one of
Shingwaukonse's four wives.

First Anglican church at Sault Ste Marie, on the 'British' side of the rapids. Used as both a school and a house of worship, it was located on the property of fur trader Charles Oakes Ermatinger.

Kaygayosh, younger brother of Shingabaw'osin and, before 1836, Shingwaukonse's mentor in the *Midéwiwin* (Grand Medicine Society)

Métis near Sault rapids with a wooden canoe, dipnet, and whitefish

From left: A man identified by elders at Garden River as possibly being William B. Robinson in Native garb, Shingwaukonse, and Nebenagoching (1849)

Visitors to Montreal (*Illustrated London News*, 15 September 1849). *From left:*
Shingwaukonse, Nebenagoching, and Menissinowenninne (The Man of the Island).
The latter may be the same person whom elders identified as William B. Robinson in
the photograph opposite.

Dodems drawn by leaders at Garden River on an affidavit they signed in 1850 in the
presence of Joseph Wilson, with John Bell acting as interpreter. The document shows
Shingwaukonse's sprightly Plover *dodem*, Kabaosa's (Caibaiosai's) more reserved Crane
dodem (bottom), and Piabetassung's Hawk *dodem*.

Ash ke po ge gosh   Leech Lake
Mach i ga bow   Half of the Lake
Wai in ge gum   Red Lake
Mi ge ge   Eve ne ba go shish
He no shause   Lake Courtueile
Otha wuh Ko Ki shik   Puck wai a wau
Ya bause   Fol a vou
Ki chi he ne se   Puck arai a wau
Me so po do   Chippewa River
A mose   Lake du Flamba
He nis te meau   Trout Lake
Waub un i mi ki   Turtle Portage
Dan ge be   Lac Chetec
Ma ta go mi
O kan de Kan
Muk ud day bin aco   Antonogau
Ma shin a way   Bad Rive
Sha ga ya saense
Ki besh Kunk   Roin River
Mik ney ke quah   Fond du Lac

On behalf of the above chiefs I have inquired of the Salt St Marie & Garden River Chief if they would be willing to alow the American Indians to come out and settle on there lands they are willing with your consent to alow it. we must ask your leave

Mah Ke day pense
Ogishtai say He will say yease alone when you and the Governor has given your consent
There are two of our People all to geather

Petition sent by the southwestern Ojibwa leaders, under Ogista's auspices, to the Indian department 1852. Notice that the name of the head chief of Leech Lake, Minnesota, Eschekebugecoshe (Ashkepogegosh), leads the list.

Buhkwujjenene, or 'Wild Man,' one of Shingwaukonse's sons and successors at Garden
River. Oil painting by J.W. Foster

That, only four of us agreed to join his
Band - Myself (Ethan Biron), my brother
Alexis Biron, John Bell and Antoine Cadotte.
All the other Half-breeds said, that they were
already Indians enough without binding themselves
to be under an Indian Chief. And they all
left the Council-town.

Joshua Biron's statement, made to John Driver and then relayed to E.B. Borron, regarding events affecting the Métis in 1849. Biron emphasizes that only four Métis, all of whom were related to Shingwaukonse by marriage, joined the Garden River band in 1849.

Lord Lorne's visit to Garden River in 1881. Oil painting by Sydney Prior Hall

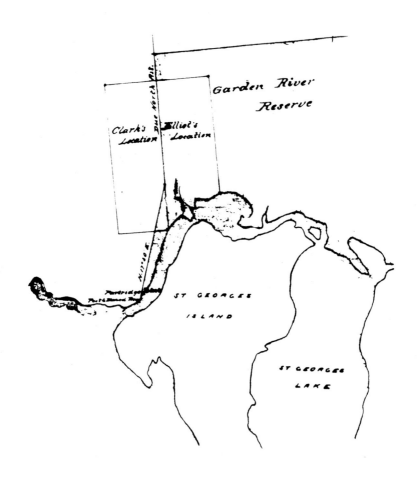

Tracing of the western boundary of Garden River Reserve, 1889

Ogista, also known as Chief Little Pine or 'Augustan,' one of Shingwaukonse's sons and successors. Oil painting by E.F. Wilson

Garden River, circa 1896. Watercolour by William Armstrong. Notice the wooden houses, stores, and mining company buildings.

GARDEN RIVER

Photograph of a gravehouse in Garden River taken in 1933. Notice the 'gothic' ornamentation.

St John's Anglican Church, Garden River

The Longfellow window, St John's Anglican Church, Garden River

The Garden River cast of what became known as the 'Hiawatha pageant,' on tour in Michigan in 1904. The play, performed in the Ojibwa language, draws on themes from Longfellow's epic poem *Hiawatha*. In this production, George Kabaosa, a great-grandson of Shingwaukonse, plays the lead role.

George Kabaosa and his family in front of their house on Sugar Island

John Askin, one of Shingwaukonse's sons, at Garden River, circa 1915

The Struggle for Aboriginal Rights

The Aboriginal Rights Debate

In an editorial in January 1850 the prominent Toronto newspaper the *Globe* commented on the Ojibwa's demands. Native claims, the *Globe* declared, were an obstruction to national development. The earth might 'be the Lord's and the fulness thereof,' but the rewards should fall to those with the enterprise to exploit the resources: 'The principle of depriving the Indians of lands which they could not use, in order that white men should teach them to bring forth the fruits God has provided for the sustenance of man, may be an unjust one; but like many unjust principles, it has been ratified and sanctioned by time and common practice. It is now too late to discover and blame it.'[1]

According to the *Globe*, the Ojibwa were unenterprising wanderers entrenched in a narrow economic niche with no claims whatsoever to proprietorship over land, minerals, timber, or fisheries. The most vocal advocates of Native claims at Sault Ste Marie were the Métis, who might be given land grants by way of charity, but that was all the recognition the newspaper felt the issue warranted. Indian wigwams, the *Globe* maintained, 'were now to be seen on the Michipicoten River, now beyond Fort William, and often in the prairies of the west, or in the forests of the north. It seems difficult to reconcile oneself to the idea of a nomad race like this, raising serious claims to the exclusive possession of a vast tract of country ...'[2] To uphold this contention the *Globe* printed extracts from D.B. Papineau's report of 4 November 1847, complete with all the erroneous ethnographic data related by John W. McNaughton.

The *Globe* had raised the question of Aboriginal rights to the status of a public debate, and Macdonell proved quick to take up the challenge. The lawyer had his own views on the Ojibwa position – drawn from Native oral testimony, Schoolcraft's writings, and descriptions of the treaties Britain had made with the Ojibwa from 1790 to 1836 – and he set out to debate the *Globe*'s position in a series of articles in the *Patriot.* The Ojibwa themselves held that they had come from Wabenong, land of the east, he began, and belonged to a people called the Algonquin, a 'generic term for the primitive stock of tribes in the north.' The Ojibwa were the most powerful and extensive nation which had emerged from this primary matrix. They called themselves Odjibwag, 'which appears to denote a peculiarity in the voice or utterance.' They had constituted a form of political entity in the past and had fought together as such, Macdonell claimed, citing an abbreviated version of a legend which is still current among elders at Garden River:[3] '12 nations from the South and from the West combined to drive out the Chippewa, twice they attacked and twice they were defeated by the Chippewas.'[4]

Macdonell emphasized that the Ojibwa boasted that they had never been a conquered nation and that Papineau's report stemmed wholly from political expediency. And Papineau's source for the claim that the Ojibwa came from the Mississippi 'would be a curiosity to ascertain,' the lawyer contended. The head chiefs at Sault Ste Marie had maintained territorial prerogatives over tracts in the vicinity of the rapids for centuries. One of these chiefs, Keokonse, over a hundred years old in 1850, had been present at the taking of Michilimackinac in 1763 and remembered the Ojibwa's transactions with the French. Far from being a 'small and contemptible set of refugees,' the Ojibwa were the owners 'since time immemorial' of land to which 'no other party can show the shadow of title or claim.'[5]

On 23 December, in a letter to Robert Bruce, Macdonell described his role with regard to the Ojibwa in patron-client terms; however, his statements suggested a reciprocal relationship different from the usual one between lawyer and client: 'I have lived among the Indians some little time and am received among them as one of their own people. The chiefs of the different bands upon the Lake have reposed a trust and confidence in me which I deem worthy of attention.'[6]

With an intensity of purpose evidently inspired by Shingwaukonse's shamanistic vision, Macdonell set out to formulate a case for Aboriginal right which he expected to test in the courts late in the spring of 1850. By this time it was apparent that Vidal's divide-and-conquer technique had failed. The three American Ojibwa (one being the head chief Oshawano), five American Métis, twelve Canadian Ojibwa, thirteen Canadian

Métis, and one French Canadian whom MacTavish recorded as accompanying the Macdonells and Metcalfe to Mica Bay[7] gradually came to be seen as the vanguard of a broadly based Native protest movement. Ironside had previously argued that even though 'measures had been taken to incite the wild Indians of the Head of Lake Superior' to join the Mica Bay expedition, the unrest was but a temporary phenomenon and would soon abate.[8] Three months later, MacTavish apprised Sir George Simpson of 'talk of 2000 Indians coming down in the spring from up the country, some of them from Saskatchewan.' The chief factor felt that the situation had grown ludicrous. Probably 'they will also have an auxiliary corps of Esquimaux,' he remarked wryly.[9]

Throughout the fall and winter of 1849 the magistracy at Sault Ste Marie contended that Macdonell had been manipulating matters to suit his own advantage, even to the point of persuading Little Pine and his party to walk '300 miles in snowshoes ... [while] smelling damages ...'[10] By March, however, matters seemed less certain. 'I should say he was a little cracked,' Capt. Ashley Cooper of the Second Rifle Brigade wrote to his superiors in explanation of the lawyer's behaviour. According to Cooper, Macdonell intended going back to Mica Bay with 'his chiefs.' Meanwhile, Bonner, angered by the chief justice's refusal to admit his charges of conspiracy and armed insurrection, applied to the captain for guns and ten thousand rounds of ammunition in order to take back the mine by force.[11]

On 14 March Macdonell informed Superintendent Bruce that under statute 2 Vict. Cap. 15, passed in October 1838 for the protection of Indian lands, the Crown must appoint a commissioner to preserve the Sault tract from trespass. He said he had been authorized to convey this message by Little Pine and several other Native leaders who, 'should they acquiesce [in Bonner's repossession of the mines] would be virtually acknowledging that they had not the right to the lands ...' Dispossession of the Quebec and Lake Superior Mining Association's operation, he continued, had occurred in response to Vidal's denial of the principle of Aboriginal right. The Ojibwa had no desire to stop the course of legitimate enterprise in the Upper Great Lakes region. An offer to lease the mine to the company for a token fee until a settlement had been effected with the government had been rejected by Bonner. Once the existence of Aboriginal rights was recognized, Macdonell stressed, the company would be 'enabled to proceed with their works at once.'[12]

While MacTavish and Cooper might scoff at Macdonell's effusive idealism, the lawyer remained steadfast in his promise to assist the Ojibwa until negotiations had begun. William B. Robinson, who had been appointed in January to negotiate with the Ojibwa, wrote to Macdonell on 9 May 'warning him of the trouble he wd bring on himself' if he persisted in upholding the validity of the Ojibwa takeover of the Mica Bay mine.[13] Robinson, who spent twelve days in the Sault during May, was brother of Chief Justice John Beverley Robinson (hence, another of Macdonell's in-laws) and a clever political appointment on the part of the Reform ministry. He had been a familiar figure to the Garden River Ojibwa in his role as manager at Bruce Mines, and it was through Robinson that Shingwaukonse had been able to submit a petition to the Executive Council for travelling expenses during the previous winter. As a Tory, Robinson would shield the government from the brunt of attacks should negotiations fail, and his relationship with Macdonell helped prevent an unbreachable schism between the treaty-making party and the defenders of Aboriginal rights at Mica Bay.

The lines between the two sides nevertheless remained sharply drawn. On 31 May, Macdonell informed the Indian Department that, Robinson's caution notwithstanding, Little Pine had no intention of backing down on the claims issue. Should Bonner succeed in fortifying mining locations north of the Sault in defiance of Shingwaukonse's wishes, the goodwill towards the government recently re-established by Robinson's overtures would not last.[14] Frederick O'Meara, a frequent visitor to Garden River at this time, grew concerned that the government would fail to impress on the Ojibwa's minds the 'enormity' of the 'traitorous' aims of those who had taken over the mine. On ill-founded suspicions, the missionary warned the residents of Garden River and Thessalon that, unless they took care, they would be implicated in the guilt of 'unquiet men ... attempting to revolutionize the Province.' Since Little Pine had been 'duped' by those disloyal to the Queen, his followers would be well advised to have nothing more to do with their chief as long as he continued to have dealings with the two Macdonells.[15]

The Ojibwa along the north shore of Lake Huron responded to O'Meara's meddling by sending Waubesemie, who resided at Manitowaning, to Ironside with a memorial from three prominent head chiefs, Mishiquongai, Shawanoseway, and Ainenonduck, requesting that O'Meara be removed from the district.[16] Although these men held O'Meara to be arrogant, disrespectful of their authority as leaders, and guilty of several petty offences, such as the theft of bricks from Ironside's property at the Anglican Manitoulin Island Establishment, there could be little doubt that O'Meara's position on the claims issue was their main grievance.

Although O'Meara attempted to procure a statement from Little Pine negating these allegations, Wilson transmitted a request to the Indian Department in August from Shingwaukonse, Piabetassung, and Kabaosa demanding that the priest be prevented from attending treaty negotiations.[17]

To offset fears implanted by O'Meara and to gain an ally who would vouch for his loyalty to the Crown, Little Pine asked McMurray to be present at the treaty negotiations.[18] On the whole, however, the chief did not seem overly concerned about aspersions which might be cast on his allegiance to queen and country. While Shingwaukonse set about rallying supporters, old Keokonse meanwhile complained to Ironside about trespassers on his lands at Thessalon. He also expected the Indian Department to approve the lease of an island he and 'his immediate successors' had made to Alex Cameron, a local trader.[19] Each chief seemed confident that his territorial prerogatives would soon be recognized by the government.

The Robinson Treaties of 1850

Following the distribution of presents in late August, William B. Robinson arrived at Sault Ste Marie to implement the policy laid out in its essentials by Vidal the previous fall. His instructions almost exclusively concerned compensation money. In April the Committee of the Executive Council had granted £5,000 for an immediate cash payment and determined that a perpetual annuity would be drawn from annual interest on a capital fund of £25,000.[20] Robinson had also been told to secure the cession of as much land north of Lakes Huron and Superior as possible, especially the territory around Mica Bay and Michipicoten 'where the Quebec Mining Company have commenced operations.'

Since May, Robinson had been continuing Vidal's scheme of isolating Little Pine from his allies. In this tactic he found a firm supporter in Sir George Simpson, who willingly acquiesced in furthering the government's 'business with the Indians.'[21] It was good economic policy for the governor of the Hudson's Bay Company to reduce the number of free traders in the Upper Great Lakes area, and in 1850 no one threatened his organization's monopoly status more than Macdonell and his Métis backers. Company agents needed little urging to spread rumours among bands at Nipigon, Michipicoten, and Fort William that support for Little Pine and Macdonell constituted nothing less than a rejection of the authority of the Crown.[22]

This tactic brought immediate results. While Shingwaukonse's and

Keokonse's bands remained relatively unaffected, since they were not particularly dependent on the Hudson's Bay Company trade, more westerly groups lacked other trade options. It was therefore not surprising that, torn between the pressure exerted by the Hudson's Bay Company on the one hand and his commitment to the alliance with Little Pine on the other, Peau de Chat grew listless and finally ill at the Sault. When Lord Elgin, who had arrived to give the proceedings added dignity and publicly authorize Robinson to act as an agent of the Queen, visited Peau de Chat's lodge on 31 August, the Native leader immediately 'expressed his disappointment in proceedings at Mica Bay ... and professed much respect and attachment to Queen and her representatives.' Head chief Totomenai also stated that 'he would not consent to give Michipicoten to the Whites who asked for it, but would cede it to the Queen.'[23] According to oral tradition at Garden River, Little Pine exhorted the Ojibwa to protect their prerogatives, warning, 'We must act. They are weak now. They will be more powerful soon.'[24] But to leaders faced with a monopoly situation, 'they' had grown too powerful already.

The question of previous land grants made by the Sault Ste Marie band to the French and British since 1750 proved to be a delicate one. In 1850 a Mr Barhams of Port Hope, Ontario, had submitted a claim to land at the rapids, which he contended had been granted by the Great Crane to Alexander Henry the Elder.[25] Little Pine also wanted the government to recognize his allocations of land along the Garden River to his eldest son, Tegoosh, and the plots to the Anglican and Roman Catholic churches. Robinson chose to ignore both Barhams' and Little Pine's petitions. In consequence, the mission and Tegoosh claims, in particular, remained controversial issues for years.

The commissioner also rejected all Native petitions for government assistance in Native mining and logging enterprises. When Shingwaukonse threatened to go to England to complain to Queen Victoria concerning the government's reluctance even to consider his proposals, Robinson retorted that the chief and his people 'could take such a step if they pleased.' The official even suggested that, to quiet the chief, the government should consider building the chief a new house. After that, he asserted, nothing more would be heard of the London expedition.[26]

Robinson felt he had left the Ojibwa few grounds for complaint. In his speeches and in the treaty he drafted, he stated that the Native population would be able to continue hunting and fishing on ceded lands not yet sold or leased by the Crown. He also outlined potential benefits the Ojibwa might experience in having growing mining towns nearby, since such centres would afford markets for whatever surplus produce they might wish to sell. Finally, in conformity with a suggestion made earlier by Vidal, he included a provision in the treaty which would secure the Native people an annuity of £1 or more per capita should revenue from the ceded district enable the government, without loss, to increase the payments. Robinson undoubtedly inserted this 'escalation clause' expressly to placate Little Pine.[27]

Robinson then used his control over distribution of treaty payments to drive a final wedge between Shingwaukonse and the other Native leaders attending the ceremonies. When Little Pine disagreed with the manner in which the negotiations had been conducted, Robinson replied that the majority of the chiefs had agreed to the government's terms and that those who signed the agreement would receive money. Those who did not could expect nothing. Otherwise, the commissioner showed little interest in the composition of the annuity lists, even though his two interpreters, George Johnston and John William Keating, placed the American head chief Oshawano, or 'Cassaquadung,' and numerous Métis individuals under their Ojibwa names on the band rolls.[28]

Robinson, then, on the basis of geographic criteria alone, arbitrarily divided the bands of Lake Superior from those of Lake Huron, and drafted a final treaty, the Robinson-Superior Treaty, which was signed on 7 September 1850 by the chiefs and head men residing on Lake Superior. Reluctantly, and only after presenting a petition requesting that certain Métis be either granted land or secured in their present holdings at the Sault, Shingwaukonse placed his mark on a second treaty document, the Robinson-Huron treaty, duplicating almost exactly the terms of the first, on 9 September. Thirty-seven chiefs and head men signed after him.[29]

A Brief Reprieve

During the course of treaty negotiations Shingwaukonse repeatedly impressed on Robinson that, as the Canadian government refused to hear the Native side on the claims issue, the chief intended to travel to England to present the Ojibwa's case to the Crown. At the time, the commissioner regarded Little Pine's declarations as empty threats, employed to win political leverage.[30] Robinson's scepticism failed to weaken the chief's resolve to meet with Queen Victoria. In November 1850, Ironside reported to Bruce that not only was the leader still thinking of going to England, but also, according to Shingwaukonse's 'confidential interpreter,' who kept Ironside abreast of news at the Sault, the Garden River band had already collected £200 for the trip. Waubesemie from Manito-waning would travel with Shingwaukonse.[31]

Unforeseen legal events intervened to postpone the trip. By April 1851, Attorney General Robert Baldwin had overturned the chief justice's decision on the Mica Bay issue, and Shingwaukonse had to appear for the spring assizes in Toronto, only to have the case bound over a second time. George Johnston, who was collecting data for Schoolcraft's voluminous ethnographic and statistical work on the Native people of the United States, also engaged the chief's time. Little Pine and Nebenagoching made several trips to Manitoulin Island to solicit Ironside's help in purchasing equipment for the development of the agricultural, fishing, and logging industries at the Sault. And Shingwaukonse requisitioned thousands of boards and nails, a team of oxen, two horses, a plough, saws of various sizes, a number of padlocks, and 'irons' for a sawmill. Nebenagoching, on behalf of his band, which in 1850 had reserved Whitefish Island at the Canadian rapids as a fishing station, ordered a hundred pounds of net thread to advance the Native commercial fishery. Economic prospects for both bands began to brighten.[32]

The Garden River people gradually shed their disappointment over the setbacks to Little Pine's scheme. This rise in morale was hastened by interest shown by the Methodists in the welfare of the community. In the spring of 1851, the Reverend George McDougall, a young and energetic man, had arrived at the Native village to be greeted by a formal address from Ogista. Ogista outlined some of the plans the Ojibwa were contemplating to improve their economy. Potatoes, oats, turnips, and carrots all grew fairly well on the reserve, Ogista explained, and concluded by appealing to the missionary to help the band make agriculture at Garden River a profitable enterprise.[33]

The band would not be disappointed. Under Methodist direction, the Ojibwa built forty new houses. And despite the sandy soil and poor climate, which combined insufficient spring and summer rainfall with wet harvest seasons, agriculture flourished. By 1852 a chapel, a school, and a small agricultural training institution had been established. The missionary procured seed and supplies from Church, the merchant on Sugar Island, who was also a Methodist. While there were still major difficulties to be overcome in providing relief for needy families during the early spring, by April 1853 McDougall could write that 'in a few years they will be happy people, enjoying the Blessings of this life and salvation.'[34]

The Methodist presence also provided an outlet for the pent-up pressures and disappointments of the preceding years. At camp meetings the Ojibwa could call on a powerful, but benign cosmological being for aid. It was relatively easy for Ogista, well versed in invoking the *manido.sug* of his traditional religion, to turn his oratorical powers to pleading for God's grace. A large, handsome man, Ogista possessed a deep, rich voice and a commanding yet lyrical oratorical style which quickly gained the admiration of the Methodist clergy. One listener noted that even his 'gestures were graceful and appropriate ... exactly suited to the character of the expression.'[35]

His participation in Methodist activities afforded Ogista an opportunity to redeem himself in the eyes of his family and his community. He had been severely chastised, almost ostracized, for rash criticisms of his father, whom in 1849 he had publicly denounced before Anderson and Vidal for disloyalty to the Crown.[36] He had tried to raise himself in others' estimation by bold actions and words, and by ingratiating himself with local government officials. Ogista had wanted to test his own talents for leadership, to steal prestige from his dominant father. Probably while intoxicated, Ogista had even physically attacked the elderly chief. Jealousy of Buhkwujjenene for his close attachment to Shingwaukonse and the Anglican Church had also roused Ogista's ire.[37] With the Methodist presence, however, his behaviour changed, and he discovered a new sense of purpose in encouraging the pursuit of agriculture and the construction of cabins.

For two years, agriculture advanced steadily in response to an economic upturn induced by a brief logging boom. In the spring of 1853, the merchant Church secured a contract to supply lumber for the construction of the American ship canal at the American rapids. As a result, in 1500 cords of wood were cut and hauled by the Methodists, community morale rose, and the use of 'firewater' diminished.[38]

This prosperity was shortlived, however. New government policies on the disposal of timber and minerals on the Garden River reserve undermined efforts to maintain a well-organized, industrious community. While the Methodist movement emphasized farming, environmental conditions were generally unfavourable for agriculture. Farming had to be supplemented by other seasonal activities. McDougall soon recognized this, and strongly supported logging. In their turn, however, Ojibwa loggers became the target of extraordinarily harsh treatment by mining interests, and the Methodists seemed powerless to resist these attacks.

Competition from the Mining Companies

The Robinson Treaties stipulated that wherever the government had bargained, before 1850, to sell locations on unceded land, such sales might be completed following fulfilment of all conditions by the purchasers of the sites. In August 1852, therefore, George Desbarats, the agent responsible for the Lemoine and Simpson locations, pressed the government to compel the Ojibwa to 'give up their land quietly' and abide by the treaty.[39] Such appeals became imbued with urgency after the passing, on 23 March 1853, of an Order-in-Council stipulating that, after 1 May 1853, all overdue payments would be called within six months. If the sales were not completed, the locations would revert to the province, not to the Native bands. William H. Palmer, Rankin's agent, forced to act on the Elliot and Clark claims, informed the Indian Department that he would not voluntarily support Church's logging endeavours or the American canal project. He would take a lawyer's advice on the subject of the timber.[40]

The Indian Department at first tried to effect a compromise between the mining companies and the Native people. When Desbarats offered payment for the Lemoine and Simpson locations, the department suggested that, as the mineral outcroppings lay north of the Ojibwa settlement, the locations might be resurveyed to accommodate the village in front. Garden River, it was argued, had long been the residence of 'an influential band of Indians,' and their removal might be 'productive of very serious consequences and discontent among them.'[41] Desbarats, however, refused to agree to the suggestion.

The Robinson Treaties had deprived the Native peoples of clear title to both land and resources. The Reverend William McMurray, who recognized this flaw immediately, argued that chiefs should be restored a measure of their former authority, while rights to reserve territory should be vested in the band.[42] Native leaders likewise anticipated that they could suffer from lack of rights, and the government's gradual withdrawal of presents aggravated their concern. In 1852, the value of presents given to the bands was only three-quarters of their value in previous years. The three most prominent speakers, Shingwaukonse of the Ojibwa, Mocomanish of the Ottawa, and Wawcousai of the Potawatomi, voiced their fear that, once distributions had ceased altogether, they would no longer be recognized as representatives of distinct peoples. Little Pine directed his speech to Keating, asking him to convey the following plea to the governor general: 'We salute you. We beg you to believe what we say for though we cannot put down our thoughts on paper as you, our wampams [wampums] and the records of our old men are all as undying as your writings and they do not deceive.'[43]

Appeals to the governor general were in vain. In November 1850, Elgin had informed Lord Grey, his relative in the Colonial Office, that as the

House of Commons refused to consider proposals for the continuation of the presents, Canada 'must make the best of it.'[44] This meant devising a rationale to justify diminution and final cessation of the distributions. The expense of the presents was cited as the main reason, but the Canadian government also observed that the act of giving them indicated that the recipients deserved special recognition as members of groups. The practice, it was reported, tended 'to uphold the cherished belief of independence as a separate People and is consequently inimical to the habits and mode of life of ordinary subjects.'[45] Bruce directed Ironside to impress upon Little Pine and the other chiefs the uselessness of any further petitions of this nature.[46]

Superintendent General Bruce also severely reprimanded Macdonell for attempting to represent the Ojibwa legally, since, Bruce emphasized, all communications had to pass through Indian Department officials as long as Native persons continued 'to participate in the Queen's Royal Bounty.'[47] To this, Macdonell retorted that Lord Elgin had been willing to listen to his appeals on behalf of Native people in 1849. Furthermore, no laws, the lawyer argued, prevented Native leaders from seeking legal assistance. Should a contrary principle be assumed, he continued, 'you virtually deny the Indian redress of every grievance and would compel him to submit to every wrong [to] which the neglect or ignorance of the Indian Department might subject him.'[48] Extension of presents to Native people arose from the desire of colonial governments to ensure peaceful trade with the indigenous peoples and to reward services in time of war, and, Macdonell asserted, should in no way exclude the Ojibwa from exercising basic rights.

In addition to threatening the injury to Native rights and prerogatives described by Macdonell, the collapse of the transactional system by which bands were given presents in return for their political and economic loyalty to British colonial institutions deprived the Ojibwa of a dependable source of provisions and goods which in the past had helped carry them over hard times. Because of the growing scarcity of game and fur-bearing animals, the Ojibwa, particularly the interior bands, desperately needed the assistance. In April 1851 Ironside noted great numbers of people, weakened by hunger, coming from the interior to the coast for the first time. Those who made it to Manitowaning received rations, but the agent feared that many had perished *en route.*[49] At the same time, the Hudson's Bay Company counteracted this coastward movement by attempting to prevent bands from meeting other traders. The major inducement used to encourage bands to remain stationary was liquor.

Wemyss Simpson, a cousin of Sir George Simpson posted at La Cloche after 1852, frankly declared that he wanted to keep the Native people out of the clutches of the missionaries, since the priests would inform on him for selling whisky to the Ojibwa. Officially, the Hudson's Bay Company prohibited the sale of spirits, but at the post under young Simpson's charge any pretence of upholding this law was abandoned.[50] Ironside, too, upheld the double standard, which severely punished white and Native free traders for selling liquor but turned a blind eye to the company's infractions. In 1852, Wemyss Simpson became Ironside's son-in-law, and these two, along with Joseph Wilson, John William Keating, and Keating's associates, Arthur Rankin, James Cuthbertson, and Arthur Maitland, formed a powerful clique hostile to all organizations, particularly missions and Native bands, which challenged their economic and political hegemony along the north shore of Lakes Huron and Superior. This group sought to make the coastal bands into wage labourers economically dependent on the Hudson's Bay Company and the mining enterprises.

O'Meara recognized that the economic changes introduced by the province at the insistence of the Hudson's Bay Company and the mining companies posed a real threat to the Native community. In July 1851, encouraged by signs that the Ojibwa would not submit tamely to the threat, the missionary, at Little Pine's request, witnessed the signing of a contract for the cutting and sale of pine timber between the Sugar Island merchant Church and the Garden River band. The Ojibwa agreed to keep Church's establishment 'supplied with logs for sawing' for ten years, while the merchant would pay £25 annually to Little Pine to protect the timber from exploitation by other commercial agencies. The Ojibwa would be paid for logs they wished to sell, and Church promised to saw a certain quota of the timber hauled to his mill into boards for the band's use, free of charge.[51]

O'Meara felt the transaction to be a good one and recommended that Church receive government permission to buy timber from the band and arrange for the payment of timber dues to the Indian Department. Ironside, on the other hand, immediately opposed allowing any American to maintain close economic ties with British Native bands and criticized O'Meara for agreeing to the arrangement. In response, Shingwaukonse asked Allan Macdonell to assist his band in erecting a sawmill with the irons they had recently purchased with their annuity. It became clear that the nationality of the buyer was not really the issue, however, since Macdonell wrote to the Indian Department several times for permission to begin the mill but received no reply.[52]

The government still had to deflect public interest from the Aboriginal rights issues that had been raised in the press. For this reason, it took no immediate action on either the mining companies' grievances or Church's and Macdonell's petitions. In the interim, Shingwaukonse and eleven others of his band were brought to Toronto in May for eleven days, taken on tours of the Niagara region, housed and fed in a comfortable hotel, and then asked to apologize for their participation in the dispossession of the Quebec and Lake Superior Mining Association. Whether the required statement was obtained by coercion or not remains a moot point. Nevertheless, Little Pine and his party received an official pardon signed by the attorney general, Robert Baldwin, stating that the Queen's forgiveness had saved the Ojibwa from being 'indicted by the Mining Companies or their agents.'[53] Press releases, which stressed the kindly manner in which the Ojibwa delegation had been treated in the metropolis, apparently succeeded in quelling public curiosity about the Aboriginal rights issue.

Manipulation of Reserve Boundaries

Keating meanwhile had begun devising ways in which he might ingratiate himself with the influential Tory Arthur Rankin, and others in the mining field, by using his knowledge of the Native language and Native affairs to help the miners acquire title to their locations. While he failed to secure the position of protector of Native lands, he was successful in early 1852 in persuading the Crown Lands commissioner to employ him to work with the government surveyor, John Stoughton Dennis, in laying out reserve boundaries.[54] According to an Order-in-Council passed in June 1852, Keating was an assistant acting in an undefined capacity, but his goal was to have some say in the positioning of survey lines. To advertise his potential worth to the government as well as to further his own aims, he promised, whenever disputes arose between government agents and Native people, to contact the head chiefs and have them point out the boundaries of their reserves. In July he acquired the permission he coveted. Keating now wielded considerable power. Sir George Simpson's promise to assist the surveying party gave Keating added authority.[55] In August, the former mining explorer set out with Dennis to impose his own form of order on the frontier.

For the Hudson's Bay Company and Rankin and his associates, maintaining monopoly conditions meant opposing Macdonell, who continued his explorations around the Sault Ste Marie district with Native assistance.[56] To prevent Macdonell from becoming a serious competitor, Rankin and his party wanted uncontested access to two mineral locations, the first embracing the Clark location at Garden River, and the second lying just east of the Quebec and Lake Superior Mining Company operations at Mica Bay. Rankin looked to Keating to do as much as possible to end Native control in these two areas.

Keating's solution proved clever and deceitful. On 6 August, he and Dennis decided they would begin by surveying Little Pine's reserve and then work east along the coast of Georgian Bay, marking off reserves as they went.[57] Six days later, Keating held a council with the chief and principal men at Garden River during which a dispute arose over the proposed survey. Keating acted on his own interpretation of the manner in which the boundaries should be laid out – an interpretation which had little in common with the limits set out in the treaty. Under Keating's direction, Dennis ran the western boundary to Partridge Point, but at an angle S. 11 30' W. for 245 chains, instead of due north. This contradicted the treaty, which described the reserve as extending 'from Partridge Point to Masquenonge Bay, inland ten miles, throughout the whole distance ... and also [including] Squirrel Island.'[58]

In order to expand the size of the tract eastward to match his claim that the area of the reserve was approximately 130,000 acres, Keating had the eastern boundary run to Masquenonge Bay at an angle N. 44 30' E. for 1000 chains before it continued due north another 960 chains to a maple boundary. From this point, the border extended west 1260.5 chains until it intersected a line projected north from the western side of the Simpson location. It ran down this boundary 387 chains due south until it met and continued along the line running to Partridge Point. Keating's manipulations excluded almost all the original Clark location, except for a small triangle of land in the south-east corner, from Native proprietorship.[59]

Defiance, Self-Interest, and Decision Making: Native Responses to U.S. Indian Policy

The Ojibwa bands residing south of the American border had experienced an unsettled existence for almost half a century. Those who signed treaties with the U.S. government in 1837, 1842, and 1847 had no guarantee that they would be allowed to remain on their traditional territories. Even before the War of 1812, rivalries among the Hudson's Bay Company, the North West Company, and the American fur interests had created a turbulent dynamic which hampered attempts by western Native

leaders to develop linkages which would ensure long-term band autonomy. Often pressured to participate in conflicts which seemed to serve
neither their own nor their bands' interests, many chiefs had opted for
neutrality. This stance had influenced their activities during the War of
1812, when chiefs such as Eschekebugecoshe of Leech Lake had avoided
the conflict even when urged to join by the British authorities.[60]

Defiant demonstrations of group autonomy also permeated bands'
relationships with missionaries. Renewed emphasis on the conservative
Midéwiwin religion evidently arose as a reaction to the widespread cult
movements which flourished at the turn of the nineteenth century. This
probably accounted for the cool response of Eschekebugecoshe's Leech
Lake Pillagers to the teachings of the Reverend William Boutwell, the
Episcopalian missionary who had been sent to labour among them
between 1833 and 1837.[61] A similar defiance characterized Eschekebugecoshe's remarks to Schoolcraft following the U.S. government's implementation of its new trading policy in the 1830s.

Speaking of the authority exercised over his people's country for the
purpose of trade, he asserted: 'The Americans are not our masters; the
country is ours.' He next demanded that traders be allowed to visit his
band who would sell their goods more cheaply, and added that the
Ojibwa wanted more than one trader at each trading post.[62]

Such pronouncements reflected the views of many head chiefs residing
west of Lake Superior, near the headwaters of the Mississippi. Deep political rifts divided the south-western bands. The self-interest of one or two
major Native leaders contributed to these divisions, although irresponsible behaviour on the part of at least one government official was also a
contributing factor. According to Lynman Warren, a trader at La Pointe,
the Indian agent at St Peter's, Minnesota, had involved Hole-in-the-Day, a
Pillager, in a series of petty intrigues in order to secure Native agreement
to a land surrender in 1837. Hole-in-the-Day had come down twenty days
before the negotiations had even begun and, according to Warren, had
'in fact, made the treaty.'[63]

Hole-in-the-Day may have chosen to exploit opportunities for personal
aggrandizement when the occasion arose. Yet, even so, a strong desire for
personal advantage at the expense of others still remained unusual
among Native leaders. The adage that the sins of the fathers are visited on
the sons tended to be particularly true in the case of Hole-in-the-Day's
family, for his son, who succeeded him, also an anomaly among Ojibwa
power-holders, manipulated the course of treaty negotiations in his own
favour. The son first sponsored an abortive revolt against the American

government over a minor aspect of trade policy, then demanded, and received, the lion's share of annuity payments at a treaty made in 1867. His legacy was no less unsettling. James G. Smith, the anthropologist who has studied the career of Hole-in-the-Day the Younger, concluded that the 'self-aggrandizement, arrogance, and lack of consideration for the welfare of his band that characterized his career are remembered and partially account for the contemporary suspicion of the elected leaders [at White Earth, Minnesota, today].'[64]

While this Pillager chief's actions were an exception to the rule, the careers of the two men nevertheless indicate the kind of problems self-interested leaders could inflict on their communities. The activities of both had negative repercussions throughout the Upper Great Lakes region for many years. Tensions within and among bands, lingering in the wake of the elder Hole-in-the-Day's irresponsible politics in 1837, created an emotional climate wherein any chief could readily be suspected of seeking private advantage, to his group's cost.

Many bands had serious internal disputes about whether Ojibwa leaders should bow to the will of the state or rise to oppose it. Even Eschekebuge-coshe was suspected of complicity with the government, for, according to Schoolcraft, 'through the importunity of the sub-agent, who gave [him] ... a flag and medal ... [at a peace treaty with the Dakota, he] was obliged to flee his country for his life, and remain away nearly two years.'[65]

Nevertheless, most chiefs persevered in seeking remedies for their people's problems. In the late 1840s, several western band leaders formed a delegation to Washington asking for a retrocession of a tract they had formerly ceded under the La Pointe treaty of 1842. While Schoolcraft dismissed the delegation as a party organized by an entrepreneur to exhibit Native individuals in the metropolis for profit, at least one of these Ojibwa delegates, Kenisteno, would soon join the ranks of Ojibwa wishing to join Little Pine's settlement near Sault Ste Marie.[66] In April 1850, John S. Livermore, the American subagent stationed at La Pointe, Wisconsin,[67] sent out a circular warning that the Ojibwa might soon have to move westward. In response, Kenisteno decided to launch an appeal to his fellow Ojibwa on the Canadian side. In these tumultuous times leaders such as Eschekebugecoshe and Kenisteno saw in Shingwaukonse's vision of a Canadian 'homeland' hope that a refuge might yet be found away from the encroachments of resource exploration and exploitation. There was a chance, too, that political strength might issue peacefully out of the pursuit of new, long-term goals.

Little Pine, meanwhile, needed a person he could trust to act as an intermediary between the Ojibwa leaders and the Indian Department. Believing that Keating would act on their behalf, Shingwaukonse revealed to the agent the plans he was discussing with the western leaders. Not long afterward, Keating reported to his superiors that a wampum belt had been sent to Little Pine from the western chiefs heralding an exodus of American Ojibwa.[68] The chief had acted as a spokesman for this Native-controlled emigration scheme for more than a decade. Now the time had come to translate design into action. At the distribution of presents the same year, Ironside received a petition of the same nature from Muckedaypenasse, writing on behalf of six major south-western Ojibwa leaders – Eschekebugecoshe of Leech Lake; Iabanse or 'Little Buck' of Rice Lake; Kenisteno or 'The Cree' of Trout Lake; Okandikan or 'The Net Buoy' of Ontonogan; Ahmous or 'The Little Bee' of Lac du Flambeau; Shaganashense or 'The Little Englishman' of Grand Portage – and ten other prominent chiefs.[69] Ogista, who had acted as Shingwaukonse's *mishinawa* (messenger) in the matter, made arrangements to welcome the migrants onto the Sault lands as soon as the governor general granted his permission.

The news that Macdonell's earlier statements about a projected influx of Ojibwa to the north shores of Lakes Superior and Huron had not been wild fancy took government officials temporarily aback. Most felt that any increase in the concentration of Native people on the western frontier had to be stopped at once. On 27 August 1852, Superintendent General Bruce instructed Ironside to inform Shingwaukonse and Nebenagoching that the governor general strongly disapproved of their scheme. His communication closed with the admonition that the chiefs 'will not fail to perceive in this proposition a strong proof of the advantages they enjoy from being under the protection of the British Crown.'[70] To the head chiefs, this spuriously benevolent answer deprived them of one of their foremost leadership prerogatives: the right to provide a refuge for their allies in their time of need.

From the government standpoint, this evidence of a strong Native alliance highlighted a need for more stringent policy measures to suppress any nascent Native frontier movements. References to the general appeals that had once been extended by the Indian Department for American bands to remove to Manitoulin Island and elsewhere ceased after 1852. Instead, the department took a radically new line: that Manitoulin Island had always been reserved principally for Native people from the north shore of Lake Huron.[71] Most officials recognized that this was untrue, but endorsed the lie for reasons of political expediency and frontier security.

The next summer, Keating set out with James W. Bridgland to survey the Batchewana reserve on Lake Superior. Because of the value of the mineral deposits in the northern sector of this tract, Keating was not inclined to be generous in estimating its area. The treaty, he claimed, granted Nebenagoching 'more [territory] than the chief could ever [have] had a claim to.'[72] As usual, Keating remained on the outlook for simmering disagreements among bands, or else instigated conflicts that he then encouraged for his own purposes.

He did not have to wait long. The arbitrary political divisions Robinson had imposed in the north-eastern sector of Lake Superior in order to split up Little Pine's alliance had produced considerable discord, which Keating now exploited. He did so in part by proposing to bestow privileges on certain Lake Superior chiefs who had previously helped him explore for minerals. In 1853 he had recommended that Totomenai, for instance, should be allowed to lease mineral locations on the Michipicoten reserve on terms similar to those obtained in Cornwall, 'where the Lord of the Manor always retains the Royalty, tho' his returns vary with the profit of the mine.'[73] Another rift Keating exploited was between the Batchewana and Goulais Bay Native communities. These groups had petitioned the Indian Department to allow them to receive their annuities at Sault Ste Marie, since the rapids were closer to them than Michipicoten, where payment would be made by the Hudson's Bay Company.[74] These groups may also have wished to escape the company's monopoly control. When, in May 1852, without consulting the Native peoples, the government placed both the Batchewana and Goulais Bay bands under the authority of Nebenagoching, all three bands resented the decision, since each considered itself to be politically autonomous.[75] When Keating came among them in 1853, he argued that tensions arising from this source had engendered conflicts over group territorial boundaries. A wooden standard bearing the *dodem* of the Crane, which marked the southern limit of the Batchewana reserve tract, had been torn down by 'Bears,' who denied that the 'Cranes' had jurisdiction over them.[76] This 'dispute' gave Keating another opportunity to take control.

Keating maintained that it would be best merely to mark the extent of the Batchewana reserve by monuments, and thus leave the position of the survey lines on the ground ambiguous. He cited the expense and difficulty of transporting equipment over rocky terrain as reasons for this decision. The Native people would not care, he claimed, for they were only concerned about hunting and fishing. In his field reports he stressed the importance of the fisheries and argued that, if they could be secured for the Native people, the land could be taken from the Ojibwa without difficulty.[77]

This time Keating judged the area of the reserve to be 184 square miles. To enclose a space sufficient to embrace this extent of territory, he had Bridgland run a line from Wanakekenging, or Pancake Bay, on Lake Superior, N. 85 E. for eleven miles. A second and parallel boundary considerably south of the first extended from a point a short distance above Gros Cap for ten miles east into the interior. According to a map submitted to the Crown Lands Department in 1853, the eastern boundary, running north and south, intersected the two latter lines perpendicularly.[78] Marking the tract's boundaries in this way secured the mining companies' access to the mineral beds lying east of Mica Bay. By running the northern boundary just south of the iron and copper outcroppings, rather than 'ten miles throughout the whole,' which would have included these sites, Keating's mining associates could begin their staking of locations at once.

Silencing Macdonell on the Issue of Aboriginal Rights

Keating feared strenuous opposition from only one source – Allan Macdonell. Macdonell's continued petitioning early in 1853 for permission to aid the Ojibwa in erecting a sawmill demonstrated that he still considered himself an ally and representative of the Garden River band.[79] Keating knew he could count on local support to assist him in severing Macdonell's relations with the Ojibwa. In May 1853, Ironside had written to Bruce that the Ojibwa expected the lawyer to arrive at the Sault within a month. This 'frequent tampering with the Indians by unauthorized persons,' the agent emphasized, 'tends more than anything else to do away with that influence over them which it is necessary should be possessed by all those who have the care of them and their well-being at heart.'[80] The Indian agent also complained that O'Meara and the Anglican catechist, Buhkwujjenene, had emerged as leading instigators of Native discontent over the terms of the treaty. Effectively countering the missionary, however, would prove more difficult than silencing Macdonell. It would be by indirectly threatening the lawyer that the government would finally procure a halt to Little Pine's plans for the immediate alteration of the Robinson Treaties.

Throughout the spring of 1853, Shingwaukonse was busy preparing for his journey to England. In March, Wilson had proclaimed the chief to be afflicted with gangrene in the back and 'not expected to live,'[81] but by early June the old warrior had sufficiently roused himself to set out for Toronto. He had been advanced £70 by Church to supplement the £200 or more the Garden River Ojibwa had raised for the expedition. He also had made arrangements with Native leaders in communities along the north shore of Lake Huron to contribute further sums as the delegation progressed eastward. Shingwaukonse had been authorized by his people to apprise Macdonell of their plans regarding the treaty and to request legal advice before proceeding on to the Atlantic Coast. Yet in this last attempt to gain recognition for his vision, the chief was to face only bitter shock and disappointment.

The cause of this sudden reversal in Little Pine's activities lay in a bill introduced into the Legislative Assembly by the attorney general, Robert Baldwin, regarding the administration of justice in the unorganized parts of Upper Canada. George Brown of the *Globe* in Toronto had sent Allan Macdonell a copy of the bill in April. 'It appears to me that it would have been ... appropriately entitled an Act to procure the conviction of Allan Macdonell,' its recipient responded gravely to Brown.[82] Clause nine warned that 'any person inciting Indians or half-breeds frequenting or residing in such tracts of country ... to the disturbance of the public peace ... shall be guilty of a felony, and upon conviction thereof shall be sentenced for not more than five years nor less than two years in the Provincial Penitentiary.'[83] This, for the lawyer, was bad enough, but given his idealism and deep concern for the Native peoples, other sections disturbed him as greatly. He found clause ten particularly offensive, as it maintained that a sheriff or magistrate had the power to choose jurors without reference to the mode of selection prescribed by the Upper Canada Jurors Act. But most of all, the bill prescribed severe penalties for anyone associated with the campaign for Native rights. Macdonell was taken aback, since he had hoped for the extension of a legal system which would enhance the rights of the Native community. Many Métis, including the 'Birons, La Fonds, La Batt, Le Blanc, Fontaine, Jolinaux & & ...' had been educated in Montreal or elsewhere, and among them, he charged, 'may be found men superior to Mr. Atty. Genl. in education as well as intellect.'[84]

In April 1853, Macdonell could still afford to condemn the bill as a 'high handed act' of tyranny. Only after it had passed into law on 14 June 1853 as *An Act to Make Better Provision for the Administration of Justice in the Unorganized Tracts of Country in Upper Canada* (16 Vict. Cap. 176)[85] did he fully realize that, though the Ojibwa had received a pardon, he had not. In consequence, he might be tried within the Provisional District of Algoma under the terms of the new act. This meant that, for his security, he would have to adopt a radically different relationship to Little Pine than he had formerly assumed. In a letter dated 15 June – the day after the act became law – Macdonell informed Bruce that he had met with Shingwaukonse and three other Ojibwa at his Toronto residence, and had branded the chief's plans to continue to England as 'madness and folly.'[86]

Macdonell feared the consequences of even the slightest concurrence with Little Pine's scheme. 'How the project originated with them I know not,' he cautiously proceeded, 'nor have I enquired of them, nor would I have volunteered to advise them at all did I not feel convinced that the advice which I have tendered them will not be at variance with your views of the matter ...,' In this tortuous manner Macdonell sought to extricate himself from an awkward position. His letter exhibited neither the pithy turns of phrase nor the clarity of argument of his earlier communications to the Indian Department. Given their situation, he concluded ponderously, the Native people had better commit themselves exclusively to farming.[87]

A Legacy of Indeterminacy

Following this disappointing encounter with their former ally, Shingwaukonse and his party left Toronto to return to Garden River. Their despondency may have been alleviated in part by the excitement and religious fervour of a Methodist camp meeting held in August on Waubashine Island, lying south-east of their village. George McDougall's report of the occasion hinted at none of the bitterness which must have been felt by the delegation on their return from Toronto. The missionary lauded the drawing power of the Methodist gospel, which had rallied over forty Native converts from Saugeen under the missionary Conrad Van Dusen, sixteen bateaux of people from the Mahyahmakong (Pequaming) mission at L'Anse, and several families from west of the Keweenaw Peninsula. Amid what he viewed as sublime natural surroundings, McDougall confidently asserted that Methodist preachers like Peter Jones expunged all traces of evil 'superstition' to reveal everywhere the miraculous workings of the hand of God. To McDougall, the Garden River community in 1853 had a capacity for 'piety, frugality and industry' which surpassed all other Methodist Native missions within Canada.[88]

Although emotional religious appeals might give a temporary lift to morale, material progress without legal rights or protection was only a superficial boon. During 1853, the Native community encountered a series of obstacles to further economic development. Every major resource field was affected. Shingwaukonse complained that, due to pressures from commercial fishing organizations, his people had been 'obliged to change their encampment in consequence of threats [which] ... prevented [them] from making their usual fishing which is their chief dependence for the winter.'[89] Even though both Wilson and Keating advocated government reservation of traditional Native fishing grounds as compensation for depriving the Ojibwa of almost all other important sources of income, nothing was ever done about these recommendations.

Meanwhile, local mining companies continued to petition the Crown Lands Department to prohibit Indians from cutting timber on the mineral locations, which at Garden River included the entire waterfront. The only secure claim the Ojibwa had to their land base lay in a letter written in 1850 to Superintendent Bruce by William B. Robinson pledging that the government would not sell the Simpson and Lemoine locations. Because of the close association between McDougall and Church, the miners directed their accusations about taking logs primarily at the Methodist Ojibwa, who were punished harshly over the next four years for what their missionary had formerly viewed as 'industry.' William Palmer even demanded that the government make an example of their leaders.[90]

Shingwaukonse immediately desired to be informed of the exact nature and standing of the privileges exercised by the various mining companies.[91] He believed that Cuthbertson, Maitland, and Rankin had been selling pine off his reserve too cheaply. In October, Shingwaukonse had been told that not one of the agencies claiming locations had paid the £1130 still owing on each allotment of 6400 acres, but this did not mean that pressure from companies seeking title to the locations would abate. Keating's intervention in the survey had seen to that. With his assistance, the Clark location had been freed from Native proprietorship. Now that Rankin and his associates had a strong bid to a claim at Garden River, they were not likely to tolerate any campaigns for Native rights.

Soon afterwards, Shingwaukonse entered the final stage of his illness, with Wilson arranging for him to be placed under medical supervision.[92] Even so, he continued to work to realize his vision. Among his eldest sons, Ogista was a Methodist, Buhkwujjenene an Anglican, and Tegoosh a Roman Catholic. The diverse religious allegiances of his sons were of less concern to Little Pine, however, than their ability to maintain useful links between his band and agencies and institutions external to Ojibwa society. He therefore dictated a form of 'will' to James Chance, who had learned the Ojibwa language from O'Meara, in which he requested Chance to ensure that the Anglican Church upheld Buhkwujjenene's status as chief.[93] He then distributed his medals to Ogista and Buhkwujjenene, thus denoting that he wished them to carry on his work. The terms of the Robinson Treaties had made Shingwaukonse uneasy. He had sought to do everything he could to restore to the Ojibwa people some measure of their independence within the nation state. When he died, in March 1854, he transmitted this intensity of purpose to his sons.

In 1853, Chance took over direction of the Anglican mission (left vacant since Gustavus Anderson's departure from Garden River in October 1849) and immediately set out to establish Buhkwujjenene as head chief, in compliance with Little Pine's last wishes. With O'Meara's backing, Chance broached the subject at once. He mentioned it to Ironside and other government officials at the chief's funeral, as Shingwaukonse's body was being laid in its traditional wooden enclosure on the west bank of the Garden River, with a long black pennant suspended from a pole nearby to symbolize the death of a head chief. But Ironside and Wilson resented Chance's interference, remembering the trouble they had previously had with O'Meara's dogged support for Buhkwujjenene's decision to go to England with Little Pine. Moreover, Ironside and Wilson had already chosen Ogista as their candidate for Little Pine's successor. When Chance pressed the point, Wilson snapped at him, heedless of the solemnity of the occasion, saying 'I'll be d——d if it shall be so.'[94]

On 10 December 1855, Ironside recommended to Viscount Bury, Elgin's successor as governor general, that Ogista be recognized as head man of the Garden River band in accord with 'the well understood custom' that the eldest son succeeded the father.[95] The Indian Department replied that Chance had already informed them differently[96] and there the matter stood. The local government agents and the Anglican missionaries each regarded a different man as head chief. The Indian Department decided not to interfere at once, but to wait upon events.

Chapter Six

Testing the Untried Mettle: Ogista's Rise to Leadership

A Master Strategist

Unlike his father, Ogista could not demonstrate his appropriateness for leadership in the traditional manner by pointing to his past war exploits or claiming the support of a council of elders. Oral traditions at Garden River hold that Ogista initially not only lacked experience but also failed to attain the vision necessary to assume the heavy burden inherited from his father. He needed 'power,' yet when he fasted as a youth he had grown ill, so he had attempted to gain respect by adopting an air of bravado. His occasional indecisiveness, too, confused his followers. He was successful, however, in maintaining his father's contacts with leaders of the western bands and, through the Methodist movement, with notable Native individuals at Saugeen and Rama in Ontario, and at L'Anse in Michigan.[1]

Ogista focused on bringing Western education within the reach of the Ojibwa people, in order to strengthen and enhance Native culture rather than to supersede Native values. Because of his requests for educational assistance, Methodist missionaries thought he supported their policy of assimilation[2] and were surprised when, in 1857, he transferred his allegiance elsewhere. While his sudden changes in stance on such matters sometimes provoked conflict within the Garden River community, the band recognized that the chief's strengths outweighed his failings. If he proved weak as a policy maker, he shone as a strategist. He deflected threats to his group's prerogatives by at first appearing to favour his adversaries' requests and then, when the time was right, demanding important concessions as a condition of his support. He was most successful in negotiating at the local level, where his charismatic intensity impressed both Indian agents and missionaries. It was not until well after

Confederation that the substance and not merely the style of his speeches gained the ear of senior government bureaucrats.

Confronting Monopoly Strength

Ogista's bellicose, ill-timed actions in 1854 soon attracted attention. Shingwaukonse's death had left a vacuum in the existing power relationships among Native leaders within the Upper Great Lakes region. In an attempt to gain recognition as Little Pine's successor, Ogista, supported by Nebenagoching, led an expedition in the fall of 1854 against the Quebec and Lake Superior Mining Association's operations on Michipicoten Island.[3] During this affair, concealed Native marksmen fired several shots past working miners. In response, the Crown Lands agent, Joseph Wilson, notified his superiors that steps might have to be taken to subdue what he saw as a discontented and potentially volatile Native population. When there was no immediate reply to his appeal, in 1855 the agent and magistrate turned to the Hudson's Bay Company for help in enforcing law and order on the frontier.

While Ogista's and Nebenagoching's expedition of 1854 may have shown the Native community that Shingwaukonse's son could pursue a strong course of action, the attack on the Michipicoten mine could not have been undertaken at a worse time from the standpoint of Native interests. Wilson used the incident as justification for establishing a police force at Sault Ste Marie for the purpose of arresting 'rowdies' and anyone who opposed government resource policies. Meanwhile the Hudson's Bay factor at La Cloche, Wemyss Simpson, saw the episode as an excuse to solicit government backing to prevent free trade, ensuring his company's monopoly and keeping the Sault bands, like the bands west of Sault Ste Marie, economically dependent on him.

Sir George Simpson planned to relocate the La Cloche post to Little Current on Manitoulin Island, since the La Cloche station stood on a mine site he was interested in developing. Simpson realized that securing government permission to reside on unceded Indian territory at Little Current would allow his company to control the sale of fuel and supplies to steamers plying the waters along the northern coast of Lake Huron. When informed by Wilson of the attack on the Michipicoten mine, Sir George Simpson sent a petition to the Executive Council warning of impending trouble among the Native bands of the Upper Great Lakes.[4] Allowing the Hudson's Bay Company to hire Native labour at Little Current, he argued, would set a precedent for the kind of relationship which might be established between the company and Native people elsewhere along the coast, and would ensure peace. Although economic dependency had not characterized the Lake Huron trade during the early decades of the nineteenth century, Simpson nevertheless claimed that outbreaks of violence had never occurred when his company 'used to have exclusive control.'[5]

Wilson, Wemyss Simpson, and Simpson's father-in-law, George Ironside,[6] upheld Simpson's decision to move the trading post from La Cloche to Little Current.[7] The only dissenting voice came from O'Meara, who in 1854 had encouraged George Abatossaway, an educated Ottawa from Mackinac Island, to move with his band of about one hundred people to Little Current and open a store for the steamer trade. Abatossaway, who had been considering joining the Garden River band, decided instead to follow the missionary's advice, and within a few years had developed a prosperous business.[8] By 1856, both the Indian superintendent, L. Oliphant, and Froome Talford, a commissioner involved in a special investigation into Native concerns in the province in 1855, recommended that government protection should be extended to Abatossaway's enterprise.[9] But the government's position had changed radically as a result of Simpson's petition to the Executive Council, and O'Meara, knowing that Simpson's 'peace-keeping' arguments were a cover for his scheme to destroy competition, feared for the economic future of the Little Current band.

A new wave of resource exploration after 1856 triggered competition between the local land agent and the missionaries for control of the Garden River reserve. To avoid being manipulated by either side, Ogista formed temporary alliances with the first one, then the other. His continuous defence of his band's prerogatives provided room to manoeuvre for other members of his group, especially his brother Buhkwujjenene, allowing them to develop creative resource policies. At the same time, the group also had ways of calling their leader to account when he disregarded the interests of his people. A head man suspected of complicity with one external agency or another might be compelled to declare his position openly at a public council. Their ability to ensure a reciprocity of interest between leadership and group enabled bands in the Sault Ste Marie area to withstand forces seeking to undermine their decision-making powers and their political standing.

The challenges facing these groups rapidly intensified. Following the appointment of Robert Pennefather to the position of Superintendent of the Indian Department in 1856, the Indian Department fell increasingly under the influence of the Hudson's Bay Company and the mining interests. When Wilson again petitioned for troops to aid in the suppression of crime in the Algoma District, the Executive Council immediately dispatched a sergeant and six men of the Pensioner Corps to act as special constables under the magistrate's direction.[10] Meanwhile, in support of Simpson's policies, Ironside at Manitowaning purposely delayed annuity payments, on the grounds that lack of money over the winter would keep the Native people from purchasing goods from free traders.[11] The government justified its policy of depriving the band at Little Current of its main source of livelihood by arguing that, as all Native people on unceded territory had a 'joint interest in the soil,' no one group could appropriate profits from communally owned lands and resources for its exclusive benefit.[12] The Hudson's Bay Company was subject to no such restriction, and in October 1856, the Executive Council passed an Order-in-Council granting Sir George Simpson permission to proceed with his new trading establishment.[13] Simpson and his allies also argued that, as whole bands had disappeared into the interior and never returned to the coast, monies reserved for them by the Hudson's Bay Company out of their annuities had been accumulating. To keep money circulating in districts controlled by the company's monopoly, it was maintained that this surplus capital should 'be considered forfeited' and distributed among individuals most nearly related to the persons who were reported missing.[14] The principle that all Native individuals held a joint interest in annuity monies, as well as in land and resources, deterred groups from making major expenditures on tools or other equipment.

As a further hindrance to the development of Aboriginal enterprise, Pennefather sent a circular to all Native communities in May of 1856 stating that any individuals who were party to an 'irregular or private bargain' to sell land, timber, or other major merchantable resource would forfeit their annuities.[15] This new stipulation weakened the Ojibwa's defence against external encroachment on their land and resources. In response, mining companies, believing the Ojibwa to be rendered economically impotent by the new policy, redoubled their efforts to secure the mineral locations. According to the Methodist missionary at Garden River, the government's stance had dealt the band a harsh blow morally and psychologically. Industry, the Reverend George McDougall noted in 1857, had ceased entirely as a result of the Ojibwa's uncertainty about their lands. Prices of staples such as pork and flour had skyrocketed because of the mining boom, and even the mission faced financial difficulties. McDougall admitted that these distressing circumstances weakened his motivation to work. 'The past,' he wrote nostalgically, 'were seasons of pleasing remembrance.'[16]

Pressure for the Surrender of the Reserves

Rankin's agent, Palmer, recommended the abolition of the reserve system. Such land, he asserted in 1853, constituted hindrances to progress and the public good. Because of Canada's willingness to set aside large tracts for the Native people, shutting out entrepreneurs, the United States had drawn ahead in the race for resource development. On the Batchewana tract lay valuable fisheries, iron, gold, and copper outcroppings, and 'not less than one million acres of the finest arable land.' Palmer impressed upon Froome Talford the belief that Canada's destiny lay in 'throwing open the portals ... to the energies of our conquering race.' According to Palmer, the best resource areas in the country lay near Sault Ste Marie. As for the Native people, he stated, they sit around in a 'state of starvation ... too lazy to set their nets ... [or] to plant a few potatoes on shore. In fact they are but the feeble remnant of a wretched mongrel brood that in a few years will be extinct.'[17]

The Ojibwa could expect little government protection from the consequences of resource policies implemented on their reserves by the Crown Lands Department, of which the Indian Department was to constitute a subdivision after 1860. Wilson's combined roles as Crown Lands agent, collector of customs, magistrate, and protector of Native lands gave him immense power over resources on reserves.

On behalf of Palmer, Maitland, and Cuthbertson, Wilson informed the Indian Department that Allan Macdonell still conducted explorations in a manner which interfered with the smooth operation of the reserve system, which was designed to isolate the Native people from the course of national development. The magistrate had been unable to pry any information from Nebenagoching concerning Macdonell's activities, but he had convinced Mishkeash, subchief at Goulais Bay, to talk. From this source he had learned that Macdonell had entered into an agreement with Nebenagoching regarding several mining locations, a contract, Wilson informed the government, he intended to discourage. By promising to establish a commercial fishery at Goulais Bay, Wilson persuaded Mishkeash to observe and report on Macdonell's movements and transactions. In September 1857, the agent had written to the Indian Department for permission to lease a portion of the Batchewana reserve for a fishery station, but his request was refused. He nevertheless allowed a small group of American entrepreneurs to carry on operations illegally, in order to retain Mishkeash as an informant.[18]

Wilson outdid even Keating in the granting and withholding of privileges to further his own goals. To procure Nebenagoching's demotion from leadership, the agent sent his departmental superiors a petition from the Goulais Bay band containing complaints against their head chief.[19] The foremost of these grievances concerned the payment of annuity monies by Nebenagoching to Ojibwa who had accepted treaty money and other assistance from the United States.[20] When Nebenagoching learned that Pennefather had been enquiring into his handling of band finances, the head chief in April submitted a testimony accounting for all the monies under his charge, clearing himself of the accusations made against him. While Wilson claimed to be committed to the preservation of peace and order, his activities produced the opposite result. Wilson promoted Mishkeash, while Ironside upheld Nebenagoching. The Batchewana chief and subchief were thus embroiled in the competition between Wilson and Ironside during 1857 for the coveted position of commissioner at the upcoming treaty negotiations. Strains and stresses produced by Wilson's favouring of Mishkeash over Nebenagoching and his promotion of the illegal fishery at Goulais Bay against the wishes of the majority of the Batchewana band led to an outbreak of violence. At a festivity held near the Goulais River by the owners of the illicit enterprise, Apequash, Mishkeash's brother, was accused of pandering to Wilson. Enraged, Apequash stabbed his accuser in the chest. This incident frightened Wilson, who feared an investigation should the injured man die.[21] Fortunately for Wilson, two of the men involved in the illegal fishery were doctors, and the knife had glanced off a rib, so the man's life was saved.

Macdonell encouraged the Native community to prepare and sign a petition demanding that the magistrate be removed from office. Intending once again to clear himself, Wilson became increasingly draconian in his dealings with the Aboriginal population, at the same time maligning Macdonell 'for wanting to join the country and become a true half-breed.'[22] Wilson knew that speed in effecting the surrender of the reserves was essential to enable the mining interests he supported to acquire further locations in addition to those Keating had helped them secure. In order to prevent further difficulties, Wilson set out to silence Nebenagoching by threatening the head chief with penitentiary should he reveal anything of the agent's affairs to other government officials.[23]

In response to pressure from the mining interests, the Canadian government pushed for the surrender of the entire Batchewana and Garden River reserves. When approached by Commissioners Talford and Worthington on the subject, Nebenagoching at first agreed to the cession, provided that the Batchewana Bay and Goulais Bay people could retain

reserves near their traditional fisheries. Indian Affairs refused the suggestion: the tract promised to be far too valuable for the purposes of lumbering and mining. Keating, appointed commissioner in charge of obtaining
the surrenders, imposed his own conditions, as usual, on the negotiating
forum. Should the Batchewana or Goulais bands refuse to cede their
lands, he maintained, they would simply be left out of the compensation
payment of £300 offered for the Batchewana tract.[24]

Mishkeash at this point found an unexpected ally in the Baptist missionary James D. Cameron, Jr. A man given to vehement expression of his
views, Cameron roundly denounced to Pennefather Keating's handling
of the whole affair, and stressed that the Native community no longer
trusted the commissioner. Keating, Cameron fumed, had proven beyond
a doubt that he would go to any lengths to aid his mining associates. During negotiations held in September of 1857 he had even concluded a
council by shouting at Mishkeash that he cared little whether the Goulais
Bay group signed the treaty or not, and branded the whole band as 'fools
without prefixes.'[25]

Given the power of the mining lobby, there was no way in which the
politically unrepresented Ojibwa could hope to retain their reserves in
their entirety. In order to placate the dissident bands at Goulais and
Batchewana, Keating, Wilson, and Simpson decided to grant them the
option to reserve a sum from their compensation payment to purchase
eighty acres of land per family. The Batchewana tract would thus be freed
from Native control and the Ojibwa compelled, at their own expense, to
incorporate into the Western system of landholding.

By this time, Mishkeash realized that he had few alternatives and
agreed to abide by these terms, since even Cameron seemed satisfied with
the compromise.[26] Wilson had proven to be a false friend to the Goulais
Bay chief over the fishery, since it became apparent that, once the miners
staked their claims, the Batchewana reserve would be ceded from under
both the American entrepreneurs and their Native associates. Because of
the illicit nature of their fishery operations, neither party would be able
to seek legal redress.

There were still two matters, however, which prevented the miners
from securing their claims. First, Nebenagoching refused to have anything to do with Keating, stressing that he and his people would negotiate
only with the superintendent general of the Indian Department.[27] Second, while Ogista had agreed to allow each family belonging to Nebenagoching's band to settle on forty acres at Garden River, he made it
clear that the balance of the reserve lying beyond the allotments to be

surveyed must not be taken from the Ojibwa. The government objected. As a compromise, Keating suggested the surrender of only the sector of the Garden River reserve north and east of Echo Lake and the Echo River, an area that included the Wilson mine site, among others. This surrender could be achieved most rapidly, he believed, by allowing the Ojibwa permits to cut timber on their reserve if they agreed to the government's terms, but withholding such 'privileges' if the band refused.[28]

Wilson had already demonstrated that he could be swift and determined in punishing offenders who cut timber on mineral locations on the reserves. In February 1857, when Charles Biron was caught by the magistrate and his military pensioners removing 'six long pine planks' from the Elliot site, Wilson held Biron up as an example of how 'half-breeds' who had 'been permitted to receive Indian presents, partake of annuity and reside on the reserve' plundered valuable resources.[29] His allegation that most offenders were Métis were of doubtful validity. For similar offences, he had previously levied harsh penalties on the less adversarial – and hence more vulnerable – Methodist Ojibwa, compelling them to emigrate to Sugar Island, Saugeen, and L'Anse. As a result, there were far fewer Ojibwa families living at Garden River than in former years.

Ironside and Wilson worked together to force further Ojibwa removals. Pennefather had requested that lists be compiled of individuals whose attachments to bands passed through their mother's line, a formidable task, since so many of the younger generation had exercised matrilineal rights in becoming members.[30] Because Ironside knew that the Superintendent General's primary goal was to reduce the size of bands on the frontier, rather than to establish hard and fast principles regulating band membership, he decided, instead, to split the Garden River band into two groups based on occupational, rather than genealogical criteria. Family heads received an ultimatum: either they remained in Canada and did not cut timber, or else they removed to the United States and relinquished all attachment to the reserve and the Canadian government.[31]

It was a hard choice for those confronted with the decision. Incentives to move to the United States had briefly existed when rumours spread that Native peoples might be given the vote in the 1856 Michigan elections.[32] Prior to the election day, American citizenship and the vote had come to be viewed as a panacea for all the trials the Native peoples had recently experienced – a hope which died when the Ojibwa were barred from exercising the franchise. Following their disappointment in 1856, some Ojibwa hoped to hasten the extension of the vote by volunteering to fight in the Civil War.[33] Although Ojibwa did volunteer, even this dream faded. Taking advantage of politically unrepresented Native land holders, A. Fitch, the corrupt and arrogant Indian agent at the American Sault, distributed Ojibwa allotments to his political cronies for patronage purposes, while barring avenues by which the Native peoples could sue for redress.[34] In the midst of this turmoil, bands which could live near Church's establishment on Sugar Island or attach themselves to one of the larger mission settlements in the Upper Great Lakes area gained a measure of protection from speculators, dishonest officials, and the threats of the mining companies. McDougall protested feebly but felt he could do little in the long run against the powerful clique headed by Wilson, and in 1857 he left Garden River. No protection was provided by his successors, Thomas Hurlburt, David Sawyer, and Allan Salt,[35] and the Methodist mission limped on with a rapidly declining population until it closed in 1866. Meanwhile, Biron's arrest precipitated a major clash between Ogista and the Crown Lands agent. During this confrontation, Ogista, possibly due to the political lethargy of the Methodist movement at Garden River and grieved by the death of a son sent home from Alnwick Industrial School with tuberculosis,[36] turned against Methodism and its assimilationist attitudes. After 1857, he dispensed with missionary backing, carrying on alone in his fight against the assault on his people's rights and territorial prerogatives.

When Keating approached the chief in the fall of 1857 about licences to cut timber, to be granted in exchange for the Garden River tract, Ogista shouted at him, 'No white man shall plant his foot on our Reserve and carry on any work there.'[37] Wilson endeavoured to crush this resistance by preventing the Ojibwa from removing any timber whatsoever, and by early spring the next year the leader seemed to have 'broken.' The band could not hold out, with the high price of food, and many families were starving. On 2 February, Wilson forwarded a petition, dated 26 January 1858, in which Ogista and Buhkwujjenene agreed to uphold an official prohibition against the taking of timber by any Native person who was in any way associated with Church's enterprise. Despite the Ojibwa's hardships, Ogista still insisted on one condition: only after his band had received the money owing from the sale of the mining locations would he agree to surrender land or resources.[38]

The petition raised a storm of controversy in May between the Crown Lands Department and the Indian Department. L.S. Sicotte, the commissioner of Crown Lands, claimed that the 'spirit of the [Robinson-Huron] Treaty gave government complete control over conditions' under which the locations were to be sold. Any Native intervention in the process,

Sicotte argued, could only be deemed detrimental to the national good.[39] Yet William Spragge, deputy superintendent of the department, contended that the locations had already been forfeited and that the initial deposit of £150 should be paid to the Ojibwa.[40] To Sicotte, Spragge's suggestion constituted political heresy. Most of the deposit money, he argued, had been spent on surveying the reserves, while the Ojibwa's 'violence' against miners on Lake Superior invalidated their claim to the remainder. 'Mercy might seem meet' with regard to the government's extension of the deadline for the final payments on the locations, he concluded, for it was important to the public interest 'not to abandon the reserves to the Indians, but rather to obtain all their property.'[41]

Pennefather eventually healed the breach between Sicotte and Spragge by reminding both contenders that to ensure rapid progress towards surrender 'it would not be advisable to hamper any negotiations ... with subconditions as the recognition of these [Ojibwa] mining claims.[42] As an added incentive to compel Native compliance, the Superintendent General directed Ironside to inform the Ojibwa that the government would no longer fund any medical, school, or contingency expenses out of annuities. The sale of their land would be used to form a fund to provide for such expenditures.[43]

Richard Carney: Unwitting and Unwilling Champion of Aboriginal Rights

Keating's and Wilson's shrewd plans for the eventual abolition of both the Garden River and Batchewana reserves collapsed because of the unforeseen intervention of a third party, the merchant and magistrate Richard Carney. In 1856, Carney had arrived at Sault Ste Marie from Owen Sound and had been appointed, like Wilson and Simpson, as a protector of Indian lands. A well-meaning but hardly bold or creative thinker, Carney viewed the extinguishment of the reserve system as a giant leap forward for 'civilization' in Algoma. To Carney, order on the frontier would accompany the surveying of farm lots for the promotion of settlement and the enforcement of regulations for cutting timber. On 3 September 1858, he set out for Garden River with orders from the Indian Department to organize a mode of collecting dues on timber cut on the reserve. His report of a council held with Ogista and Buhkwuj-jenene indicated that he had never before encountered Ojibwa with such a sophisticated grasp of policy making or such a strong determination to pursue their goal of securing their community's future.[44]

Ogista demanded to see Carney's credentials, which the magistrate produced. Then, with Allan Salt acting as interpreter, the chief recounted the difficulties his band had experienced in having their rights to land and resources recognized. He began by showing the magistrate the letter Sir George Arthur had sent to his father in 1839 promising to provide farming assistance. Such aid, Ogista stressed, had never come, even though Little Pine had agreed to convert to Christianity. Ogista made it clear that his people's adherence to the Christian faith depended as much on their economic welfare as on their spiritual morale. Prior to 1853 they had had at least some hope for a better future; but since the prohibition on cutting wood, the very survival of the settlement was in jeopardy: '[When] the Constable seized Logs and Boards ... we gave up working, and we were at a loss what to do to sustain life, so in consequence of this many ... went away, going to different parts, so the Govt. breaks up our settlement and we are still in the same way, the Indians are scattered, those that went away have not come back. There are Three Churches here and all are nearly empty.'[45]

Buhkwujjenene, the next speaker, asserted that although the Robinson Treaties stipulated that the distribution of annuities was to occur at a place and time convenient to all concerned, Ironside had charged the band for transporting the money to the Sault. Payments were always late. Why is it, Buhkwujjenene asked, when the journey to Toronto took only two days, that the Ojibwa's 'money winters just half way?'[46] He further recounted that under the new system of distributing annuities on a per-capita basis, each person received less than one dollar, while the system itself prevented the band from acquiring a surplus for development. To enable his group to monitor their own expenditures, Buhkwujjenene wanted the government to furnish annual accounts to the band and establish a date when the Ojibwa could expect their annuities each year.

> Resuming the role of spokesman, Ogista declared that the Ojibwa regarded their surrender of rights over territory and resources in 1850 to have in no way detracted from prerogatives they continued to exercise pertaining to their reserves: I know the boundary lines of my Reserve, and within them is my Land, the reason I reserved this was that I might have the benefit of it, it is my property, it was not given to the Govt ... [From the] Land that was surrendered beyond the Reserves I have never taken anything nor do I know that my Boys have taken anything off it.[47]

The head chief stated that he had been collecting information regarding several mineral locations on the Garden River reserve which had been in the process of being sold to Montreal companies for more than a decade. Six hundred dollars had been paid on each site, but none of the interested parties had so far completed the conditions of sale. Ogista thus deemed the locations to be forfeit, and demanded the principal and interest to be paid immediately to his band. He also explained that his father had ordered sawmill irons, costing $136, out of the annuity, but that government intervention had prevented the band from setting up its own logging industry. He desired the Indian Department to exchange the irons for a yoke of oxen. Finally, he asked Carney if there were any possibility of a merchant settling at Garden River in competition with Church.

Carney replied that such was unlikely since Church was too well established, and maintained instead that regulations should allow the band to continue trading with the Sugar Island merchant. Naïvely, the official believed that the main problem in selling wood to Church lay with the absence of a clear policy for levying dues on timber taken from reserves. He also sympathized with Ogista's view regarding the mining locations. It was 'preposterous' to expect any business person to sell valuable property on being told that all the proceeds had already been expended in surveying the location. The money should be paid to the band.[48]

Carney also tried to be a peacemaker between sectors of the original Garden River band divided by external policies, although at times he felt almost overwhelmed by the complexity of the problems involved in the task. Tensions arising from Ironside's exclusion of Ojibwa families who had traded with Church, or who had accepted money or land from the American government, sparked antagonisms which led to witchcraft scares.[49] The magistrate soon learned that the American head chiefs, Oshawano and Kebay Nodin, had been trying to exclude Piabetassung and his band from sharing in whatever monetary compensation might be paid by Washington for the surrender of the American reserve at the rapids.[50] Piabetassung was not accepted by leaders or their allies on either side of the international border, and he asked the magistrate to help him keep his status as a 'British' chief, even though he lived on Sugar Island. Since to assist Piabetassung would contravene government policy, there was little Carney could do. Ironside's superiors had allowed him to use his own discretion in striking names off the annuity lists, and in so doing, Ironside had tried to gauge the temper of the Garden River and Thessalon Ojibwa towards Piabetassung and his band, whose interests were closely tied to Church's trading establishment. Ogista's growing determination to sever all economic ties with Church and to form alternative trade relationships on the Canadian side prevented reconciliation between the two sectors of Little Pine's formerly unified band. Intermarriage and business transactions between the two groups continued, but politically each band would henceforth remain autonomous.[51]

Carney had better success in instigating a system at Garden River of evaluating improvements to 'property' made by Ojibwa individuals who had decided, under the pressure of Ironside's ultimatums, to move to Sugar Island. Buhkwujjenene had asked the magistrate to protect a number of houses from being dismantled or otherwise severely injured by those evacuating them, since their former inhabitants had made the choice to leave of their own free will. Their occupants, Buhkwujjenene explained to the magistrate, had shared in prerogatives associated with membership in Little Pine's band but, by their departure, had demonstrated loss of confidence in band policy and so forfeited all their rights to band-controlled resources.

This bothered Carney, who felt that Buhkwujjenene's stance was unfair. To encourage what he termed a 'better spirit,' as well as prevent material losses to certain individuals, he reminded Buhkwujjenene that those who had left the band had also increased each remaining member's share of the annuity, so that those moving into the houses should be willing to pay for improvements. Buhkwujjenene hesitated in replying, since he suspected that such an externally imposed scheme might undermine the band leader's authority over the allocation of houses. After consultation with others, however, he finally agreed to Carney's suggestion, provided that the head chief and his principal men were notified whenever such a transaction took place. In this manner, the Garden River band's leadership acquired new regulatory powers.[52]

As a result, try as he might during 1858 to promote Ojibwa assimilation into mainstream society, events forced Carney to suggest arrangements that would strengthen and develop local band government. His support of Ogista's claim to the mineral locations unwittingly led him to uphold the principle of Aboriginal right, which immediately aroused the ire of Wilson and his clique. Wilson contemptuously treated Carney's good-natured overtures of assistance to the bands as unwarranted interference in matters which should not concern him, Carney at first took the insult personally, rather than seeing that it reflected Wilson's stress on the utility of according Native people low status, especially with regard to rights over merchantable resources. To signify that his intentions were honourable, and that he had no interest in becoming entangled in what he viewed as petty power politics, Carney requested the Indian Department to send a black pennant to Garden River in his name to be suspended over Little Pine's grave to replace one that had blown away. Even so, Wilson's continued assaults on Carney weakened Carney's support for Ogista, and by June 1859, the agent's attitude to the head chief and his band had changed radically. These Ojibwa, he contended, constituted nothing less than 'sharp cunning traders' whom he felt 'romantics' had let off too lightly by exempting them from punishment, especially for defaulting on payments to merchants. For an 'untutored savage,' he continued, 'it might do,' but property or possessions belonging to Garden River offenders should be confiscated or else 'two thirds of the population [will be] arrested in their place.'[53] For the government to impose a land allotment system on the reserve, he continued, would grant creditors a lien on Native offenders and so whip order into what the magistrate had come to regard as the chaotic state of Ojibwa society.

Carney's portrayal of Aboriginal bands as irresponsible, easily manipulated sources of potential disruption on the frontier derived exclusively from his fears that Wilson would ruin his career by maligning Carney as he had regularly maligned Macdonell. As early as January 1859, Wilson made it clear that Carney had seriously erred in raising the issue of Aboriginal right and probably had opposed government policy in more ways than one. In consequence, Carney's actions lost their initial integrity, direction, and force. To raise himself in the estimation of the Indian Department he suggested that offering Ogista a salary might compel the chief to surrender the reserve in the spring. To justify providing Ogista with this stipend, Carney quoted the leader as saying: 'the Queen of England and the President of the United States have salaries and why should he not?' If the head chief wished to be paid for doing 'the Tribe's business in his own way,' Carney suggested to Pennefather, 'why not pay him for doing it in the manner the government desired?' Ogista, however, refused to be bought and terminated all further intercourse with Carney, citing the excuse that a '*che.amung* [*che.ogima*, or great chief] was coming,' and that only with this great chief would the band conduct business.[54]

Despite Carney's change in attitude in the late fall of 1858, his initial actions benefited all the bands, including those of Nebenagoching and Mishkcash. After Carney's detailed description of Buhkwujjenene's grievances about annuity payments, Ironside was reprimanded in January 1859 for withholding annuities.[55] Nebenagoching had his authority restored after levying charges, with Carney's assistance, against the operators of the illegal fishery. Just before the time appointed for the trial, Carney tried to prevent the case from being heard, fearing the hostility of Wilson and his clique. Nebenagoching nevertheless remained adamant, and, lest Wilson misrepresent him to his superiors, Carney sent a detailed account of the trial proceedings to the Indian Department.

Carney could not bring himself to accuse Wilson directly, and instead transferred the blame for instigating the fishery from Wilson to Mishkeash. Mishkeash, he claimed, had 'blackmailed' the illicit company's agent, S.N. Beach, who, because of his anomalous position in the eyes of the law could not defend himself and so suffered heavy losses. As a result, Mishkeash and his group had grown prosperous, whereas before they 'had been anything but.' Beach, Carney argued, had meanwhile been so imbued with romantic notions of the 'noble that he readily fell prey to Native chicanery.' As a result, the magistrate recorded that he would levy only a token punishment on the illegal enterprise, especially since the defendant, Beach, 'pleaded he could bring such exculpatory evidence before the Department which he hoped would lead His Excellency, the Govr. Genl. to remit the Fines wholly or in part.'[56] This was as close as Carney dared come to pointing an accusing finger at Wilson.

Throughout the hearing, it had been Carney, not Beach or the Ojibwa, who faced the hardest trial. Feeling unable to impose sentence on the party whom he felt was most responsible for the offence, Carney chose leniency towards both Beach and himself as the safest course. By contrast, Mishkeash faced a less severe judgment from his own people, and it is possible that Carney's detailed description of the proceedings and their outcome was an attempt to atone in some measure for succumbing to Wilson's intimidation and using Mishkeash as a scapegoat.

Immediately after the hearing, the head chiefs summoned Mishkeash before the entire Native community, and Buhkwujjenene admonished him for participating in the illicit fishery. Buhkwujjenene stressed that all the Ojibwa knew that during the trial Mishkeash had been uttering falsehoods and that, in so doing, the subchief had shamed his listeners as well as himself. On hearing these words, Carney concluded, Mishkeash broke down and 'cried bitterly.'[57]

In providing an opportunity for Nebenagoching to exercise his authority, and for Mishkeash to admit his wrong, the trial served a cathartic purpose and so helped to reintegrate the Native community. During the treaty negotiations which followed, the Ojibwa leaders could focus strictly on securing specific advantages for the groups they regarded as being under their express protection. Mishkeash, on resuming his status as an influential head chief, arranged to purchase eighty acres on behalf of each family at Goulais Bay. Ogista agreed to act as Totomenai's spokesman concerning the Michipicoten band's need for suitable land to plant vegetables.[58] At the request of the Batchewana, Garden River, and Thessalon peoples, Nebenagoching elicited a promise from William Gibbard, the provincial fisheries inspector, to secure for the Ojibwa exclusive use of the fishery just east of Point Thessalon, in addition to their fishery station on Whitefish Island at the rapids. Head chiefs anticipated that revenues would accrue to their groups from leases and sales, particularly of mining locations, on the ceded portions of the reserves. An expansive optimism prevailed which increased the Native leaders' willingness to share their present and anticipated resources. When Ironside promised to prevent the balance of unceded reserve territory from being taken from the Ojibwa once the surveys were made, Ogista and Buhkwujjenene on 14 June 1859 agreed to the suggestion that they offer a portion of their reserve to families from Goulais Bay and Thessalon who were interested in settling at Garden River. Then, at the agent's prompting, they went on to speak directly to the Batchewana group. We grant to you, they declared, 'an equal share of land to what we have and promise to consider you in all respects as members of our Band.'[59]

Growth of a Resistance Movement

During treaty negotiations in the spring of 1859, the head chiefs tried to stave off the likelihood of future clashes between their bands and officials of the Crown Lands Department by appealing for government protection for many facets of their developing economy. It was to no avail. The issue of Native proprietorship over land and resources, which Pennefather had suspended for expediency's sake during the treaty proceedings, flared into life again following the surrenders. Under the cessions known as the 'Pennefather Treaties,' conducted on 9 June 1859 with the Garden River and Batchewana bands, and two days later, on 11 June, with the Thessalon band, the entire Batchewana tract, except for Whitefish Island, as well as more than half the original area of the Garden River and Thessalon reserves, passed from Aboriginal to Crown control. These agreements, as ratified, neither defined nor entrenched the rights extended to incomers to Garden River by the Garden River chiefs, an omission noted by Carney only four days after the invitation had been made.[60] They further failed to ensure that each family would receive lands. The only surveys of allotments on the reserves during the nineteenth century took place in 1866, when the government laid out 'Shinguicouse Township' in response to pressure from lumbering interests who wished to secure land for a sawmill at the mouth of the Garden River, and in 1870, when the eighty-acre lots at Garden River and Batchewana were finally surveyed.[61]

Not one of the promises made by officials to encourage the Ojibwa to agree to the surrenders was ever honoured. Gibbard immediately swept aside his verbal agreement with Nebenagoching regarding the Thessalon fishery with a nonchalance that amazed even Ironside; Gibbard then leased the location to an American party.[62]

By this time, the Hudson's Bay Company store at Little Current, allegedly established 'to give stimulus to the industry of the Indians of that neighbourhood,' had driven Abatossaway out of business and then sold out to yet another external business interest. Disoriented by these events, Abatossaway turned to the government for assistance and protection, but instead was pressured to act as an informer against other Native leaders who were resisting similar efforts to destroy their people's economic independence. At the same time, Pennefather pointedly reminded Ironside that if chiefs were 'found guilty of any transaction for the sale of timber,' they must be removed from office.[63]

While the Pennefather Treaties attempted to inaugurate a system of individualized land holding on reserves, Ogista soon felt that the disadvantages of such an option, given the prevailing social attitudes towards Native people, outweighed the advantages. Chosen as a delegate to meet the Prince of Wales at Sarnia in September 1860, Ogista attended a meeting of the Grand Council – a forum for discussion and debate among south-eastern Ontario Ojibwa operating under Methodist missionary auspices – while waiting for the Prince's arrival. Discussion centred on the grievances of two Ojibwa individuals, David Sawyer and Catherine Sutton, both of whom had purchased land holdings at Owen Sound but had been unable to retain them because of Indian Department rulings prohibiting persons of Indian status from holding property in fee simple. While at the time Ogista refrained from offering an opinion on the case,[64] the character of the complaint could hardly have failed to register with the head chief, particularly as he knew Sawyer personally through the latter's association with the Methodist mission at Garden River.

News of such incidents bred fear and bitterness among Native people living along the north shore of Lake Huron. Gradually, the Canadian Upper Great Lakes Native community began to resolve itself into two groups, one willing to accede to government direction in local band affairs, the other denouncing all compromise and threatening violence if resource laws were enacted on territory where traditional prerogatives held sway. Resistance to the government was centred at Wikwemikong, Manitoulin Island. As early as 28 February 1859, Samuel Kichikemeg, a leading Wikwemikong chief, informed John Aisance, son of the Roman Catholic head chief of the same name who had died in 1847, that he was reluctant to join in to the Grand Council which was to be held that year at Rama, suggesting that the council reflected government rather than Native attitudes and opinions.[65] The Jesuit fathers Choné and Kohler at Wikwemikong tried to keep discontent focused on a single political issue, such as Native control over fishing locations.[66] The Muskoka bands wavered in their allegiance, and then joined the Rama camp, mainly on the instigation of Rama's head chief, William Yellowhead.[67] The final split into sides came when the government announced its intention in 1860 to secure the surrender of Manitoulin Island. In response, the Wikwemikong contingent assumed a 'garrison mentality,' asserted the moral rightness of their position, and expelled anyone – Native or white – who dared question the validity of their cause.[68] At a meeting held at Mechkewanong, Manitoulin Island, in 1861, those dedicated to obstructing the government's settlement and resource policies swore to 'eat out of one dish' and never cede the island.[69]

As in 1846, in preparing the frontier for further resource development the government ignored the substance of Native grievances. In its determination to implement of its resource policies, the province sought to deprive the indigenous peoples of all claim to political, economic, or cultural distinctiveness. When Richard Carney and his son John were appointed early in 1861 to gather data for a census, they were instructed to focus almost entirely on each band's degree of advancement towards 'civilization.' Western moral and organizational principles shaped the census takers' focus on such issues as the number of 'retainers under each chief' or the ratio of 'illegitimate' to 'legitimate' children within each band.[70]

Alert to threats to their integrity as independent groups, the Ojibwa refused to meet with officials, or else sought to confuse the enumerators by providing false information. Ironside reported to Richard Carney in May that from Spanish River, on the north shore of Lake Huron, west to Sault Ste Marie, the Ojibwa and Ottawa were so incensed by the questions of the census takers that there was almost no hope of completing the forms. John Carney admitted that the Ojibwa interviewed had deliberately given misleading information, and that the sheets he had filled out for the Garden River, Batchewana, and Goulais Bay bands were full of inaccuracies and omissions.[71]

At this time more than one-half of the population of Sault Ste Marie was of Native extraction. During his ennumerating activities, John Carney registered 475 out of a total of 850 individuals residing between Garden River and Goulais Bay as 'Indian.'[72] While Richard Carney and his son made no distinction between 'Métis' and 'Indians,' other official opinions differed on this point. For instance, John Prince, appointed as judge of the Algoma District in 1858, held that Native families at the rapids fell into two categories, based on his own predominantly late-eighteenth-century view of the social order. The judge perceived 'Indians' as belonging to the domain of the 'wild' and 'untutored,' while the term 'half-breed' he used to describe undisciplined, unstable social elements which, he contended, constituted a 'pest to the whole country.'[73] From his diaries, it is evident that Prince's categories were based primarily on residence and settlement patterns. Métis owned strip farms at the rapids, while 'Indians' lived in nucleated villages like the one at Garden River. In Prince's view, a Métis who joined the Garden River settlement became an 'Indian,' and as land prices at the rapids were likely to rise with the approach of the settlement frontier, the more Métis who could be convinced to become 'Indian,' the more control men like Prince and Wilson could exercise over territory for the purpose of land speculations.

Pennefather's policies of 1857 and 1858 had resulted in the exclusion of 133 individuals from the Garden River annuity list by 1860.[74] Under Prince, however, band membership rose, as social, legal, and economic incentives were used to induce Métis to sell their holdings cheaply at the Sault and move to Garden River. By October 1862, the judge noted approvingly that 'a good many ... half-breeds ... had annuity paid to them by Capt. Ironside.'[75]

Métis who moved to Garden River were sympathetic to the mood of resistance promoted by the Roman Catholic Ottawa at Wikwemikong, and official fears escalated as more was learned about the extent of Native resistance. Carney reported that almost all the residents at Garden River had grown distrustful of the local magistracy. Nebenagoching had instructed his band to cease all agricultural work in protest against Gibbard's stance on the fishery, and he and Ogista had contacted the governor general about their grievances. Rumours spread, meanwhile, of a growing militant disposition among the bands. It was known that Canadian Ojibwa had been encouraged to join the rebels in the Civil War, while circulars directed to Hudson's Bay Company posts on Lakes Huron and Superior warned that guns and ammunition had allegedly been sent to arm the Sioux uprising in Minnesota.[76]

In accordance with instructions from his department, Ironside drew up lists of Manitoulin Island Native people who opposed the government.[77] The western sector of Manitoulin Island was surrendered on 6 October 1862, mainly by chiefs whose territorial prerogatives extended over tracts on the neighbouring mainland, but who had resided much of the time after 1836 at Manitowaning or its outlying settlements. This event simply strengthened the resolve of Native people at Wikwemikong not to cede the territory surrounding their settlement. Abatossaway warned that, at a council held at Wikwemikong the previous spring, the majority present had agreed 'to prevent any surveyors coming to the Island,' and to obstruct the work of any survey parties. To prevent harm not only to the surveyors, but also to the chiefs who had agreed to the 1862 treaty, Abatossaway appealed to the Indian Department for protection for himself and his band.[78]

Wilson advocated that troops be stationed at Sault Ste Marie to subdue the growing unrest.[79] The provincial fisheries inspector, Gibbard, also supported the use of force, and on 23 July 1863 Gibbard and a party of six constables armed with revolvers briefly confronted an angry crowd at Wikwemikong, although no one was injured in the fray.[80] Prince, however, felt that his duty to the Crown demanded strict enforcement of provincial resource regulations, and by 1864 he had developed a plan for inducing the Ojibwa to cede all their timber. He used a loophole in the Pennefather Treaties first noted by Carney in 1859 as a wedge to divide the Garden River community by restricting Nebenagoching and his band to an enclave west of the original settlement and prohibiting their access to timber as a merchantable commodity: 'I am of the opinion [Prince informed Wilson] that the Batchewana Bay and Goulais Bay Indians are entitled to a Grant by way of occupation only of 40 acres of the Garden River reserve, but that they have no right to cut timber for sale thereon or to controul [sic] Or interfere with the chiefs of the Garden River band in any way ...'[81] Prince thus abruptly dispensed with the promise of equal rights extended by Ogista and Buhkwujjenene to Nebenagochings people only five years before. His action met with no resistance, since the only man who might have questioned his course, George Ironside, had died in 1863. The judge's unilateral decision on this matter was to constitute the most serious pre-Confederation encroachment on a Garden River head chief's right to regulate his group's membership.

Wilson also considered splitting the Garden River community into privileged and non-privileged factions in order to secure a timber surrender, although he felt the division should be made along religious lines, between Anglicans and Roman Catholics, rather than between bands. In a letter of 20 January 1864 to Charles Dupont, Wilson, Ironside's successor at the Manitowaning Indian Agency, claimed that, to his 'surprise,' Nebenagoching and his people were Roman Catholic, whereas Ogista's band was primarily Protestant. Wilson's idea was to grant only Protestants timber licences. 'You and I must work together' on this, he prompted Dupont.[82]

Despite such tactics and Prince's refusal to help prevent miners from selling timber from the unceded Elliot location, Ogista still regarded the Crown as essentially a benign, protective power which could be called upon whenever his people were in distress. Ogista was confirmed in this view when Deputy Superintendent Spragge intervened to help settle the band's long-standing dispute with the Garden River Mining Company over the Lemoine and Simpson locations.[83] From the remoteness of his Montreal office, Spragge had little idea of the exact nature of the problem on the frontier, but he favoured segregating Native peoples in locations far from the main thrust of resource development. Following a review of the miners' case by the Executive Council, George Desbarats on behalf of the Garden River Mining Company agreed to relinquish his claims provided the province returned his initial deposit on the sites, a proposal the government accepted.[84] Spragge considered that an important intermediary step towards the integration of bands into the capitalist economy would be to allow the Indians to cut and sell 'firewood of ordinary descriptions' until their forests could be ceded to timber companies. He expected the Ojibwa to respond positively to his suggestions, since dues collected on the wood might contribute to a capital fund, from which interest could be drawn and paid to them annually. Such a scheme governed cutting operations at Caughnawaga, Spragge asserted, and might serve as a model for a similar system at Garden River. Finally, he recommended that Ogista receive a team of oxen, and seed, to encourage the chief to agree to his scheme.[85]

Support for the Band from Missionaries and Merchants

In obedience to Spragge's instructions, Wilson drew up a schedule of dues for the band to pay on 'ship's knees' – used in wooden ship construction – as well as shingle timber and cordwood for the American market. Meanwhile, with Dupont's assistance, Ogista persuaded a Canadian merchant by the name of John Davidson to open a store and build a wharf near the mouth of the Garden River. Another trader, John Cousins, was allowed to operate a smaller store and wharf nearby. The Reverend Edward Sollows, the Methodist clergyman at Bruce Mines, felt that major steps had been taken. The differences between the Ojibwa and the government had been 'amicably settled' he noted in June 1863. Stores had been built and full employment provided to the Garden River residents at last.[86]

Because he favoured Spragge's system for allowing Native people to cut and sell their own timber on their reserves, Ogista baulked at Wilson's attempts to effect a timber cession, and instead instructed every head of family in his band to mark out allotments to cut timber on the Elliot location. Like the Wikwemikong contingent, his group would unite to oppose encroaching resource policies.[87] He had formidable help. Both Roman Catholic and Anglican missionaries supported the Ojibwa leader's position. This made Wilson more determined then ever to sow seeds of dissension between the two denominations. 'I am certain that the Priests are at the bottom of all, they feel themselves outflanked by me as to the ownership of the Reserve,' he informed Dupont in February 1864.[88]

According to Ogista, the Ojibwas reason for rejecting the government demands arose from their belief that the bands alone should control resources on reserves.[89] Annoyed at this intelligence, Wilson seized all the logs the Garden River community had cut during the spring. Although he had intended making the confiscation while the head chief was away on a two-week caribou-hunting expedition, Church, sympathetic to Ogista's position, prevailed upon the leader to stay and challenge Wilson's right to take the wood.[90]

Under Prince's influence, Wilson switched from seizing logs to apprehending Native offenders. The judge stressed that the Ojibwa could be compelled to serve as jurors, be forced to observe game laws of which he was the author, and be indicted and fined for failing to observe provincial timber regulations.[91] But the judge feared Ojibwa hostility. 'There are dangerous times looming in the distance for us who live here among the Indians and halfbreeds,' he cautioned.[92] In March 1864, when Sollows claimed that members of the Garden River band had threatened to 'shoot any government officer who goes down on the reserve and interferes with them,' Dupont, aware of Prince's feelings on the matter, advocated taking strong measures if necessary.[93] Should the magistrates meet with resistance, he argued, they 'might make an example of some prominent one [leader] amongst them and arrest and punish him, for inciting them to disloyalty and resistance of the laws.'[94]

Although Allan Macdonell escaped being prosecuted under the act Baldwin had passed in 1853 to curb Native unrest, Garden River Native leaders were not so fortunate. During the summer of 1864, Charles Biron, an educated member of Ogista's band, was apprehended for resisting the resource laws and sent to the penitentiary at Penetanguishene. When the band sought assistance from the Indian Department for Biron's defence, they were told that the law absolved the government from all responsibility in the case. According to Spragge, the matter was not one in which the department 'was officially called upon to interfere.'[95]

Although Wilson, Dupont, and Prince employed all the legal weaponry at their disposal, they could only diffuse the intensity of the Native resistance movement; they could not eradicate it completely. Sporadic outbursts of violence continued until as late as 1875.[96] The magistrates found themselves quixotically arrayed against a shifting, indistinct 'foe,' since the issue at stake was not resources *per se*, but the future status of Native groups within the Canadian nation. The clashes over fishing rights, timber cutting, and the survey were superficial symptoms of a greater and deeper problem. In an address to a council at Wikwemikong in 1864, one head chief poignantly described the fears which motivated his opposition to the government: 'The Whites when they come will do labour and make money ... and to you, my friends, will be given all the lowest, meanest work to do as servants, such as carrying water, cutting wood, cleaning stables ...'[97]

Aboriginal leaders contended that their commitment to retaining a degree of control over land and resources derived from the responsibility they felt for their rising generation. Abatossaway, who favoured accommodation, stated that his band also wished to be respected as a group, and to have the right to determine its own future and keep most of what it held. With respect to their political activities during the mid-1860s, bands differed only as to means, not in their ultimate goals. It was mainly through this mutual reaffirmation of commitment to the survival of cherished values that sustained resistance to the government began to fade. A lessening of discontent at Sault Ste Marie also ensued following the removal from office of the notorious U.S. Indian agent, A. Fitch. The Honourable D.C. Leach, his successor, recommended the immediate granting of patents to check the worst abuses of Fitch's former allotment system.[98]

At this point, two events caused a temporary suspension of the magistrate's actions against Native people who contravened the resource laws. During the summer of 1864, forest fires along the north shore of Lake Huron destroyed millions of acres of timber.[99] A smallpox epidemic among the settler and Native populations followed this first catastrophe, and officials had to devote all their attention to implementing quarantine laws and provisioning the afflicted.[100] During this break in the ongoing struggle over conflicting notions of resource proprietorship, provincial land surveyor George B. Kirkpatrick laboured over a fire-scarred landscape adjusting the boundaries of the Garden River reserve. His work met with no resistance.[101]

According to the Pennefather Treaty of 1859, the western border began at Partridge Point, as already stated in the Robinson-Huron Treaty, and ran due north. Halfway along its original length, it was expected to intersect with a new northern boundary line, set down by Kirkpatrick, which would extend due east to a specified maple boundary, and then proceed southeast to Onigaming, or 'The Portage,' on the west shore of Echo Lake. It was not long, however, before William Shebakezick, Kirkpatrick's guide, reported to Ogista and Buhkwujjenene that the survey did not conform to Ojibwa expectations. The western boundary ran at an angle rather than due north, and the northern boundary did not strike Onigaming but instead fell half a mile south of the portage.[102]

Anomalies in the Garden River survey aroused Nebenagoching's suspicions about the boundaries of the Batchewana tract, which were also rerun in 1864. On the last day of the year, 31 December, Wilson, at Nebenagoching's request, informed Spragge that the Ojibwa expected the eastern boundary to extend inland ten miles from the coast. Just north of the surveyed boundary several mineral locations had recently been staked by Maitland and four other mining entrepreneurs – Begley, Mansfield, Duffield, and Bethune. Nebenagoching claimed that these sites lay on the reserve. The main reason he had agreed to the tract's cession was to gain the revenue from the sale of these lands.

Nebenagoching, Wilson admitted to Spragge, 'is quite correct.' Wilson had been present at the negotiations for the Pennefather Treaties and had distinctly heard Keating tell the Native assembly that the Batchewana reserve included the mineral outcroppings in question. 'Better give the Indians a few miles than be accused by them of this ... and be attacked in the press for a breach of faith,' the magistrate cautioned.[103] He obviously disliked being directly confronted by the chiefs on this issue, for he knew as well as Keating the reasons why the surveys deviated from the descriptions of the tracts originally presented to the Indians in 1850.

In the spring of 1865, Wilson again endeavoured to negotiate a timber cession at Garden River, this time armed with a slightly different strategy. Father Auguste Kohler, SJ, had taken umbrage at Charles Biron's arrest for cutting timber. The band, the priest asserted, had maintained its own code for organizing its economic pursuits 'since time immemorial,' which the priests understood and respected. Quarrels on such matters should be settled in a 'fatherly way' outside the courts.[104]

Wilson and Dupont realized they might be bested in an argument with the Jesuits, and in consequence the political position of Nebenagoching's people immediately grew stronger. These two officials, although both Protestant, could direct their attacks against members of any denomination, and after 1865 simply changed the target of their invective from the Roman Catholic to the Anglican mission.

Strange Bedfellows

Wilson soon found a chink in the armour of Anglican missionary opposition to his schemes. Chance had aspirations of 'regaining' Garden River from the Roman Catholics and Methodists solely for the purposes of a Church of England mission. This bellicose advocate of Low Church doctrine, O'Meara's protégé, had begun to criticize the Roman Catholics from the pulpit in a manner which annoyed even the religiously lethargic Prince.[105] The missionary also identified Wilson's recognition of Ogista as head chief as a hindrance to the progress of his vision for the future of the community. By siding with Ogista as well as the Jesuits, Wilson felt he could place Chance on the defensive and so force Chance to support government resource policies.

Chance considered Ogista to be proud, unstable, easily manipulated, given to drinking, entertainments, dancing, and ceremonies unseemly for an Anglican.[106] No friend of Wilson or Dupont, the missionary maintained that the Native leader demeaned himself by associating with these officials. Since Wilson had arranged for Ogista to receive oxen and seed, Chance decided to destroy any influence this gave Wilson by deposing Ogista and establishing Buhkwujjenene as head chief in his place.

Wilson immediately countered Chance by supporting Ogista. Meanwhile, the magistrate directed missionary attention, in general, away from the resource issue and the problem with reserve boundaries by highlighting ambiguities in both missions' rights to occupy land on the reserve. Wilson's first move in this strategy was to gain Ogista as an ally against Chance. This was not difficult once Ogista knew of Chance's plan to depose him. In June, Chance complained to Spragge that Ogista had brought whisky onto the reserve and promoted a drunken spree in which several people were injured. Spragge told Dupont about Chance's complaint, Dupont informed Wilson, and Wilson passed the news along to Ogista.[107] Wilson thus felt he could count on Ogista's support during the next stage of his plan.

During the summer, while Chance and Buhkwujjenene were attending an Anglican synod in the southern part of the province, Wilson claimed that some grassy grounds belonging to the Church of England obstructed a public road and got Ogista and Father Baxter, SJ, to knock the Anglican mission fences down.[108] Shingwaukonse's Roman Catholic son, Tegoosh, and the Jesuits suggested a compromise which would allow for a road to run between the Anglican and Jesuit missions. This involved moving the fences and a barn several metres. In November, Dupont wrote to Spragge that the matter had been settled.[109]

But Wilson knew his opponent too well to assume he was defeated. On discovering that the Jesuits had been permitted to enclose a portion of the point lying below their main premises, Chance decided not to let the matter drop. At the spring assizes, Father Baxter, encouraged by Wilson, indicted the Anglican missionary for trespass. Wilson refused to give evidence, and Ogista, although he admitted he was uncertain about the facts, stated that a road *might* have existed twenty years ago. No land title was held by the Roman Catholic or the Anglican missions, apart from the deeds drawn up by Shingwaukonse in 1848 and subsequently invalidated by Vidal's survey. A trial therefore ensued based on interpretations of Little Pine's original wishes and the location of the chief's grave relative to the alleged road, which seemed to run directly over the burial plot.[110]

Not until July 1866 did Chance figure out that the fences had been knocked down not because of interdenominational rivalry but because the government wanted control of the reserve and its resources. In directing a claim to the Indian Department for damages incurred during the indictment proceedings, Chance blamed the government officials wholly for the incident. 'If Mr. Wilson and the chief had not acted as they did,' he argued, 'the Jesuits would never have ventured to proceed against our church mission.'[111]

Buhkwujjenene Intervenes on Behalf of Direct Democracy

Chance pressed for Buhkwujjenene's installation as head chief not only because of the special charge the missionary felt Shingwaukonse had laid on him, but also because he liked and approved of Buhkwujjenene personally. Buhkwujjenene and his wife had helped Chance in innumerable ways when the clergyman first arrived at Garden River, even to the point of giving him their own dwelling. Dignified and congenial, Buhkwujjenene exhibited many gracious mannerisms, such as bowing deeply from the waist when taking leave of a person. He also had a shrewd, almost meticulous mind for business affairs, which Chance admired but could not easily emulate. For these reasons, Chance became increasingly committed to making Buhkwujjenene the head of his projected mission settlement.

In response to Chance's and Buhkwujjenene's appeals the preceding year, the Anglican Church Mission Society had sent a delegation to Garden River in August 1866 to determine the feasibility of attaining fee simple title to a site for an industrial school.[112] Native complaints concerning the survey had prompted Alexander Campbell, commissioner of Crown Lands and superintendent general of the Indian Department, to visit the community at about the same time. Campbell had no interest in maintaining reserves and felt they should be surrendered as soon as it was practically possible. Nebenagoching's strong arguments for having the Batchewana tract resurveyed, however, temporarily disarmed him. To win time, Campbell replied that he would respond at a later date through Chance and Kohler.[113]

Campbell then decided to forgo further discussion with the chiefs by accepting both the Batchewana survey and the non-payment of monies from mining sales to the Batchewana band as a *fait accompli*. According to Keating's report of 1853, Campbell informed the missionaries that the Batchewana tract enclosed 184 square miles, a statement confirmed by Order-in-Council on 18 July 1854. Technical difficulties and the expense of surveying over rocky terrain had prevented the interior boundary from following the line of the coast. With blunt frankness, probably because he knew Kohler and Chance would readily detect the conflict of interest which engendered the dispute, Campbell concluded: 'The sales [of mining locations] have been made, and it is now impossible to make any changes even if the Treaty have the interpretation which the Indian Sare [Sayer or Nebenagoching] contends for.'[114]

Campbell's communications only succeeded in strengthening mission opposition to the government's unilateral decisions. Fathers Kohler and Baxter sought to obtain title to territory on behalf of the Goulais Bay and Batchewana bands. Since the government refrained from surveying these reserves until 1870, the Roman Catholic missionaries provided invaluable assistance in defending the Ojibwa's land base against encroaching mining and timber interests. Chance, meanwhile, aided Buhkwujjenene in pursuing specific grievances with Campbell about annuity payments and resource management at Garden River. Under the Robinson Treaties, Buhkwujjenene held, each band was entitled to receive an annual lump sum for improvements as well as for distribution to individuals. He also requested information about land sales and the timber licensing system.

Campbell replied in October 1866 that, in 1850, the population affected by the Robinson Treaties had numbered 1,422, but by 1865, according to the census of that year, it had risen to 2,285.[115] This increase in annuitants had reduced payments to less than one dollar per person. While the Superintendent General failed to address Buhkwujjenene's query about group versus individual payments, he admonished the Garden River band for drawing, through Spragge, one hundred dollars for oxen and seed which, he declared, had injured all the other annuitants sharing in the £600 allocated by treaty.

As for the interest which had accrued from land sales, only one township, McDonald, had been laid out in the vicinity of the Sault. The amount received by the Indian Department by 1866 had been only $572.88 – too small a sum to draw any interest worth considering. Campbell also argued that Spragge had misled the Ojibwa into believing that arrangements for cutting timber similar to those prevailing at Caughnawaga could be attained for Garden River. Yet wood on the Caughnawaga reserve had been cut and sold under provisions of a special Order-in-Council. No such permission could be secured for lands lying north of Lake Huron.[116]

Through Buhkwujjenene's influence, Chance came to favour the promotion of lumbering over agriculture. It was unrealistic, given the climate and lack of assistance, the missionary maintained, to expect all the Ojibwa to become farmers. To deny them access to other resources on the reserve was cruel and unjust. Chance rarely minced words, even when writing to Campbell. The governor general, he stressed, might as well sign their death warrant at once, or issue an Order-in-Council to drive the Ojibwa off the reserve, as persist in prohibiting them from cutting wood.

Chance demanded that the chiefs in council should exercise complete managerial control over the dispersal of timber at Garden River.[117] When Campbell rejected this suggestion, the clergyman altered his position to allow the Indian Department to govern the allocation of timber licences.[118] Chance felt that his success as an intermediary between the Ojibwa and the government would aid the cause of his mission, and so endeavoured to gain Ojibwa compliance with government licencing terms. In this he failed, however. Ogista refused to listen to the views of Chance or anyone else on timber management, and in the fall left for the United States until May of 1867. During Ogista's absence, Chance compiled a list of grievances against the leader, including among them Ogista's 'wandering' propensities. He submitted the list to Campbell and requested that an inquiry be made into Ogista's fitness for leadership.[119]

In late May, Spragge instructed Dupont to investigate Ogista's activities. Dupont arrived at Garden River on a Friday without prior warning and remained until noon the next day to hear complaints about the leader. Receiving none, he returned to Manitowaning. News of what had taken place enraged Chance, since he had not been notified of the agent's visit.

He also considered Dupont to be a mere instrument of Wilson. The whole affair, he maintained, had been a farce.[120]

Buhkwujjenene soon found that Chance's ardent support of his policies at times could prove to be more of a liability than an asset. In June 1867, he and his brother Ogista had had a private disagreement about whether or not more land should be ceded from their reserve. Buhkwujjenene had opposed the government's issuing of a patent to Rankin for the Clark location on 1 April 1865, while Ogista had argued that the sale would increase band revenue. Buhkwujjenene feared that such unconditional sales might lead to an undermining of band government and the Ojibwa's commitment to direct democracy.[121] Chance, while not particularly wishing to challenge traditional band leadership, nevertheless, through the incautious pursuit of his own mission's goals, so severely threatened the local band system that Buhkwujjenene found himself compelled to side with his brother against the missionary in spite of Chance's strong support of the resource policies which he favoured.

The events that caused Buhkwujjenene's change of position began when Rankin made overtures to Ogista and John Bell, Jr, about the purchase of the Elliot location. While Ogista wavered about whether or not he would agree to the mine sale, John Wigwas – evidently a son of old Megissanequa, one of Shingwaukonse's sons-in-law – Joseph Tegoosh, and several others who acted as delegates for both the Roman Catholic and Anglican congregations agreed to surrender three chains of land on either side of Peltier Creek, west of the Garden River, to the Roman Catholic mission as a location for a grist mill.[122] Ogista himself had been pressing for a grist mill since 1864, but Chance refused to believe that the head chief's involvement in the negotiations was not instigated by the Jesuits. 'I ... protest against any surrender of land by Augista [sic] to Mr. Rankin or Priest Kohler as illegal,' Chance proclaimed to Campbell. The Jesuit mill could not possibly assist the entire community but would, he held, only foster factional dispute.[123] Chance achieved his aim. Though cession of the mill site occurred on 9 July 1867, no mill was ever built.

The missionary's next move was to try to prevent the band from associating with Wilson and his clique. Chance declared to Campbell that Wilson's and Keating's activities would force him to use all his influence in opposing Wemyss Simpson, the Conservative candidate for Algoma and another of Wilson's cronies, in the upcoming election.[124] By September 1867 the missionary smugly reported that although Keating and his son-in-law had pitched their tent near Ogista's dwelling, their attempts to win Native electoral support for Simpson would fail, since 'Carney had decided not to rescue Indian votes ...'[125] Chance's and Carney's opposition to Simpson, may well have caused the Ojibwa to lose the franchise they might otherwise have exercised in Canada's first federal election.

It was not long before Chance demanded that the inquiry into Ogista's leadership be resumed. To invalidate Ironside's statement of 1855 that, as an eldest son, Ogista should succeed his father, Chance obtained statements from McMurray, O'Meara, and Thomas G. Anderson to the effect that laws of patrilineal descent and primogeniture did not obtain among the Ojibwa. McMurray substantiated Chance's statements that the head chief governed the transmission of the office himself, O'Meara gave his opinion that patrilineality had been grafted onto the Ojibwa system, and Anderson testified that in the past he had frequently been called upon by a band to recognize a younger son or a nephew as a head chief's successor.[126]

Confronted by this additional data, Spragge instructed Dupont to return to Garden River and collect oral testimonies which might justify government implementation of an electoral system.[127] Chance recoiled at this, since Spragge had disregarded his claim that Buhkwujjenene's moral character was superior to Ogista's. Recognizing the shift in premise, the missionary hastened to point out that he had never authorized an inquiry into the 'validity of chieftainship' but only into the moral foundations on which it should be based.[128]

Dupont recorded comments verbatim from the Ojibwa and sent them to Deputy Superintendent Spragge.[129] From a cursory reading of Dupont's submissions, Spragge found that not one negative statement had been uttered against Ogista. Even Buhkwujjenene had maintained that he was satisfied with his brother as chief. Several band members stated that they could not understand why Chance complained about Ogista's drinking when Buhkwujjenene himself took liquor occasionally and at times had been intoxicated.[130]

According to one affidavit by Thomas Simpson, a mining acquaintance of Wilson's, Buhkwujjenene had been given ten dollars by Dupont. Spragge felt this could indicate that Buhkwujjenene was as willing to accept government 'gifts' as Chance had accused Ogista of being. Or, conversely, it might reflect on the investigating team, for it was very possible, the Deputy Superintendent maintained, that Dupont was paying Buhkwujjenene 'to shut his mouth.'[131]

Neither Chance nor Spragge was prepared to draw any final conclusions from such unsatisfactory evidence. For the time being, however, Chance had to lay aside his pursuit of Ogista's removal, as Buhkwujjenene needed his help in examining new resource regulations. The secretary of state, Hector Langevin, had proposed to Wilson that Native people should pay full dues on all timber cut, but that licences and ground rent might be purchased at half the price charged to white persons, 'to encourage industry.'[132] Ogista refused even to consider these terms. Buhkwujjenene at the same time explained to Chance that the dues were too high for small family operations working in the bush. Wilson, Buhkwujjenene held, had been selling land on the ceded part of the reserve for four years at twenty cents an acre. How could the Ojibwa hope to compete with settlers who could cut and sell timber from their own lands without the burden of dues or rent?[133]

Chance informed the government that the prices of provisions had escalated, while the Native people under the Robinson-Huron Treaty had the lowest annuities of Native people anywhere in Canada. The strictness of the terms forced families from Garden River to seek employment in the United States.[134] Finally, on 8 June 1868, the missionary forwarded a petition to Langevin from Buhkwujjenene, Waubmama, and Bell asking them to view Ogista's resistance merely as a temporary protest against overly harsh measures, and to relax the offending regulations.[135]

Wilson and Dupont stressed that local band government on the reserve was growing stronger. The government's answer was to strike intractable individuals off the annuity lists or to arrest them. 'Indians who [since 1850] came from the American side of the line must be required to leave the Reserve,' Langevin directed.[136] Due to the 'anomalous state of things occasioned by many new names,' Wilson was instructed to draw up lists for both Ogista's and Nebenagoching's bands and then delete those who could be placed in the category 'intruder.'[137] Wilson, evidently confused about the criteria for striking persons off the rolls, argued that certain Métis should be allowed to remain on the lists since 'they have enough Indian blood to constitute them as Indians.'[138] So ambiguous were the criteria for allowing exclusion from the group that decisions came to be based mainly on Wilson's personal whims. The missionaries proved the greatest check on officialdom's activities in this regard. In November, when three Garden River residents were arrested under the law forbidding the inciting of Native unrest and sent to the penitentiary, Chance could hardly believe the severity of the terms. If Wilson or Dupont ever again dared to use such oppressive measures to curtail men's ability to earn an honest living, the priest raged, he would 'appeal to the Christian public.'[139]

As an accompaniment to this callous disregard of human dignity and rights, intensive resource development on the reserves continued unchecked. Under the provisions of the *General Mining Act* (32 Vict., cap. 34) of 1869, a miner could pay one dollar per acre for full subsurface rights and reap potential profits without having to pay royalties, taxes, or duties.[140] Large lumbering companies were ready and waiting to harvest the rich pine from the Garden River and Batchewana lands. It thus was essential for the Crown Lands Department to determine the exact state of leadership at Garden River and identify any potential weaknesses that would be exploited to gain further surrenders. It was an unfavourable time for the band to have Chance raise the issue of leadership once again, and yet he did.

In August 1869, William Plummer, a Sault Ste Marie merchant and a special commissioner for the Indian Department, arrived at Garden River on Chance's and Spragge's instructions to investigate the leadership issue. Plummer invited the chiefs, head men, and missionaries to a council and explained that grave charges had been brought against Ogista. Not one Native person spoke.[141]

Finally, Ogista himself rose and demanded to learn the name of his accuser. Waubmama, eldest son of the Crane chief Muckedayoquot, also denounced the secrecy with which threats had been made against the chief. The individuals should identify themselves. Yet it was Buhkwujjenene – the rival chief – who dealt the harshest blow to Chance's arguments for Ogista's removal. The band sought peace on the issue of leadership, Buhkwujjenene maintained, for his father had ordained it. No one person could proclaim the meaning of the old chief's will with regard to leadership succession within the band. He and his brother *both* enjoyed prerogatives bestowed by their father and exercised with the consent of their people: 'My father Shingwauk gave Augustin [Ogista] that medal he wears and desired I also should be a chief like him and enjoy all the benefits attaching to a chieftainship ... in witness of which he gave this paper [the will or testament of 1854].' Thus, acting as his brother's advocate before the assembly, he declared that the charges against Ogista were false. With these words Buhkwujjenene ended, once and for all, external attacks on Ogista's leadership.[142]

Resilience, Change, and New Challenges

Increasingly sophisticated Native resistance to the unilateral implementation of resource regulations on reserve lands promoted the development of organizational structures capable of protecting and creating policies worthy of serious government consideration. Ogista had shown courage in his stand against the imposed measures, although from the government standpoint the immediate consequence appeared to be merely a deadlock between Wilson and an intractable Native leader. A second, dynamic impulse favouring negotiation and compromise followed, to which both the Anglican and the Roman Catholic missionaries willingly lent their support. This new surge of political enthusiasm, which arising out of band consensus, adopted the petition as its instrument.

Tested by the confrontation with Chance, Ogista emerged more influential than ever before. He had received the sanction of head men according to traditional custom. Through him, the band leadership system had weathered assaults from both hostile political forces and a narrow Victorian moral code. This powerful exhibition of the strength of the reciprocal ties between the chief and his band showed the futility of attempting to drive a wedge between community leaders, and both the government and the missionaries ended their attacks on Ogista.

Following this event, Plummer showed a willingness to negotiate with this strong political entity. The arrests and seizing of wood which had continued until May 1869 now ceased. Ogista and his band agreed to cede Squirrel Island to Duncan G. MacDonald for $272, and to sell the timber on the surrendered part of the reserve to George Danson, but only under certain conditions. Both entrepreneurial parties promised to follow the letter of the agreement exactly, which stipulated that if no sawmill was built by MacDonald, Squirrel Island must return to the band, and that Danson must hire and train Native labour. When it became apparent that Danson had no intention of fulfilling his contract, his licence was soon revoked.[143]

Ogista took the lead in promoting several projects on the reserve. After one last boundary dispute between Chance and Baxter, during which Ogista and Tegoosh intervened to delineate the limits of each mission as they believed their father had established them, Chance left Garden River to assume a new ministerial position at Niagara-on-the-Lake. His going upset Ogista, who had been hoping for the establishment of the industrial school which Chance, Buhkwujjenene, and the Church Missionary Society had been considering since 1866.

In 1869 Ogista believed he had been blessed by a vision for the future of his community similar to the one his father had experienced. An opportunity to communicate his desire directly to the upper echelons of the Anglican hierarchy arose in 1870, when the Reverend Edward F. Wilson, pastor from Sarnia, stopped at Garden River briefly *en route* from visiting the Red River with Col. G. Wolseley's expedition. Without telling anyone of his intentions, Ogista embarked on the steamer bearing Wilson homeward to Sarnia and there prevailed on Wilson to aid him in publicly expressing his views to Canadian metropolitan society.

Ogista's adventures in southern Ontario drew press attention, especially after Wilson had Ogista's narrative of his own experiences published in a pamphlet entitled *Little Pine's Journal*.[144] The Red River uprising, however, had made the Ontario public reluctant to encourage new missionary undertakings for Native people. James Beaven, William B. Robinson, and Frederick O'Meara lent verbal support, but Wilson believed that sufficient funds to build a school could only be raised in England. When Ogista cited his old age as a reason for staying home, Wilson persuaded Buhkwujjenene to accompany him in Ogista's stead.

Wilson had his own ideas about Ogista's reasons for wanting an industrial school built at Garden River. To Wilson, Ogista represented in his demeanour and oratorial powers the epitome of the 'noble savage': the raw metal which would be forged into the Christian Man by Wilson's efforts. Ogista, the missionary believed, had been summoned by the Divine Will to approach the Anglican Church for assistance; Wilson felt chosen to act as a catalyst in the 'elevation' of this Ojibwa leader and his people.

On assuming charge of the Garden River Anglican mission, Wilson formally recognized Ogista as head chief, and encouraged the leader to gain a surrender of land for an industrial school.[145] The band granted approximately eighty acres to the Anglican Church in May 1871, and a smaller allotment to the Roman Catholic mission. Ogista wanted to gain access to Western education for his band, but even as early as 1874 it seemed that Wilson and the chief had divergent visions for the future of the Ojibwa. The head chief repeatedly expressed fears about the demise of the Ojibwa as a distinct people, expressing his concern symbolically through the image of the setting sun. Yet his statement failed to move Wilson, who worked towards the assimilation of the Native people into the trades and the rural working class.

On 3 December 1873, Ogista reported to the Indian Department that the band had recognized him as head chief by universal acclamation and requested a salary. Almost as a footnote, he added that the industrial school, completed in the early fall of 1873, had burned down. According to the leader, the cause had been arson, the 'work of some bad people.'[146] Wilson arranged for another residential school to be built at Sault Ste Marie, and in 1874 invited the Earl of Dufferin to lay the cornerstone. Even though by this time the head chief opposed the missionary's assimilationist schemes, Wilson nevertheless continued to uphold the leader as the initiator of his industrial school system at Sault Ste Marie.

Ogista continued to search for avenues that would afford Native people a measure of self-determination within the nation state. Wilson, by contrast, seeing the Native community only as a limiting milieu, sought to establish a highly regimented learning environment 'purged' of 'uncivilized' cultural elements. Between these two perspectives lay a great gulf filled with contradiction and misunderstanding.

Chapter Seven

Challenging the System from Within

At the time of Confederation, economic development was a primary objective at Garden River. Yet the manner in which this community proceeded towards its economic goals differed radically from the assimilationist program for reserves set out by Parliament after 1867. A reorganized Indian Department – placed under the Department of the Secretary of State until 1873, and after that under the Ministry of the Interior – stressed the implementation on reserves of a system of individual property holding which would eventually release government from involvement in the economic affairs of the Aboriginal people altogether. Native populations fell under a regime of 'internal colonialism'[1] which made them wards of the state in a country that had once been their own. The Ojibwa determinedly resisted this externally imposed policy in order to keep their group identity. However, as long as restrictive laws curtailed their access to minerals and timber on their reserves, they were prevented from employing revenue from these resources to assist in establishing a group-controlled economic base.

Testing for Native Proprietorship of Minerals, 1873–1875

Despite regulations prohibiting Native people from mining and selling minerals, many band members had considerable experience as mining explorers. Members of Nebenagoching's kin group and the Jones, Nolin, and Bell families were eagerly sought after by mining company agents, among them Judge John Prince. Other family heads maintained territories containing mineral deposits in the bush and engaged in black-market transactions. Ogista mined a tract that contained iron exposures two kilometres from the coast between the Garden and Echo Rivers, but resented the fact that he could not legally sell the mineral. Like his father, he believed the reserve and its resources belonged to the Ojibwa by right.

Possibly on the advice of Simon J. Dawson, a politician well known to the Garden River people in the 1870s,[2] Ogista decided to try to establish a precedent which would allow bands rights to minerals. The time seemed auspicious for such a move. Not only were the principal band members at Garden River willing to let their chief test the system by bringing his own holdings on the market, but Native leaders westward to Lake of the Woods had begun to reaffirm a commitment to the idea of Native control over mineral resources. For instance, at the Northwest Angle treaty negotiations in September 1873, during which Native proprietorship of mineral resources arose as a major issue, the Ojibwa leader Mawedopenais spoke in favour of Native control.[3]

As long as Ogista and his band retained control over the negotiating forum in their dealings with miners, precedents to safeguard Aboriginal ownership of minerals seemed to be within reach. Yet when one particularly influential American mining entrepreneur, James Wilkinson, began to stake far more territory than the band originally intended to alienate, the Ojibwa lacked the power to curtail his activities and could expect no government protection. Ottawa's reaction to the Ojibwa's predicament was to try to exploit the weakness of the band's position to gain a surrender of the entire reserve. This affair began in the fall of 1873, after Ogista had permitted Wilkinson to conduct several days' explorations on the reserve. Soon afterward, John Askin also brought iron holdings onto the market, but offered them to Philetus Swift Church rather than to Wilkinson. When the band limited the area available for mining purposes to four hundred acres, Church abided by the conditions, but Wilkinson refused to restrict his survey and staked three large locations, one of which enclosed two smaller sites claimed by Church.[4]

Ottawa initially tried to resolve the conflict between the two mining interests by determining which party had first offered payment to Ogista for his explorer's right. Wilkinson maintained that he had been the first, upbraided Church and Church's agent, Tegoosh, for interfering, and promised to pay Ogista handsomely for his support in the dispute. Yet neither the chief nor his band would play favourites.[5]

When it became evident that the leader was not interested in money but in trying to force a decision about the issue of Native proprietorship over mineral resources, the head chief's evidence was found to be 'too contradictory to be admissible.' Church's case suffered, since the merchant had respected band decisions and had even considered leasing the locations for five years with the privilege of renewing the transaction from time to time – an option, suggested by Ogista, which resembled the conditions granted to Macdonell in 1849. Wilkinson, by contrast, emphasized that he had paid Ogista solely 'to make him interested in obtaining a surrender to the Crown.' It had been a self-interested gesture; no legal principles or precedents had been involved.[6] Yet when Ottawa suddenly asked for the surrender of the whole reserve, the head chief terminated all further negotiations. Shielded by this decisive action on the part of their leader, the band, led by Ogista's son Jarvis, petitioned the minister of the interior, stating that they had decided to sell 1,200 acres of mineral land – enough for both contenders – but no more, on condition that the government recognized Ogista's explorer's rights.

In October, Church's son, Philetus Munsen Church, and Wilkinson, Ogista, Jarvis, and William Driver – Ogista's son-in-law and interpreter – met in Ottawa with the superintendent general of the Indian Department. The government would agree to only one course. The Indian Department would reserve the right to dispose of the locations 'to whomsoever it would be most advantageous and proper to sell,' and in November the band unconditionally ceded 1,200 acres.[7] Ogista's testing of the system had resulted merely in an unsatisfactory compromise. The band had not been able to retain control over either the manner in which the land would be alienated, the size of the locations, or the person to whom they would be allocated. No new ground had been broken.

Native Resistance to Missionary-Controlled Farming Communities

The band could expect little assistance in its quest for economic and political self-determination from missionaries who upheld the government's assimilation program. In 1874, both the Anglicans and the Methodists briefly reconsidered the idea of establishing isolated model farming communities. Their efforts, however, were defeated by the Ojibwa's lack of interest in the scheme, the scarcity of funds, and the Hudson's Bay Company's policy of encouraging bands north of Sault Ste Marie to stay in the interior.[8]

Ogista's attitude demonstrated how far Native support for missionary-governed settlements had declined since the 1850s. During 1874, in the hope of reviving a farming–mission community at Garden River, the Methodists laid claim to the buildings they had vacated eight years earlier. The result was a two-year dispute with George Menissino, whose family now lived in the mission house, and Ogista, who demanded that the Methodists pay for improvements made by his brother. This confrontation marked the end of the Methodist presence at Garden River. Although the mission continued to claim the land surrounding an old graveyard, the mission house reverted to the band, and one of Buhkwujjenene's daughters, her husband, and their children occupied the premises.[9]

Economic and Political Pressures, 1875–1877

In 1875 no work existed on the reserve and times were harsh. The mining locations ceded in 1874 provided neither employment nor a market for Native produce. Instead of building on Squirrel Island, Duncan G. MacDonald, in association with Messrs McRae, Craig and Company, had erected a sawmill on a seven-acre tract (surrendered by the band in 1872) on the east side of the mouth of the Garden River and used the island offshore to graze horses.[10] The mill operated for only three years before it went into receivership.

Until 1879, when the Conservative government implemented its famous 'national policy' of economic tariffs to protect Canadian businesses from American competition, lumbering suffered a slump which forced many sawmills along the north shores of Lakes Huron and Superior to close down. As a result, young men seeking work were compelled to migrate to mills in Michigan, Wisconsin, and Minnesota. Since by law a band member remaining more than five years in the United States could be struck off the annuity lists, seasonal migration became a necessity. Marriages took place with women from communities lying south or west of Lake Superior, and kinship ties were carefully maintained year after year. Eventually, whole families travelled by schooner from settlement to settlement around Lake Michigan and Lake Superior. Oral traditions from Garden River imply that the spring exodus grew to be a social as well as an economic event, as stops at various communities *en route* to the mills provided opportunities to establish new contacts and revitalize the old.

For those who remained at Garden River, the absence of wage labour continued until 1879 when Duncan G. MacDonald assigned the sawmill and its associated timber limit north of the reserve to John Spry, an American lumberman with a milling establishment on Neebish Island in the St Mary's channel. Hardship also resulted from an Order-in-Council in 1875 which prohibited fishing in October, the month when the community depended on the sale of catches for their winter supply of pork and flour.[11]

During these years, the Ojibwa complained not only about the lack of employment opportunities and the new fishing regulations, but also about their meagre annuities. The Garden River Ojibwa joined other bands on Lake Superior in sending a petition through Simon J. Dawson to the Indian Department asking that their annuities be raised to four dollars per capita in accordance with the escalation clause in the Robinson Treaties. Dawson expressed contempt for the law which denied the Native people revenue from resources upon their reserves. Native title was not one of mere occupancy or courtesy, he stormed, 'but of right – conferred by the Imperial Government – long before Ontario had any existence.'[12]

To add insult to injury, band funds were successfully appropriated by a shrewd politician for his own purposes. Edward Barnes Borron, former mine manager at Bruce Mines and in 1874 MP for Algoma, argued that should the Ojibwa's petition be granted, band income from the sale of ceded lands might be used for the construction of a road from Sault Ste Marie to Batchewana Bay. The estimated cost of this road was $45,960 – a large sum at the time. Arguing that the road would benefit the Native people because it would offer more land for colonization and sale, Borron persuaded the Executive Council to pass an order directing that half the burden of the road's cost fall on the Batchewana band's capital fund.[13] The Native population thus once again found their meagre resources depleted by events outside their immediate control.

By 1875, government fishing regulations, low annuities, and Borron's capture of band funds were only three among a growing number of irritants confronting Native leaders. Head chiefs repeatedly asserted that, in practice, the spirit of the Robinson and Pennefather Treaties had been totally disregarded. Boundary descriptions had not been respected; provincial laws encroached on the bands' internal affairs. Although Ogista was well aware of Rankin's manipulation of the reserve's western boundary, he was also incensed by inaccuracies in the 1864 survey of the northern boundary. The imposition of external regulations concerning band membership fuelled additional discontent. In accordance with the terms of the General Enfranchisement Act of 1869, William Van Abbott, who was appointed Indian Lands agent at Sault Ste Marie in 1872, began removing from annuity lists the names of Ojibwa women who had married non-band members. In response, Ogista, Nebenagoching, and Buhkwujjenene immediately asked Van Abbott to write to Ottawa asking that the women be allowed to be 'reclaimed' by the band and that Vict. 31, cap. 12 'be repealed.'[14]

The Ojibwa also received four dollars per capita annuity for the first time in 1875. This, however, did not solve difficulties arising from their lack of control over capital funds. To rectify this problem, several Lake Superior bands petitioned Governor General Lord Dufferin for arrears owing to them under the 1850 treaties. Access to lump-sum payments, their document stressed, was needed to permit the purchase of agricultural implements.[15]

Borron supported the Ojibwa in this new campaign, since promises of arrears payments could act as inducements to encourage further land cessions, especially at a time of economic hardship when younger Ojibwa no longer knew how to trap or hunt. Ottawa, on receiving Borron's communication, instructed Van Abbott to initiate attempts to gain a surrender of the reserve. Although the agent agreed that arrears might smooth the pathway to surrender, he did not share Borron's anticipation that economic difficulties would hasten band compliance. Achievement of this goal, he cautioned, might still prove to be 'a work of time.'[16]

Instead of helping the Garden River band to resolve its political and economic difficulties, the missionary Edward F. Wilson at first proved unsympathetic. Not only did the Anglican missionary have no confidence in Ogista's plans for his community, he also backed increased government intervention in every facet of reserve life. If the Ojibwa would not see for themselves what was good for them, he declared, 'they should be made to do so.'[17] Wilson wholeheartedly advocated schemes to force children away from their families, place them in boarding schools, and indoctrinate them in such a way that they would not wish to return to their former way of life. He remained far more anxious about the willingness of mainstream society to welcome these newly 'civilized' and 'Christianized' entrants than about the havoc wreaked on Native families by his unthinking paternalism. A 'kindly' feeling existed towards Native children in Canada, he argued. It was only the 'undisciplined behaviour of Native people' which prevented them from 'intermixing with the white people.'[18]

Missionary and government attitudes exacerbated the effects of the harsh winter of 1877. Fish catches failed in the autumn, and merchants would extend no advances for provisions without government guarantees.[19] Even so, Ottawa rejected the Ojibwa's appeal for advances on their spring annuities.[20] Extreme distress was narrowly averted by employment offered by the Victoria Mining Company, which operated silver workings in Duncan Township north of the Garden River reserve. In the spring of 1877 the band had granted the company a sixty-six-foot strip across the reserve. Although the mine apparently paid no money for the land, the company hired Native labour throughout the fall and early winter to construct a road along the ceded allowance.[21]

The federal government's emphasis on eradicating special Indian status and dispensing with the reserve system only made Ogista more determined to resist growing threats to the survival of his father's plan for the future. Ottawa commissioned a check survey on mineral locations on ceded territory at Garden River preparatory to an intensive promotion of land sales both north and west of the reserve boundaries established in 1864. The idea was to induce the Native people to accept forty acres per family and surrender the balance of their land. In response to these instructions, Van Abbott called a meeting at Garden River in June 1878. Ogista adamantly resisted the agent's proposals: 'I thank the Government for asking the surrender of my reserve while I am living. It will never come out of my heart to surrender. The Reserve was from Partridge Point to Echo Lake. This is what my father reserved. I hope while I live my Band will never consent.[22]

To Inherit the Kingdom

Ogista held that to solve the problems confronting his band he and his people must seek spiritual guidance. To the Ojibwa, human aid alone could not solve difficulties of such magnitude. Improved conditions would be achieved primarily through re-establishing positive linkages with powerful spiritual agencies, and only secondarily from developing strategies to further specific political ends. By the spring of 1878, the spirit of renewal was so strong among both the Roman Catholics and the Anglicans that it astonished even the crusty evangelical Wilson, and caused him to question the validity of his own assimilationist views.

In a letter to his father written in February 1878, Wilson maintained that, unprompted by any act on his part, Garden River had experienced a spiritual awakening.[23] He further proposed that the settlement might stand as a centre of evangelical rebirth; money must be raised to strengthen the mission and build a new church. To Wilson, the power of the Divine Spirit had finally appeared to infuse events about him, after years in which the priest admitted he had experienced disillusionment and doubt. At last, he concluded, he heard the voice of God speaking, with the whole Native community as His instrument.

The symbolic power with which the Native people vested the biblical use of the term 'nation' at a prayer meeting at Ogista's house on 5 February particularly struck the missionary. Wilson had chosen his text from Matthew, chapter 25: 'And before him shall be gathered all nations: and he shall separate them one from another ... Then shall the King say unto them on his right hand, Come ye blessed of my Father, inherit the kingdom prepared for you from the foundation of the world.'[24]

The central theme of the role of the nations before the throne of grace profoundly affected the old chief who, 'though very hoarse with a bad cold, knelt upon his bed and made a most touching prayer': 'O God, we have heard wonderful news to-night ... We thank thee God for this wonderful news ... and yet how little do we prepare for these great events ... On which side of the great King will we Garden Rivers be? ... God grant that we may be prepared.'[25]

Ogista immediately began planning a course of action based on his father's original vision, but with significant additions. The Ojibwa would continue to test and press the system to yield up precedents for the existence of Aboriginal right, yet interspersed with this intensive political activity would be a gentler appeal to government and the missions. Emphasis on spiritual revitalization and harmony of intent encouraged Ogista to bring Ottawa officials and many band representatives together in one large gathering to promote what he hoped might be mutual aims. To this end, the Garden River head chief invited Native leaders from Fort William, Manitoulin, Saugeen, Nipissing, Magnetawan, Mississauga, and Parry Island to meet at Garden River on 1 July. He also requested Ottawa to send a delegation and monies, to be drawn on the band's capital fund, to finance the meeting.[26]

Van Abbott attended the last session of the council on 7 July and found among these assembled sixty-seven representatives from different bands who stated they were there without money or provisions.[27] Since no government authorities other than Van Abbott had arrived, the assembly decided to send a delegation to Ottawa in the fall. Ogista and Buhkwujjenene were appointed from Garden River; Nebenagoching would represent the Batchewana band; Bwanakeyosh and Peter Keokonse, Keokonse's son, would attend on behalf of the Thessalon people. A son of the deceased Lake Huron head chief named Megis, who had signed the Robinson-Huron Treaty on behalf of the Parry Island band; a son of the deceased head chief Tagwaninini from Wikwemikong; the notable Manitoulin head chief William Kenoshameg; and, from Muskoka, David Aisance – all important leaders in the Great Lakes Native community – planned to join Ogista on his journey to the capital.[28]

When Ogista informed Van Abbott of his intentions, the agent replied that the band would receive no money for travelling expenses, nor would they be welcome at Ottawa. The head chief paid no attention. The delegates, anticipating such opposition, had arranged for the journey to be funded by the Grand Council, the forerunner of the present-day Union of Ontario Native people, whose secretary, Moses Madwayosh, had the money ready and waiting at Collingwood. Following the delegation's departure in late September, Van Abbott informed the minister of the interior that the Native people were carrying a wampum belt which, they hoped, would move the government to recognize them as a loyal and independent people under the Crown.

The belt, six feet long and six inches wide, depicted twenty-four Native people holding a rope attached to a boat. This wampum, Van Abbott continued, had been given to the Ojibwa by representatives of the British Crown in 1764. Enclosed with the agent's letter was a message from the Garden River band stating that the Native people in their alliance with the British had 'bled from head to foot' for their country. In fighting on the side of the British forces during the War of 1812 they had honoured a promise they had made to the British authorities in 1764 that they would fight at the King's command. For this assistance, the Aboriginal people had received presents which they appreciated 'as much as the white does his money and land.'[29]

The Canadian government impressed on Van Abbott that under no circumstances should the Native delegation be allowed to proceed to Ottawa. There was no need, it was argued, and in any case Native people had no right to make such demands. The Ojibwa might describe the wampum belt as a 'treaty,' noted David Laird, the superintendent general of Indian Department, contemptuously in a letter to the Indian Lands agent; but those officials who had encouraged Native faith in messages represented by symbols worked in shell lacked the authority to make such vain 'promises.' The minister also said that the bands were presumptuous for requesting a 'written agreement ... assuring them that they were entitled to Reserves' as well as official guarantees that no further surveys would be conducted without Native consent. Laird concluded by asserting that he alone had the power to subdivide reserves whenever it might be 'necessary' or 'in the interest of a band.'[30]

Undeterred by Van Abbott's warnings that they would not be received at Ottawa, the Native delegates requested and obtained an audience in the fall with the governor general, Lord Lorne, in Ottawa. Lorne received his Native guests graciously and promised to visit several of their communities, including Garden River, on a forthcoming expedition to Red River he was planning for 1881. The delegation stressed their hostility to the allotment system intended for their reserves; but owing to Lorne's sympathetic manner, they decided not to voyage to England to present their grievances in person to the Queen – a course they earlier had been considering as a last resort. Lorne instead assured them of the inviolate nature of their special relationship to the Crown. Lord Lorne's promise to meet with the band leaders in the near future also provided exactly the excuse Ogista needed to prevent the surrender of the Garden River reserve. And it came none too soon. Arthur Rankin had been called upon by John A. Macdonald, minister of the interior and superintendent general of Indian Department in the new Conservative government formed in the autumn of 1878, to raise once again the matter of ceding the reserve.[31] Ogista maintained that no surrender would take place unless Lorne himself were willing to open negotiations. Rankin meanwhile tried unsuccessfully to purchase the Elliot location, as well as 400 additional acres for a marble mine, located due north of the mouth of the Garden River. By refusing to deal with any individual except Lorne, the Ojibwa had stripped Rankin of government authorization for his essentially self-interested schemes. Ogista then, with a tenacity that startled Ottawa, opposed Rankin's right to a small triangle of land of 345 acres whose 'hypotenuse' followed the reserve's western boundary where it crossed the Clark location.[32]

The second meeting with Lord Lorne took place at Garden River on 31 July 1881 amid considerable ceremony. Head men bearing long staves formed a double column flanking the path from a central dais to the wharf where Lorne's vessel had docked. Tall, portly, and dressed in traditional attire,[33] Ogista came forward to greet the Governor General. With the aid of an interpreter, the chief repeated the Ojibwa's grievances regarding the loss of hunting and fishing rights and incorrect reserve boundaries, as well as their desire for payment of treaty arrears. He concluded by handing Lorne a petition.[34] Although the band was afterwards branded in the Canadian press as 'chronic grumblers,' Simon J. Dawson, now the MP for Algoma, refused to accept this judgment. Under similar circumstances, he wrote to John A. Macdonald, 'Whites would grumble in a far more audible manner.'[35]

Native Commitment to Independent Action

Irregularities and legal anomalies intended to undermine the Ojibwa's ability to keep their land became targets for Native attack. When, in May 1882, Nebenagoching demanded another survey of the northern boundary of the Batchewana reserve, Ottawa's examination of the documents pertaining to this issue revealed a confusing array of area designations of the territory ceded by the Batchewana band in 1859. Apparently in response to Joseph Wilson's private suggestions after 1860, Keating's estimation of 184 square miles had been increased to 300 square miles by Order-in-Council on 22 July 1859. In 1866, Alexander Campbell gave yet another figure, of 250 square miles.[36]

Nebenagoching railed at the idea that none of these estimates compelled an adjustment of the northern boundary to include the mining locations sold on the ceded Batchewana tract between 1859 and 1880. Owing to Keating's shrewd manipulation of the survey, Ottawa could ignore the issue of whether or not minerals fell under Native proprietorship. The government characterized the supposed amount of territory surrendered by the Batchewana people as 'liberal.'[37] Nebenagoching nevertheless felt betrayed and made no secret of his attitudes on the issue.

At the same time both the Batchewana and Garden River bands combined to oppose Rankin's takeover of Partridge Point, which fell within the triangle of land fought for by Ogista between 1877 and 1880. In April 1883, two families, the Cadottes and the Perraults – the first belonging to the Garden River band and the second to the Batchewana band – were served with writs of eviction from farmlands they had occupied for more than twenty years. Ogista and Nebenagoching appealed to the Department of Indian Affairs (established formally in 1880) to intervene. In response, Ottawa began an examination of documents pertaining to the sale of the Clark location and decided that the boundaries of the mining location and reserve were too ambiguous to permit a government stand on the case. The complainants, Ottawa maintained, nevertheless had recourse to the courts.[38] This boundary dispute led Ogista, John Ogista, Buhkwujjenene, Nebenagoching, Nebenagoching's son Edward, Mishkeash and his brother Gagiosh, and Waubmama to attend the Grand Council held in 1884 at Cape Croker. They expected to find a sympathetic audience. Yet when they discovered that at Ottawa's instigation the council would devote its time exclusively to discussing the Indian Acts – especially amendments relating to enfranchisement – Ogista grew contemptuous of the gathering.

After listening to one municipal scheme for subdividing reserves and for subjecting Native landowners to a property tax, Ogista proclaimed that he 'blamed the Native people of the East and South who were well educated, for having these laws passed.' When the subject of exclusion from band rolls of Native people who accepted enfranchisement and women who married non-band members came up later, Ogista felt that he might arouse productive controversy by revealing the limitations on

Native choice produced by these either-or situations. 'Let the women and the enfranchised go,' he characterized this attitude. 'I will give them nothing.' The fact that Native leaders living to the south could relinquish responsibility for those they were expected to protect appeared to Ogista to be not only negligence but also weakness.[39]

Instead of voting on the issues, the northern delegates soon unanimously voiced opposition to the character of the meeting and prepared to leave. The eight were angered by criticisms by south-eastern leaders that northern bands were backward, wishing to reject the virtues of education and the franchise, and preferring to live 'in the woods or wilderness.' It was only through the intervention of Chief Solomon James of Parry Island that this breach was healed. James chastised the council for trying to impose inflexible ideological and moral constraints on all bands in the province. And, ultimately, the wisdom of James's views was acknowledged.

Ogista responded by expressing his gratitude for James's intervention. 'I decided to come to the Council and make my parting friendly,' he began, 'but I find you have retained my presence among you and I thank you all.' Ogista then limited the rest of his speech to two points. First, he stated, as a head chief he intended to retain control of his band's membership, and second, mining interests had not only broken their promises to his people but had manipulated reserve boundaries. He concluded by requesting that his message be conveyed to Indian Affairs at once.[40]

Band Responses to Divisive External Pressures

The band was now experiencing formidable difficulties in maintaining lines of communication with Ottawa. Van Abbott endeavoured diligently to promote Indian Affairs policies after he learned in 1884 that the superintendent general of Indian Affairs had been considering replacing him with a younger man who would strongly encourage farming among the Ojibwa.[41] Knowing that the Native communities rejected government systems of land allotment, Van Abbott sought to convey the impression of total compliance to Ottawa's agricultural schemes by preventing Ojibwa grievances from reaching Indian Affairs. This he did by levying such severe punishments on certain educated and influential band members for even minor infractions of the Indian Acts – especially those clauses pertaining to membership qualifications and transmission of property – that he silenced complaints at the source. Oral traditions at Garden River stress that Waubmama was one of these victims, and examination of the documentary evidence substantiates the Ojibwa elders' statements.[42] Van

Abbott understood enough of the Ojibwa authority structure to know that by suppressing the activities of an influential family head, in this case the leading member of the Crane *dodem* at Garden River, he could intimidate heads of other *dodemic* groups without noticeably infringing the band's traditional leadership system.

Van Abbott's manipulations ultimately failed in their intent to break the band down into factions, since the groups immediately took steps to prevent such an outcome. The Ojibwa knew they needed a new organizational vehicle for the development and promotion of their ideas and policies, yet they had no desire to deprive their band in any way of the structural continuity and tradition of protective service residing in the person of their head chief. On 17 April 1885, the band therefore petitioned Indian Affairs to permit the election of several subchiefs, while the position of head chief would continue to be filled in the traditional way. This suggestion for granting the group increased responsibility over its internal affairs nevertheless floundered owing to Ottawa's imposition of an either-or framework on band decision making. There was no legal precedent, the government insisted, for allowing an individual such as Ogista 'to retain his powers as chief in the event of the Band adopting systematic election in the appointment of chiefs.'[43] The band's interest in strengthening its local government by reconciling the old and the new was thus temporarily set aside, and attention was directed towards yet another external challenge.

A Time for Sacrifice – Ogista's Last Years

Both the Garden River and the Batchewana bands resented their lack of control over the government's use of their capital funds, and decided to counter the threat to their economic future as a group by adopting a policy of passive resistance. The drain on the Batchewana revenues for road construction had grown so intense that by 1886 Ottawa's decision to expend $400 annually for a schoolteacher's salary terminated interest payments to the band altogether.[44] It was little wonder that both bands fought against Indian Affairs' unilateral allocation of additional monies from their funds to promote white colonization. According to Ottawa, Native peoples could directly participate in voting money only for the purposes of education, medical expenses, and roads.[45]

Ogista, in order to discourage persons in his band from breaking with his group's policy of unified resistance to the government's control of Native revenue, blocked attempts by the agent to grant funds from the band's revenue, even for individual needs. Although the chief tried to aid in extreme cases, it still happened that sick, elderly, or destitute persons who lacked assistance from close kin or friends could suffer as long as this government–band deadlock continued.[46] At the same time, Native leaders fully supported the government's drive to encourage settlement, provided that public works did not drain their group's coffers, since sale of ceded reserve lands would result in an increase in Ojibwa capital funds. In 1885 the *Algoma Pioneer* could confidently proclaim, 'Come to Algoma. No Indian Troubles Here.'[47] The bands as a group meanwhile experienced hardship for the sake of gaining future rights to share in the potential benefits of Ottawa's policies. This form of 'sacrifice' at Garden River only ended, its goal unattained, when the period of intense settlement drew to a close.

During the last three years of his life, Ogista devoted himself entirely to delaying the activities of encroaching interests so that Jarvis Ogista, his son, and Buhkwujjenene could investigate each threat as it arose and seek to preserve band interests from injury. When in 1887 the Canadian Pacific Railway (CPR) surveyed an allowance for a spur line to Sault Ste Marie which would cut through the community's best agricultural land, Buhkwujjenene contacted Indian Affairs asking that the line be moved north half a mile to avoid several farms.[48] When requested by Ottawa to make inquiries, Van Abbott held that the complaint had been 'grossly exaggerated.' As a result, families affected by the railway's construction received minimal compensation for damages. The lack of consideration for Ojibwa views on this occasion fostered tensions which pervaded all future relations between the band and the CPR.[49]

Within a year of this survey the band reported that the railway had been removing gravel from four pits. Two of these pits were located near Waubashine Island, the third bordered the Root River, and the fourth and largest lay near the Garden River. Ogista set out determinedly to vindicate Native rights in the face of this new aggressor. The band, meanwhile, collected information, charged the CPR twenty-five cents for each truckload already removed from the four sites, and levied a royalty of 3 per cent on all future gravel sales.[50]

To give his band's demands bite, Ogista maintained that the CPR had acted illegally in coming onto the reserve without notifying his people, and that no surrender for the railway allowance would take place until payment was made for the gravel. Seriously ill and having to be carried to meetings on a bed, the head chief declared that although he had personally been forbidden by Van Abbott to communicate with Ottawa on the subject, he expected that his people would persevere in pressing for official recognition of their rights in this matter after he was gone.[51]

Ogista's Influence on the Reverend E.F. Wilson

Ogista died on 23 December 1890, and almost immediately land for the railway allowance, a station, and all four gravel pits was expropriated under the terms of the Railway Act.[52] Never once during his final years had the head chief failed to defend the prerogatives vested in him by his father. He had consistently upheld the notion that there must be either consent or conquest before any relinquishment of Native right might be said to have occurred on unceded territory. Within Sault Ste Marie society, however, Ogista would not be particularly remembered for his efforts to secure a measure of Native self-determination.

So entrenched in Anglican circles at Sault Ste Marie was a notion that Ogista represented an 'elevated Indian' who had been redeemed from heathenism through Christianity that a debate arose over a statement allegedly spoken by the chief on his deathbed. When, on 31 January 1891, the *Sault Express* quoted the leader as saying he would reappear 'as a sturgeon in a small lake at the back of the houses,' the Reverend James Irvine, resident missionary at Garden River, charged that Ogista could never have uttered such words. To Irvine, once the transition from 'savage' to 'saved' was made, no Christian chief could continue to hold traditional Native beliefs, even though the newspaper's editor contended that data for the article had been drawn from a 'reliable' source and 'had been corroborated.'[53]

Irvine's attitudes undoubtedly prevented him from understanding Native goals and aspirations. Wilson, however, was beginning to show less myopia on this subject than his Anglican colleague. During the late 1880s in his *Algoma Missionary News and Shingwauk Journal*, Wilson had highlighted instances of Native conformity to English cultural traditions. Descriptions of Yuletide feasts at Garden River stressed the importance of 'roast beef, plum pudding, tarts, preserves and jellies' to the occasion. The *Journal* depicted 'cottages' surrounded by gardens, fences, and 'flowering shrubs.'[54] Nevertheless, although one article might claim that 'not much difference [existed] between houses of these Native people and those of our British working class,'[55] by 1890 Wilson eventually had to admit that such resemblances remained principally superficial.

The missionary could not avoid knowing that he was dealing with a culture very different from his own. Whole villages, including persons whom he had considered converted Christians, could suddenly vacate a region because 'a number had died.'[56] Wilson also found that Native people often refused to work for him without pay, and at times openly questioned the integrity of the missionary's intentions: 'There is something about the Indian character which makes them exceeding difficult to work with [Wilson asserted]. He won't believe you are acting for his good [and] not your own profit.'[57] Wilson held that even the catechist Buhkwujjenene exhibited these particular failings. During their travels together in England, the missionary reminisced, 'it was hard to convince our swarthy companion that the money was going to be applied to the purpose for which it was given ... [Buhkwujjenene] seemed to think at least a portion should find its way into his pocket for his personal use.'[58]

Ever since Wilson's experience at Ogista's house in 1878, the clergyman had been passing through a transitional point in his career; subsequent events further increased his sense of being in limbo. Ottawa ceased promoting industrial schools, since it held that the graduates of these institutions competed for employment with white tradesmen and immigrant labour. Indian Affairs showed a diminishing interest in his educational projects, as did the Native people themselves, with many withdrawing their children from his industrial institutions. Wilson therefore began to revise many of his former ideas and seek new solutions. By 1890 he had even begun to favour a measure of Native self-determination.[59]

More than a decade before, Wilson and Ogista had both interpreted the concept of 'kingdom' to mean a state inherited by nations faithful to the Divine Will. Their cultural backgrounds led them to choose radically different ways of achieving this goal. Yet one thing was certain. Wilson had been far more changed by his labours among the Native peoples than Ogista had been altered ideologically by his contact with late-nineteenth-century British social doctrines.

In his later years, Wilson reconstructed a new vision of the future of Native society from his experiences in the mission field. By contrast, Ogista chose temporarily to relinquish linkages with external agencies which provided material advantages but threatened the political, social, and economic autonomy of his people. Hardship might result in the short term, but the Ojibwa hoped that in the end the rewards would be more than adequate compensation for the difficulties experienced.

E.B. Borron Employs the Shingwaukonse Legend to Enhance His Own Definition of Indian Status

The issue of providing for payments according to the 'escalation clause' in the Robinson Treaties – an issue which harked back to a time when the old Province of Canada could, without serious loss, sustain a yearly outlay of four dollars per capita – became a bone of contention between Ottawa and Ontario. Ontario, in control of revenue from Crown lands, and hence faced with the likelihood of having to capitalize a fund to satisfy the Native claim, wished to keep expenditures as low as possible. For this reason the province sent E.B. Borron to Garden River to collect data which might justify slashing the size of the annuity lists.

Borron's approach to his task entailed establishing grounds for the existence in 1850 of a charter group. From this starting point, he argued, it would be possible to determine, by a system of patrilineal reckoning, who were and who were not qualified annuitants. There would be no consideration of the historical factors which led to drastic reductions in group membership after 1858 or social pressures which compelled Métis to fill the dwindling ranks.

In four reports written between December 1891 and October 1894 Borron submitted what he held to be a strong case for halving the number of annuitants.[60] Evidence to substantiate his views was derived from two sources: from oral testimonies gathered by John Driver, brother of Ogista's son-in-law William; and from a report written by William B. Robinson in which the commissioner set out his rationale for including the escalation clause in the treaties. Conditions for data collecting were not ideal. Driver had encountered difficulties in eliciting information. Both Buhkwujjenene and Nebenagoching had proved reluctant to speak with him, probably as much from anger at Borron's appropriation of band funds in 1864 as from a desire to impede the inquiry. As a result, only sketchy information could be obtained regarding the nature of relations between Shingwaukonse's band and the Métis.

On the basis of this information, Borron asserted that Little Pine in 1849 had acted as the catalyst in a process by which 'half-breeds' became endowed with Indian status. By promising Indian presents and land to Métis who assisted him in dispossessing the Quebec and Lake Superior Mining Association, Little Pine, Borron suggested, epitomized the impracticality of a charismatic leader who cared little for the escalating costs incurred by the province with an increase in the number of those claiming Indian status. Yet Borron's assumptions were wrong. It was not true that the Mica Bay takeover had brought large numbers of Métis into the bands. Individuals who participated in the expedition to the mine had been drawn from several bands, as well as from the Métis community at the rapids, but the system of recruitment adopted by Little Pine in the fall of 1849 had in no way changed the traditional mode of determining permanent group membership. The exercise of dyadic kin attachments to Shingwaukonse's nodal core group still constituted the most frequent manner in which individuals had joined the Garden River band after 1849. Little Pine might have granted permission for non-band members to reside on his territory, but this did not necessarily entitle them to share in all band prerogatives.

Borron also claimed that William B. Robinson had endorsed the inclusion on annuity rolls of certain Métis families for political reasons. It would have been expedient in 1850, the politician argued, to placate Métis such as the Birons who seemed to wield considerable influence within the Ojibwa population. Yet Borron either did not realize or simply ignored the fact that kinship ties existed between Shingwaukonse's own family and that of the Biron family.

To support his claim that the Ojibwa should not be allowed to have control over the membership of their own bands, Borron drew a contrast between 'Métis' – who, he argued, had been incorporated by 1850 into the capitalist commercial system, since they always trapped, fished, or made maple sugar for sale – and 'Indians' – whose social organization he felt derived solely from their individualistic system of hunting territories. Yet his statements concerning the deterministic influence exercised by one particular mode of land tenure on social composition applied far better to interior groups, which had grown dependent on the Hudson's Bay Company, than to the more economically autonomous coastal bands. Borron refused to admit the possibility that leaders like Shingwaukonse could exercise prerogatives over land and resources on behalf of their bands, simply because to have done so would have undermined his principal contention that Native groups in general lacked internal mechanisms capable of regulating their membership.

A Crisis in Leadership, 1891–1897

While lying on his deathbed, Ogista had asked Van Abbott to recognize his son Jarvis Ogista as head chief, but the agent had remained noncommittal, merely stating that such a decision would have to rest with the band alone. Then, soon after the chief's death, the agent imposed an electoral system on the Garden River community. The elected leadership which resulted was composed of a chief, Buhkwujjenene, and four councillors to represent the 437 band members.[61] School attendance, roads, and community health were the band's only responsibilities. It had little control over reserve resources or the regulation of band membership.

Buhkwujjenene had no intention of allowing these constraints to hinder his effectiveness as chief. In July 1891 he petitioned for two of his sons-in-law and Tegoosh's wife and children to be placed on the annuity list.[62] Ottawa refused his request, just at the time when Borron's investigations were causing concern that others, too, might be denied such rights. The consequences proved dramatic. Borron's stress on the ambiguous nature of 'Indian status' at Garden River gave Van Abbott leeway to manipulate band membership to his own advantage. In consequence, bitter interfamily disputes arose. As the decline in the powers of the chief and council became increasingly apparent, band members launched attacks on both the external decree and the local agent who had imposed it.

By 1896, at least three Ojibwa families had hired lawyers and attempted to secure title to their land holdings at Garden River on grounds of length of tenure.[63] Other instances of strife, one involving a son-in-law of Buhkwujjenene, gave rise to witchcraft attacks on Native persons who seemed to support Ottawa's policy of forcing individuals to leave the reserve.[64] In every case, however, the underlying cause of discord was the fact that the band's leaders had been deprived of their power to initiate policies, regulate activities, and protect band interests. Buhkwujjenene declared that because of the prevailing lack of respect for 'the authority of the ancient chiefs,' too many people acted in a self-interested manner, 'like whites.'[65]

Subsequent events, in the end, made it possible to prevent the band from breaking into adversarial cliques. Probably most influential in averting chaos was the outcome of a legal dispute, in the course of which the Native plaintiff, Joseph Tegoosh, recalled precedents Shingwaukonse had established in 1848 and 1849 to govern land holding at Garden River. In the fall of 1891, Van Abbott had permitted Joseph Nowquagezick, who had moved to Garden River from Manitoulin Island as a child and been raised by the Anglican missionaries, to build on a lot claimed by the Tegoosh family. In response, Joseph Tegoosh produced the land deed dictated by his grandfather, Little Pine, in December 1848. It was obvious from this document that Shingwaukonse had granted land lying east of the Garden River to his son Tegoosh, confident that he possessed full authority to do so according to the traditions of his people. 'Nongom nimina ondjiiw ogimawiian,' Shingwaukonse had stated: 'I now give [the land] to him in my quality as chief.'[66]

As this case proceeded towards a settlement in which the Tegoosh family agreed to relinquish nine acres to Nowquagezick, Ottawa grew increasingly reluctant to interfere in the affair. It had been revealed that two Christian missions had acquired title to lands at Garden River on the grounds that their allotments had been reserved to them by Little Pine years before. The issue of how much weight should be granted to the territorial prerogatives exercised by Shingwaukonse prior to 1850 threatened to resurrect the whole question of Aboriginal rights with a vengeance. Van Abbott, too, apparently decided it to be an opportune time, given the desire of Native individuals to test the validity of such precedents in the courts, to stop manipulating band lists and withdrawing residency rights.

By late 1896, the agent also knew that he faced strong opposition from both the Garden River and the Batchewana bands which could jeopardize his career. This opposition occasionally took the form of public indignation, but was mostly of a covert nature. In November, Ottawa received a petition, signed by Nebenagoching, demanding Van Abbott's removal from office, although, when later questioned, the chief denied knowledge of the complaint. The agent had been seen publicly intoxicated, the document submitted, had charged fees for services which it was his duty to perform, had withheld annuities, and had too freely stuck names off the band lists. In response, and without Van Abbott's knowledge, Ottawa instructed A. Dingman, an inspector of Indian reserves who was then looking into the Tegoosh case, to conduct an investigation into Van Abbott's activities.[67] Dingman found that the agent was suffering from overwork, illness, poor pay, and lack of confidence about his ability to do his job. The Department of Indian Affairs and the two bands agreed to permit Van Abbott to remain at his post until he was eligible for full pension. Van Abbott then stopped his former oppressive practices, began to rely substantially on an educated Native constabulary to maintain order on reserves, and became an impartial intermediary in disputes between the band and Ottawa over timber.[68]

Van Abbott's change in behaviour alleviated much of the fear and concern at Garden River. Ottawa's rejection of Borron's recommendations as too harsh and radical removed a second source of contention. Instead, Commissioner A. Macrae, who visited Garden River in August 1897, suggested that certain individuals might be given 'non-transferable status' – meaning that their children might not be entitled to Indian status – but that the government should not significantly alter the existing band lists.[69] In this more congenial atmosphere, the leadership returned wholeheartedly to pressing for a measure of managerial control over reserve resources.

The band wished to increase opportunities for small-scale family logging operations and advocated a re-survey of the northern boundary to include a tract of 12,616 acres – known as the 'Indian Strip' – covered by the Spry timber lease.[70] Following a flurry of petitions and the visit of a

Native delegation to Ottawa in July 1895, Indian Affairs agreed to move the east-west boundary northward, provided that the band granted $350 for the purpose from their capital funds of $47,068.[71] Buhkwujjenene and his councillors readily agreed.

When it became apparent in October 1896 that a far larger sum would be requested by Ottawa for subdividing the township of Duncan, north of the reserve, Buhkwujjenene vetoed the earlier transaction and demanded that the reserve's western boundary first be run north from Partridge Point before any further negotiations regarding the northern line took place. By this act the chief demonstrated to his band that its leadership could still respond to challenges and bring matters to a standstill until a consensus could be reached. On 9 February 1897, Buhkwujjenene and twelve others walked out of a council meeting, with the result that thirty-four of the forty-seven voting band members originally present agreed to a survey, which cost the band $3,787.[72] In this manner, leadership deferred to the wishes of the group, which viewed the return of the 'Indian Strip' as a potential source of future revenue, and registered its dislike of Ottawa's terms. Meanwhile, Ottawa upheld the continuation of the Spry lease until the company cleared the land of its timber.

Disappointed with Ottawa's rejection of their bid for an improved economic future for their community, the Ojibwa nevertheless continued the struggle to develop their local economy in other ways. When the sawmill at the mouth of the Garden River burned down in 1891, it became necessary for the band to make arrangements with local lumbering firms to secure employment during the fall and winter months, in contravention of the law prohibiting Native people from conducting their own businesses.[73] Despite the formidable odds, however, in the end Ojibwa persistence triumphed.

Trials and Tribulations of the Timber Trade during the 1890s

Logging provided a valued source of Native income for several reasons. It added an extra option to the Ojibwa's traditional fall and winter activities, allowing them to participate in mainstream commercial society without radically altering the composition of the kin-based winter hunting group or undermining the system of family hunting and trapping territories. The establishment of timber quotas small enough to discourage intensive cutting allowed male work groups to intersperse logging with other bush employments such as caribou and moose hunting, trapping, fishing, maple sugar gathering, mineral exploration, and guiding.

Provisioning camps for the winter remained a major difficulty, since provincial fishing laws prohibited taking fish in the autumn when fish were most abundant, and merchants were often reluctant to extend credit. The once bountiful Whitefish Island fishery also had grown less productive because wastes dumped by steamers near the rapids had polluted the water. Finally, in 1898, the island was expropriated under the terms of the Railway Act, although certain residents were permitted to retain property holdings until 1905.[74] The decline of this fishery brought new challenges, since it threatened to leave band members increasingly at the mercy of the local merchants in the spring and fall. Not surprisingly, a search for alternatives to the sale of fish as a means of supplying their winter bush camps ranked high among Ojibwa priorities by the 1890s. Government attitudes towards Native logging operations did not help matters. Ottawa was parsimonious with permission to take timber off the reserve, extending the privilege only to bands in straitened economic circumstances. When Buhkwujjenene directed Van Abbott in the fall of 1891 to inform Ottawa of the band's desire to cut two thousand cords of spruce, Ottawa reacted by requesting a report stating 'whether [the] Native people absolutely [were] in need of such a privilege.'[75]

This state of affairs persisted for over five years. When crop failure compelled Buhkwujjenene in October 1896 to petition the prime minister, Sir Wilfrid Laurier, for a general cutting licence, it was expected that sympathy for the band's plight as winter approached would move government to act quickly to alleviate economic distress.[76] In anticipation of a favourable reply, family groups moved to their logging territories, set up wigwams and shanties, and cut haulage ways.

This time Ottawa curtailed logging operations for an entire winter. The resulting lack of funds so crippled farming activities the following spring that the Ojibwa were forced to apply for government assistance to tide them over to the next year. When a timber buyer described the Ojibwa's method of parcelling out reserve land to Hayter Reed, the superintendent general of Indian affairs, Reed raised objections to the family territorial system. He felt that this mode of organization failed to clear the land properly for division into farms. By allowing the Ojibwa to cut 'promiscuously,' he argued, 'only the best and most accessible [timber] would be taken,' disputes would arise, and 'the risk of fire [would be] increased.'[77] To curtail production until the Ojibwa demonstrated a greater readiness to assume agricultural pursuits, Reed stipulated that, while timber had to be block cut, not more than 500,000 board feet of pine might be removed by the Native people during the winter. Gradually, modification of the terrain would force the Ojibwa to adopt the farming economy the government had been unsuccessfully trying to impose on them for over half a century.

The agent in November received a map of the reserve graphed out in allotments, each two miles wide. No work, Reed ordered, might be undertaken until the agent had marked out the reserve according to plan and had ascribed a berth, to be block cut, to each work group. In reply, Van Abbott, who by 1896 had come to question the feasibility of Ottawa's Indian policy, argued that the arrangement suited neither the buyer nor the Native people. The original contract with H.P. Fremlin, the timber merchant, had called for one million board feet of pine. To Abbott, '500,000 board feet would go a very short way among the 70 or more Native people who may require work.'[78]

Familiar with the topography of the reserve, the band stressed that its own system of land allocations suited the rugged character of the countryside. Much of the timber lay scattered in valleys, a factor that militated against block cutting. As for Ottawa's emphasis on conservation, the Ojibwa replied that bush fires annually destroyed far more timber than they could take out. They appealed for permission to begin work at once, with no changes in their mode of operations, since most families had already erected bush camps, and groups lacking horses or oxen would have no means of transporting logs once ice choked the rivers.

Their arguments were to no avail. Indian Affairs rejected the contract with Fremlin because it was an agreement the band had made itself. Ottawa then negotiated a new contract, but by this time it was too late for work to begin. By February the Ojibwa were so deeply in debt to merchants for provisions that they could not afford seed for spring planting. Jarvis Ogista, Buhkwujjenene's spokesman, appealed to Indian Affairs for help, stating that a 'sentiment of humanity,' if nothing else, should impel Ottawa to draw monies from the Garden River capital fund for seed potatoes.[79]

By depriving the Ojibwa of earnings from logging, the government had eradicated the band's insurance against hardships occasioned by crop failure. Yet Ottawa refused Jarvis's request, referring to the same policy which had driven Abatossaway out of business in 1859. 'The Department does not agree that the whole band should pay for seed requested by a few,' its reply stated.[80]

When, at Jarvis's prompting, Father G. Artus, SJ, and Van Abbott voiced strong support for the grants, Ottawa reluctantly agreed to forward $325 to be repaid with an interest rate of 6 per cent per annum. By May, however, neither money nor seed had arrived, and it was too late to plant potatoes. Not surprisingly, tempers at Garden River ran high. 'I wish to tell you,' Jarvis informed Reed, 'that ... if next winter our people is [*sic*] starving as they have been the last one we will hold the Department of Indian Affairs responsible.'[81]

When matters did not improve the following winter, Jarvis, who had been elected chief in 1897, attempted to have Father Artus appointed as adviser to the band. Ottawa immediately objected, on the grounds that such a course might foster interdenominational rivalries.

It was clear that the Ojibwa would have to take independent action to change government perceptions of their economic competencies. Eventually, they were able to effect significant changes in Ottawa's policy and have some of the restrictions on their enterprises temporarily removed.

The band's first step was taken during the winter of 1901–2, after one timber company refused to grant advances for provisions unless the local agent officially guaranteed that the Ojibwa people would cut 30,000 cedar and tamarack ties. William Nichols, Van Abbott's successor, had less experience in arranging such deals than his predecessor or the Ojibwa themselves. He not only agreed to authorize the work but also permitted the band to negotiate its own contract with the company.[82] The Ojibwa resolved to cut the ties eight feet long and six inches thick, and to sell their finished product at twenty-one cents per tie, minus dues. Delivery would take place along the St Mary's River, the Echo River, and the CPR rail line. In 1901 both the company and Indian Affairs seemed satisfied with the arrangement. The following January, however, the company suddenly refused to pay for any ties under six and one-half inches thick, and stipulated that the rail line would constitute the only acceptable delivery point, whereupon the band's new chief, Charles Cadotte, accused the firm of breaking the contract. At the same time, the government had doubled the dues on each tie, charging four cents instead of the two cents they charged whites. Cadotte demanded to know the reason why.[83]

Ottawa replied that the company required ties over six inches thick to prevent the Ojibwa from inadvertently cutting them under six inches at the narrow end. Other arguments were equally petty. It was suggested that, while the contract might have allowed ties to be delivered to the banks of the Echo River, in the final analysis 'the tenderer had the option of choosing the locality,' not the band. With regard to the charging of double dues, Indian Affairs reiterated that the timber belonged to all members of the band, 'men, women and children in equal shares.' The government justified the increased dues, which were theoretically destined for the band's capital fund, by arguing that workers should 'not be allowed to appropriate the full value of the timber for their own use and benefit, and thus deprive the nonworkers of their share of interest therein.'[84] Given Borron's sweeping appropriation of Indian funds in 1874, this must have seemed like the last straw. Yet, instead of reacting with anger, the band maintained a calm, businesslike demeanour.

The usual diameter of cedar and tamarack trees at Garden River, Cadotte explained, enabled a man to make only two ties six-and-one-half inches thick from a single log, whereas from the same log one could obtain three ties six inches thick. The chief particularly resented having women, children, and the elderly used as an excuse to deprive Native leadership of decision-making powers over proceeds from reserve lands. Yet the chief's response was measured. Band members 'not taking ties were employed in other lucrative manner,' he asserted, 'and ... the whole band really reaped the benefit of the work on the ties.'[85] Double dues were therefore unnecessary. There was no open condemnation of Ottawa, only a straightforward account of why, from the band's perspective, the government policy was seen to conserve neither revenue nor resources.

The band also gained an ally in its Indian agent, William L. Nichols. New to the situation, Nichols was shocked by the cycle of seasonal hardship imposed upon the Ojibwa. Conservation of resource revenue counted for far more to Ottawa than community welfare, he noted. To alleviate distress, he began drawing on his 'own means' to assist Native families who, as a consequence, were soon 'doing better than they had [done] before under similar circumstances.'[86] The band's patience and Nichols's confidence were rewarded. The company expressed satisfaction with the 30,000 ties delivered to the CPR and stated that it hoped to enter into future contracts with the band. The Ojibwa had proven that they could manage their own business affairs in a way that the government found difficult to criticize. As a result, Ottawa relaxed its policies regarding dues and quotas.

Soon afterward, the band negotiated a lucrative contract with another company, Burton Brothers of Barrie, which gained Ottawa's approval for its policies for handling supplies, haulage teams, timber scaling, and any disputes which might arise. In a more generous vein than his predecessors Hayter Reed and James Smart, Frank Pedley, the new superintendent general of Indian Affairs, gave Nichols leave to issue timber permits to Native people 'for such quantities as each applicant could be reasonably expected to produce.'[87] Not only had the band preserved its organizational and territorial systems, it had also improved the government's attitude to Native interests.

Building on Established Foundations

By the turn of the century, a more congenial economic and political climate, as well as a heightened public interest in things Native, provided Ojibwa individuals with novel opportunities to draw on their stores of traditional lore. About 1900, George Kabaosa, a great-grandson of Little Pine, assisted L.O. Lawrence, an immigration officer at Sault Ste Marie, in incorporating themes from Henry Wadsworth Longfellow's epic poem *Hiawatha* into a play in the Ojibwa language.[88] First performed in 1900 by an all-Native cast in a natural setting at Kensington Point, east of Garden River, the play attracted considerable local acclaim. Longfellow's granddaughter attended the production and was so impressed that she donated a stained-glass window to St John's Church, built on Anglican mission ground in 1882, as a memorial to Buhkwujjenene, who died in 1900. Yet, like Longfellow's poem itself, L.O. Lawrence's treatment of Native themes reflected a romanticized view of a vanished past rather than the realities or potentialities of the present.

A false view of historical events blinded the public to the band's rapidly developing political and economic competencies. A new intensity of purpose pervaded the wording of petitions sent to Ottawa in the first decades of the twentieth century. Old-fashioned oratory gave way to a more modern style of expression as young Ojibwa used English, the dominant language, to defend their traditional prerogatives. One such communication, for example, designated the Garden River reserve as a 'primogenitive habatation [*sic*], on which Indians should be granted 'full rights' to resources, especially timber.[89]

New pressures demanded that grievances be conveyed with succinctness and force. In 1906 the Algoma Advisory Union, a precursor of the Sault Ste Marie Chamber of Commerce, complained that as the Garden River population had failed to clear large farms, even though forests on all sides of their reserve were being levelled by timber companies, Ottawa should expropriate the reserve, as others had recommended many times before. The union, composed of several prominent Sault Ste Marie residents, petitioned Prime Minister Laurier to terminate the reserve system so that the municipality might extend eastward beyond Partridge Point.[90]

William Nichols and the Garden River Band Council mounted a sustained opposition, sending a delegation composed of Chief George Menissino, John Askin, Alex Wabanosa, and William J. Pine to Ottawa in November of 1906. As a result, the union had to be content by 1910 with an Order-in-Council allowing construction of a trunk road across the reserve, but no additional surrender of territory. After four lengthy years of negotiations, the Ojibwa obtained a ruling exempting them from hav-

ing to contribute labour or funds, either for construction or maintenance, to the enterprise. The band also secured acceptance of the
condition that, should the road cease to be used for public conveyance,
the land allowance would revert to the band.[91] The encroachments of
modern capitalist society would come only so far, and no farther.

Chapter Eight

Preserving a Distinct Community

For many years the Garden River and Batchewana leaders fostered a lively political dynamic on the frontier, and their campaigns had important consequences for the future. In the early 1870s, they influenced the struggle for recognition of Aboriginal rights to minerals led by chiefs in the Lake of the Woods area who were also deeply concerned about their people's economic future.[1] These western Ojibwa leaders nevertheless had far less room to negotiate than had their Upper Great Lakes counterparts a generation before. Beginning in 1871, the federal government employed the format of the Robinson Treaties in drafting a series of land cession agreements, known as the 'numbered treaties,' by which Ottawa systematically extinguished Native title throughout Manitoba, the western prairie provinces, and vast tracts of the Canadian north. Bands also faced increased government intervention in their internal affairs. The Indian Act of 1880 endowed a newly established Department of Indian Affairs with powers to impose a uniform system of elected chiefs and councils on bands, tribes, and chiefdoms, regardless of the manner in which these groups formerly had governed themselves. The passing of the Indian Advancement Act four years later authorized the government to depose any chiefs considered 'unfit' to discharge their duties effectively.[2] By 1900, administration of Indian affairs would be dominated by what one historian has termed a 'narrow vision' of what Native peoples were and could become.[3]

As time progressed the Sault Native community also faced new internal problems. Batchewana leaders understandably chafed against the social and political limitations which had been placed on them since their removal from the Sault in 1859 and began a search for a new land base close to, but separate from, the Garden River reserve. During the late nineteenth century, however, the bands usually remained united in pursuit of their goals, and for many years both bands continued to work together to enhance their store of occupational expertise and skills.

Developments in the Sphere of Community Activities

Traditional social organization, skills, and values continued to inform the band's ongoing struggle to defend and develop the economic potential of its diversified resource base. The winter kin-based hunting, trapping, and logging group had already resisted pressures to reshape the community's potential workforce into exclusively male, company-controlled work teams. Each fall, once the chief and council concluded their negotiations with the timber merchants about provisions, quotas, prices, and locations for delivery, traditional family groups set out for their bush camps, where, along with their other winter activities, they would cut timber until the spring. It was a way of life which they had followed since before 1850, and it would continue at Garden River until well into the first decades of the twentieth century.

The father or eldest respected man presided over the labour of his sons and sons-in-law. Alternatively, a man might remain in the settlement during the winter and send only his sons, along with a sledge, equipment, and, if he owned one, a team of horses or oxen, which were a source of family independence and pride. Most men looked forward to the day when they might purchase their own teams, reflecting a cultural emphasis on the ability of the male head of the family to secure the means to operate his own family business. This emphasis continues in the twentieth century, with the focus today on owningheavy equipment such as trucks and even small bulldozers. A third option in the late nineteenth century, adopted by younger, unmarried men, was to seek employment off the reserve from jobbers or in company-owned logging camps.

The opening of roads, haulage routes, and skidways facilitated the use of teams, sleighs, and carts for transportation in the bush, rather than the traditional toboggans, sleds, and dog teams. After maple sugaring in the early spring, men prepared and planted their fields using the same teams that had hauled logs during the winter. Traditional religious attitudes towards seasonal transitions and their characteristic economic activities persisted in spite of technological changes. For instance, men with recognized spiritual powers conducted spring rituals, presented offerings and petitions to the invigorated spiritual agencies of the universe, and burned tobacco in the fields. During the *sahsahguhwejegawin*, a spring feast of thanksgiving and sacrifice, offerings were suspended from poles or elevated on a platform. It was believed that burning tobacco in the fields ensured a good harvest.[4]

Throughout the summer many men sought wage employment. Others who owned boats and nets engaged in the commercial fishery. Still others, often apprenticed to French or Métis kin or trained at an industrial school, practised a trade such as boatbuilding, carpentry, shoemaking, harness making, or blacksmithing.

Summer was also the time for mining. Since an act passed in 1888 stated that no royalties could accrue to the Garden River band's credit from mining on reserves, the band possessed little initiative to lease or sell its mineral lands. Instead, members of the Sayer (or Sayers), Jones, Nolin, Bell, and Pine families transferred whatever practical skills they had learned as mineral explorers to the working of small family-owned iron, copper, and silver ore operations on the ceded townships of Laird and Duncan, or on the Batchewana tract. At least one family also quarried local marble, and ore and marble sales became a welcome source of extra capital. Mines came to be circulated over time within kin groups; a man might reassign his location to his brother, and his brother transfer the mine to his brother-in-law, and so on.[5]

During the fall, men who had been working off the reserve returned to their community for the harvest and haying on marshes along the Root River and at Echo Bay. The season of maturation received ceremonial recognition from family heads. Suitable plants were ready for gathering in the fields, forests, and water by the community's medical practitioners. For families who intended to remain in the settlement during the winter, firewood had to be chopped and stacked. As not all groups who left for the bush participated in logging, men who pursued alternative occupations, such as hunting or trapping inland, collected bark and, with the assistance of their wives, constructed canoes for their upriver journeys.

From conversations during the early 1980s with elders at Garden River, it became clear that the Ojibwa cognitive system endowed new bush activities north of Lakes Huron or Superior with meaning transferred from valued traditional occupations. Lowering 'pointers' – or supply craft used in the logging industry – at high water season down the White, Puckasaw, Montreal, and Mississauga Rivers demanded not only skills similar to those required in the rapids fishery, but also a fortitude developed with the help of spiritual protectors. The 'river' was an evocative symbol of the individual's life, as to reach one's destination along its course meant heeding spiritual as well as material guides. Successful performance indicated achievement of a harmonious relationship between economic necessity, acquired technological knowledge, and one's personal goals, and reflected a man's sense of identity and well-being, since such competence arose from an inner spiritual balance.[6]

Women's Activities

Women joined their husbands in the bush, unless they were caring for young children, school-age youngsters, elderly kin, or livestock on a day-to-day basis, activities which precluded their leaving the settlement in winter. At the winter camps they, and the children who accompanied them, fished, trapped, and prepared hides. On returning to the community in April, they and their husbands engaged in maple sugaring and, during the summer months, tended the maturing field crops.[7]

With the assistance of male members of the household, women procured needed raw materials to make and repair garments, footwear, baskets, and handicrafts for family use and sale. They picked berries and dried them in the sun. Because men were often employed in wage labour away from the community in the summer, women formed the core of the family group during this season, in a reversal of the winter pattern. In the autumn, female family members dried and smoked fish and preserved the harvest of field and garden for winter consumption.

While women tended to be more conservative than men, the division of labour by gender was not rigid. Men and women could perform many of the occupations traditionally associated with the other sex. This usually was less a matter of choice than necessity, owing to the often prolonged separation of men from their families. The assumption of predominantly male roles by women also was evident in the political and religious spheres. The female family head could assume the status of a speaker or group leader, especially if she possessed recognized medicine powers or if the family lacked a senior male member as a result of absence, sickness, or death.[8]

Occupational Interdependence Throughout the Seasonal Cycle

In his study of the north-eastern Cree community at Mistassini, Quebec, during the late 1970s, anthropologist Adrian Tanner demonstrated that the unwillingness of trade monopolies to equip and provision family hunting groups made the Cree dependent on government subsidies to maintain their winter fur production.[9] Tanner's findings in this regard furnish a late example of the economic dependence on monopolies and government that was appearing among bands west of Sault Ste Marie by 1850. By contrast, the Garden River band was able to protect and develop a diversified local economy characterized by a number of seasonally appropriate activities, none of which dominated the annual cycle. The band simply refused to accept Alexander Vidal's dismissal of Shingwaukonse's claims to merchantable resources other than fur, even though Vidal's views shaped the Canadian legal system's definition of Native rights over land and resources for more than a century. The vitality of the Garden River economy was crucial to the community's political autonomy, as the degree to which Native proprietorship over valuable resources was recognized by government and merchants tended to define the scope of the band's decision-making powers.

The availability of wage labour, the community's proximity to sources of purchasable foods, and the ready convertibility of many local resources into saleable merchandise at nearby markets made Garden River residents less vulnerable economically than fur-producing interior bands. After 1900, each phase of the annual cycle at Garden River was characterized by an occupation capable of providing monetary returns, from which a portion necessarily was reserved and reinvested in the next endeavour. Fishing in the fall purchased provisions for winter logging, which in turn produced money to buy seed for spring planting, and so on.

Band leaders promoted summer employment on the reserve to provide funds to supplement cash returns from market gardening, one of the most risky ventures within the cycle. Crop failure was not uncommon, while insurance was unknown. Other activities usually could tide the band over a bad harvest, but the combination of a poor growing season and government policies which curtailed production in another sector, such as logging or fishing, could have severe consequences.

Little Systems and Broad Minds

Ojibwa leadership at Garden River retained remarkably well its strength of purpose in battling the forces of change and the restrictive legislation that threatened Native community goals. The subject could arouse considerable emotion in elders who personally participated in the struggle: 'What is his right? It [the governing power] can be wrong even if it wears a crown of gold. And what is gold if it means that? He's stepping over God.'[10] Yet, by 1900, there was reason to hope. William Nichols, the Indian agent, refused to force native people into a narrow economic

niche as many of his predecessors had. Owing to his relatively liberal outlook, he came to respect the competencies inherent in the community
and sought to encourage them. Two of his successors, Thomas G. Wigg
and Murdock MacLellan, followed his lead. All three officials at various
times after 1910 upheld a claim laid by the Garden River Band Council to
gravel beds lying along the Garden River just north of the CPR's own ballast pit. Construction of the trunk road had raised the demand for gravel,
and hence its price. The Garden River deposits constituted some of the
finest grade of stone readily accessible within Algoma.[11]

At first the incident seemed a minor one, at least superficially, to both
the local agent and Ottawa. It concerned the removal of stone from the
reserve for commercial purposes without band permission. As debate
over the issue gained momentum, however, it grew apparent that more
was at stake than merely a Native bid for a potentially lucrative short-term
source of income. Principles were involved which had been and would
continue to be of enduring significance to the Ojibwa.

The Gravel Pit Dispute

George Kabaosa had complained to Indian Affairs as early as 1897 that the
CPR had been removing gravel from band property and selling it to local
buyers. By the spring of 1911, so much crushed stone had been shipped
from a 32.3-acre site north of the Garden River pit that Charles Cadotte,
the elected chief, demanded that an official measurement of the amount
removed be made.[12] Under Cadotte's leadership, the band hired a team of
lawyers, Messrs Goodman and Galbraith, conducted a careful inquiry into
prevailing gravel prices, secured an affidavit from a local company to support their contentions, and charged the CPR $25,513, or eight cents per
cubic yard, for the 318,924 cubic yards of stone taken by trespass.[13]

The CPR, which had built a spur line into the ballast pit, immediately
protested that the price was 'excessive' and refused to pay. In response,
Ottawa dispatched J.G. Ramsden, inspector of Indian reserves, to Garden
River to make a thorough investigation into the matter. Ramsden went
straight to work. After consulting with MacLellan and Wigg, the two local
Native agents, who both described the band's demands as 'fair and just,'
Ramsden devised an ingenious alternative scheme which would prevent
alienation of either land or resources in this instance, and which would
transform the gravel into a source of ongoing revenue for the Garden
River community. By this plan, the price to be charged would be reduced
from eight cents to two cents per cubic yard, but the railway would be

required to pay a fixed sum of $150 per acre for injury to reserve property and a royalty of $1.50 per carload on all gravel to be shipped from the area in the future.[14]

The band concurred with Ramsden's proposals. His terms embodied the strongest precedent to date for the legitimacy of Native control over a resource lying within reserve boundaries. Confidently assuming that negotiations would focus exclusively on the issue of trespass, the Ojibwa prepared for Indian Affairs to submit the case for arbitration before federal, provincial, CPR, and band representatives. In January 1913, band councillor John Askin asked for a copy of the Arbitration Agreement to study prior to the band's appointment of a negotiator, although there seemed little doubt that Ramsden would be the band's first choice. Not only would a forum arise for the testing of the existence of principles basic to Aboriginal prerogatives, but the CPR, one of the most powerful agents of national unification, would be taking a place alongside Canada, Ontario, and the Native representatives on the stand. If the Ojibwa secured their claim the event would have a profound impact on Canadian Native policy.

Sudden realization of the momentous consequences to Native status if the Ojibwa claim were admitted shook both Ottawa and the CPR from their former lethargy. Indian Affairs immediately appointed A.D. McNabb, a far less flexible man than either MacLellan or Wigg, to the position of Native agent. McNabb referred to the Native spokesmen as interfering nuisances or 'agitators' and refused to consider the Native claim seriously. This agent personified the new authoritarian attitude which stemmed from the federal government's desire to prevent any further steps towards Native self-determination.

What the Native community viewed as a dispute concerning control over resources, Ottawa ultimately narrowed down to a mere question of whether or not more reserve land should be alienated. Ramsden had presented a number of reasons why the federal government should retain the land base on behalf of the band, but the issue of actual proprietorship had not been debated. Indian Affairs and the CPR were careful to prevent such a debate from occurring.

The fact that the band was also in the midst of negotiations with another firm, the Superior Dock and Dredge Company, was used to weaken its case. The Ojibwa were in the process of agreeing to sell a quarry site to the local gravel company in the hope of securing a long-term employer of Native labour. Sensing a commercial rival, the CPR pressured Ottawa to sidestep Ramsden's position regarding royalties. This Indian Affairs did by relegating the Ojibwa to the status of mere 'occupiers' of the land. Ottawa then dispensed with the charge of trespass, the CPR expropriated the 32.3 acres, and the board of arbitrators – which did not include J.G. Ramsden – became responsible only for determining the land's value. The final appraisal was not generous. In the end, the band received only $5,282 for the land and gravel, minus $1,293 for legal costs.[15]

The Wild Man's Stone

Knowledge that the basis of negotiations with the CPR had been altered without their consent fired the band's opposition to the cession of a trap-rock bluff lying north of Squirrel Island. The bluff was known as the *Buhkwujjenenewabick*, or 'wild man's stone.' Two rival companies wanted the site for a quarry and, as in the past, Ottawa reserved all rights over the disposition of the territory once it was surrendered. The Ojibwa retaliated by stating that cessions they had made previously, while supposedly for their 'benefit,' had turned out to be sacrifices for which they had received little or no return. The quarry ceded to the Superior Dock and Dredge Company had failed even to provide a source of employment, since the firm had been driven out of business by competition from the CPR pits.[16] Band leaders informed W.R. White, head of the team sent to survey the face of the *Buhkwujjenenewabick*, of their annoyance at losing Squirrel Island, the Clark location, the gravel pits, and especially Partridge Point, which had been subdivided in 1902 for settlement. They demanded redress for at least one of their grievances. White reported to Ottawa that the Ojibwa refused to authorize any further sales until the western boundary of their reserve was run due north from Partridge Point in accordance with the terms of the Robinson-Huron Treaty.[17]

It was not until the gravel companies themselves began offering incentives to encourage agreement to the cession, however, that Ottawa's resistance began to wane. Reserve residents received guarantees that employment, including insurance benefits, would become available to them. Not only would boundaries set down by the chief and council be respected, but also, if the site ceased to be used for quarrying purposes, it would revert to the band. Eventually, the terms grew sufficiently advantageous that to refuse them would mean rejecting an important opportunity for local development. So, finally, the Garden River Ojibwa agreed to surrender.[18]

Norman Jones, a Garden River resident who worked at the quarry during its operation, claimed that according to oral tradition all parties who trespassed beyond the geographic limits set forth in the 1914 agreement would have incurred punishment from the *Buhkwujjenene.sug* or little wild men who 'owned' the *Buhkwujjenenewabick*. Shot with 'seed' or 'cork' by the wild men, a person who ignored the boundaries laid out by the con-tract's terms, would become 'crazy.'[19] This propensity to translate geo-graphic landscape into symbolic space endowed the incident at the quarry with heightened significance. Even though negotiations had concerned the cession of nothing more glamorous than gravel, the consequences of the agreement would be recited in legend by later gen-erations. Paralleling in certain respects the Mica Bay mine takeover of 1849, events surrounding the *Buhkwujjenenewabick* in 1914 attained mythi-cal appeal and provided symbolic as well as practical precedents for future action.

Curbing the Dynamism: New Economic Policies and the Course of Band Development

The conditions the Garden River band were able to impose on the sale of crushed stone from the *Buhkwujjenenewabick* drew the group as close as it had ever come to being able to exercise full proprietorship over a resource other than fur. It was to be the last such gain for many years. After 1913, A.D. McNabb deliberately refused to record in the band min-utes any of the speeches made in council pertaining to issues of resource control on the reserve.[20] He also constantly maligned Ojibwa leaders, most notably George Kabaosa.[21] By refusing to acknowledge Native sug-gestions and grievances, and by imposing a rigid agricultural policy on the developing community, the agent temporarily checked the band's progress towards self-determination. As a result divisions emerged within the Garden River community similar to those that had appeared in 1857 and 1896.

McNabb encouraged agriculture with great zeal. Ottawa promoted farming on reserves as part of a campaign for a 'New Ontario' of the north, in keeping with the emphasis on social and economic reform which followed the First World War. The band gained some advantages from new arrangements for loans, financed out of band funds at an annual rate of 6 per cent interest, for the purchasing of seed, draft horses, and farming equipment.[22] As well, local merchants, the Union Agricultural Society, and other groups organized campaigns to promote increased agricultural production.[23] Major difficulties also from this focus on a single economic activity, however.

Some Ojibwa families found they could not meet their payments for horses, oxen, and other purchases, especially since, despite McNabb's high expectations, crop failure remained a frequent problem. No crop insurance existed and, when band members fell deeply into debt, Ottawa could threaten to take 'drastic measures' to collect on loans.[24] Among proponents of agriculture, optimism triumphed over realism. Niggardly financing, often poor equipment, and pressure for intensive cultivation of crops such as strawberries, which were unsuited to either the climate or the soil, continually hampered the campaign.[25] A survey of allotments made by the surveying team of Lang and Ross showed that by 1916 family heads held from six to fifteen acres, but rarely more – the same ratio of land to single family group as had existed at the time of the 1861 census.[26]

In activities other than agriculture, McNabb regarded the Native people as mere gleaners in the wake of major resource industries. In 1913, when the American firm which held exclusive timber rights on the Batchewana tract ceased all cutting operations owing to a law stipulating that all wood pulp be manufactured in Canada, McNabb suggested that Ottawa terminate the company's licence altogether and allow the band what meagre returns still might be wrestled from the cut-over countryside.[27] At the same time he stringently opposed Kabaosa's campaign to attain Ojibwa management over timber resources on reserves, and turned a deaf ear to associated Native demands for the cancellation of the Spry lease on the Indian Strip. Despite sustained pressure from the Garden River band for control over the Strip, formally identified by Ottawa in 1895 as part of the unceded reserve, the tract did not revert to the Ojibwa until 1932.[28]

Ottawa's support for a single occupation – farming – rather than for the local economic system as a whole, with its seasonally integrated and interrelated activities, fostered ignorance of what was happening 'on the ground.' Even McNabb had little grasp of the overall picture, a fact which produced glaring contradictions and inconsistencies in his accounts of how the Native economy functioned over time. For instance, in 1913 he described the Goulais Bay band as eking out a 'very precarious living' from fishing, whereas only three years later he proclaimed that the same people were 'expert fishermen' who derived 'a good living' from their occupation.[29] McNabb also argued that 'excellent' soil conditions allowed agriculture to flourish at Garden River, whereas an American Indian agent visiting the community at approximately the same time wrote that no farming existed 'outside of small garden, [as] nearly all the able bodied Natives [were] working at fairly good wages at river driving or loading timber on vessels.'[30]

This policy bias towards agriculture and away from group resource management proved extremely injurious to the previously harmonious relationship between the Batchewana and Garden River Bands. McNabb, in seeking to control the reserve environment by promoting farming, interacted exclusively with the Garden River Band Council and so deprived the Batchewana leaders of a forum in which to voice ideas and grievances. This threatened to force Batchewana band members into a caste-like situation offensive to the Ojibwa, who valued free and direct democratic expression within the group. McNabb thus revived Joseph Wilson's earlier policy of fostering internal dissension by depriving one band of rights while extending privileges to the other.

At first the Batchewana Band Council wholeheartedly supported the Garden River people's drive to rectify inaccuracies in reserve boundaries, and backed George Kabaosa's campaign to gain group access to timber on the Indian Strip. There was a strong spirit of shared interest and intent. As the First World War progressed, members of both bands emphasized their desire to attain full citizenship rights and often enrolled in the services expressly for this purpose. Those who remained at home similarly shared in the quest for human freedoms which they knew had been denied them or, as in the case of the franchise, withdrawn

When, in March 1916, the dynamic George Kabaosa was compelled to step down after his election as Garden River chief owing to Ottawa's refusal to approve 'of any of the candidates,' relations between the two groups dramatically worsened.[31] With Kabaosa out of the way, a variety of externally imposed conditions led to extreme hardship for certain residents at Garden River, especially those whose names failed to appear on the Garden River annuity list. Documentary evidence suggests that niggling sanctions imposed on Batchewana band members living at Garden River regulated even the 'proper' attainment and use of firewood.[32] Oral traditions refer to this period as the time of the 'clean up' or 'purge.'[33] However, because the exclusion of one segment of a community contravened fundamental Ojibwa values, the bands immediately looked for ways out of the dilemma. Neither band would submit to the government policies which bred the conflict. When worsening tensions between the two groups led to disputes over which leader – Shingwaukonse or Nebenagoching – had acted as principal head chief at Sault Ste Marie in 1850, the Batchewana band finally decided to relocate and purchase part of the original Clark location which was then on the market.[34] Despite the schism, an underlying unity still linked the Batchewana Band Council and its former host group. Both bodies gave individual families considerable freedom to choose which group they would ultimately belong to. Hence, former members of the Batchewana band were able to join the Garden River group, and vice versa.

Mechanisms for Maintaining Positive Interrelations with Government and Industry

The Garden River band responded to the inflexibility of government policy after 1913 by dividing its leadership into two sectors, one to uphold positive linkages with the government and the other to press as hard as was reasonably possible for changes in keeping with Native goals and values. Superficially, it appeared that political factions had arisen, but in practice allowed the Ojibwa to continue, even this arrangement permitted a degree of political activity without the danger of alienating McNabb or Ottawa. The responsibility for maintaining good relations with the government usually fell to an elderly and respected Native individual who already had earned a reputation in the council forum and so chose to relinquish the more active role to younger men. This practice allowed the Ojibwa to continue, even under conditions of internal colonialism, the tradition of civil chieftainship which they had practised long before 1850.

John Askin assumed this role about 1913 and held it until his death in 1919. A dignified orator, respectful to government policies without being subservient, Askin maintained a stance that furnished a core of stability and continuity within a repressive milieu. In 1912, McNabb had distrusted Askin, since he had seen the seventy-six-year-old subchief as the 'ruling spirit' behind the band's opposition to the CPR during the gravel dispute. Yet by 1915, the agent had swung around radically in regarding Askin as an ally and expressing gratitude for the 'able assistance he has always rendered the agent since taking office.'[35]

In his speeches as a counsellor and spokesperson, Askin always found it necessary to play down his own past as a lumberman in urging the Ojibwa to farm exclusively. In March 1916, McNabb recorded that Askin had gone so far as to accuse J.L. Kennedy, the local timber buyer, of 'raking off the farmers.'[36] Yet this seemingly strong ideological commitment to agriculture on the part of an individual whose age and status in the community allowed him to adopt a stance somewhat at variance with the complexities of the situation proved to be important to the band's welfare. Askin's purported commitment made it next to impossible for outside interests to appropriate the Ojibwa's land base. If the subchief had not taken the position he did, Garden River might well have lost 4,000 acres of prime agricultural property west of the Echo River to a government-run prison farm, on the grounds that the Ojibwa lacked the initiative to work the land.[37]

While the chief and council at Garden River remained firm in their determination to pursue community goals, the band leadership by 1913 found it difficult to live up to its full potential. So much energy had to be diverted towards protecting whatever gains had been made between 1906 and 1912 that speakers like Askin spent much of their time simply defending the status quo. This problem was caused largely by the continued ideological positioning of 'Indians' as a group seeking to stem the tide of national development and subvert the 'public good.' This distorted view shaped policy and let to anomalies and contradictions pertaining to Native title to land and resources, and especially to the relegation of bands to the position of 'occupants' rather than proprietors of reserves.

Simon J. Dawson, as well as legal experts involved in investigating Native claims disputes, found that the province's contravention of hunting and fishing rights which had been extended to Natives people under the Robinson Treaties actually brought the powers of the Crown to extend such prerogatives into question.[38] The constitutional significance of such findings discouraged their full exploration until new ways of thinking could foster more complex legal structures designed to shield the Crown's delegated rights.

Because the Robinson agreements provided the model for later treaties made between Native peoples and the Crown, and, as such, had a major bearing on Canada's relationship with its Native people, Native groups continuously tested the capacity of these agreements to uphold Aboriginal rights. The history of the Garden River community is a long story of attempts to break legal barriers, set up after 1849, by creating new precedents. Both Ogista's sale of the Wilkinson location and the gravel pit dispute of 1914 were directed towards this end. Although the band's protests failed in their primary goal, they led to minor triumphs in the negotiating forum. As a result, conditions inserted in agreements with outside agencies came increasingly nearer to recognizing Native proprietorship over land and resources on reserves, regardless of prevailing law.

The denial of rights to bands which traditionally exercised territorial prerogatives and possessed a form of government based on direct participatory democracy, and whose leaders were held responsible to the group through a system of responsive reciprocal ties, created many problems for the Garden River community over the years. In the 1850s, shrewd officials pretending to be Shingwaukonse's friends worked for their own economic advancement, manipulating reserve boundaries in the belief that the eventual collapse of the band's organization and the destruction of its territorial base would serve to conceal their handiwork. In the name of retrenchment and band control, moreover, Ottawa made group membership dependent on receipt of annuities, rather than vice versa, as had formerly been the case. This threatened to end the Garden River community as a vital, developing entity by dividing it into opposing groups, competing for money and other material benefits to compensate for a lack of rights. When it was found that sowing dissension could not halt the momentum towards self-determination, the government adopted harsher measures, and in 1916 deprived Garden River of its leadership altogether until a suitable degree of compliance with government wishes was restored.

Despite such setbacks, however, by 1916 the Ojibwa had demonstrated that in the face of formidable odds they could still maintain a milieu in which they could develop their social, economic, and political culture. Restrictive policies could be gradually changed and the consequences of ignorance and dishonesty rectified through the combined efforts of Native leaders and sympathetic government, legal, commercial, and religious agencies. Most important, band leaders were able to retain Little Pine's faith that indigenous peoples might function as semi-autonomous, self-determining groups within the Canadian nation.

Chapter Nine

A Unifying Vision

Between 1827 and 1853 an alliance arose among Native leaders from north of Lake Huron and around Lake Superior to the Red River and the headwaters of the Mississippi. Its objective was to find ways in which bands could seek reconciliation with the emerging Canadian state in order to participate in its development. This policy, according to a local Garden River legend, originated with a 'gift' bestowed on Shingwaukonse in a dream which gave him insight into the rifts in intention and understanding which divided political agencies, both Native and white, as well as the power to assist in healing them.

A leader such as Shingwaukonse owed his reputation to his skill in identifying the causes of disruption within the universe and his ability to find ways to deal with these disturbances. In practising divination, a leader first had to secure a vision granting the requisite 'blessing' from spirit agencies, and then obtain authorization from his group to employ his special 'gift.' The leader's reciprocal relationship with the spirits was the source of his power, but it was equally important for him to achieve 'balance' in using this power within the sphere of social and political action. The flow of power, often regulated through ritual, was channelled through superior human power-holders whose main task was not to compete with other powers but to maintain harmony in the cosmos. Human power-holders had therefore to be wary of signs of change and adjust their own position and strategies accordingly.

Since the Ojibwa believed that 'sufficient good' depended on the possession of 'sufficient power,' lack of good meant some agency was temporarily obstructing the flow of power and, in turn, access to resources.[1] On the other hand, proper alignment with the power source ensured that necessities required by a band would continue to be supplied. In 1846

Little Pine believed that spiritual agencies had responded to his pleas for help, and felt optimistic, in the midst of seeming want, that there was hope for his people's future.

The failure of the Shawnee uprising had demonstrated the futility of trying to resist white encroachment onto Native territory. Instead, Shingwaukonse devised a policy of reserving certain lands and resources exclusively for the benefit of his people. He emphasized his past loyalty to Britain and argued that his followers, like other Loyalist groups, deserved to occupy their territory unmolested. Recognizing limitation as symptomatic rather than causal, the chief set out to encourage the government to assist him in founding an Ojibwa settlement, similar to Methodist farming communities in south-eastern Ontario, but which would exercise managerial jurisdiction over local lumber and mining operations, as well as promote farming. To aid in securing his goal, Little Pine surrounded himself in 1848 with Native allies, interpreters, Métis and French traders, and, in the case of Allan Macdonell, a lawyer and entrepreneur. Head chiefs from other bands acted in a similar manner by claiming timber and minerals on behalf of their own groups.

Fearful of large concentrations of Native people on the western frontier, both Canada and the United States ignored Shingwaukonse's appeals. His plans regarding lumbering and mining on lands over which he exercised regulatory control met with resistance on the grounds that the Ojibwa lacked sound organizational skills. To allow Native people to exploit timber or minerals on their reserves, it was maintained, would lead to chaos and wastage of the resource. Policy makers refused to believe that bands could act responsibly, a radical reversal of the way in which British authorities had regarded the Ojibwa, as military allies, during the period of intercolonial rivalries only a generation earlier.

Although government opposed his scheme, so confident was the chief of the rightness of his vision that he invited Ojibwa from around Lake Superior, as well as the French and Métis at the Sault, to join with him and Allan Macdonell in dispossessing mining operations at Mica Bay, north of Sault Ste Marie. This act launched a public discussion of Aboriginal rights, and between 1850 and 1852 there was a lively press debate about Native relationships with the land and its resources. This controversy ended abruptly in June 1853 with the passing of a bill, introduced by Attorney General Robert Baldwin, which provided for harsh legal action against any instigator of Native discontent within the Algoma district.

With this new law, the process of maturation in Ojibwa leadership and policies which had continued for two hundred years was forced 'under-

ground,' into band councils. Dynamic leadership continued out of the
public eye, and new organizational forms evolved as chiefs retained, elaborated, and defended their prerogatives despite formidable difficulties.
The cautious candour, flexibility, and innovativeness of Ojibwa leadership after 1850 enabled it to survive until today with its integrity intact.

Traditional Ojibwa Leadership: Its Prerogatives and Responsibilities

Entities referred to as *dodemic* groups and defined by agnatic or, less
frequently, cognatic descent principles influenced the Ojibwa leadership
tradition – the prerogatives and responsibilities of leadership and its
transmission from one generation to the next. Although the Ojibwa
belief system had always allowed for transfer of group traditions and symbols between generations, incentives for specific social changes arose during the seventeenth century. It has been maintained that any stress on
unilineal descent principles or primogeniture derived primarily from
organizational concepts introduced by the French and British and
grafted onto the Native system. During the colonial period, Native leaders assumed the status of a 'forest aristocracy' in their relationship with
external authorities, who presented them with medals and other accoutrements of rank. With the close of the colonial era, however, these ceremonial exchanges ceased. This led to a renewed emphasis on traditional
leadership principles which upheld, as a norm, reciprocity of interest
between a head man and his group, and encouraged a leader to protect
his people even when to do so involved personal risk.

Not all scholars would agree with this perspective, however. For example, Charles A. Bishop has presented the intriguing hypothesis that trade
relations structured the internal nature of Ojibwa groups.[2] Yet Shingwaukonse's campaign in the twilight of the trading era, rooted as it was in
traditional Ojibwa ideas about power and its proper recognition, calls
into question the suggestion that structured systems of trade relations
were primary social determinants. Reducing such a vital element of the
Ojibwa belief system as the *dodem* to something akin to a modern company's logo, as Bishop does, highlights it function as a group designator
(as well as an individual identifier in matters related to marriage and the
extension of kin obligations to non-kin), but ignores its ideological role
in the Ojibwa's response to economic and political change. Shingwaukonse employed his *dodem* only when he saw his role as preserving a cherished cultural milieu.

The scope of political and economic prerogatives exercised by an

Ojibwa group leader went far beyond the range of responsibilities of either the head of a winter hunting group or a trading chief. While in some ways the band leader seemed to be an elaborated version of the hunting group head, especially with regard to controlling access to local resources, the role of the head chief was less concerned with economic activities *per se* than with band membership and preserving a milieu that facilitated harmonious interaction among several extended family groups. The Ojibwa *ogima* acted as a coordinator, as well as a policy maker and diplomat. Many anthropologists regard this role of chief as coordinator as a mere epiphenomenon of the historic era. Nevertheless, investigators' views vary on this point according to the weight each scholar attributes to the modifying influence exerted on proto-Ojibwa organization by European contact and his or her view of the pre-1760 Upper Great Lakes environment as either harsh or diversified and capable of sustaining an 'original affluent society.'[3] Because of insufficient early historical data, the nature of leadership among proto-Ojibwa peoples has been the subject of a controversy based more on theory than on empirical historical evidence. It is generally accepted that precarious environmental conditions promoted organizational flexibility among the proto-Ojibwa, although rival interpretations of later influences on Ojibwa history persist.

One ethnological trend has been to view band leadership among Algonquian-speaking groups as emerging from a primitive organizational form stressing individualism. John M. Cooper[4] has regarded the hunting territory system recorded earlier for the Montagnais of Quebec as indicative of an individualistic tendency among all north-eastern Algonquian-speaking peoples – a tendency which, he claims, had existed since 'time immemorial.' In its political economy, Cooper claims, the family hunting group approximated a 'minute state,' while the jural authority exercised by chiefs, where such leaders existed at all, permitted them only to adjust boundaries and intervene in disputes. In Cooper's view, the importance of the 'band' versus the family group developed in the forum of government–Native relations. Following this development, he argues, 'the family would not be so nearly identical with the "state,"' leadership would come to wield a wider and more pervasive influence, and changes would take place in land tenure, so that 'the line between band sovereignty and ownership in severalty would be more distinctly and sharply drawn.'[5]

A focus on the 'band' revived following Julian Steward's assertion that this group may have constituted the original political and economic unit among Algonquian-speaking peoples after all, and that emphasis upon the family and individualized territorial system stemmed from fur trade relations.[6] Diamond Jenness has also explored this line of argument, and later studies have tended to uphold this premise in the historical context.[7] Scholars have recognized a major difference between the form of individualized land tenure exhibited by Native societies which principally exploited beaver for trade, and the territorial attachment of wider-ranging hunting peoples who pursued migratory big game such as barren ground caribou.[8] Eleanor Leacock and, later, Robert Murphy and Julian Steward, by drawing a distinction between use value and exchange value, have suggested that the focus on securing animals for their pelts fostered an irreversible dependency on trade goods and an emphasis on individualism in both the economic and social spheres of interaction.[9]

By contrast, Edward S. Rogers has warned against relying too heavily on ecological and trade factors to explain the nature of historic organizational forms. Among the Ojibwa, notes, the population could fall considerably below the carrying capacity of the resource base.[10] This has led him to suggest that rarely examined cultural variables, such as the predominance of witchcraft, influenced the distance separating groups and the extent of their territorial base. Yet other scholars[11] have argued that capitalist mercantilism could still explain such phenomena. Dispersion of peoples northward from the Upper Great Lakes area as a result of the fur trade, they maintain, led to a breakdown of formerly territorially based clans, but allowed for the retention of certain associated structural forms: for instance, the existence, in attenuated form, of an ancient system of clan chiefs and clan tenure.

Within the last two decades, however, there has been a return to the idea that individual initiative within the family group may always have constituted an important influence on social dynamics among northern Algonquian-speakers. Richard Preston, while maintaining that the Cree transfer traditional economic, political, and religious skills between generations most readily within the small social unit, also notes that certain individuals expanded the range of their economic and political competencies to meet challenges created by the nation-building project of white society.[12] Similarly, Adrian Tanner has challenged Leacock's unilineal model and case for the inevitability of economic dependency in the eastern subarctic by arguing that subsistence activities still seasonally predominated over production for exchange among the Mistassini Cree. Capitalism, Tanner claims, has modified the Cree cognitive structure and social organization to a far lesser degree than was earlier thought.[13] More recently, Harvey Feit has employed both qualitative and quantitative data to develop a model for assessing the viability of hunting societies in the Canadian north. Feit's work not only demonstrates that hunting constitutes a feasible economic occupation, but also suggests ways in which Native leaders might interact with government and other external agencies in revitalizing, developing, and protecting the hunting sector of Canada's boreal forest economy.[14] In the 1990s, facets of Aboriginal social and political structures are coming increasingly to be viewed as feasible bases for the development in the twenty-first century of distinct Aboriginal governmental institutions within the modern state.[15]

Other scholars, by focusing almost exclusively on the flexibility of Ojibwa social organization in response to inimical external forces, have tended to see Native leadership not as a creative force, but as a dependent variable within a constantly adapting social system. Following the tenets of conflict theory, James G.E. Smith has posited that principles of opposition guided competition for scarce resources and that, in the ensuing strife, individuals arose who assumed the rank of leaders. In Smith's view, leadership remained diffuse in its powers throughout the historic era because structural elaboration of the authority hierarchy within the hunting group failed to resolve tensions arising from demonstrations of personal initiative. In using the term 'nodal core' to describe the central social, economic, and political unit around which consanguines and affines coalesce, mainly in response to external stimuli, Smith suggests that social organization conformed to the economic base, the population varied according to the availability of resources, and leadership depended on the acquisition and distribution of scarce material assets with an eye to building a strong political entity to challenge the competition. Such a system, predicated on the notion of 'limited good,' maintained the egalitarian character of bands by keeping everyone at the same level of economic and political advancement.[16]

While Smith's analysis may identify problems that existed among the Ojibwa under the reserve system, his approach fails to consider the influence of intercolonial rivalry on the leadership during the French regime and the early British colonial era. Head chiefs gained prominence when they were regarded by the competing colonial powers as courtable military allies. As such men frequently acted as brigade leaders in the fur trade, they had access to material goods which rapidly became a form of currency exchanged among influential power-holders to maintain of a balance of power within the Upper Great Lakes Native community.

During periods of heightened intercolonial tension, head chiefs of strategically placed western bands would even occasionally become mediators between European contestants. At the same time, political strategies devised by these men to preserve their groups' autonomy during negotiations with external authorities also informed the manner in which chiefs regulated the trade milieu in their bands' favour. Ojibwa leaders controlled access to the entrances of major inland waterways, and hence resources along such routes. Colonial authorities borrowed heavily from eighteenth-century European concepts of status and tenure in defining and recognizing the nature of these prerogatives, vested in head chiefs, and communicated these ideas to the Native people as well. After 1760, John Askin, Sr, a sympathetic friend to both the Ojibwa and the Ottawa, sought to have these rights recognized in British and American law, a goal also pursued by his son, John Askin, Jr, and later by Allan Macdonell and William Ermatinger. All these men came to be attacked for their stance on this issue by the new breed of British officials who came to power after the War of 1812. Following the period of intercolonial rivalry most Native agents had little respect for indigenous leadership prerogatives and, by the 1840s, with the Aboriginal peoples shackled by a system of internal colonialism, governments went so far as to claim that such rights had never existed.

Shingwaukonse rose to prominence at a time when the old order in the Upper Great Lakes Native community was passing away. He demonstrated that Ojibwa head chiefs, exposed to new ideas, could overcome the odds and develop the skills they needed to bring about social change. It is important that Little Pine's followers supported his plans: otherwise his policies would not have become firmly embedded in the oral traditions passed down from generation to generation at Garden River. Other power-holders also proved receptive to his ideas, since he acted in accordance with traditional values which all understood and wished to preserve. As well, the nineteenth-century political climate in Canada helped preserve the influence of Shingwaukonse's policies, particularly those regarding land and resource management on reserves, after his death. Following American precedents set in the late 1850s, when U.S. officials allocated farm acreages in the vicinity of Sault Ste Marie to Ojibwa individuals and families, Canadian authorities attempted to subdivide Native lands north of Lake Huron in 1858. Further inducements for Native peoples to abandon their reserves included promises of the extension of the franchise and other citizenship rights to those who agreed to support a system of individualized land tenure. Yet because power over Native affairs in Canada was diffused among several decision makers, there were significant opportunities for effective Native resistance to government policies. This was not the case in the United States, where Washington's power over Native lands was shown, for instance, in the late 1880s when Indian reservations were unilaterally subdivided under the terms of the Dawes General Allotment Act. Canadian Native policy did not neatly parallel American policy. When pressured by mining and logging companies to dispense with the reserve system, Canadian officials responded with far more flexibility and willingness to compromise than their American counterparts. Despite the political strength of groups contending against Ojibwa interests, opportunities remained for negotiation and a measure of Native influence over policy.

The fact that the structure of Ojibwa society survived the radical changes occurring in late-nineteenth-century Canada testifies to its resilience. While its survival may be partly due to its flexibility, cultural factors also played a part. Mary Black-Rogers has offered a perspective on Ojibwa intergroup relationships which both complements and modifies James G.E. Smith's earlier stance on Ojibwa social dynamics. Smith's focus on competition and self-interest as the basis for action is replaced by a focus on Ojibwa values and beliefs. In Black-Rogers's view, the Ojibwas place a high value on personal qualities that facilitate relationships based not on competition, but on the offering of respect on one side and acceptance of responsibility on the other. Although Black-Rogers discerns a hierarchy among power-holders, she has also observed that power waxes and wanes in response to external events. Drawing on Black-Rogers's argument that 'power' may be viewed as an ability to retain a measure of control over circumstances, often on behalf of others as well as oneself, I suggest that the nature of Ojibwa culture encouraged individuals to work to preserve an environment congenial to group interests.[17] This was Little Pine's aim, and to some degree leaders at Garden River are still judged by their success in serving group interests.

Leadership Capable of Meeting Challenges

Although this study is predominantly historical in approach, it also attempts to examine how the Ojibwa system of thought and values influenced the strategies adopted by Shingwaukonse and his successors. Throughout the period under examination, spurred by cultural imperatives which emphasized the importance of maintaining independence and control in the face of difficulties, ambitious men devised creative solutions to the often formidable problems confronting the Ojibwa. In their actions, however, these leaders adhered closely to the tenets of their culture's power-belief system.

Shingwaukonse, for instance, appealed to colonial authorities, state officials, and representatives of a range of religious denominations for assistance in promoting his settlement scheme; and yet he would accept aid only if it furthered Native goals. Missionary and government policies which threatened to force the Ojibwa into a social, economic, or political niche incompatible with the Ojibwa's own cultural interests were resisted. In the early 1840s, Little Pine found it necessary to distance himself from the agencies he had previously courted. When his strategies brought results contrary to his band's interests, he sought to form new alignments more congenial to group wishes.

During this period of semi-isolation, the chief meditated on ways in which he might promote peaceful accommodation between whites and Native people so that bands might continue to retain their integrity as groups. In 1846, he forcefully challenged the province's right to implement a monolithic development policy – a policy regulating mining and lumbering in the Lake Huron and Lake Superior regions – because it made no provision for the recognition of Aboriginal claims. By taking over a mine on the north-eastern coast of Lake Superior in the fall of 1849, Shingwaukonse and his allies caused the government to reverse its former position and, in 1850, to implement a system of reserves north of Lakes Huron and Superior.

In taking over the mine, the chief drew upon Native legends about the powerful spirits protecting the mine in order to give the Native resistance movement special symbolic appeal. At the same time, he and his allies could count on the support of Allan Macdonell, a former shareholder in the dispossessed mining company, who opposed monopoly control over resource development on the western frontier and was willing to defend Aboriginal rights in spite of the risk to his own career. Macdonell's presence as a mediator well known to government, miners, and the Ojibwa reduced the likelihood of violence while the mine was under Native control in the fall and winter of 1849–50.

Despite Little Pine's determination to protect his people's rights, the Native people gained no recognition for their traditional prerogatives in 1850, apart from the admission in the Robinson Treaties that Native people might retain hunting and fishing rights on ceded lands not yet sold or leased by the government. The government negotiator, William B. Robinson, shrewdly used prevailing metropolitan stereotypes of the 'Indian' as solely a hunter-gatherer in order to gain public support for the Robinson

Treaties. The role of Native people as independent entrepreneurs in the fur trade, commercial fishing, lumbering, and mining was ignored, as was their invaluable contribution to early resource development.

The interest groups which dominated Canadian politics after 1850 also raised formidable obstacles to Native aspirations. Large mining companies were foremost in political power among the resource industries north of Lakes Huron and Superior. Prominent political figures and business magnates such as Sir George Simpson and Arthur Rankin owned shares in mineral locations and were not about to allow Native 'presumptions' to hinder their enterprise. These monopolistic concerns co-opted local government agents to help them deprive the Native people of their few remaining rights.

Shingwaukonse realized the magnitude of this threat to local band government when, shortly before his death in 1854, his decision to lay his band's grievances before the Crown in England was so vehemently opposed by the Indian Department. Between 1854 and 1857 the government, in the name of efficient resource management and social control, destroyed the viable community economies which Little Pine and George Abatossaway had been fostering at Garden River and Little Current. There was little band chiefs could do, however, for the penalties imposed under an act passed in the legislature in June 1853 made it extremely risky for sympathetic missionaries and entrepreneurs to defend Native enterprises.

From 1857 to 1865, the political constraints imposed on band leaders sparked a resistance movement, centred at Wikwemikong, which threatened violence against those who questioned its aims. Yet, like Little Pine in earlier years, this group preferred peaceful measures and petitioned the Queen to restore to bands a degree of their former authority over their people and lands.

Despite resistance, however, the dominant ideology continued to prevail and gradually permeated all legal definitions and interpretations of the relationship of Native peoples to land and resources. Mere hunters, fishers, and gatherers, it was maintained, could never initiate complex projects, and were incapable of formulating a coherent concept of liberty. Bands also suffered under the mainstream legal system, as their traditional economies were shattered by the legal circumscription of band-regulated hunting and fishing. Missionary journals tell a sad tale of starvation, sickness, and removals during these years. Meanwhile, until 1865 policy makers held that Natives had no clear rights to marketable resources other than fur, and that under the reserve system, title to land constituted a mere 'courtesy' extended by the Crown. Such ambiguous, contradictory, and basically denigrating perceptions of the Native economy and system of land tenure persisted in spite of strong criticisms after 1873 by Simon J. Dawson, MP for Algoma.[18]

Head chiefs and their bands fought to preserve the operation of the traditional management system, which ensured that all heads of family groups within the band had access to available resources, while continuously seeking to expand the range of resources open to exploitation by Natives. It was an uphill battle. In 1873, Ogista and several head chiefs from Lake Superior unsuccessfully pressed for a degree of local band control over mineral locations. By this time, Ogista and Buhkwujjenene had ceased to contest the government's right to collect timber duties from band members engaged in lumbering, although both men knew that what government agents called 'conservation' referred principally to a conservation of revenues and had little to do with the preservation of a long-term yield. When the dues came to be oppressive, many family heads who 'owned' territories containing timber and minerals simply sold the resources on the black market. Insensitive government policies thus encouraged covert defiance of the law, with band members, local merchants, and even missionaries aiding in the deception.

Whether engaged in legal or illicit lumbering, however, the Ojibwa early on adopted the 'family territory system' to regulate their operations on the reserve, and the local Indian Lands agent was usually too occupied with other matters to attempt to interfere in Native bush activities. This mode of production occasionally gained admiration from local entrepreneurs, although such approval, when broadly publicized, carried with it liabilities for the system. For instance, when one timber merchant in 1896 informed Ottawa that the Native people maintained their own method of parcelling out areas for cutting timber which not only conformed well to the topography of the land but also incorporated a share system regulated by the chief and principal men, he unwittingly became an informer. Instead of being commended for responding constructively to local conditions, both the entrepreneur and the local agent were reprimanded for their leniency and for disregarding policy, and were instructed to implement a grid system of timber berths at once, regardless of the wishes of the Ojibwa. The government relented only when the band, through its chief and council, explained the practical reasons for their system of resource management. Once assured that the Native system was rational and effective and did not conflict with neighbouring, large-scale company operations, Ottawa gave the band more autonomy than the letter of the law allowed, both in the methods of resource exploitation and in its transactions with buyers.

During roughly the same period, local agents also began permitting Native individuals to hold mining locations on ceded lands.[19] While this constituted a departure from Shingwaukonse's original plan, in which timber and minerals would be group-controlled resources supplying revenue for the whole band, the private operations provided locatees with cash supplements which could be used to purchase supplies for winter trapping or logging, or materials to fashion agricultural implements. By the 1890s, the local band economy had come to be characterized by a series of seasonally appropriate activities, in which a portion of the surplus returns from one employment was necessarily reinvested in preparations for the next. Mining, like temporary wage labour, offered a source of funds to cope with emergencies without depleting the band's limited capital.

At no time did the Garden River band ever conform to a model of Ojibwa society as primarily passive, albeit flexible in responding to external pressures. The group was able to exercise its prerogatives over land and resources not because protective legislation had confirmed its rights, but because Native people themselves had fought hard for their rights. Ojibwa leaders had expended their energies, time, and money to encourage government, missionary, commercial, and legal agencies to support their people's goals. Their persistence and courage occasionally won the respectful admiration of local officials and clergy. Although the cumulative effect of such outside support was important, it was not by itself powerful enough to make policy more responsive to Aboriginal needs and aspirations. In 1857, 1877, 1884, and 1905, formidable external political interests pressured the government to dispense altogether with the reserve system in the vicinity of Sault Ste Marie. It was the Garden River leaders who after 1859 forced Ottawa to recognize the band's special relationship to land and resources and allow it to retain its land base almost intact. At the same time, the Ojibwa, with the cooperation of local government officials, merchants, and company agents, maintained much of the non-capitalistic character of their system of production.

For these reasons, it may not be accurate to view the preservation of the land base as the most important reason for the continuing integrity of the group over time. Rather, the group's persistence seems to have stemmed directly from the character of the relationship between the band and its leadership, with custom requiring the leaders to make their intentions and goals public so that they could be made continuously responsible to those for whom they acted. This reciprocal relationship enabled the group as a whole to develop organizational forms capable of upholding, elaborating, and defending prerogatives over the land and resources required for the 'sufficient good' of all concerned – even where the rights in question had never been encoded in Canadian law. During the course of research on this study, it became evident to me that groups are to a large extent defined by their history and the use they make of their inherited values, organizational traits, and symbols. While cultural precedents may be adaptable to new social contexts, however, they require favourable conditions in which to evolve.

Traditional and Modern Manifestations of Leadership

While the relationship between power-holder and group has persisted at Garden River until the present day, the responsibility for decision making has tended to shift back and forth from leader to band, depending on external circumstances. The present study suggests that, before 1850, when the reserve system was first established north of Lakes Huron and Superior, Shingwaukonse's followers had few leadership responsibilities or powers apart from the control the heads of the hunting groups had over winter hunting activities. Constant vigilance in the interests of the group was mainly the responsibility of the most prominent power-holder. This individual's family unit formed a 'nodal core' to which other family groups were attached through agnatic, affinal, or cognatic kin ties. Little Pine's band, through consensus, could impose checks and balances on its chief's prerogatives and options, but Shingwaukonse remained the primary actor, especially in the sphere of external affairs.

The chief, in consultation with his principal men, also retained the right of admitting new individuals to the reciprocal relationship between him and his group. The 'band' thus could not properly be considered a residence unit, since it was primarily relationship-based rather than location-based. An individual might 'belong' to a band and yet not reside with the group for long periods of time.[20] At any one time, moreover, group size might expand or contract, depending on the degree of competency exhibited by its leader in sustaining a political, economic, and social milieu favourable to the perpetuation of valued group interests and activities.

Under stable conditions, a hierarchy existed composed of subchiefs who recognized the primacy of a head chief. Well into the late nineteenth century, the Garden River 'band' could still be described as a body of individuals united under a prominent leader. Similarly, the Sault band on the British side was united under the headship of Nebenagoching. Shing-waukonse and his band were inseparable: he had brought the group into existence and sought to sustain it. After his death, this group became vastly reduced in size as family groups broke off and joined other bands, mainly in response to divisive government policies.

There were no instances of bitter religious strife during the period under study. Though occasional rifts arose between members of different Christian denominations, these did not affect the Native community as strongly as they did the small white community, which was continually plagued by religious disagreements. After 1835, very few self-described 'pagans' existed, and only one, Oquaio, can be identified in the documentary record. In the Batchewana Band census for 1865, Oquaio, or Neck of Earth, a well-known hunter and medicine practitioner of the Loon *dodem* in the Goulais Bay area north of the Sault, registered his religious preferences as 'pagan.'[21] No serious splits seemed to have arisen between this 'traditionalist' and the Methodist, Roman Catholic, or Anglican Ojibwa, who referred to themselves generally as 'Christians.' In fact, the relatively strong religious orientation of both the Ojibwa and Métis at the rapids seems to have acted more as a unifying than a dividing factor. Exceptions to this rule occurred during private disputes involving shamanistic reprisal, especially when one of the contestants hailed from a neighbouring community. In 1858 and 1859, Shingwaukonse's grandson, Edward Piabetassung, who lived on Sugar Island, engaged in a property dispute with a man from Thessalon, Kechenebaunewbau, who was reputed to be a *djiski*.[22]

The theory developed by Robert J. Berkhofer, Jr, that differences or gradations of belief historically almost always generated divisions within Aboriginal communities, thus is not borne out by Garden River history.[23] For one thing, the Sault hardly constituted a 'virgin' field for Christian missionary endeavours, even in the 1830s. To this population, the teachings of missionaries of the various denominations were not startling or even particularly new. Garden River, moreover, was never a 'mission establishment.' Its roots were in the fur trade, for which it had acted as an important way-station *en route* to the west. In this respect, it should be analysed in the light of what is known about various 'composite' French and Métis Great Lakes communities.[24] Even so, it fits none of these models particularly well, since before 1858 its leadership held distinctly Ojibwa values and goals regarding land and resource use. The community's Native leaders were continually looking around and borrowing from other sources, while retaining what they wished to keep. Sault Native leadership was so well organized and had such a solid political base during the period under study that missionaries were often the ones experiencing a degree of political dependency.

At Garden River, any rifts between Methodists, Roman Catholics, and Anglicans evinced little of the sectarian bitterness and strife that afflicted the government-sponsored missions. At the mission at the Narrows on Lake Simcoe and at the Manitowaning Establishment on Manitoulin Island, political power struggles often focused on peripheral issues rather than economic questions directly affecting the group's survival. Finally, the Sault Native community, with its unity in ethnic diversity, was never prone to the 'garrison mentality' which plagued its more ethnically homogeneous Wikwemikong neighbours whenever eastern Manitoulin Island Native fisheries and cornfields were threatened by outside resource interests. A small island population forms a rather specific eco-logical case in any event, but to the Roman Catholic Odawa population, isolated within the Ojibwa 'sea,' protection of their local fisheries was especially crucial. No doubt the assistance offered during these years by the Roman Catholic Métis and Ojibwa from the Sault area was much appreciated, and may even have encouraged some 'opening up' of the Wikwemikong community to Ojibwa influences.

As Paul Landau eloquently writes in *The Realm of the World: Language, Gender and Christianity in a Southern African Kingdom*, 'On a basic level, any-thing unfamiliar demands the contours of a boundary, even if egotisti-cally drawn ...'[25] In the Sault region this statement applies equally well to Aboriginal people and to colonial administrators, since it refers more to cultural perspective than to belief. Shingwaukonse, a noted practitioner of both the *Midéwiwin* and the *djiskuiwin* in his young manhood, still 'grew' throughout his lifetime, learning not only where prevailing bound-aries lay, but also how one could subtly shift and even at times erase them. This growth depended on two things: getting to know the 'other,' even at considerable personal risk to himself; and relinquishing an overt attach-ment to denomination, since as a 'model' Church of England chief he had at various times encountered opposition even from his own close family members. Unlike Landau's 'ordinary persons' in Botswana and GammaNgwato, who relied on Christian beliefs, practices, and networks, Shingwaukonse continued to rely for his elevated status within the broad Great Lakes Native community on his reputation as a traditional *Midéwi-win* practitioner, especially after the death in 1836 of his mentor, Kay-gayosh. The Ojibwa cognitive system ultimately proved more effective in furthering his goals than Christianity, since Native thought did not encourage overt expression of beliefs. By the 1870s, however, resource issues had superseded religious issues to such a degree that the chief's political heirs would be judged far more by their ability to protect and enhance their people's resource base than by their religious preferences.

The religious differences which divided the Garden River and Batchewana bands in the 1830s were eroded by close relationships and continual interaction between the bands, a trend Shingwaukonse acknowledged shortly before his death by granting lands to both the Anglican and Roman Catholic churches. It was not religious difference but traditional leadership organization which kept the Garden River and Batchewana bands distinct from one another, even after 1859 when both groups resided at Garden River. Nebenagoching's people retained their own chief and council, and maintained their own band account. When the population of both bands rose significantly in the early decades of the twentieth century, the Batchewana leaders waged a determined campaign to secure their own community base at the Sault. This heralded the onset of about five years of interband rivalry in the late 1930s, with both groups competing for government and public attention in order to achieve their respective goals.[26] Ultimately, the Batchewana chief and council were successful in obtaining a suitable land base. As soon as Arthur Rankin's old mining location came up for sale, the Batchewana First Nation purchased it with their own band monies – the first of several such properties the Batchewana chief and council would acquire along the eastern boundary of Sault Ste Marie.

Before 1850, Ojibwa bands in the Sault vicinity were governed by a flexible band model which permitted fusion and fission in response to changing external and internal conditions.[27] The Robinson Treaties proceedings changed all this by establishing registered charter groups. Another major alteration in the government's concept of 'band' organization occurred in 1874 when, following urgent petitioning by the Natives of the Robinson Treaties area, distribution of annuities ceased to be based on the sharing of a fixed lump sum among all recipients. The adoption of the four-dollar per capita annuity raised questions about rights to these monies which, in the interests of government economy, ultimately led to the encoding of the principle of *partus sequiter patrem* – rights reckoned by inheritance in the male line – in the Indian Act of 1876. It was this 'limited good' offered by Ottawa, more than any other single factor, which created at Garden River a legally defined 'band' in place of the more flexible traditional 'band' model. Locally, however, the traditional 'band' persisted and became the decision-making band unit. Although this entity was often mistakenly viewed by Indian Affairs officials as synonymous with the legally defined 'band,' the latter remained separate from its static twin in much the same way as the living organism exists apart from its shell.[28]

Tensions arising at Garden River from time to time, as the band grew and individual and group interests diverged, were gradually relieved by the leader's efforts to attain control of sufficient resources to meet the needs of all band members. At this time the 'band' emerged as a political entity functioning in its own right, with the petition serving as its major tool. Together, traditional power-holders, elected leaders, and the 'band' sought to ensure that resources exploited by outside agencies furnished capital returns to the group in the form of royalties, interest, dues, or employment opportunities. In this way no sources of revenue on the reserve were totally alienated. In several agreements with resource companies, the Ojibwa insisted that, once external utilization of quarries or timber berths ended and revenues ceased to flow into group coffers, the land would revert to the band.

The system for electing a chief and council implemented by Ottawa in 1891 in response to band petitions was an improvement over the traditional system. The new system allowed leadership to be drawn from a broad pool of diverse talents and skills, enabling the band to cope more effectively with the increasingly complex issues pertaining to the allocation and protection of reserve land and resources. At the same time, the band developed a procedural framework within which precedents for dealing with recurring issues could be set and improved upon through discussion and debate. This process of bureaucratization, while certainly not unique among the Ojibwa, began to evolve independently of direct external pressures as early as 1885 at Garden River, as a result of the band's determination to further its goals in a manner which mainstream society would recognize and respect and which would also ensure the band a measure of political autonomy.

The Divided Mantle

Despite the organizational changes mentioned above, the traditional value system, designed to uphold reciprocal respect relations among responsible power-holders both seen and unseen, still informed Ojibwa thinking to a significant degree. Its persistence strengthened resistance to the ethic of individual and intergroup competition and provided a focus for both individual and group initiative. This observation contradicts the finding that Native peoples who leave the strictly hunting and trapping way of life tend to relinquish their traditional beliefs. Instead, it supports a position which regards Native thought systems as potential sources of wisdom for mainstream society. While this position has some affinity with approaches which highlight the creative power of belief systems, it also stresses the need for historical investigation of how such thought systems actually affect group behaviour over time. Such evidence is needed to help legitimize claims for the creative potential of specific world views.

The Native belief system constitutes a level of reality which, according to elders at Garden River, is not open to negotiation since it holds the key to Ojibwa distinctiveness. Older individuals at Garden River voiced concern that the modern emphasis on group boundary maintenance might detract from the concept of 'power' as primarily a creative principle within the core of living things, and so divert attention from their culture's stress on the need for individualized expressions of respect towards sources of such power. Yet, while wary of attempts at description which might define the belief system too narrowly, one elder metaphorically expressed confidence and pride in the resilience of his value system, comparing it to a tree which throughout many seasons has been able to retain its vitality: 'When I was last down at the graveyard they say those old pines there, they get weak [or blasted] at the centre. But just the other day they cut one down and you know, it was solid, solid right through.'[29]

The importance of maintaining Garden River as a milieu congenial to the survival of Ojibwa cultural values remains a persistent theme in the traditions recounted by Garden River elders. The transactional responses necessary to maintain such a climate changed, yet basic values did not. The decline of the fur trade and the advent of mining and timbering heralded an extensive elaboration of ideology, but no radical departures in fundamental cultural premises. Since so many aspects of their traditional spiritual beliefs continued to inform Native responses to external political, economic, and religious agencies, *adiso.ka.nag* concerning Shingwaukonse remained powerful cultural transmitting mediums for the aims which this Ojibwa leader upheld during his lifetime. 'Shingwaukonse the Man' has been replaced by 'Shingwaukonse the Prophet,' a legendary figure whose vision of the future is gradually being realized through the actions of successive generations.[30] To this chief, as to his followers, mineral deposits, timber, and fish were as much gifts as the animals had been – gifts to be taken, treated with respect, and used in meaningful exchanges which transcended the merely commercial. To emphasize the importance which this value system still holds for Ojibwa today, one of Shingwaukonse's great-grandsons recounted the following story about the chief's beliefs, stressing the significance of its message for future generations:

> Manido are all valuable. Everything was put in for a purpose. That's what he said. If you run into any trouble you're the cause of it. You can bring distur-bance. Only you can make a good thing or bad thing of yourself. He was really smart, just like a minister. He told others, 'You be proud of these gifts. Don't make fun of anything. Don't waste anything. It's not for sale. If you throw it away, I'll live naked.'[31]

His descendants are expected to maintain the tradition, and they gen-erally do, even though they may not participate directly in politics. In this common endeavour to maintain and develop a group milieu, founded on values the chief upheld, the claims of individual and group are recon-ciled under one 'mantle,' and Shingwaukonse's faith in his people and culture and his confidence and hope for the future live on.

What does the history of Garden River reveal about the leadership of Shingwaukonse and his successors? Was it ultimately weak and ineffec-tual, or surprisingly resilient in the face of a restrictive legal system enshrined in successive Indian Acts? Whatever the verdict, it is true that Shingwaukonse remained faithful to his vision for the future and to tradi-tional group values and norms. After 1850, Garden River leaders were portrayed as obstructing the public good whenever they espoused any economic occupation other than trapping or farming, no matter how they framed their appeals. Even modern social science models have been unfair to Native communities, focusing too narrowly on transactions involving the extraction and exchange of only one or two subsistence-level resources, such as fur, fish, or farm produce. Yet Ojibwa culture has always favoured the use of a wide range of resources and has encouraged communities to seek assistance in developing management skills and technological infrastructures. The Ojibwa sought to protect what they had until they could develop it fully, on their own terms, and their leaders worked tirelessly to ensure sustained returns from their local resource base.

Canadian Native policy in practice often tended to treat reserves as unprotected common lands where, in the absence of concerted Native resistance, what has been termed 'the tragedy of the commons' would almost certainly have been played out.[32] The small but important gains made by Native people contradict the claim that the Ojibwa were inher-ently incapable of managing economic resources. In the 1920s, the Garden River First Nation won an important victory when the government approved an agreement made with the local quarrying company which gave employment to band members, provided insurance benefits, and ensured that when the site ceased to be worked it would revert to the band. Ultimately, all parties benefited, and the Ojibwa showed themselves to be a responsible and just host group to outside entrepreneurial interests that were willing to negotiate in good faith and respect the terms of the agreement.[33] Such instances provide welcome precedents today when government–community co-management has become a key concept in forming policies relating to economic development on Aboriginal lands.

For almost a century and a half, Shingwaukonse's goals inspired Native decision making in the Sault region, and they continue to do so. In the words of a Garden River resident – one of Shingwaukonse's direct descendants:

> He was a brave man, he wasn't scared of disruption. He knew he might fail. But that didn't stop him. As one story said, he had a purpose, a gift. He followed his goals. He couldn't turn back. 'And then what kind of man would I be?' he said. 'You cannot leave the path. You wouldn't be remembered.'[34]

Notes

ABBREVIATIONS

AO   Archives of Ontario
MNR   Ontario, Ministry of Natural Resources, Surveys and Mapping
              Branch, Peterborough
MTPL   Metropolitan Toronto Public Library, Baldwin Room
NA   National Archives, Washington, D.C.
NAC   National Archives of Canada, Ottawa
Vidal Papers Regional Collections, University of Western Ontario, London,
              Alexander Vidal Papers

CHAPTER 1   Little Pine: Man, Leader, and Legend

1 Schoolcraft held that the *Wabano* was a relatively recent ceremony, held at dusk, and derived from a 'degraded' form of the *Midéwiwin*. Schoolcraft, *The Red Race in America*, 114–15. Information on the *Midéwiwin* may be obtained from Hoffman, 'The Midéwiwin or "Grand Medicine Society" of the Ojibwa,' and Dewdney, *The Sacred Scrolls of the Southern Ojibway*.
2 Schoolcraft, *Personal Memoirs*, 110.
3 Despite his own deliberate gift-giving manipulations, Schoolcraft often branded the Ojibwa as dishonest and acquisitive, and registered surprise that chiefs rarely followed his agency directives. Six years after his office meeting with Shingwaukonse in 1822, his diary for 18 August 1828 recorded a mixture of dismay and reluctant admiration for the seemingly cavalier way in which the chief, even though participating in an earlier gift distribution, had skirted his wishes: 'The giving of public presents on the 5th had evidently led to his visit, although he had not pursued the policy expected of him, so far as his influ-

ence reached among the Chippewas on the American shores of the straits. He made a speech well suited to his position, and glossed off with some fine generalities, avoiding commitments on main points and making them on minor ones, concluding with a string of wampum. I smoked and shook hands with him, and accepted his tenders of friendship by repledging the pipe, but narrowed his visit to official proprieties, and refused his wampum.' Schoolcraft, *Personal Memoirs*, 306.

4 Schoolcraft's interest in the old Sault chief Great Crane, and his progeny, sprang wholly from the agent's intention to resort to patrilineal reckoning and primogeniture to determine leadership succession at the rapids following the death of a leader by the name of Kaygayosh in 1836. According to Schoolcraft: 'Gitcheojeedebun [Great Crane], had four sons, namely, Maidosagee, Bwoinais, Nawgichigomee and Kezhawokumijishkum. Maidosagee, being the eldest, had nine sons, called Shingabawossin, Sizzah, Kaugayosh [Kaygayosh], Nattaowa, Ussaba [Sassaba], Wabidjejauk [Waubejechauk], Muckadaywuckwuk [Muckedayoquot], Wabidjejaukons, and Odjeeg. On the principles of Indian descent, these were all Cranes of the proper mark, but the chieftainship would descend in the line of the eldest chief's children.' Schoolcraft, *Personal Memoirs*, 590.

5 The English word 'totem' derives from the Ojibwa term *dode.men* or *dodem*. The *dodemic* system still uses symbols derived from the natural world, both faunal and floral. It can be quite difficult to determine exactly which unit is being described in early-nineteenth-century writings, since, in common parlance among white settlers until the 1830s, a *dodemic* group was often called a 'tribe,' but then so also was the extended family nodal core group which formed the main economic unit among the Ojibwa.

6 Thwaites, ed., *Jesuit Relations and Allied Documents*, 18:229–31.

7 Schenck, 'Identifying the Ojibwa.' According to oral tradition, the Outchibous band at Sault Ste Marie split around 1670, with a prominent chief of the Crane *dodem* migrating to Chequamegon, near La Pointe, Wisconsin. Warren, *History of the Ojibway Nation*, 316–17.

8 National Archives of Canada (hereafter NAC) MG 1, Archives nationales, Archives des colonies, Correspondance generale, Canada (CllA), F-19: 43r, 'Marks of the various Indian villages. Ratification of the Peace, August 4, 1701.'

9 Schoolcraft, *Personal Memoirs*, 110.

10 Frost, *Sketches of Indian Life*, 51. Tughwahna may have been a brother of Maidosagee, the head chief at Sault Ste Marie during the late eighteenth century, since an individual by the name of 'Tugauhanas' acted as Maidosagee's spokesman at Detroit in 1779. NAC, RG 10, vol. 16, 113, 'Papers relating to the West-

ern Indians at Detroit,' 6 June 1779. It may also have been the same person whose name, rendered 'Tacoanais,' appears on a land surrender made by the Ojibwa to the North West Company in 1798. AO, MS 75, Russell Papers, 'Surrender of land at Sault Ste. Marie to the Northwest Company,' 10 August 1798.

11 The first recorded instance of Little Pine's use of the Plover *dodem* is in a letter to a missionary in 1844. AO, MG 35, Strachan Papers, 'Shingwaukonse to the Reverend William McMurray,' 13 May 1844.

12 Interviews with ex-chief Richard Pine, Sr, ex-councillor Fred Pine, Sr, and ex-councillor Dan Pine, Sr, June 1982. The word at Garden River for Plover is *chu.e.skwe.ske.wa*. Although Lewis Henry Morgan argues that the word *chueskweskewa* designates the 'Snipe gens,' the word for snipe at Garden River is *muhno-menekashe*. Paul Pine, Ogista's son, who resided at Marquette in Michigan, acted as a guide during Morgan's researches into beaver habits – and probably during Morgan's mineral exploring as well – and may have given Morgan the information on the *chueskweskewa dodem*. Morgan, *Ancient Society*, 166.

13 Historical evidence for hunting territories, based on a group allotment scheme, dates from around 1700. Baron de Lahontan wrote that the Ojibwa would 'choose rather to die from hunger than to straggle out of the Bounds alloted to them, or to steal the beasts that are taken in their neighbours trap.' Thwaites, ed., *Baron de Lahontan, Some Voyages to North America*, 2:482. Schoolcraft provided valuable information on territorial allotment around 1791, the year his father-in-law, John Johnston, first encountered Chief Waubojeeg, whose territory is being described, near present-day La Pointe, Wisconsin: 'It is a rule of the chase, that each hunter has a portion of the country assigned to him, on which he alone may hunt; and there are conventional laws which decide all questions of right and priority in stalking and killing game. In these questions, the chief exercises a proper authority, and it is thus in the power of one of these forest governors and magistrates, where they happen to be men of sound sense, judgement and manly independence, to make themselves felt and known, and to become true benefactors to their tribes.' Schoolcraft, *The Indian in His Wigwam*, 142.

14 Kohl, *Kitchi-Gami*, 407.

15 Rogers and James G.E. Smith, 'Cultural Ecology in the Canadian Shield Sub-arctic.'

16 Blair, ed., *The Indian Tribes of the Upper Mississippi Valley and Region of the Great Lakes*, 1:309–10.

17 Interviews with Dan Pine, Sr, Richard Pine, Sr, and Fred Pine, Sr, August 1982.

18 Shingabaw'osin actually translates as 'the stone through which one [sees something].'

19 James G.E. Smith, personal communication, 16 October 1989.

20 Frost, *Sketches of Indian Life*, 142.
21 Interview with ex-councillor Frederick E. Pine, Sr, in August 1983.
22 Kohl, *Kitchi-Gami*, 161–2; Schoolcraft, *Historical and Statistical Information*, 3:62; McKenney, *Sketches of a Tour to the Lakes*, 235.
23 Winchell, *The Aborigines of Minnesota*, 532.
24 The division between interior peoples [*muskego*] and lake peoples is still recognized at Garden River today, particularly linguistically, with regard to slight differences in inflection. Toby Morantz examines the role of trading captains near James Bay in 'James Bay Trading Captains of the Eighteenth Century: New Perspectives on Algonquian Social Organization.'
25 Occasions such as a major treaty signing between the Ojibwa and representatives of the American government at Fond du Lac, Minnesota, in August 1826 placed strains on this form of leadership. These government-sponsored events often took place at locations a considerable distance from bands residing in the eastern sector of the Lake Superior region. Confronted by unfamiliar government policies, chiefs from these groups had to make decisions on issues vitally affecting their people in situations where traditional checks and balances on a leader's power failed to work effectively. Although Shingabaw'osin represented the entire Sault band, he travelled the long route to Fond du Lac accompanied by only a small retinue, and during the course of negotiations may have spoken mainly for himself and a few close kin rather than for his group as a whole. The consequences of this externally imposed distancing of a power-holder from the band for which he was responsible posed a threat to the traditional system. In one of his most radical statements of 1826, Shingabaw'osin acquiesced in the Americans' desire to exploit the copper resources on Ojibwa lands, in spite of vehement opposition from the Plover, a chief whose band's territory along the Ontonagon River lay in the midst of rich copper-bearing country just west of the base of the Keweenaw Peninsula. The Plover, after referring to an Ojibwa belief that exposures of this metal were protected by spirit guardians and that unsanctioned use by Aboriginal peoples as well as whites could lead to severe reprisals by these beings, stated that copper constituted a gift from the Great Spirit which could be proclaimed the property of no one man. Shingabaw'osin's unconditional support for American policy regarding the alienation of copper reserves may have been interpreted by American officialdom as a wise decision by an enlightened chief, but for certain Native leaders, such as the Plover, it stood as an unwarranted abrogation of authority by a single power-holder. Washington, National Archives (henceforth NA), RG 75, T 494, Reel 10, 'Ratified Treaty No. 145. Documents Relating to the Negotiation of the Treaty of August 5, 1826 with the Chippewa [Ojibwa] Indians.'

26 Shingwaukonse married a pair of sisters. NAC, RG 10, vol. 2631, file 128, 145, pt 0. Shawanapenasse is mentioned in AO, MU 275, Harry D. Blanchard Collection, M. Section Papers, 1766–1932, 'Letter to Richard Carney from Garden River chief inquiring as to his right as a chief, dated October 12, 1858.'

27 Richard White, *The Middle Ground.*

28 Interviews with Dan Pine, Sr, Richard Pine, Sr, and Fred Pine, Sr, August 1982.

29 Black[-Rogers], 'Ojibwa Power Belief System,' 141–51.

30 Hallowell, 'Ojibwa Ontology, Behaviour and World View,' 19–52.

31 Black[-Rogers], 'Ojibwa Power Belief System', 147.

32 Ibid., 146.

33 Preston, 'Reticence and Self-Expression'; Adrian Tanner, *Bringing Home Animals,* 69.

34 Warren, *History of the Ojibway Nation,* 89–90.

35 Daniel Erskine Pine, Sr, born in 1900, was the son of John Askin, who was born in 1836.

36 Although many Garden River residents no longer engage full time in economic pursuits as hunters, fishers, traders, and harvesters of furs and other bush resources, significant aspects of the traditional outlook persist. Concern was felt during the initial stages of this study that retrieval of oral data on traditional attitudes regarding leadership might constitute a problem. It was anticipated that elders at Garden River might be reluctant to discuss a subject which belonged more to the past than to the present, especially since community emphasis was on the implementation of progressive forms of local government. These apprehensions proved groundless, however, as the ethnographer found that, in addition to modern and ongoing developments in band administration, traditional concepts of leadership are still very much in evidence and Shingwaukonse remains a figure of considerable importance at Garden River. Interview with Fred Pine, Sr, 21 August 1982.

37 Ibid.

38 Prucha, *Lewis Cass and American Indian Policy,* 50.

39 George Johnston wrote of troubles Tugwaugaunay at La Pointe had in controlling hunting on his territories. When Tugwaugaunay wanted Johnston, who was appointed Indian subagent at La Pointe in 1827, to prevent Métis who were not associated with his band from taking resources from his lands, the chief found that the government chose to ban all Métis, as a racial category, from hunting, not merely those whom the chief regarded as poachers. Bayliss Library, Sault Ste Marie, Michigan, George Johnston Papers, 'George Johnston to H.R. Schoolcraft,' 6 January 1828.

40 'A Noted Indian Chief: Historical and Biographical Sketch of His Remarkable Career,' *Sault Star,* 10 June 1899. Nebenagoching's father, Waubejechauk, or

White Crane, was one of Maidosagee's sons. In 1897 an Indian Lands agent at Sault Ste Marie, Ontario, referred to a conversation he had with Nebenagoching in the French language. NAC, RG 10, vol. 1954, file 4472, 482895. Nebenagoching's mother, born a Perrault, may have remarried a Sayer after the death of her first husband, Waubejechauk. Both Tegoosh and Buhk-wujjenene, two of Little Pine's sons, also could speak some French and had been taught by missionaries to read Ojibwa. Wilson, *Missionary Work among the Ojibway Indians*, 246.

41 Interview with Dan Pine, Sr, 13 June 1983. Prince Napoleon, a cousin of Napoleon III, visited Sault Ste Marie in 1861. At this time the Métis were 'isolated among and scorned by the Anglo-Saxon population.' The prince's aide-de-camp regarded the Ojibwa, on the other hand, as a people whose 'silence conceals a certain contempt for the onlookers and a real pride.' Ferri, *Prince Bonaparte in America, 1861*, 199–201.

42 Kohl, *Kitchi-Gami*, 377.

43 Interview with Dan Pine, Sr, 10 June 1983. Ten days is an extraordinarily long time for a vision fast.

44 Kohl, *Kitchi-Gami*, 375–6.

45 It is interesting to note that the 'Vision of Ogauns' recorded by Diamond Jenness in the Parry Sound area of Ontario contains much that is reminiscent of Shingwaukonse's vision and would have dated from around the same period. Jenness, *The Ojibwa Indians of Parry Island*, 55–9.

46 Fred Pine, Sr, held that *ujew*, the Ojibwa word for hill, formed the root of the word. The name translates as 'He [the sun] who is rising over the hill.' The sun could 'see' all things on earth, and exercised a powerful regulatory control within the Ojibwa cosmos. Interview with ex-councillor Frederick E. Pine, Sr, 10 June 1983.

47 Ibid.

48 Ibid.

49 Mason, ed., *Schoolcraft's Expedition to Lake Itasca*, 86.

50 NAC, RG 10, vol. 26, 14987, 'Journal Census par Charles Gaultier, 1791.'

51 During his years at L'Arbre Croche and Mackinac, Askin, Sr, had three children, John, Jr, Madelaine, and Catherine, by an Ottawa or Ojibwa woman, prior to his marriage in 1722 to Marie Archange Barthe of Detroit. The collections of Askin Papers in the Burton Historical Collection, Detroit Public Library, the Ontario Archives in Toronto, and the National Archives in Ottawa make no mention of Shingwaukonse. Few records of Askin's early life survive, however.

52 Burton Historical Collection, Detroit Public Library, J.B. Barthe Papers, Account Book.

53 Mason, ed., *Schoolcraft's Expedition to Lake Itasca*, 149. The name 'Lavoine' was employed on a petition to the lieutenant-governor. Catholic Archdiocesan Centre Archives, Toronto, Bishop Alexander Macdonell Papers, AC 2402, 'To His Excellency Sir John Colborne, K.B., 1835.'

54 Burton Historical Collection, Detroit Public Library, J.B. Barthe Papers, Barthe MS Ledger. In 1778 Lavoine Barthe moved west, possibly to settle in the vicinity of the Wisconsin portage. Quaife, ed., *John Askin Papers*, 1:143.

55 Interview with Dan Pine, Sr, 13 June 1983. 'Alavoine' was used as a Christian name in both the Chevalier and Barthe families.

56 Schoolcraft, *Summary Narrative*, 6.

57 Genealogical data were taken from the records of St John's Anglican Church, Garden River, the Roman Catholic Church Register of Assinins (formerly L'Anse) Indian Catholic Mission in Michigan, Methodist Church records at L'Anse, and the Pine family Bible, kept by John Askin's wife, Cecilia Shawan. This Bible is now in the possession of a daughter of Dan Pine, Sr. Relevant information also was obtained from 'Report of Baptisms, Marriages and Burials at Sault Ste Marie, 6th October 1833 – 15th March, 1835,' Society for Converting and Civilizing the Indians of Upper Canada, *Fifth Annual Report*, 1835.

58 Interview with Fred Pine, Sr, 17 November 1983.

59 Wise, 'The Indian Diplomacy of John Graves Simcoe,' 36–44.

60 Charles M. Johnston, ed., *The Valley of the Six Nations*, xxxvi–xxxviii.

61 NAC, RG 10, vol. 8, 8525, 'A.M. McKee, Deputy Minister of Indian Affairs, to the Commissioner of the United States,' 27 July 1793.

62 There was a short period when British traders, and indeed all persons of British descent, feared for their safety. Even the situation of John Tanner, an American captive of the Ottawa, became precarious at Mackinac Island after his adoptive Indian father, Tawgaweninne, became seriously injured in a fight: 'When I saw this, I became alarmed for my own safety, and, I knew *Me.to.saw.gea*, an Ojibway chief, was then on the island, with a party going against the whites; and, as I had understood they had sought opportunity to kill me, I thought my situation unsafe.' James, ed., *A Narrative of the Captivity and Adventures of John Tanner*, 20. When traders made arrangements which showed they were disposed to respect Native prerogatives, these attacks on traders ceased. In 1797, the Hudson's Bay Company opened a post at Michipicoten, north of the Sault. The willingness shown by Maidosagee's band in 1798 to cede St Joseph Island to the British government for a garrison post, and land on the north shore of the St Mary's straits to the North West Company also demonstrated that accommodation had been reached. Relations between the Ojibwa and the British grew more amiable. John Johnston, who entered the Lake Superior trade in 1791 and eventually settled at Sault Ste

Marie, even came to know Maidosagee well enough to entertain the chief, prior to 1810, as a frequent house guest. Schoolcraft, *The Literary Voyager, or Muzzeniegan*, 109. Yet not all traders fared so well. John Sayers in 1797, who may not have obtained the sanction of the Crane band for his occupation of land at Sault Ste Marie, suffered the destruction of all his buildings. So great were his losses at the Ojibwa's hands that he gave up his activities as an independent trader and entered the employ of the North West Company. Yet independent traders felt uneasy about Crane reprisals against British traders for only a year or so. In 1794 Maidosagee's band granted 192 acres of land 'forever' to Jean Baptiste Nolin for 'four kegs of nine gallons each of Rum and sixteen-pound weight of tobacco.' The date and nature of this transaction is interesting, since the property had previously been purchased by Nolin from another trader, Jean Baptiste Barthe. Nolin's need to obtain a deed from the Native people – possibly the first made since the land transactions authorized by Robert Rogers at Mackinac in the 1760s – appears to have originated in the Ojibwa's heightened determination to exercise a degree of control over the disposition of lands at Sault Ste Marie. By intimidating threats and hostile acts, the Ojibwa compelled the resident commercial population to recognize the existence of Aboriginal right. Confronted on both sides of the border by encroaching state powers, which by 1794 seemed increasingly likely to sacrifice Native interests to their own nation-building goals, the Native people struck back by demanding that their special prerogatives be respected. This unrest most certainly stemmed in part from the northward spread of ideas originating with Brant and the 'western confederacy,' since in 1798 the North West Company contended that it would be difficult to obtain a land surrender at the rapids 'without the interference of Brant.' Bitterness over the failure of the confederacy to prevent alienation of territory west of the Ohio, news of the Americans' intention to garrison Mackinac, and Britain's apparent lack of concern for Native interests, engendered additional Indian resentment. One thing is certain. Trade rivalries exerted little influence over Native activities at the Sault during these years. The Ojibwa were concerned with inducing all whites, British or American, to recognize their territorial rights.

Britain's first step after the signing of the Treaty of Ghent was to move the western post from St Joseph Island to Drummond Island. The station at St Joseph had been partly a concession to Native demands. While difficult to defend from attack by water, it had proven to be easily accessible to the Lake Superior bands, and lay near important fisheries. By 1815, however, Native interests had a low priority, with William McGillivray of the North West Company the only voice calling for consideration of more than purely strategic factors in the choice of the location for the garrison. While the fluctuating sense of responsibility towards the Native people exhibited by the British colonial government contrasts sharply with Washington's economically based post-1800 Native policy, it also shows that the Ojibwa had far greater challenges to meet after the end of the War of 1812 than those arising solely from the expediencies of trade. Burton Historical Collection, Detroit Public Library, J.B. Nolin Papers, 'Articles of Agreement between Jean Baptiste Nolan and Quesgoitacameguiscame, sic Tamesa Mestosaguis and Bouniche,' 15 September 1794; 'Rep. No. 42, 20th Congress, House of Representatives. Land Cessions in Michigan. Committee on Public Lands,' 2 January 1828, 452; 'Regarding Communication through the Falls of St. Mary's,' 8 November 1798. NAC, RG 10, vol. 1, 'Communication from Sally Aince to Brother Brant,' 26 January 1795. NAC, RG 10, vol. 9, 8830.

63 The Sault band were back on reasonably good terms with the British by June of 1798, when they participated with two other bands in the signing of a treaty ceding St Joseph Island. NAC, MG 19-F, Claus Papers, vol. 7, 262–3, 'Captain Lamothe to the Superintendent of Indian Affairs,' nd [1797]. In 1798, land plots were surrendered at Fort William to the Hudson's Bay Company and at the Sault to the North West Company. NAC, RG 10, vol. 20, 'Report of Commissioners A. Vidal and T.G. Anderson on a Visit to the Indians on the North Shore of Lakes Huron and Superior for the purpose of investigating their claims to territory bordering on those Lakes, 1849,' Appendix E. Typescript copy in the Archives of Ontario, Toronto.

64 A useful source for understanding the reasons behind the ephemerality of this movement is Cave 'The Failure of the Shawnee Prophet's Witch-Hunt.'

65 Warren, *History of the Ojibway Nation*, 324.

66 Edmunds, *The Shawnee Prophet*, 76.

67 Danziger, *Chippewa of Lake Superior.*

68 Interview with Fred Pine, Sr, 9 May 1984.

69 NAC, RG 10, vol. 27, 16/0/79, 'John Askin to William Claus,' 8 May 1810.

70 Quaife, ed., *John Askin Papers*, 1:550.

71 Interview with Fred Pine, Sr, 12 July 1982; interview with Richard Pine, Sr, 13 July, 1982.

72 Cumberland, *Catalogue and Notes of the Oronhyatekha Historical Collection*, 26.

73 NAC, RG 8, C-676, 201, 'John Askin to William Claus,' 18 July 1812.

74 Askin maintained that about seven hundred Natives left for Detroit in August 1812. Wood, ed., *Select British Documents*, 1:436–7. Shingwaukonse received a medal for his participation in the Detroit campaign. NAC, RG 10, vol. 264, 'List of receivers of medals for engagement at Detroit, Chateauguay and Chrysler's Farm, 30th November, 1848.'

75 Wood, ed., *Select British Documents*, 1:506–8, General Isaac Brock to Lord Liverpool, 29 August 1812.

76 In one of these engagements Waubejechauk, Nebenagoching's father, lost his life. Schoolcraft states that Waubejechauk fell at the Battle of the Thames. Schoolcraft, *Summary Narrative*, 79. See also the *Sault Star*, 28 December 1957. A statement regarding the defection at Fort Miami appears in NAC, RG 8, C-671, 106–7, 'A.C. Muir to General Proctor,' 30 September 1812.

77 NAC, RG 10, vol. 416, 5942, 'Petition of William Shinquaconce et al.,' 20 August 1846.

78 Schoolcraft, *Summary Narrative*, 79.

79 NAC, RG 10, vol. 416, 5942. 'Petition of William Shinquaconce et al.,' 20 August 1812.

80 Washington, D.C., *Treaties between the United States of America, and Several Indian Tribes from 1778 to 1837*, 276–7.

81 Quaife, ed., *John Askin Papers*, 1:69ff. Askin's death evidently affected Little Pine, for he named one of his sons John Askin.

82 NAC, RG 8, C-258, 399, 'Lt.-Colonel Robert McDouall regarding Captain Payne's survey of Drummond Island, October 1815.'

83 A document preserved in the Sayer, or Nebenagoching, family reads: 'In consequence of Wa-ba-che-chake, a Chippewa of the Sault St Mary's having been killed in battle during the late war with the Americans at Fort George, his title and marks of distinction thereby falling to his son, Ne-ban-a-aw-bay, a boy of eight years of age, we the subscribers do hereby with the advice and consent of his tribe here assembled invest the said Ne-ban-a-aw-bay with the title and marks of distinction belonging to his late father. Drummond Island, the 29th day of June, 1819 Joe Maramette Major commanding W. McKay Sup. Indian Affairs, D.J.'

84 In company with Shingwaukonse and several others, Nebenagoching visited Montreal in 1849 and had his watercolour portrait done by Cornelius Krieghoff. His name in Ojibwa has been translated as 'Rays protruding from one side in an imbalanced way like the Moon "Holding Water."'

85 Interview with Fred Pine, Sr, 12 August 1983.

86 Schoolcraft, *Personal Memoirs*, 632.

87 George Johnston, 'Reminiscences.' That the American military, and not whites in general, were the target is evident from correspondence of Hudson's Bay Company employees on the Canadian side. For instance, Factor John Silveright noted in 1821 that both Major Winnett from Drummond Island and the Earl of Dalhousie passed through the St Mary's straits without incident on a trout-fishing excursion to Gros Cap, north of Sault Ste Marie. NAC, MG 19-A21, Hargrave Papers, vol. 1, series 1, 3, 'John Silveright to James Hargrave,' September 1821.

88 Bald, *The Seigniory at Sault Ste Marie*, Bayliss and Bayliss, *River of Destiny*, 42–4.

89 Wise, 'The American Revolution and Indian History.'

90 *Wisconsin Historical Society Collections*, 5:412.

91 *Michigan Pioneer and Historical Collections*, 12:909.

92 Schoolcraft, *Summary Narrative*, 76–7.

93 Ibid., 76–9.

94 *Michigan Pioneer and Historical Collections*, 18:609–10.

95 Schoolcraft, *Summary Narrative*, 79–80.

96 *Michigan Pioneer and Historical Collections*, 12:605–8.

97 Ibid., 18:611.

98 *Wisconsin Historical Society Collections*, 8:181.

99 Schoolcraft, *Personal Memoirs*, 96.

100 Marano, 'Windigo Psychosis.'

101 Field notes, 13 August 1982. Wolves are not quite witches according to the elders interviewed, although Richard Pine, Sr, admitted that Sassaba probably was becoming 'unbalanced, sort of like a windigo.'

102 Schoolcraft, *Personal Memoirs*, 248.

103 Schoolcraft, *The Red Race in America*, 299.

104 Schoolcraft, *Historical and Statistical Information* 1:361–81.

105 Schoolcraft, *Historical and Statistical Information* 3:85. The pictograph in question, at Agawa Canyon, takes in one of thirteen 'panels' of such inscribed drawings facing the waters of Lake Superior, separated from the waves only by a rocky ledge. It recalls the voyage across Lake Superior of Myeengun, or the Wolf, who was a *Midéwiwin* practioner. See Rajnovich, *Reading Rock Art*, 42–3.

106 Dan Pine, Sr, and Fred Pine, Sr, both stated that Little Pine traded west of Lake Superior before the outbreak of the War of 1812.

107 Initiated into the *Midéwiwin* at an early age, Marksman later went to Ebenezer College in Jacksonville, Illinois, and became a Methodist preacher at Pequaming, L'Anse, in Michigan. Pitezal, *Lights and Shades of Missionary Life*, 1–16.

108 NAC, RG 75, Records of the Michigan Superintendency 1814–51, vol. 2, FM-2 (1), Roll 67, 105–6, 'George Johnston to H.R. Schoolcraft,' 15 May 1827.

109 Schoolcraft, *Personal Memoirs*, 248–9.

CHAPTER 2   For the King and the King's Church

1 Canada (Province of), *Journals of the Legislative Assembly*, 1847, App. T, 'Report on the Affairs of the Indians of Canada,' 'To the Chippewas of Sault Ste. Marie and Lake Superior.'

2 Ibid., 'Minutes of Speeches Made by the Different Tribes of Indians in reply to Lieutenant-Colonel Mackay's of the 11th of July, 1829.'

3 Little Pine argued in 1833 that the British government had promised houses. Waddilove, *The Stewart Missions*, 103–4.
4 'Minutes of Speeches made ... the 11th of July, 1829.' See note 2.
5 Schoolcraft, *Personal Memoirs*, 251.
6 Mason, ed., *Schoolcraft's Expedition to Lake Itasca*, 147–9.
7 Benjamin Slight, a Methodist missionary, wrote: 'The Indians consider it rude to call a man by his proper name in common discourse. They always give him the quality he has with respect to the speaker, but when there is between them no relation or affinity, they use the term of brother or uncle, nephew or cousin, acording to each other's age or the feeling they possess towards the person they address.' Slight, *Indian Researches*, 82ff.
8 NA, RG 75, MI, F. M-2, Roll 71, 'Francis Audrain to Schoolcraft,' 25 September 1833.
9 Mason, ed., *Schoolcraft's Expedition to Lake Itasca*, 315.
10 Although Shingwaukonse seems to have been close to Michael Cadotte's family, particularly Louis Cadotte, who became his personal interpreter in 1846, he apparently initially opposed Buhkwujjenene's marriage to Marguerite (or Margaret) Cadotte. The reason has never been entirely clear. Buhkwujjenene continued to profess the Anglican faith, and no other religious impediments seem to have been present. Frost, *Sketches of Indian Life*, 87.
11 Metropolitan Toronto Public Library. Baldwin Room (hereafter MTPL), Thomas G. Anderson Papers, S29, 'Testimony of John Bell.'
12 Interview with Richard Pine, Sr, and Fred Pine, Sr, 14 August 1982.
13 Little Pine made frequent references to the confusing array of religious opinions and creeds which confronted him during these years. See, for example, Elliot, *Indian Missionary Reminiscences*, 157–8.
14 Kohl, *Kitchi-Gami*, 384.
15 NAC, RG 10, vol. 5, 'Sir Thomas Kempt to Sir John Colborne,' 18 February 1829.
16 Surtees, 'Land Cessions, 1763–1830.'
17 Rezek, *History of the Diocese of Sault Ste. Marie and Marquette*, 245.
18 Verwyst, *Life and Labors of Rt. Rev. Frederic Baraga*, 1–15.
19 Copway, *The Traditional History and Characteristic Sketches of the Ojibway Nation*, 197.
20 NA, RG 75, MI, Roll 71:84, 'Extract of a letter of Francis Audrain,' 22 June 1833.
21 Grant, *Moon of Wintertime*, 280ff.
22 Elliot, *Indian Missionary Reminiscences*, 157.
23 Ibid., 157–8.
24 Ibid., 159.

25 Shingwaukonse often referred to Yellowhead as 'brother' or 'cousin.' See, for example, Slight, *Indian Researches*, 82ff.

26 Slight, *Indian Researches*, 78–83.

27 See, for example, Bolt, *Thomas Crosby and the Tsimshian*, and Devens, *Countering Colonization*.

28 Graham, *Medicine Man to Missionary*, 5.

29 Clarke Library, Central Michigan University, Bingham Papers, Journal Two, 17 December 1832.

30 Ibid.

31 Ibid., 22 January.

32 Bingham employed John Tanner, the well-known Saginaw captive, as an interpreter during the early 1830s. After 1840 Bingham's interpreter was Louis Cadotte.

33 Clarke Library, Central Michigan University, Bingham Papers, Journal Two, 24 January 1833.

34 Waddilove, *The Stewart Missions*, 24. The Sault area had been regarded as a suitable site for Anglican endeavours even before the War of 1812. MTPL, Scadding Collection, Correspondence Regarding the Application of Mr John Johnston in 1810 for a Missionary to be sent to Sault Ste Marie: Jacob Mountain, Bishop of Quebec, to Charles Manners, Archbishop of Canterbury, 11 November 1810.

35 Cameron describes the teacher as his 'cousin.' This may have been William Cameron, who later became an independent trader at the Sault, although there is some argument that William was James's brother. J.D. Cameron, Jr, accepted baptism from Bingham on 2 May 1832. Clarke Library, Central Michigan University, Bingham Papers, Journal Two. For notice of his removal from the Anglican mission, see Society for Converting and Civilizing the Indians *Second Annual Report*, 1832.

36 HBCA, MG 20, B/109/a/3/1829–30, La Cloche Post Journals.

37 Waddilove, *The Stewart Missions*, 27.

38 HBCA, MG 20, B/109/a/5/1831–2, La Cloche Post Journals.

39 Society for Converting and Civilizing the Indians, *Second Annual Report*, 1832, Appendix.

40 Maclean, 'An Irish Apostle and Archdeacon in Canada,' 51.

41 Ibid.

42 Waddilove, *The Stewart Missions*, 103.

43 Ibid., 104.

44 Salisbury, 'Transactions or Transactors?'

45 Waddilove, *The Stewart Missions*, 86.

46 Ibid., 104.

47 This made McMurray brother-in-law to Henry Rowe Schoolcraft, since School-craft had married Charlotte's sister, Jane.
48 Burton Historical Collection, Detroit Public Library, George Johnston Papers, 'McMurray to George Johnston,' 7 May 1833.
49 NA, RG 75, MI, Roll 71: 68, 'Elbert Herring to Schoolcraft,' 20 June 1833.
50 NA, RG 75, MI, Roll 71: 48, 'Francis Audrain to Schoolcraft,' 13 June 1833.
51 Society for Converting and Civilizing the Indians, *Third Annual Report*, 1833.
52 Burton Historical Collection, Detroit Public Library, George Johnston Papers, 'McMurray to George Johnston,' 7 May 1833.
53 Kohl, *Kitchi-Gami*, 382. Kaygayosh did not accept Anglican baptism until he was on his deathbed in 1836. Schoolcraft, *Personal Memoirs*, 570. Schoolcraft writes about an occasion in January 1827 when Shingwaukonse arranged for the agent to participate in a *Midéwiwin* ceremony held in the agent's own office. Although there were several *Midéwiwin* practitioners present, Shing-waukonse acted as the main functionary. After sealing off the office from external influences by drawing the blinds and locking the door, the chief began singing phrases represented by figures carved into wooden 'song boards,' designated as mnemonic aids. The chief, according to Schoolcraft, also performed 'transformations of legerdemain.' Schoolcraft, *The Literary Voyageur or Muzzeniegan*, 36–7.
54 'The Venerable Archdeacon McMurray,' *Algoma Missionary News*, January 1892.
55 Society for Converting and Civilizing the Indians, *Fifth Annual Report*, 1835, 'Journal of the Missionary to the Sault Ste. Mary, ended July 22, 1835.'
56 Ibid.
57 This wampum belt, just over a metre long, was on the auction block at Sotheby's in New York during the week of 18 to 25 May 1997. The belt, which is narrow, has thirteen diagonal rows of white shell beads crossing a field of purple shell beads. The ends (one of which is frayed) were both originally dec-orated with a fringe-like design having seven horizontal white indentations. It is probably older than 1833. It was presented for a price, along with a letter designating its provenance, to the British Museum in the spring of 1997. When the British Museum would not pay the price, it was sent to New York to auction. I am indebted to Mr Robin Brock of Toronto for this information, along with the pages of the Sotheby's catalogue referring to the item.
58 Society for Converting and Civilizing the Indians, *Third Annual Report*, 1833.
59 Ibid.
60 Maclean, 'An Irish Apostle and Archdeacon in Canada,' 51.
61 Society for Converting and Civilizing the Indians, *Fourth Annual Report*, 1834, 'Report presented to the Society at its meeting at Upper Canada College, Toronto, December 27th, 1834.'

62 HBCA, MG 20, B/194/b/10/1835–6, Sault Ste Marie Post, Correspondence Books, 'William Nourse to Bethune, 29 July 1835.'

63 Society for Converting and Civilizing the Indians, *Fourth Annual Report*, 1834.

64 Ibid.

65 HBCA, MG 20, B/194/a/8/1834–5, Sault Ste Marie Post Journals, '30 September, 1834.'

66 HBCA, MG 20, B/194/b/10/1835–6, Sault Ste Marie Post, Correspondence Books, 'William Nourse to Angus Bethune, 12 April 1836.'

67 HBCA, MG 20, B/194/a/8/1834–5, Sault Ste Marie Post Journals, '9 March 1835.'

68 Waddilove, *The Stewart Missions*, 86.

69 Society for Converting and Civilizing the Indians, *Fourth Annual Report*, 1834.

70 Ibid.

71 Frost, *Sketches of Indian Life*, 59–60.

72 MTPL, Anderson Papers, S29, 'Anderson's Journal, 1835,' Typescript: 7.

73 AO, MG 35, Strachan Papers, 'T.G. Anderson to Captain G. Phillpots,' 18 July 1835.

74 Anglican Heritage Collection, Bishophurst, Sault Ste Marie, Reverend Canon Colloton Papers, 'Extract from the Reverend G.A. Anderson's Report of the Sault Ste. Marie and Garden River Mission, January 1849,' Typescript.

75 HBCA, MG 20, B/194/e/8/1835, Report on the District of Sault Ste Marie.

76 HBCA, MG 20, B/194/b/9/1834–5, Sault Ste Marie Post, Correspondence Books, 'Nourse to Mr. Denis Laronde,' 2 December 1834.

77 Catholic Archdiocesan Archives, Toronto, AC 2402, Bishop Macdonell Papers, 'To His Excellency, Sir John Colborne, K.B., 1835.'

78 MTPL, Anderson Papers, S29, 'Anderson's Journal, 1835.'

79 AO, MG 35, Strachan Papers, 'T.G. Anderson to Captain Phillpots,' 18 July 1835.

80 Ibid.

81 Ibid.

82 AO, Captain T.G. Anderson Papers 1814–1822, MS23, Reel 1, 'Indian Council,' 14 July 1822.

83 Catholic Archdiocesan Archives, Toronto, AC-16, Bishop Macdonell Papers, 'John Bell to Bishop Macdonell,' 8 April 1834.

84 AO, MG 35, Strachan Papers, 'Thomas G. Anderson to Captain G. Phillpots,' 18 July 1835.

85 NA, RG 75, MI, Roll 69: 51–2, 'Petition of Chiefs to Andrew Jackson,' 15 September 1834.

86 Schoolcraft, *Historical and Statistical Information*, 1:112.

87 Schoolcraft, *Personal Memoirs*, 524.

88 AO, MU 838, Mis. MSS, transcript copy, 'Diary of Thomas G. Anderson, Visiting Superintendent of Indian Affairs at Cobourg, 5 September, 1849.'

89 The first division lay about Miscotosaugeen, or Hay Lake, nine miles below the rapids; the second embraced sixty acres reserved for the home band at the rapids, and the third lay on the Tahquamenon River, the site of Shingabaw'osin's former summer lodge. Schoolcraft, *Personal Memoirs*, 570–1.

90 NA, M. 234–422/422, 'Testimony of Mary Oboshawbawnoqua.' Enclosed with letter from 'Major W.V. Cobbs to C.A. Harris, Commissioner of Indian Affairs,' March 1837. A copy of this document is housed in the archives of St Peter's Cathedral, Marquette, Michigan. Francis Oshawano was the son of Akewenzee Oshawano, who in turn was the son of Kezhawokumijishkum, a son of Great Crane.

91 NA, RG 75, M234, Roll 415: 619, 'James Ord to James L. Schoolcraft,' 5 June 1838.

92 Clifton, 'Wisconsin Death March.'

93 Burpee, ed., *Journals and Letters of Pierre Gaultier de Varennes de La Vérendrye*, 73; Jenness, *The Indians of Canada*, 277.

94 British Parliamentary Paper No. 323, 1839, 101, 'William H. Higgins, Secretary to the Aborigines' Protection Society, and Augustus D'Este and Samuel Blackburn, on behalf of the Committee. Enclosed with a letter to Sir George Arthur, K.C.B., from Lord Glenelg,' 22 August 1838.

95 AO, MG 35, Strachan Papers, 'Charles Elliot to Bishop John Strachan,' 12 October 1837.

96 Society for Converting and Civilizing the Indians, *Seventh Annual Report*, 1839.

CHAPTER 3   Years of Testing and Trial

1 Prior to 1830 the British Sault itself was still very much an unorganized frontier community. Though intermarriages had taken place between Ojibwa, French, British, and Métis residents, yet the Aboriginal community still remained spatially and occupationally distinct from its white and Métis neighbours. Relatively untrammelled by external laws or social mores, it conformed poorly to modern frontier social models, for it fitted neither the image of an exclusively fur-trading hunter-gatherer society, nor that of a cohesive multiethnic community similar to those identified by Richard White in his 1994 study, *The Middle Ground*. The best one can say is that it was an Aboriginal society in transition, whose leaders were in many respects naïve because they could remember when their people had been integral to events in the Upper Great Lakes region. They expected to be consulted and heard during the birth pangs of the new emerging social order, in much the same way as they

had been at the height of the fur trade or during the major intercolonial wars. On the American side of the St Mary's channel, Métis often acted as intermediaries in negotiations with the government. Canadian officials in the 1830s, however, refused to recognize the Métis as a class, and thus Métis had to become 'Indians' in order to participate in campaigns for Native rights.

2 Nebenagoching's plot is shown on Alexander Vidal's MNR 1846 Town Plot Survey of Sault Ste Marie, at the Archives of Ontario. For a list of male heads of families belonging to the French and Métis population at the British Sault in 1849, see AO, MU 1465 27/32/9, Irving Papers, 'Population of Sault Ste Marie in 1849,' information collection by E.B. Borron in 1893.

3 Records of St John's Anglican Church, Garden River. Records of Church of the Immaculate Heart of Mary, Garden River.

4 As Robert K. Thomas has pointed out, a unique Métis language, but not a Métis consciousness similar to that of the New Nation at Red River, developed at the Sault. Robert K. Thomas, 'Afterward,' 248.

5 NAC, RG 10, vol 612, 215, 'George Vardon to J.M. Higginson,' 16 April 1848.

6 Interview with Fred Pine, Sr, 30 August 1983. The missionary Frederick Frost also provides examples of the use of bow and arrows at the turn of the twentieth century. Frost, *Sketches of Indian Life.*

7 NA, RG 75, M234, Roll 415: 619, 'James Ord to James R. Schoolcraft,' 5 June 1838.

8 NA, RG 75, 'Schoolcraft to C.A. Harris ... enclosing an extract of a Letter dated Sault Ste Marie,' 20 August 1837, Records of the Michigan Superintendency, Letters sent 18 July 1835–26 June 1839, 300.

9 Ibid.

10 MTPL, James Givens Papers, 'First Speech of Chinquakous – Young Pine,' 1838.

11 MTPL, James Givens Papers, 'The Speech of Ottanwish after hearing the address of Chinquakous,' 1838.

12 Jameson, *Winter Studies and Summer Rambles in Canada* 3:286.

13 Ibid., 3:275.

14 Ibid., 3:237–8.

15 Arthur, ed., *The Thunder Bay District.*

16 MTPL, James Givens Papers, 'The Reply of Ching-qua-konse, A Chippewa Chief,' 1838.

17 E.J. Pratt Library, Victoria College, University of Toronto, Diary of the Reverend James Evans, 11 July–17 November 1838.

18 Landon, 'Letters of the Rev. James Evans, Methodist Missionary,' 'Evans to Stinson,' 20 August 1838, 52–3.

19 E.J. Pratt Library, Victoria College, Diary of the Reverend James Evans, 72–4.
20 Ibid., 107.
21 Shingwaukonse was at the trading post of Vincent Roy at Vermillion Lake during these years. Akiwenzie, who was with him, is likely Akiwenzie ['Elder bowed near the Ground'] Oshawano. Fulford, 'The Pictographic Account Book of an Ojibwa Fur Trader,' 191.
22 NAC, RG 10, vol. 124, 69819–20, 'T.G. Anderson to S.P. Jarvis,' 1 March 1838.
23 MTPL, James Givens Papers, 'Second Speech of Chinkquakons and Reply,' 1838.
24 NAC, RG 1, E5, ECO file 1157, vol. 8, 1848, 'Extract from a letter from Sir George Arthur, Lieu. Governor, to Chief Shinquackouse, dated Govt. House, York, 19 Sept., 1839.' I am indebted to Joe Boissoneau, Sr, and John Biron, interviewed in fall 1982, for information about the kinds of skills the Métis could contribute to Little Pine's settlement.
25 NAC, RG 10, vol. 124, 69712–13, 'Anderson to Jarvis,' 23 May 1840. Little Pine's decision to ask the British government to extend presents to the Métis also logically complemented Anderson's belief that Métis on the western frontier not in receipt of the queen's bounty might prove disloyal. NAC, RG 10, vol. 124, 69676–9, 'Anderson to Jarvis,' 17 December 1838.
26 McNab, 'Herman Merivale and Colonial Office Indian Policy in the Mid-Nineteenth Century.'
27 The government's new policy orientation relegated the Native person to the level of a non-rational being, unable to formulate consistent policy. British Parliamentary Papers, *Journals of the Legislative Assembly*, 1844–5, App. EEE, 'Report on Affairs of the Indians of Canada'; *Journals of the Legislative Assembly*, 1847, App. T, App. 94, 'Report on the Affairs of the Indians in Canada.'
28 NAC, RG 10, vol. 124, 69698, 'Anderson to the Rev'd M. Proulz at Wikwemikong,' 10 May 1839; NAC, RG 10, vol. 124, 69698, 'Anderson to Jarvis,' 24 December 1838; NAC, RG 10, vol. 124, 69773–5, 'Anderson to Jarvis,' 8 June 1842.
29 AO, MG 35, Strachan Papers, 'The Reverend F.A. O'Meara to Bishop Strachan,' 11 October 1839.
30 The well-known La Pointe chief, Keche Besheke, wrote to Shingwaukonse, who had evidently been urging the southwestern Ojibwa to remain loyal to the British and not take American treaty money. The letter is reproduced in full to give an idea of the sort of communications which passed between Shingwaukonse and his allies:

> My Dear Friend Shingwauk I received your letter that you forwarded to me by Capn Wood, I am very satisfied to hear that your family is well as also yourself. My dear Chief I remember well what I told you last summer.

I have always the same mind I don't alter it. I love too much my mouth and my heart. My pipe I sent you shall remember you of my faithfulness. I also tell you my Dear Chief that nobody can + will be the master of me. I am my own Master. They tell me that our agent when he arrives to this place will intreat me to go to Prairie du Chien this summer. But I tell you that I will certainly not go but I intend to go down this summer to see our English friends for the last time as they will give us presents this summer only and then no more. I intend to go down to Mahnitowahno in the month of June next. I like more to go down to see the Red Coat than to receive here a little money. So I will go down. Never believe My dear Chief that any body is master of me and the Americans never shall be. The half-breeds that came to La Pointe last summer know all our chiefs, and almost all our Indians tormented me last summer – even our Traders spoke ill of me. I can tell you for my person that I will certainly go. I think altho' that the chief Ashkebuggecooshe [of Leech Lake] and his young men will arrive this spring and go down with me. I hear this chief and his young men are very poor this winter that they are almost freezing to death so I think he will go down to see our English friends for the last time. The chiefs from the interior asked me to wait for them [and] that they would go along with me. I told them that I will start from here early in June, if they arrive in due season we will go down in company. Perhaps also Aiahbens will go down, he said so. For me I go down to keep my word. I honor my own word very much and always wish to keep it. If I live I will see you next summer. My dear Shingwauk, we are poor. I do not know what we shall eat during the journey but still I will go. I wish you good health my Dear Friend and good health to all your family and our friends.

Your Friend Kache Whashke

AO, MG 35, Strachan Papers, 'The Reverend F.A. O'Meara to Bishop Strachan,' 31 October 1839. Besheke accepted Christianity only shortly before his death: *Wisconsin Historical Society Collections*, 3:365–9. Anna Jameson relates Keche Besheke to the name 'Whashke' or 'Wayish.ki': Jameson, *Winter Studies and Summer Rambles in Canada*, 3:202–3.

31 AO, MG 35, Strachan Papers, 'O'Meara to Strachan,' 31 October 1839. In 1838, 110 Ojibwa came to the British present distribution from Bay de Nock: 47 from Drummond Island, 123 from the American Sault, 38 from Point St Ignace, and 34 from Green Bay. None however came either from La Pointe or from the headwaters of the Mississippi River, since the distribution of American annuities conflicted with the British present giving. NAC, RG 10, vol. 124, 69777, 'Return of Indians who received presents at Manatowauning in August

1838.' According to government reports, the Ottawas of Manitoulin Island in 1838 numbered 268 souls, and the Ojibwa of the Sault and St Joseph Island, 189 souls. Fish was regarded as the main food of all these bands. NAC, RG 10, vol. 124, 69836; NAC, RG 10, vol. 124, 69845.

32 AO, MG 35, Strachan Papers, 'O'Meara to the Reverend H.J. Grasett,' 5 June 1839.

33 AO, MG 35, Strachan Papers, 'O'Meara to Bishop Strachan,' 30 October 1839.

34 Ibid.

35 Capp, *The Story of Baw-a-ting,* 175.

36 Millman, 'Frederick Augustus O'Meara,' *Dictionary of Canadian Biography* (1982) vol. 11, 552–4.

37 AO, MG 35, Strachan Papers, 'O'Meara to Strachan,' 3 October 1839.

38 AO, MG 35, Strachan Papers, 'Report of F.A. O'Meara covering period June–September, 1839,' 3 October 1839.

39 AO, MG 35, Strachan Papers, 'O'Meara to Strachan, enclosing a copy of Report sent May 4th, 1840, to the Secretary of the Upper Canada Clergy Society.'

40 Ibid.

41 AO, MG 35, Srachan Papers, 'O'Meara to Grasett,' 17 March 1840.

42 Ibid.

43 AO, MG 35, Strachan Papers, 'Report of F.A. O'Meara, Sault Ste Marie, to the Upper Canada Clergy Society, dated 4th May, 1840, sent to the Bishop of Toronto, 7th Oct., 1841.'

44 AO, MG 35, Strachan Papers, 'O'Meara to Strachan,' 20 October 1841.

45 NAC, RG 10, vol. 145, 83747–50, 'Report on the Manitowaning and Sault Mission by the Rev. O'Meara,' 1841; NAC, RG 10, vol. 124, 69722–4, 'Anderson to Jarvis,' 9 March 1841. A claim for the Ermatinger estate had been submitted to the government by the Ermatinger family on 11 August 1843. NAC, RG 10, vol. 124, 69765–7. James Fraser was acting as agent for Charles Oakes Ermatinger's son, William. In response, Shingwaukonse prevailed on O'Meara to draft a petition to the governor general requesting that land belonging to the Ermatinger estate revert to the Ojibwa. Little Pine led the list of signatories, but of the other chiefs who signed the document, only two, Mishkeash and Nowquagabo, hailed from the Canadian side. The others, among them Kebay Nodin, Saboo, Ogemapenasse, and Ahbetahkezick, had been associated with Shingabaw'osin's band in the 1830s. NAC, RG 10, vol. 120, 4809, 'To the Governor in Chief of Upper Canada [Canada West].' With the assistance of Joseph Wilson, newly appointed Crown Lands agent and collector of customs, Little Pine sent a second petition in October. Capp, *The Story of Baw-a-ting,* 175–6.

46 AO, MG 35, Strachan Papers, 'O'Meara to Strachan,' 19 January 1841.

47 Ibid.

48 AO, MG 35, Strachan Papers, 'O'Meara to Strachan,' 20 October 1841; 'O'Meara to Grasett,' 8 January 1840; 'F. Wilson Jones to Grasett,' 11 November 1840.

49 British Parliamentary Papers, *Journals of the Legislative Assembly*, 1847, App. T, no. 94, 'Report on the Affairs of the Indians in Canada,' 'Copy of a letter sent by Thomas G. Anderson, Esquire, to Shinquakonce.'

50 Ibid.

51 Ibid.

52 Ibid. Anderson felt any import problems were counterbalanced by the fact that Natives could bring their own private property duty free across the international border under the terms of the Jay Treaty of 1795–6. For this reason, he rejected a proposal to consider entering goods for the Ojibwa duty free at Manitowaning, which, he argued, would only promote the liquor traffic.

53 British Parliamentary Papers, *Sessional Papers*, App. 21, no. 25, 1858, 'Answers to Queries put by the Commissioners for Indian Affairs to the Reverend F.A. O'Meara.'

54 AO, MG 35, Strachan Papers, 'O'Meara to Strachan,' 19 January 1840.

55 Clarke Library, Central Michigan University, Bingham Journal, 14 November 1841.

56 AO, MG 35, Strachan Papers, 'O'Meara to Strachan,' 21 October 1841.

57 Van Gennep, *The Rites of Passage*.

58 NAC, RG 10, vol. 124, 69733–4, 'Anderson to Jarvis,' September 1841.

59 MTPL, Thomas G. Anderson Papers, S29, 'Statement of John Bell.'

60 Ibid.

61 Ibid.

62 Interview with Fred Pine, Sr, 5 January 1984.

63 NA, RG 75, M234, Roll 771: 15, 'James Ord to Robert Stuart,' 1 September 1842.

64 AO, MG 35, Strachan Papers, 'Report of the Rev. Frederick A. O'Meara,' 17 October 1842.

65 Clarke Library, Central Michigan University, Bingham Papers, Box A, Bingham Journal, 24 January 1846.

66 AO, MG 35, Strachan Papers, 'Strachan to his wife, Ann Strachan,' 10 August 1842.

67 AO, MG 35, Strachan Papers, 'Strachan to John Beverley Robinson,' 11 August 1842.

68 Clarke Library, Central Michigan University, Bingham Papers, Bingham Journal, 27 November 1842.

69 AO, MG 35, Strachan Papers, 'Report of the Reverend F.A. O'Meara,' 19 December 1843.

70 Clarke Library, Central Michigan University, Bingham Papers, Bingham Journal, 6 March 1843.

71 See for example, NAC, RG 10, vol. 32: 19143–6, 'Speech of Katawabidai, Drummond Island,' 16 July 1816. AO MS 23, Reel 1, T.G. Anderson Papers, 1814–22, 'Speech of Katawabidai at Drummond Island,' 9 June 1822.

72 Mang'osid was only a spokesperson at Fond du Lac, but he was a powerful *Midéwiwin* practitioner. Conversations with Fred Pine, Sr, in Duluth in August 1983. See also Schoolcraft, *Personal Memoirs*, 298. Rebecca Krugel traces Mang'osid's acceptance and eventual rejection of evangelical Protestant Christian teachings after 1836, when the Fond du Lac Loon chief would have been experiencing major difficulties, especially with Ermatinger's retirement from the Sault. When Mang'osid returned to his Native ways, however, he became an ally of Little Pine. Ermatinger's sons also came to support Shingwaukonse's claims in 1850, showing that by that time the two factions had decided to work together in a common cause. For Mang'osid's conversion, see Krugel, 'Religion Mixed with Politics.' There is copious information about these chiefs in both British and American historical sources.

73 AO, Strachan Papers, 'Shingwaukonse to William McMurray,' 13 May 1844.

74 Capp, *The Story of Ba-wa-ting*, 175–6.

75 O'Meara, 'Report of a Mission to the Ottawahs and Ojibwas on Lake Huron,' 37.

76 Beaven, *Recreations of a Long Vacation*, 124.

77 NAC, RG 10, vol. 150, 87003–4.

78 NAC, RG 10, vol. 159, 91444–6.

79 Wilson eventually received a formal letter of apology from Washington. Capp, *The Story of Baw-a-ting*, 180–1. The timber had been cut on the Canadian side, on Jones Island, also known as Squirrel Island. AO, Minutes of the Executive Council, 20 May 1846. Executive Council Records, Canada State Book E, 424.

80 NAC, RG 10, vol. 157, 40407, 'Shingwaukonse to George Ironside,' 20 February 1846.

81 Ibid. Shingwaukonse accused Wilson of taking what rightfully belonged to the Ojibwa. 'Colborne gave me charge of all the Lands between Batchewana Bay and Tessalon [Thessalon],' the chief argued. 'Father, our country is poor, very poor, and the little provision we got from the Americans for allowing them to cut timber was very useful to me and my people. When we had plenty of food I did not allow them to cut timber. After I refused permission, and when I did give them leave, I pointed out the place where they

should cut it. When their vessel was laid upon our side, they had then only one, they paid me twenty-five dollars every winter for leave to cut fire wood and for protection. Father since Mr. Wilson came here all this is changed. They have now five vessels laid upon the British side and my leave was not asked. They have cut firewood and I and my Indians have not been paid for it. The best timber on the British side has all disappeared since last spring.'

82 NAC, RG 10, vol. 151, 87759–60, 'Extract of a Report from Lieu. Harper, R.N., Commanding H.M.S. *Experiment*, dated Penetanguishene, 1st Sept. 1845.' Harper argued that the Métis constituted a loyal population and recommended that their lots be surveyed and land titles extended to them. He felt, however, that the Ojibwa did not 'possess authority to cede their title to the Crown' since 'it appears none of the Indians in that quarter can be regarded as descendants of the Original Tribe who inhabited the Country in question ...'

83 AO, RG 1, series A-1-6, 21678, 'Reply to Communication of Alexander Vidal,' 1846–7.

84 NAC, RG 10, vol. 151, 87762–3, 'Copy of a Report of a Committee of the Executive Council, dated 10 October, 1845.'

85 AO, RG 1, series A-1-6, 21675, 'Alexander Vidal to D.B. Papineau,' 27 April 1846. Letters Received, General Land Commissioner.

86 The government's stance was set out in the 'Report on the Affairs of the Indians in Canada,' British Parliamentary Papers, *Journals of the Legislative Assembly*, 1844–5. App. EEE.

87 The *London Illustrated News* for 25 August 1849, for instance, printed the following lines as part of a front-page article: 'In cases of absolute inferiority of structural development among the tribes we conquer, and where amalgamation of races is not expedient, or possible if it were, all that the best and wisest of men can do, is to see that the inevitable disappearance of the weaker race is left to time and nature to effect ... But, in the case of the aborigines of America ... a more exalted duty ought to have been performed. Here, there was not mental inferiority or physical incompatibility. Man for man, the accident of education excepted, they were our equals ...'

88 Leighton, 'Historical Significance of the Robinson Treaties of 1850'; Knight, 'Allan Macdonell and the Pointe au Mines–Mica Bay Affair', Owram, *Promise of Eden*, 39–40; Rogers, 'The Algonquian Farmers of Southern Ontario,' 149; Wightman and Wightman, 'The Mica Bay Affair'; Dickason, *Canada's First Nations*, 253; Telford, '"The Sound of the Rustling of the Gold Is under My Feet Where I Stand; We Have a Rich Country": A History of Aboriginal Mineral Resources in Ontario.'

CHAPTER 4   Pursuing the Great Spirit's Power

1 Anthony Hall, *1784–1984, Celebrating Together?*
2 Shingwaukonse, according to oral tradition, was blessed by the Thunderers. One who received the gifts of the Thunderers was known as Ogechedah, the 'preparing man.' Such a man had unusual powers in warfare and with certain spirits. He could even affect the cosmological order. This gift may have been the supernatural sanction which governed Shingwaukonse's actions in relation to the copper deposits north of Sault Ste Marie. According to elders at Garden River, copper in particular exercised a balancing power within the universe and, to sustain the cosmological scheme, was buried if not in use.
3 George R. Fox, 'Isle Royale Expedition.'
4 John Macdonell was engaged as an agent to John Askin in June 1778, and later went into the service of the North West Company. Quaife, ed., *John Askin Papers*, 1:92.
5 Keating's career as an Indian agent is discussed in Leighton, 'The Development of Federal Indian Policy in Canada, 1840–1890.'
6 NAC, RG 10, vol. 159, 'Keating to J.M. Higginson, Civil Secretary,' 10 June 1846.
7 NAC, RG 10, vol. 612, 'Petition of Chief Chingwauk,' 10 June 1846 (Petition No. 156). This document provides a census of Little Pine's band, which in 1846 contained 33 men, 31 women, 38 boys, and 24 girls.
8 NAC, RG 10, vol. 160, pt. 2, 92149–51, 'Ironside to George Vardon, Deputy Superintendent,' 1846.
9 Keating, while an Indian agent at Amherstburg, was appointed a protector of Indian lands in 1839. NAC, RG 10, vol. 612, 6.
10 MTPL, Articles of Association of the Quebec and Lake Superior Mining Association, 20 October 1846 (Quebec 1846).
11 One location of the Montreal Mining Company and one belonging to the Quebec and Lake Superior Mining Association lay side by side at Point Mamainse, Mica Bay, to the north of Sault Ste Marie.
12 MTPL, Montreal Mining Company Reports, Report of the Trustees of the Montreal Mining Company to the Shareholders at the Adjourned Meeting of the 30th November 1846, 1–5.
13 NAC, RG 10, vol. 612, 'Vardon to Ironside,' 29 June 1846.
14 NAC, RG 10, vol. 416, 5942, 'Petition of William Shinguaconce, Henry Shinguaconce, Thomas Shinguaconce, Joseph Nabenagoshing, Nahwaquagaboo, Francis Kewahcunce, Charles Pahyahbetahsung, John Kabaoosa, James Ahbetahkezik and George Mahgahsahsuhqua,' 1846.
15 A copy of the Order-in-Council, passed 20 May 1846, was sent to Joseph Wilson. NAC, RG 10, vol. 159, 91442–3.

16 NAC, RG 10, 'George Desbarats to Major Campbell,' 10 May 1847; 'Copy of a Report of the Committee of the Honorable the Executive Council dated the 2nd November, 1846, approved by His Excellency the Governor General in Council the same day.' Copies in Bruce Mines Museum Archives, Indian File.
17 NAC, RG 10, vol. 163, 94932, 'William Ermatinger, Attorney for Charlotte Kattawabide. Regarding claim for land at Sault Ste Marie,' 7 May 1847.
18 NAC, RG 10, vol. 123, 6190–8. 'Petition of William McMurray Chinguakose, Joseph Nabenagojing, Charles Pahyabetahsung and John Kabaoose,' 5 July 1847.
19 Ibid.
20 NAC, RG 10, vol. 166, 96644–6, 'Ironside to Major A. Campbell, Superintendent General of the Indian Department,' 25 August 1847.
21 NAC, RG 1, E5, ECO file 1157, vol. 8, 'Extract of a letter from Col. S.P. Jarvis to the Rev. Wm. McMurray dated Manitoulin Island, 3rd Aug., 1847,' in 'Appendix to the Minutes of a Council Held by T.G. Anderson, V.S.I.A., at Sault Ste Marie on Friday the 18th day of Aug., 1847.'
22 NAC, RG 10, vol. 123, 6191.
23 NAC, RG 10, vol. 166, 96644–6.
24 NAC, RG 10, vol. 163, 'Report of the Honorable Commissioner of Crown Lands regarding claims of certain Indians to territory on the shores of Lakes Huron and Superior, and embracing the subject of a letter by George Desbarats Esq., dated 10th May, 1847, claiming protection against the Indians for persons engaged in mining operations. Dated November 4, 1847.'
25 Ibid.
26 Bruce Mines Museum Archives, Indian File, 'J.D. Cameron to the Honorable James H. Price. Commissioner of Crown Lands,' 1847.
27 NAC, RG 10, vol. 612, 790–1, 'J.D. Cameron to the Governor General,' 25 March 1850. Ogista visited Washington along with the American head chiefs in connection with the fisheries issue. MTPL, Thomas G. Anderson Papers, S29, Folder B, 'The Diary of the Reverend Gustavus Anderson, 26 August 1848 to 23 May 1849.'
28 NAC, RG 10, vol. 168, 97700, 'Alexander Murray, Provincial Geologist, regarding Native claim at Thessalon,' 1848.
29 Bruce Mines Museum Archives, Indian File, 'Copy of a Report of the Commissioner of Crown Lands Relative to Indian Settlements at Garden River ... signed J.H. Price, Crown Lands Department, Montreal,' 26 April 1848.
30 Louis Cadotte was Shingwaukonse's interpreter on this occasion. NAC, RG 10, vol. 612, 338. For O'Meara's views, see O'Meara, 'Second Report of a Mission to the Ottawahs and Ojibwas on Lake Huron.'
31 NAC, RG 10, vol. 173, 100434, 'T.G. Anderson to Major Campbell,' 9 October 1849.

32 NAC, RG 1, E5, ECO file 1157, vol. 8, 'Minutes of a Council Held by T.G. Anderson, V.S.I.A., at Sault Ste. Marie on Friday the 18th of August, 1848.'

33 NAC, RG 1, E5, ECO file 1157, vol. 8, 'Council of August 19, 1848.'

34 Ibid.

35 NAC, RG 1, E5, ECO file 1157, vol. 8, 'T.G. Anderson to the Superintendent General of Indian Affairs,' 26 August 1848.

36 MTPL, Thomas G. Anderson Papers, S29, Folder D, 'T.G. Anderson to Gustavus on becoming a minister of the Church of England,' 24 July 1848.

37 NAC, RG 10, vol. 173, 100434–46, 'T.G. Anderson to Major Campbell,' 9 October 1849. By 1849 the Native population was no longer needed as a military aid to the government. This was a sudden switch, since only three years before, during the Oregon dispute, Ironside had tendered suggestions regarding the role the Ojibwa could play in any upcoming hostilities with the United States. NAC, RG 10, vol. 612, 36, 'Ironside to Indian Department,' 16 March 1846.

38 NAC, RG 10, vol. 173, 100434–46, 'Anderson to Campbell,' 9 October 1849.

39 Firth, *Symbols, Public and Private*, 404.

40 Anglican Heritage Collection, Bishophurst, Sault Ste Marie, Reverend Canon Colloton Papers, 'Extract from the Reverend G.A. Anderson's Report of the Sault Ste. Marie and Garden River Mission, January 1849.' Typescript.

41 HBCA, MG 20, B/194/b/15/1849–50, Sault Ste Marie Post, Correspondence Books, 'William MacTavish to George Simpson,' 20 September 1849.

42 MTPL, Thomas G. Anderson Papers, S29, Folder B, 'The Diary of the Reverend Gustavus Anderson, 26 August 1848, to 23 May 1849.'

43 Ibid., Entry for 22 September 1848.

44 MTPL, Thomas G. Anderson Papers, S29, Folder D: 114, 'Report to the Bishop of Toronto from Gustavus Anderson,' 3 January 1849; MTPL, Thomas G. Anderson Papers, S29, Folder C, no. 49, 'Indenture Contract of a gift of land from Indians to Rev. G. Anderson. Signed Shingwaukonce, Nebenagoching, Piabedausunk, Kabaose, Augustin, John Bell, Ogimabenaishe, Pequetchene and Mizaketosh, principal chiefs.' Years later, Gustavus wrote of this event: '[Shingwaukounce] consulted some of his people and walked over the place I had selected and said "I will give this place for a church and if you will make a writing I will sign it." I then consulted with Allan MacDonell who drew up the Document which was signed at my house at Garden River in the presence of a number of Chiefs and others who had assembled in Council ... Messrs. Wilson, McDonell and Cameron came down from the Sault together & Nebanagoching came with them. As he was an acknowledged chief of the Ojibways he was asked by Shingwaukounce to sign the document. All the signatures of the Indi-

ans were in McDonell's Handwriting – they making their totems.' NAC RG 10, vol. 7566, Garden River Band Records, 36-2-2, 'Testimonies, 1870 Inquiry. Statement of Gustavus Anderson.'

45 Rea, *Bishop Alexander Macdonell and the Politics of Upper Canada*, 32.

46 NAC [HBCA], MG 20, B/194/b/15/1849–50, Sault Ste Marie Post, Correspondence Books, 'MacTavish to A. Campbell,' 3 July 1849. NAC, RG 10, vol. 179, 103886, 'Macdonell to Bruce,' 23 December 1849.

47 Montreal *Gazette*, 7 July 1849.

48 Ibid.

49 Ibid.

50 Harper, *Krieghoff*, 54, plate 51

51 Monkman, *A Native Heritage*, 79.

52 MTPL, Thomas G. Anderson Papers, S29, 'Diary of the Reverend Gustavus Anderson,' 9 May 1849.

53 Regional Collections, University of Western Ontario, Wawanosh Family Correspondence, Box 4382, No. 6, 'To the Editor of the Chatham Chronicle, August 15, 1859.'

54 Ibid.

55 AO, MU 1391, Letter Book, W. MacTavish, 17 October 1848–25 May 1849, 'William MacTavish to James Hargrave,' 30 January 1849; NAC, Hargrave Correspondence, MG 19 (A21), Reel 76: 4005, 'William MacTavish to James Hargrave,' 30 January 1849.

56 *The Patriot*, 19 December 1849.

57 NAC [HBCA], MG 20, B/194/b/15/1849–50, Sault Ste Marie Post, Correspondence Books, 'MacTavish to George Simpson,' 10 August 1849.

58 NAC, RG 10, vol. 612, 358, 'Ironside to Campbell,' 17 September 1849.

59 NAC, RG 10, vol. 612, 401, 'J.A. Williams of the Steamer "Gore" to Robert Baldwin,' 15 November 1849.

60 AO, MU 838, 1-A-1, 'Diary of Thomas Gummersall Anderson, a visiting Supt. of Indian Affairs at this time, 1849, at Cobourg. Sept. 5th, 1849,' transcript copy: 5; NAC, RG 10, vol. 264, List of the chiefs and warriors awarded medals for their assistance in the War of 1812.

61 NAC [HBCA], MG 20, B/194/b/15/1849–50, Sault Ste Marie Post, Correspondence Books, 'MacTavish to Simpson,' 20 September 1849; AO, MU 383, 1-A-1, Extract from T.G. Anderson's Diary, last page.

62 AO, Pamphlet no. 78, 'A Journal of Proceedings on my mission to the Indians – Lake Superior and Huron, 1849, by Alexander Vidal,' transcribed by George Smith with historical notes by M. Elizabeth Arthur (Bright's Cove, Ontario 1974).

63 Regional Collections, University of Western Ontario, Alexander Vidal Papers,

CA 90N, VID 33 (hereafter Vidal Papers), Alexander Vidal, 'Memorandum of Indian Mission,' 1849.

64 Ibid.

65 *The Patriot*, 8 December 1849.

66 Vidal Papers, 'Memorandum of Indian Mission,' 1849.

67 MTPL, Thomas G. Anderson Papers, S29, 'Statement of John Bell.'

68 AO, MU 1464, 26/31/04, Irving Papers, 'Report of Commissioners A. Vidal and Thomas G. Anderson on a visit to Indians on North Shore Lake Huron & Superior for purpose of investigating their claims to territory bordering on these Lakes. Appendix. Extracts from the Notes Taken at the Conference with the Indians at Sault Ste. Marie – October 15th and 16th, 1849.'

69 Vidal Papers, 'Memorandum of Indian Mission,' 1849.

70 NAC, RG 10, vol. 2832, file 170,073-1. 'J.A. Macrae to Superintendent General of Indian Affairs,' 18 February 1899. 'Memorandum,' 1 June 1899.

71 AO, Pamphlet no. 78, 'A Journal ... by Alexander Vidal,' 1.

72 AO, MU 838, 1-A-1, 'Diary of Thomas G. Anderson,' 1849.

73 'Father Fremiot's Report to his Superior in New York.' Archives de la Société de Jésus du Canada Français. *Lettres des nouvelles missions du Canada*, 1:446–58. In Arthur, ed., *The Thunder Bay District*, 17.

74 Vidal Papers, 'Memorandum of Indian Mission,' 1849.

75 'Chief Peau de Chat's Report on His Interrogation by Visiting Indian Agent.' Archives de la Société de Jésus du Canada Français, A-1-16-1. In Arthur, ed., *The Thunder Bay District*, 17.

76 Vidal Papers, CA 90N VID 333 TSL 22 OE, Misc., 'Vidal to his father, Richard Emeric Vidal,' 17 October 1849.

77 AO, Irving Papers, MU 1464, 26/31/04, 'Report of Commissioners A. Vidal and T.G. Anderson,' 1849.

78 HBCA, MG 20, B/194/b/15/1849–50, Sault Ste Marie Post, Correspondence Books, 'MacTavish to Simpson,' 17 October 1849; 'Diary of Thomas G. Anderson,' typescript copy, 19.

79 AO, Irving Papers, 'Report of Commissioners A. Vidal and T.G. Anderson,' 1849, 7.

80 AO, Russell Papers, MS 75, Reel 5, 'Treaty with Northwest Company, Metosaki et al, 10 August, 1798, Sault Ste. Marie.'

81 HBCA, MG 20, B/194/b/15/1849–50, Sault Ste Marie Post, Correspondence Books, 'MacTavish to Simpson,' 17 October 1849.

82 AO, Irving Papers, 'Extract from Notes Taken at the Conference with the Indians at Sault Ste. Marie – October 15th and 16th, 1849.' in 'report of Commissioners A. Vidal & T.G. Anderson,' 1849.

83 Ibid.

84 Vidal Papers, 'Vidal to his father, Richard Emeric Vidal,' 17 October 1849.

85 Vidal Papers, 'Vidal to his wife, Catherine Vidal,' 23 October 1849.
86 NAC [HBCA], MG 20, B/194/b/15/1849–50, Sault Ste Marie Post, Correspondence Books, 'MacTavish to A.H. Campbell,' 11 November 1849.
87 Ibid.
88 AO, MU 1391, Letter Book, W. MacTavish, 17 October–25 May 1849, 'MacTavish to James Hargrave,' November 1848.
89 NAC [HBCA], MG 20, B/194/b/15/1849–50, Sault Ste Marie Post, Correspondence Books, 'MacTavish to George Simpson,' 12 November 1849.
90 *The Patriot*, 19 December 1849.
91 *British Colonist*, 8 February 1850. Bonner placed the blame for the attack squarely on Macdonell. There is little doubt, however, that Shingwaukonse had been using his oratorical skills, and his experience as a war chief, to muster recruits for the Mica Bay expedition years before 1849. In 1893, regarding the Mica Bay incident, Joshua Biron would state: 'Several years before the Robinson treaty was made – chief Shinguaconce of the Garden River Band called a Council – and the Half-breeds of Sault Ste. Marie were invited to attend – so we all went. The Chief told us, that if we would join his Band and be his men or soldiers – that he (the chief) would work for us, and that we would get the presents that his band was then getting. That some day he might sell his land – and that if so – his claim should be our claim – and that we half-breeds would have a right to a share of what he, the Chief, might get for it. That, only four of us, agreed to join his Band – Myself (Joshua Biron), my brother Alexis Biron, John Bell and Louison Cadotte. All the other half-breeds said that they were already Indians enough without binding themselves to be under an Indian chief: and they all left the council-room.' AO, Irving Papers, MU 1465, 27/32/10, 'Statement of Joshua Biron of Sault Ste. Marie, a Half-breed included in, or at all events paid with the Garden River Band of Indians from the year 1850 to the present time 1893. Made to John Driver and sworn to him. Testimonies included with letter from John Driver to E.B. Borron,' 5 June 1893. Shingwaukonse's use of the term 'soldiers' to describe the relationship of recruits to their chief may reflect the fact that he had spent time prior to 1812 among the buffalo-hunting peoples of the Red River district, and so adopted terminology associated with the highly corporate buffalo hunt. Yet the fact that only those Métis closely related to Little Pine's nodal core group joined the band shows that purely Ojibwa social organizational principles were operating. The Birons and the Cadottes both could activate linkages to Buhkwujjenene through Buhkwujjenene's wife, Margaret Cadotte, as well as to Nebenagoching's band through Alexis Biron's marriage to Mezai's daughter. Information from early records of the Church of the Immaculate Heart of Mary, Garden River. John Bell had married Shing-

waukonse's daughter, Marie or Mary. All those who joined the local Ojibwa bands were well-known free traders in the Upper Great Lakes area.

92 *British Colonist,* 8 February 1850.

93 NAC, RG 10, vol. 612, 393–7, 'O'Meara to Campbell,' 12 November 1849.

94 Gustavus Anderson left Garden River soon after the Mica Bay mine takeover, as he was suffering from 'nervous palpitations of the heart.' He did not return. AO, MU 838, 1A-1, Diary of Thomas G. Anderson, 1849, 38.

95 'Montreal Annexation Manifesto. To the People of Canada.' In Doughty, ed., *The Elgin-Grey Papers,* App. XVII, 6:1487–94.

96 For Macdonell's involvement in 'grandiose schemes,' as well as his role in the expansionist movement, see Swainson, 'Allan Macdonell,' *Dictionary of Canadian Biography* (1982), vol. 11, 552–4.

97 'Lord Elgin to Lord Grey, Colonial Office Secretary,' 24 December 1849 (Private), CO 42. In Doughty, ed., *The Elgin-Grey Papers,* 2:563–4.

98 The Quebec and Lake Superior Mining Association's request for a loan of £12,500 indemnity for damages was considered, and rejected, by the Committee of the Executive Council on 31 May 1850. AO, MS9, Executive Council Records, Canada State Book K, Reel 19.

99 NAC, RG 10, vol. 612, 402–3, 'T.G. Anderson to Robert Baldwin,' 16 November 1849; NAC, RG 10, vol. 612, 404–6, 'E. Meredith to Ironside,' 20 November 1849; AO, MS9, Canada, Executive Council Records, Canada State Book J, 491–3, Reel 19, 'Committee of the Executive Council,' 19 November 1849.

100 NAC, RG 10, vol. 612, 427, 'Captain Ashley Cooper to Ironside,' 15 December 1849. Captain William Ermatinger was appointed to interpret at meetings with the Ojibwa, and directed to travel with the Rifles. AO, MS9, Canada, Executive Council Records, Canada State Book J, 502, Reel 19. Expenses incurred by the government in respect to the Mica Bay affair were charged against the proceeds from the sale of the mining locations.

101 Macdonell's reply to an article by Bonner in *The Pilot* of 11 December 1849 may be found in *The Patriot* of 19 December 1849. There was a certain smugness in Tory circles on learning of the Reform government's acute embarrassment concerning the consequences of the claims affair. Although on 21 December *The Patriot,* a Tory newspaper, had indulged in rumours concerning 'killings and abductions' near the Sault, its editor two weeks later admitted that the initial statements were probably 'greatly exaggerated.' *The Patriot,* 21 November 1849, 8 December 1849.

102 *The Patriot,* 8 December 1849.

103 *The Pilot,* 1 December 1849.

104 Montreal *Gazette,* 23 November 1849. This newspaper viewed Macdonell as the champion of Native rights in the face of a presumptuous and uncaring

government authority. The commissioners, for their part, saw Macdonell as a bellicose troublemaker. AO, Irving Papers, 'Extracts from the Notes Taken at a Conference with the Indians at the Sault Ste. Marie – October 15th and 16th, 1849,' 4, in 'Report of the Commissioners A. Vidal and T.G. Anderson,' 1849.

105 *The Patriot*, 19 December 1849.
106 'Letter from Mr. Bonner, Superintendent to the Board of Directors of the Quebec Mining Company.' *British Colonist*, 8 February 1850.
107 *The Patriot*, 19 December 1849.
108 Ibid.
109 Ibid.
110 NAC, RG 10, vol. 612, 420–1, 'Statement of John Bonner before George Ironside,' 3 December 1849; NAC, RG 10, vol. 179, 103884, 'Macdonell to the Civil Secretary,' 23 December 1849; NAC, RG 10, vol. 612, 'George Ironside to the Indian Department,' 3 December 1849.
111 *The Commercial Advertiser*, (New York), 5 December 1849; Montreal *Gazette*, 12 December 1849. The story was first carried by the *Detroit Free Press* and *Tribune*, the Toronto *Patriot* and the Toronto *Globe*.
112 AO, MU 1778, Alexander Macdonell Estate Papers, Biographical Information.
113 NAC, RG 10, vol. 179, 109890, 'Macdonell to Bruce,' 21 December 1849. On January 14, Angus Macdonell served a summons on George Ironside and Archibald Cameron, manager of the Montreal Mining Company at Bruce Mines, for illegal arrests of Little Pine and his party. MTPL, Macdonell File.
114 *Detroit Free Press*, 22 December 1849. This article stated that Shingwaukonse had been present at the Battle of Queenston Heights and had been awarded a medal for bravery by the British for his participation in the War of 1812.

CHAPTER 5   The Struggle for Aboriginal Rights

1 *The Globe*, 5 January 1850.
2 Ibid.
3 Interview with Fred Pine, Sr, 20 June 1984.
4 *The Patriot*, 29 December 1849.
5 Ibid.
6 NAC, RG 10, vol. 179, 103884, 'Macdonell to Bruce,' 23 December 1849.
7 HBCA, MG 20, B/194/b/15/1849–50, 'MacTavish to A.H. Campbell,' 16 November 1849.
8 NAC, RG 10, vol. 180, 404272–4, 'Ironside to Bruce,' 10 January 1850.
9 HBCA, MG 20, B/194/b/15/1849–50, 'MacTavish to Simpson,' 1849.

10 NAC, RG 10, vol. 612, 846–50, 'Statement of the Defendants in Process. A.H. Campbell of the Montreal Mining Company,' 27 June 1850.
11 NAC, RG 8, C-1029, 4, 'A. Cooper to the War Department,' 6 March 1850.
12 NAC, RG 10, vol. 181, 105297, 'Macdonell to Bruce,' 14 March 1850.
13 AO, J.B. Robinson Papers, MU 5906, 'Diary of W.B. Robinson on a visit to the Indians to make a treaty, 9 May, 1850.'
14 NAC, RG 10, vol. 183, pt 1, 105905–6, 'Macdonell to Bruce,' 31 May 1850.
15 NAC, RG 10, vol. 612, 392–7, 'O'Meara to Campbell,' 12 November 1849.
16 NAC, RG 10, vol. 572, 'Petition of Mishiquongai, Shawanoseway and Ainenonduck,' 9 March 1850.
17 NAC, RG 10, vol. 183, pt 2, 106370, 'Wilson to Ironside,' 29 July 1850.
18 NAC, RG 10, vol. 183, pt 2, 106609–11, 'McMurray to Indian Affairs,' 24 September 1850.
19 NAC, RG 10, vol. 612, 713–14, 'Ironside to Bruce,' 5 February 1850.
20 AO, MS9, Canada Executive Council Records, State Book K, 180–2.
21 AO, MS9, Canada Executive Council Records, State Book K, 33–4.
22 AO, J.B. Robinson Papers, MU 5906, 'Diary of W.B. Robinson,' 27 August to 5 September 1850.
23 Ibid.
24 Interview with Fred Pine, Sr, 10 June 1983.
25 NAC, RG 10, vol. 123, 6617–20, 'Alexander Vidal to the Honorable Commissioner of Crown Lands,' 11 December 1849.
26 Anglican Heritage Collection Archives, Bishophurst, Sault Ste Marie, Reverend Canon Colloton Papers, 'Land transaction at Garden River to Anglican Church, 12 February [1852?].' Original was in possession of Chief William E. Pine.
27 Vidal had first suggested that treaty compensation might be limited to 'a fixed amount not to be exceeded, but open to diminution if the band decreased.' Vidal Papers, CA 9ON VID 33, 'Memorandum of Indian Mission.' By 5 December, however, Vidal realized that the intractable Shingwaukonse would have to receive at least one special concession to encourage his people to agree to the surrender. A provision therefore might be made 'if necessary, for an increase of payment upon the further discovery and development of new sources of wealth.' AO, Irving Papers, MU 1464, 26/31/04, 'Report of Commissioners A. Vidal and T.G. Anderson, 1849.'
28 AO, Irving Papers, MU 1465, 26/31/3, 'Vouchers for payments made in respect to negotiating Indian Treaties, 1850.'
29 The Robinson Treaties were presented for approval to the Governor General in Council on 29 November 1850. It was held that should bands 'at any time desire to dispose of any Mineral,' they could do so with the assistance of the

superintendent general of Indian Affairs. AO, MS9, Canada Executive Council Records, State Book K, 609.

30 NAC, RG 10, vol. 612, 673–5,'Robinson to Bruce,' 27 December 1850.

31 NAC, RG 10, vol. 572, 'Ironside to Bruce,' 20 November 1850.

32 AO, MS 91, pkg 11, George Brown Papers, Correspondence, 'Macdonell to George Brown,' 30 April 1853; Bayliss Library, Sault Ste Marie, Michigan, George Johnston Papers, 'Schoolcraft to George Johnston,' 24 May 1851: NAC, RG 10, vol. 613, 372, 'Abstract of Requisitions from the Indians,' 1851; NAC, RG 10, vol 205, 121654, Requisitions from Nebenagoching.

33 United Church Archives, Victoria University, Toronto, 'Speech of Ojesta.' In 27th Annual Report of the Missionary Society of the Wesleyan Methodist Church, June 1851–June 1852.

34 NAC, RG 10, vol. 614, 634, 'McDougall to Ironside,' 28 January 1853.

35 *The Christian Guardian*, 18 October 1854, 7.

36 AO, Irving Papers, MU 1464, 26/31/04, 'Extract from Memoranda Made at the Indian Village, Garden River, on the Second Day after the Conference at Sault Ste. Marie. Report of Commissioners A. Vidal and T.G. Anderson,' Appendix C, 2; NAC, RG 10, vol. 614, 634, 'McDougall to Ironside,' 28 January 1853; *The Christian Guardian*, 27 April 1853, 114.

37 NAC, RG 10, vol. 616, 420–2, 'James Chance to William Spragge,' 3 September 1867.

38 United Church Archives, Victoria University, 29th Annual Report of the Missionary Society of the Wesleyan Methodist Church, June 1853–June 1854.

39 NAC, RG 10, vol. 206, 121809–13, 'George Desbarats regarding the Lemoine Location, August 1852.'

40 NAC, RG 10, vol. 323, 216499, 'Palmer to Cuthbertson,' 23 August 1853.

41 NAC, RG 10, vol. 205, 1212890; NAC, vol. 206, 721809–14.

42 NA, Schoolcraft Papers, Reel 9, Appendix No. 8, 'McMurray to Schoolcraft,' 12 November 1851; Province of Canada, *Sessional Papers*, 1858, Appendix 21, 'Report of the Special Commission to Investigate Indian Affairs in Canada,' 'Letter to His Excellency,' 22 August 1855.

43 NAC, RG 10, vol. 198, pt 1, 116, 'Speech of Chingwaukonse.'

44 'Elgin to Grey, November 1, 1850.' In Doughty, ed., *The Elgin-Grey Papers*, 2: 725.

45 AO, Irving Papers, MU 1464, 26/30/14, 'Reflections on the Indian Situation in Upper Canada,' 2–3, 45 handwritten pages.

46 NAC, RG 10, vol. 206, 721870–1,'Napier to Bruce,' 25 October 1853 (Private).

47 NAC, RG 10, vol. 612,'Bruce to Macdonell,' 9 April 1850.

48 NAC, RG 10, vol. 182, 1105850–5, 'Macdonell to Bruce,' 23 May 1850; NAC, RG 10, vol. 179, 109890, 'Bruce to Macdonell,' 21 December 1849.

49 NAC, RG 10, vol. 613, 278–80, 'Ironside to Bruce,' 5 April 1851.

50 NAC, MG 19, A21, 4847, Hargrave Correspondence, 'Wemyss Simpson to James Hargrave,' 25 October 1851.

51 NAC, RG 10, vol. 191, 11383–4, 'Agreement between Shinguacouse and his Band and P.S. Church,' 1 July 1851.

52 NAC, RG 10, vol. 191, 111387–8, 'Bruce to Ironside,' 30 July 1851.

53 NAC, RG 10, vol. 188, 109891, 'Attorney General of Canada West Recommends that Indians ... be pardoned,' 22 May 1851.

54 NAC, RG 10, vol. 194, 113704, 'Keating to Bruce,' 19 February 1852.

55 NAC, RG 10, vol. 198, pt 1, 116270–3, 'Keating's Report, August, 1852.'

56 NAC, RG 10, vol. 198, pt 1, 116271–2, 'Keating to Bruce,' 6 August 1852.

57 NAC, RG 10, vol. 2211, 42451.

58 Ontario, Ministry of Natural Resources, Surveys and Mapping Branch, Peterborough (hereafter MNR), 1853 Garden River Indian Reserve No. 14, K19, 2484, by J.S. Dennis, 14 May 1853.

59 Warren, *History of the Ojibwa Indians*, 373–4.

60 Schoolcraft, *Personal Memoirs*, 295.

61 Mason, ed., *Schoolcraft's Expedition to Lake Itasca*, App. E.

62 Schoolcraft, *Personal Memoirs*, 293.

63 Ibid., 611.

64 J.G.E. Smith, *Leadership among the Southwestern Ojibwa.*

65 Schoolcraft, *Historical and Statistical Information* 5:187.

66 Ibid., 1:414–16.

67 Bruce M. White, *The Regional Context of the Removal Order of 1850.*

68 NAC, RG 10, vol. 198, pt 1, 116270–2, 'Keating to Bruce,' 6 August 1852.

69 NAC, RG 10, vol. 198, pt. 1, 116288–9, 'Captain Ironside Reports that Certain American Indians ... wish to seek an asylum under the Standard of the Red Coat,' 7 August 1852.

70 Ibid.

71 NAC, RG 10, vol. 612, 834, 'Bruce to Ironside,' 3 June 1850.

72 NAC, RG 10, vol. 205, 121916, 'Keating to Bruce,' 22 October 1853.

73 NAC, RG 10, vol. 207, 122406–25, 'Keating's Report, 1853.'

74 NAC, RG 10, vol. 196, 115151–3, 'Ironside to Bruce,' 18 May 1852.

75 Ibid.

76 NAC, RG 10, vol. 207, 122406–25, 'Keating's Report, 1853.'

77 Ibid.

78 MNR, 1854 Current Plans of Indian Reserves, Batcheewaunaung Reserve, by James W. Bridgland, May 1854.

79 NAC, RG 10, vol. 202, 119540, 'Macdonell to Bruce,' 14 April 1853.

80 NAC, RG 10, vol. 202, 120102, 'Ironside to Bruce,' 23 May 1853.

81 NAC, RG 10, vol. 201, pt 2, 119296–7, 'Wilson to Ironside,' 21 March 1853.

82 AO, MS 91, pkg 11, George Brown Papers, Correspondence, 'Macdonell to George Brown,' 30 April 1853.
83 Ibid.
84 Ibid.
85 Province of Canada, *Statutes*, 16 Vict. Cap. 176, 1853, 720–4.
86 NAC, RG 10, vol. 203, 120308–11, 'Macdonell to Bruce,' 15 June 1853.
87 Ibid.
88 *Christian Guardian*, 20 September 1854, 196.
89 NAC, RG 10, vol. 614, 647–8, 'Wilson to Indian Affairs,' 21 July 1853.
90 NAC, RG 10, vol. 205, 121525, 'Palmer to Ironside,' 10 September 1853.
91 NAC, RG 10, vol. 205, 121521, 'Ironside to Bruce,' 10 September 1853.
92 John Newton, surgeon at Mica Bay, attended the chief. NAC, RG 10, vol. 201, pt 2, 119397.
93 NAC, RG 10, vol. 333, 533–5, 'Chance to Spragge,' 6 July 1867.
94 NAC, RG 10, vol. 616, 409, 'Chance to Spragge,' 17 June 1867.
95 NAC, RG 10, vol. 222, 131771–2, 'Ironside to Viscount Bury,' 10 December 1855.
96 NAC, RG 10, vol. 614, 62, 'S.Y. Chesley to Ironside,' 20 January 1856. Chesley, evidently not able to read Ironside's handwriting in a former communication from the agent, refers to Shingwaukonse as 'Kigwakonce.'

CHAPTER 6   Testing the Untried Mettle: Ogista's Rise to Leadership

1 Information drawn from interviews with Dan Pine, Sr, and Fred Pine, Sr, in 1983 and 1984.
2 Paul Pine, Ogista's son, attended school at Sault Ste Marie and at L'Anse, Michigan. References to Paul may be found in the Bingham Papers in the Clarke Library, Central Michigan University, and in the Methodist Zeba mission records at L'Anse, indicating that he was fairly well educated. Paul acted as a guide for Lewis Henry Morgan. Ogista and Ogista's elder brother, Thomas, resided much of the time at L'Anse, as did their wives and children. George Pine, a great grandson of Shingwaukonse, became a well-known timber cruiser on the Michigan side: records of the Zeba Methodist Church Mission Society in the possession of the Reverend John Henry, Zeba. It also may be that 'Joseph Shingwauk,' who joined Francis Petosky in 1844 in running away from Upper Canada College, was one of Ogista's children.
3 This attack may have been prompted by Native anger over the government's seeming betrayal of its promise, made in 1850 by W.B. Robinson, that the Ojibwa would retain the Simpson and Lemoine locations as part of their reserve. NAC, RG 10, vol. 209, 123747–8, 'Ironside to Bruce,' 30 March 1854. *Lake Superior Journal*, 4 November 1854, 2.

4 Sir George Simpson reported that the Nipigon Ojibwa had stolen goods from St Ignace Island along the northern shore of Lake Superior. NAC, RG 10, vol. 240: 143016, 'Simpson's Report,' 1856; NAC, RG 10, vol. 227, 134976-8, 'Simpson to Indian Affairs,' 28 July 1856. Simpson stressed that the free traders, and not the Ojibwa or Métis per se, were the agents of disorder on the western frontier.

5 NAC, RG 10, vol. 227, 134976-8.

6 Ironside became Wemyss Simpson's father-in-law in 1853.

7 The matter of the HBC post was first raised in 1856. NAC, RG 10, vol. 614, 227.

8 NAC, RG 10, vol. 574, 'L. Oliphant, Superintendent General of Indian Affairs, to George Ironside,' 20 November 1854.

9 NAC, RG 10, vol. 613, 227, 'Regarding Abatossaway's enterprise at Little Current,' 19 January 1858. Oliphant tried to make the system of leasing timber berths on Indian reserves both remunerative and fair to all the bands involved, as well as the timber companies. Under pressure from influential entrepreneurs who had been interested in exploiting the timber at Thessalon and Garden River, the terms of agreements were changed under Oliphant's successor, Pennefather, to favour the companies. These changes were contested by the Roman Catholic priests at Wikwemikong and the Anglican missionary at Garden River. NAC, RG 10, vol. 614, 330, 'James Chance to the Indian Department,' 18 July 1859.

10 AO, MS9, Canada, Executive Council Records, Canada State Book Q, 350, Executive Council Minutes, 28 June 1856.

11 NAC, RG 10, vol. 226, 134663, 'Ironside to Pennefather,' 24 July 1856.

12 NAC, RG 10, vol. 226, 134663; NAC, RG 10, vol. 614, 358.

13 AO, MS9, Canada, Executive Council Records, Canada State Book R, 557-8.

14 NAC, Colonial Office Records, CO 42, vol. 613, 'H. Labouchere to Sir Edmund Head, February 20, 1856, quoted in R.J. Pennefather's Memorandum of April 7th, 1858.'

15 NAC, RG 10, vol. 614, 16, 'Regarding the Circular of May 26, 1856.'

16 Christian Guardian, 5 August 1857, 4.

17 'Copy of a letter of William H. Palmer to Froome Talford,' 2 February 1857. Copy of letter in the Garden River Band Office. Probably from NAC, RG 10.

18 NAC, RG 10, vol. 256, 140312; RG 10, vol. 248, 14690-9.

19 NAC, RG 10, vol. 241, 14290, 'Wilson to Ironside,' 30 January 1857.

20 Nebenagoching responded to the fact that Métis families had been excluded from the annuity list in 1857 by arranging for a collection to be made among his band's members and for the proceeds to be distributed to those Métis still residing among his group. NAC, RG 10, vol. 241, 143286, 'Ironside to Bruce,' 27 March 1858.

21 NAC, RG 10, vol. 249, 148472–82, 'Carney to Pennefather,' 6 Septemeber 1858.

22 NAC, MG 19, A21, 6030–1,'Wilson to Hargrave,' 11 May 1856.

23 NAC, RG 10, vol. 248, 147695, 'Carney to Pennefather,' 25 March 1859; NAC, RG 10, vol. 245, pt 2, 145638–41, 'Carney to Pennefather,' 16 October 1858.

24 NAC, RG 10, vol. 235, 139547–50, 'Keating to Pennefather,' 21 July 1857.

25 NAC, RG 10, vol. 235, 139547–50, 'Cameron to Pennefather,' 21 July 1857.

26 NAC, RG 10, vol. 247, 147044.

27 NAC, RG 10, vol. 235, 139458–61, 'Keating to Pennefather,' 8 July 1857.

28 NAC, RG 10, vol. 235, 139650–1, 'Keating to the Indian Branch,' 1857.

29 NAC, RG 10, vol. 235, 139452–4, 'Wilson to Pennefather,' 9 February 1857.

30 NAC, RG 10, vol. 235, 'Pennefather to Wilson,' 14 July 1857.

31 NAC, RG 10, vol. 247, pt. 3, 147452, 'Ironside to Pennefather,' 17 February 1859; Frost, *Sketches of Indian Life*, 293. As soon as a band's population reached approximately 150 individuals, the government would make a determined effort to split the group. Policy did not allow for large concentrations of Native people along the international border.

32 NA, RG 75, M234, Roll 405: 0269, 'George Johnston to George W. Manypenny,' 3 October 1856.

33 NA, RG 75, M234. Roll 406: 1056–7, 'Thomas C. Slaughter to W. Dole,' 27 October 1861.

34 NA, RG 75, M234, Roll 406: 0773, 'William Johnston to Commissioner,' 8 January 1860; NA, RG 75, M234, Roll 405: 0082; 'Regarding Oshawano's complaint to Henry C. Gilbert,' 31 December 1855. Fitch took office in July 1857.

35 Hurlburt was at Garden River during 1857 and 1858, Salt during 1859, while Sawyer acted as an interpreter to the mission at different times. William Harkimer resided at Garden River in 1860. Hurlburt felt that the government should abolish the operation of traditional leadership and impose an elective system on the bands. NAC, RG 10, vol. 239, pt 1, 1911860, 'Hurlburt to the Indian Department,' 22 December 1857.

36 *Christian Guardian*, 4 November 1857, 55–6.

37 NAC, RG 10, vol. 235, 139650–3, 'Keating to Indian Department,' 1857.

38 NAC, RG 10, vol. 239, pt 2, 142584–6, 'Petition dated 26 January 1858'; RG 10, vol. 239, pt 2, 142581–2.

39 NAC, RG 10, vol. 239, pt 2, 142549–52, 'I. N. Sicotte to Pennefather,' 16 February 1858.

40 NAC, RG 10, vol. 239, pt 2, 142560–4.

41 NAC, RG 10, vol. 239, pt. 2, 142549–52, 'Sicotte to Pennefather,' 16 February 1858.

42 NAC, RG 10, vol. 239, pt 2, 1421565–70, 'R.T. Pennefather, 3 March 1858.'

43 NAC, RG 10, vol. 614, 246, 'Pennefather to Ironside,' 4 June 1858.

44 NAC, RG 10, vol. 249, 148472–82, 'Carney to Pennefather,' 6 September 1858.
45 Ibid.
46 Ibid.
47 Ibid.
48 Ibid.
49 AO, Harry D. Blanchard Collection, M Section P Papers, 1766–1932, MU 234, 275, 'Information and complaint of Edward Pawyawbedeussung [son of Charles Piabetassung, and hence Shingwaukonse's grandson] of Garden River vs Kechenebaunewbeu of Thessalon.' Kechenebaunewbeu was a conjuror.
50 NA, RG 75, M 234, Roll 406: 0249–50, 'Petition of [O]Shawano, Wabojick and Kabanodin,' 2 October 1858.
51 Sugar Island was in American territory, and names of all members of the Garden River band residing on the island were deleted from the lists in 1858–9. Edward Piabetassung was a Methodist, as was Carney, and so sought Carney's help in this affair. Shingwaukonse's in-laws from his former Grand Island–Bay de Noc band, who had removed at his insistence, and who also had formerly been head men of his council, were thrown into political limbo by these changes, as they were not part of the traditional American Sault band. AO, Blanchard Collection, MU 275, 'Letter of Richard Carney on behalf of Garden River chief [Edward Piabetassung] inquiring as to his right [to be] as [a] chief. Dated October 12, 1858.' Also NAC, RG 10, vol. 247, pt 2, 11872 from the band lists.
52 Ibid.
53 NAC, RG 10, vol. 249, 148490–4,'Carney to Pennefather,' 12 June 1859.
54 NAC, RG 10, vol. 247, pt 2, 147043–6, 'Carney to Pennefather,' 28 May 1859.
55 NAC, RG 10, vol. 614, 187–8, 'S.Y. Chesley to Ironside,' 10 January 1859.
56 NAC, RG 10, vol. 248, 147690–9, 'Carney to Indian Department,' 25 March 1859.
57 Ibid.
58 NAC, RG 10, vol. 242, 143599, 'Ironside reports that chief Totomenai's band desires to exchange the reserve at Gros Cap for land either at Ahgaiwond [Agawa] or at Batchewanan Island,' 24 August 1859. NAC, RG 10, vol. 247, pt 2, 14704.
59 NAC, RG 10, vol. 573, '[Statement of] Thomas Augustin, Hd. Chief, Henry Paquetchenene, Chief,' 14 June 1859.
60 NAC, RG 10, vol. 249, 148490, 'Carney to Indian Department,' 12 June 1859.
61 MNR, 1866 Plan of Shinguiconse [township], Garden River. Wilson and MacGhee, P.L.S., December 1866.
62 Gibbard leased the fishing location to an American. NAC, RG 10, vol. 614, 332. NAC, RG 10, vol. 614, 339, 'Pennefather to Ironside,' 1 September 1859.
63 NAC, RG 10, vol. 614, 16, 'Pennefather to Ironside,' 15 July 1856. For a sum-

mary of this event, see Barry, *Georgian Bay, The Sixth Great Lake*, 74–5.

64 NAC, RG 10, vol. 256, 153974–80, 'Memorandum of the proceeding of an Indian Council held at Sarnia on the 12th September 1860'; NAC, RG 10, vol. 614, 407–9. The circular cautioned that 'No business will be transacted nor must any remarks be made upon the policy of the Government towards them [the Indians].'

65 NAC, RG 10, vol. 613, 'Kichikemeg to members of the Grand Council, Rama Reserve,' 28 February 1859.

66 Many contemporary accounts of the Wikwemikong resistance movement exist. Among these are: Conrad Van Dusen's account in chapter 28 of *The Indian Chief,* and articles in the *Globe* for 30 July 1863 and the *Canadian Illustrated News* for 8 August 1863. Owing to the pressures exerted on the government by E.B. Borron and others, in 1860 several provisions of the law which had formerly granted chiefs a degree of proprietorship over land and resources on their reserves were repealed, and the conditions regulating resource development on Crown Lands were extended to apply to timber and minerals on reserves. NAC, RG 10, vol. 254, 151940.

67 When a debate arose concerning the most suitable successor to Chief Megis of Parry Island, Yellowhead of Rama upheld James Pagahmegabow of the Caribou *dodem* against Ahwahquagezick of the Birch Bark *dodem.* There was also factionalism along religious lines, as Yellowhead and Pagahmegabow were both Methodist, while their rivals were mostly Roman Catholic. NAC, RG 10, vol. 613, 1038–9.

68 The expulsion of Chief Tehkumma and others at this time led to whole families' being left off the band rolls. NAC, RG 10, vol. 2832, file 170,073–1, 'J. Paquin to A.N. McNeill,' 26 November 1896.

69 NAC, RG 10, vol. 615, 348–50.

70 NAC, RG 10, vol. 615, 15–18, 'Instructions regarding census taking,' 1861.

71 John Carney's comments on the Agricultural Census Sheets clearly indicate this. AO, 'Census 1861. Enumeration District No. One from Westerly limit of Rankin's Mining Location in possession of Wellington Mining Company of Lake Huron to Indian Mission, Batchewana Bay, Lake Superior, District of Algoma.' Ironside reported the same problem. NAC, RG 10, vol. 254, 153183.

72 The population of Enumeration District No. 1 [Sault Ste Marie] numbered 898. That 475 'Indian' residents were listed gives an idea of the large proportion of Native residents relative to non-Native residents in 1861.

73 AO, John Prince Diary, 'November 15, 1862.'

74 The number 113 has been calculated from a census of Garden River Ojibwa for the years from 1850 to 1880 in the Aemelius Irving Collection. AO, Irving Papers, MU 1464, 26/31/03 and 04.

75 AO, John Prince Diary, 'October 21, 1862.'

76 NAC, RG 10, vol. 254, 152474–7, 'Carney to Pennefather,' 23 May 1869.
George Copway, formerly a Native Methodist missionary, was soliciting volun-
teers to join in the American Civil War. NAC, RG 10, vol. 615, 336–8. Circulars
were sent cautioning local government agents that arms may have been sent to
the Sioux around February of 1863. NAC, RG 10, vol. 302, 202351.

77 NAC, RG 10, vol. 615, 137, 'Abatossaway. Statement made before David Layton
at Manitowaning,' 26 February 1862.

78 There was a notice to have Abatossaway removed from the island, since he was
considered an informer. NAC, RG 10, vol. 615, 477.

79 NAC, RG 10, vol. 615, 389–92, 'Wilson to Dupont,' 12 February 1864.

80 The Wikwemikong resistance movement was entirely Native sponsored, with
the priests trying to channel the momentum into forms of peaceful protest
rather than outbreaks of violence. With Ironside's death in 1863 and the
appointment of his haughty successor, Charles Dupont, Native anger escalated. Dupont had little interest in protecting Native lands from settlement
and resource development, and so the contradiction inherent in the role of
the province as protector of Native interests and promoter of western-style
economic development ceased to exist. The Native people had to restore the
balance between the two roles by their own efforts, or else the development
interests invariably would win. Many contemporary accounts of this resistance exist. Among these are an account by the Native missionary Van Dusen,
articles in the *Globe* for 30 July 1863, and an article in the *Canadian Illustrated
News*, vol. 2, no. 13, 8 August 1863, 151. In the latter article, D. Blain, the lawyer for the Native people's defence argued, 'Is the fishery the property of the
Indians or not? If of the Indians, they have only done that which the law will
warrant every man in doing in protecting his property against intruders. If
the property in the fisheries be ceded to the government, the Indians are not
aware of the fact they say. I took this ground before the magistrates [Wilson,
Ironside, Layton, Carney, and Judge Prince], but they were of the opinion
that the production of the license granted by Mr. Proulx raised a presumption that the Crown was entitled to the property ... in the absence of proof to
the contrary.' In 1860, several provisions of the law which had formerly
granted chiefs a degree of proprietorship over land and resources on their
reserves were repealed, and the provisions regulating resource exploitation
on Crown lands were extended to fishing, timber, and minerals on reserves.
This triggered new fears at Garden River, as Wilson and Ironside began
ignoring the Ojibwa's interests in implementing the new policy. NAC, RG 10,
vol. 254, 151940.

81 NAC, RG 10, vol. 615, 321–2, 'Prince to Wilson,' 22 December 1863; 'NAC, RG

10, vol. 230, 136899, Appointment of Prince and Wilson to conduct sales of Indian lands and collect dues and fines on timber cut on reserves, 1863.'

82 NAC, RG 10, vol. 615, 621–3, 'Wilson to Dupont,' 20 January 1864.

83 B.H. Lemoine and George Desbarats had been very reluctant to part with their locations, but with Spragge's encouragement they did so, especially as W.B. Robinson had stipulated in 1850 that the two sites should revert to the reserve. NAC, RG 10, vol. 230, 136899.

84 AO, RG 1, L3, vol. 220(a), 16, 'Upper Canada Land Petitions,' 'G,' Bundle 9, 1858–64.

85 NAC, RG 10, vol. 615, 414–15, 'Spragge to Dupont,' 31 March 1864; NAC, RG 10, vol. 615, 429–32, 'Spragge to Dupont,' 22 April 1864; NAC, RG 10, vol. 615, 449–51, 'Spragge to Dupont,' 28 May 1864.

86 Spragge had held that trade with Church should be permitted. NAC, RG 10, vol. 615, 367–8, 399–400. 'Spragge to Dupont,' 7 May 1864. Chance, however, considered that John Cousins behaved improperly towards Native women and stated that the merchant sold spirits in his store. NAC, RG 10, vol. 324, 218397. Sollow's report is in the 39th Annual Report of the Missionary Society of the Wesleyan Methodist Church, June 1863–June 1864.

87 Ogista in 1864 asks Prince for information, NAC, vol. 284, 191329; Ogista defies Prince and Wilson, NAC, RG 10, vol. 284, 191376, 'Dupont to Spragge,' 15 March 1864; NAC, RG 10, vol. 284, 191329, 'Dupont to Wilson,' 1 March 1864.

88 NAC, RG 10, vol. 615, 389–92, 'Wilson to Dupont,' 12 February 1864.

89 NAC, RG 10, vol. 284, 191363, 'Dupont to Wilson,' 1 March 1864.

90 NAC, RG 10, vol. 615, 408, 'Church to Dupont,' 6 January 1864.

91 NAC, RG 10, vol. 615, 371–2, 'Prince to Dupont,' 6 January 1864. 'My opinion,' wrote Prince, '[is] that the Indians at Garden River are merely occupants without payment of rent.'

92 Ibid.

93 NAC, RG 10, vol. 284, 191376, 'Dupont to Spragge,' 15 March 1864. It was Dupont who suggested that Charles Biron be arrested and sent to the penitentiary at Penetanguishene. The agent also felt that the Roman Catholic priests should be penalized, since he felt they may have been promoting unrest. NAC, RG 10, vol. 284, 191581–90, 'Dupont to Spragge,' 21 November 1864. When the Wikwemikong leaders began to assert that neither Dupont nor the Crown had control over them, Dupont panicked. NAC, RG 10, vol. 284, 191581, 'Dupont to Spragge,' 21 November 1864. Whether or not a Native person actually 'murdered' Gibbard, whose body in 1863 was found floating in the waters off Manitoulin Island, was never determined. The agent made no secret of his suspicions, however. The agent even hesitated to distribute relief to bands after the forest fires and a minor smallpox epidemic which occurred in

1864, arguing instead that the Ottawa should earn their provisions by wage labour. Spragge intervened to compel the agent to assist the bands.

94 NAC, RG 10, vol. 284, 191363, 'Dupont to Indian Department,' 10 December 1863.

95 NAC, RG 10, vol. 615, 434, 'Spragge to Dupont,' 26 April 1864.

96 See, for example, 'The Collingwood Outrage,' the *Globe*, 28 October 1875. Interband conflicts occurred, but authorities were usually misled as to the cause. *Sault Express*, 6 October 1866.

97 NAC, RG 10, vol. 615, 348, 'To Our Brother Chiefs, 1864.'

98 NA, RG 75, M234, Roll 407: 0408–32, 'Leach to Dole, Commissioner of Indian Affairs,' 12 January 1864. Meanwhile, Abatossaway had not reached the end of his difficulties. A complaint levelled against him for a drunken 'spree' led the government to compel the band to leave Little Current. NAC, RG 10, vol. 515, 568, 'John Burkett to Dupont,' 1 December 1864. Spragge informed this leader that he should move to Sucker Creek, Manitoulin Island. NAC, RG 10, vol. 615, 959–62, 'Spragge to Abatossaway,' 8 September 1865. He and his band did so in 1866. NAC, RG 10, vol. 616, 267–8, 'Return of Indians.' See also NAC, RG 10, vol. 619, 45556, 'Complaint of Sarah Abatossaway [a Scottish woman who had married the chief], 1865.'

99 Richard S. Lambert and Pross, *Renewing Nature's Wealth*, 205.

100 NAC, RG 10, vol. 615, 578–80, 'Spragge to Wilson,' 22 December 1864.

101 Kirkpatrick reported that the Ojibwa wanted the boundaries to conform to the terms of the 1850 and 1859 treaties. NAC, RG 10, vol. 302, 202646. MNR, 1864 Fieldnotes, Book 823, Part 1. By G.B. Kirkpatrick.

102 NAC, RG 10, vol. 2878, file 177,991-1, pt 0, 'Lawrence Vankoughnet to G.B. Kirkpatrick,' 27 April 1893. Copy in Garden River Band File 40-3.

103 NAC, RG 10, vol. 302, 202809–12, 'Wilson to Spragge,' 1 January 1865.

104 NAC, RG 10, vol. 284, D42, Reel C-12,664, 'Auguste Kohler to Dupont,' 4 October 1864.

105 AO, Prince Diary, '20 March 1865.'

106 NAC, RG 10, vol. 324, 216822, 'Chance to Campbell,' 10 March 1865.

107 This was a second offence. The first occurred in February. NAC, RG 10, vol. 615, 875–6, 'Chance to Pennefather,' 28 February 1865.

108 NAC, RG 10, vol. 324, 216822, 'Chance to Campbell,' 10 March 1866; NAC, RG 10, vol. 615, 875–6, 'Spragge to Dupont,' 28 June 1865; NAC, RG 10, vol. 331, D3, Reel C-9581, 'Dupont to Spragge,' 2 May 1865.

109 NAC, RG 10, vol. 331, D 79, Reel C-9582, 'Dupont to Spragge,' 3 November 1865. Spragge failed to solve the difficulty immediately, but by the end of November felt it was well on its way towards being settled. NAC, RG 10, vol. 615, 1026, 'Spragge to Dupont,' 23 November 1865.

110 NAC, RG 10, vol. 615, 931, 'Chance to Dupont,' 15 August 1865; NAC, RG

10, vol. 324, 216822, 'Chance to Campbell,' 10 March 1866; NAC, RG 10, vol. 324, 216828, 'Chance to Campbell,' 28 July 1866.

111 NAC, RG 10, vol. 324, 216811, 'Chance to Campbell,' 28 July 1866.

112 NAC, RG 10, vol. 616, 134–7, 'Spragge to Dupont,' 9 August 1866. The band henceforth would receive its annuities at Garden River rather than at Sault Ste Marie.

113 NAC, RG 10, vol. 340, 378–81, 'Campbell to Kohler,' 11 October 1866.

114 Ibid.

115 NAC, RG 10, vol. 326, 218443–4.

116 NAC, RG 10, vol. 340, 578–81, 'Memorandum on the subject of Alex. Campbell's letters of 27 August and 4 September 1866.'

117 NAC, RG 10, vol. 324, 216807, 'Chance to Campbell,' 26 October 1866.

118 NAC, RG 10, vol. 616, 400–1, 'Chance to Spragge,' 21 May 1867.

119 NAC, RG 10, vol. 324, 216938–40, 'Chance to Spragge,' 21 May 1867.

120 NAC, RG 10, vol. 333, 537–40, 'Chance to Campbell,' 28 November 1866.

121 Ogista in 1864 had asked for an advance on the band annuity to construct a sawmill. NAC, RG 10, vol. 284, 191382, 'Petition,' 12 March 1864.

122 NAC, RG 10, vol. 333, 541–4, 'Chance to Spragge,' 17 June 1867. Treaties No. 110 and 111, 7 July and 9 July 1867. Bell had entered into a contract with Rankin regarding a house on Bell's Point in 1871. NAC, RG 10, vol. 2048, file 9266.

123 Ibid.

124 NAC, RG 10, vol. 616, 420–2, 'Chance to Spragge,' 3 September 1867. Allan Macdonell at the Sault ran unsuccessfully in this election.

125 NAC, RG 10, vol. 616, 420–2, 'Chance to Spragge,' 3 September 1867.

126 NAC, RG 10, vol. 33, 430–1, 'Statement of William McMurray,' 31 August 1867; NAC, RG 10, vol. 333, 514–15, 'Statement of T.G. Anderson,' 17 August 1867; NAC, RG 10, vol. 333, 517–19, 'Statement of F.A. O'Meara,' 10 August 1867.

127 NAC, RG 10, vol. 616, 518–19, 'Spragge to Dupont,' 16 August 1867.

128 NAC, RG 10, vol. 333, 498–501, 'Chance to Spragge,' 28 September 1867.

129 NAC, RG 10, vol. 333, 478–84, 'Spragge's comments on the rival claims of Ogista and Buhkwujjenene,' 1867.

130 NAC, RG 10, vol. 616, 423–4, 'Dupont to Spragge,' 8 September 1867.

131 NAC, RG 10, vol. 333, 472–3, 'Spragge's comments on the rival claims of Ogista and Buhkwujjenene,' 1867.

132 NAC, RG 10, vol. 326, 218440–1, 'Langevin to Wilson,' 13 December 1867.

133 NAC, RG 10, vol. 341, 327–30, 'Extract of Chance's letter of February 1867.'

134 NAC, RG 10, vol. 333, 537–40, 'Chance to Spragge,' 17 June 1867; NAC, RG 10, vol. 327, 218694–6, 'Chance to Langevin,' 24 November 1868.

135 NAC, RG 10, vol. 326, 218434–8, 'Indian petition,' 8 June 1868. The price of

Indian land was not to exceed twenty cents cash per acre in order to promote rapid settlement in the Algoma district. NAC, RG 10, vol. 302, 202380.

136 NAC, RG 10, vol. 617, 106, 'List of Indians and Halfbreeds residing on Garden River Reserve who may be regarded as Intruders.'

137 Wilson complained about the Ojibwa selling timber to Church. NAC, RG 10, vol. 303, 3202.

138 The act of 1869 sought to exclude those of 'less than three fourths Indian blood from the privilege of the Indian community.' NAC, RG 10, vol. 1942, file 4103.

139 NAC, RG 10, vol. 333, 537–40, 'Chance to Spragge,' 17 June 1867; NAC, vol. 327, 218694–6, 'Chance to Langevin,' 24 November 1868. Conditions were shocking, Chance related, with starvation not infrequent.

140 Nelles, *Politics of Development*, 23.

141 NAC, RG 10, vol. 333, 473, 'Regarding rival claims to leadership,' 3 August 1869; NAC, RG 10, vol. 333, 482–3, 'Statement of Augustin [Ogista]' and 'Statement of Wahbemaimai,' August 1869; NAC RG 10, vol. 333, 481, 'Statement of Pahkutchenenene,' August 1869. Taken from testimonies recorded by Charles Dupont in August 1867. In November, William Plummer was instructed to arrange for an electoral system to be implemented in conformity with the terms of the 1869 General Enfranchisement Act. The Garden River band's support for Ogista evidently made such an election unnecessary at this time.

142 NAC, RG 10, vol. 333, 481.

143 NAC, RG 10, vol. 2048, file 9321, 'Conditions with regard to the surrender of Squirrel Island,' 1873; NAC, RG 10, vol. 619, 9, 'Joseph Howe to William Plummer,' 20 January 1873. William Plummer remained visiting superintendent until June 1873, when J.C. Phipps was appointed to fill the post at the Manitowaning agency.

144 Shingwauk, *Little Pine's Journal.* Here Ogista assumes his father's Native name by adopting the European patrilineal surname system.

145 NAC, RG 10, vol. 1915, file 2697, pt 0.

146 NAC, RG 10, vol. 1915, file 2697, pt 0.

CHAPTER 7   Challenging the System from Within

1 This term was first applied in a broad sense to the context of Canada's indigenous peoples in Carstens, 'Coercion and Change.' The term was first applied to the South African context during the late 1960s and early 1970s.

2 Simon J. Dawson (1820–1902) was a special Indian Affairs commissioner in 1873. He became an MPP for Algoma in the Ontario legislature and a federal

MP in 1878. Several Garden River elders the author spoke with remembered him with affection.

3 NAC, RG 10, vol. 1846, 'Treaty No. 3 between Her Majesty the Queen and the Saulteaux Tribe of the Ojibbeway Indians at the Northwest Angle of the Lake of the Woods with Adhesions, October 3, 1873.'

4 NAC, RG 10, vol. 1938, file 3776, 'Affidavit,' 11 January 1875; NAC, RG 10, vol. 1937, file 3773; NAC, RG 10, vol. 1940, file 3940. This iron deposit had been known by the band for a long time. In 1823, John Johnston, a local Sault trader, had informed Major Joseph Delafield of the United states Boundary Commission of its location 'nine miles up the Garden River.' McElroy and Riggs, eds, *The Unfortified Boundary*, 371.

5 NAC, RG 10, vol. 1937, file 3773, 'Affidavit, John Shingwok [John Askin],' November 1874; 'Church to Indian Department,' 25 November 1875; 'Van Abbott to Indian Department,' 13 August 1874; 'Synopsis of Case.'

6 Ibid.

7 E.B. Borron was the prime impetus behind the surrender of the reserve at this time. This caused Ogista, Buhkwujjenene, Waubmama, and nine others to refuse to vote even on the surrender of the mining locations. NAC, RG 10, vol. 1938, file 3776, 'Van Abbott to the Minister of the Interior,' 19 October 1874. Mineral lands were sold for $1.50 cash per acre. NAC, RG 10, vol. 1944, file 4236. Treaty No. 140 for Mining Locations 21 M–26H was signed by the band on 25 November 1874. It was officially registered in Februrary of 1875. NAC, RG 10, file 4236, pt 0, 'To the Honorable Secretary of State,' 16 February 1875. All of these mining locations subsequently became forfeited to Ontario under the Provisional Land Tax Act of 1924. Emerson, 'Research Report on Forfeited Surrendered Lands, Garden River Reserve No. 14.' NAC, RG 10, vol. 1909, file 2372, pt 0, 'Correspondence on Wilkinson Location and its owner-ship by the University of Michigan.'

8 NAC, RG 10, vol. 1936, file 3673, 'E.F. Wilson to Clifford Sifton,' 14 July 1874. Wilson wanted the Anglican mission to be funded partly from Batchewana band capital. At the time, sixty-seven individuals resided at Batchewana Bay. The Hudson's Bay Company encouraged these Ojibwa to spend as little time on the coast as possible. 52nd Annual Report of the Missionary Society of the Wesleyan Methodist Church, June 1875 to June 1876.

9 NAC, RG 10, vol. 619, 127–9; 'E.S. Currey to J.C. Aikens,' 2 January 1873; NAC, RG 10, vol. 619, 131.

10 NAC, RG 10, vol. 2048, file 9321, 'File regarding Squirrel Island, and the building of a sawmill owned by Messrs. Craig and Company, 1872–1879.' The sale of the seven acres occurred on 17 April 1872. 'Surrender No. 165,' 1872. Morris, ed., *Indian Treaties and Surrenders*, 2:63–5.

11 NAC, RG 10, vol. 2048, file 9321.

12 AO, Irving Papers, MU 1465, 27/31/1 (1), 'Simon J. Dawson to the Secretary of H.E. the Governor General,' 7 April 1873, included with 'Petition. To His Excellency the Right Honorable Earl of Dufferin, K.C.B., Governor General of Canada in Council, 1873.' AO, Irving Papers, MU 1465, 27/31/1 (1), 'Simon J. Dawson to Colonel C. Stuart,' 7 October 1881. Dawson's family had intermarried with the Macdonells even prior to each family's emigration to Canada from Scotland. Simon J. Dawson's mother, for instance, was Anne Macdonell. It is thus not surprising for members of these two closely interrelated families to share views and interests in common. AO, Dawson Family Papers, MU 828. William Dawson, Simon's brother, had been dismissed from a post as a surveyor for what he felt were factional politics between his family and the Crown Lands commissioner, Papineau.

13 NAC, RG 10, vol. 1978, file 5978, pt 0, 'E.B. Borron to the Honorable D. Laird,' 9 April 1875.

14 NAC, RG 10, vol. 1967, file 5184, 'Council held at the English School House,' 5 August 1875.

15 AO, Irving Papers, MU 1465, 17/31/1 (1), 'To His Excellency the Right Honorable Earl Dufferin.'

16 NAC, RG 10, vol. 2028, file 8922, pt 0, 'Van Abbott to the Minister of the Interior,' 25 May 1878. Until 1878 the choice of whether or not to abandon the reserve system was left up to the Indians themselves.

17 NAC, RG 10, vol. 2023, file 8590, p 0, 'Wilson to the Indian Department,' 31 July 1877.

18 NAC, RG 10, vol. 2040, file 8949.

19 AO, Irving Papers, MU 1465, 27/31/1/ (1), 'E.B. Borron to the Honorable David Mills,' 23 November 1877.

20 NAC, RG 10, vol. 2000, file 7332, 'Van Abbott to the Minister of the Interior,' 21 November 1877; NAC, RG 10, vol. 2028, file 8924, 'Plummer to Indian Department,' 21 October 1877. I am indebted to Mr George Richardson, Toronto, for his kindness in supplying a typescript copy of the surrender from his own records. Surrender No. 166, 15 November 1877.

21 NAC, RG 10, vol. 2001, file 7392.

22 NAC, RG 10, vol. 2029, file 8922, 'Van Abbott to the Honorable Minister of the Interior,' 25 May 1878.

23 Anglican Heritage Collection Archives, Bishophurst, Sault Ste Marie, Letterbooks of E.F. Wilson, 'Edward F. Wilson to his father,' 5 February 1878.

24 Ibid.

25 Ibid.

26 NAC, RG 10, vol. 2090, file 14,067, 'Augustine Chingwauk, Chief of the Ojib-

way, to the Honorable Member of the Dominion,' 17 June 1878; 'Van Abbott
to the Honorable Minister of the Interior,' 21 June 1879.

27 NAC, RG 10, vol. 2902, file 15,434, 'Reply from the Indian Department,' 10
July 1879.

28 NAC, RG 10, vol. 2092, file 15,434, 'Van Abbott to the Indian Department,' 27
July 1879.

29 Ibid.

30 The band had requested assistance from their capital fund to cover travelling
costs in September 1879, but had received none. NAC RG 10, vol. 2092, file
15,434, 'Petition of 29 September 1879.' Funds were finally secured with the
help of the Grand Council. NAC, RG 10, vol. 2092, file 15,434, 'Moses Madwayosh to Vankoughnet,' 9 October 1878.

31 Ibid.

32 Ogista's grievances regarding the Clark location and the western boundary
resulted in Ottawa's examination of the available documentation, but little was
done. NAC, RG 10, vol. 2211, file 42,451; NAC, RG 10, vol. 2445, file 93,317,
'Aubrey White to Vankoughnet,' 7 February 1889. After reviewing Vidal's survey of the mining locations made in 1848, White concluded that 'Mr. Dennis
in running the West Boundary of the Reserve coincided with the projected
East boundary of the Clark location except where he deviated from the North
and South line to strike Partridge Point.'

33 *Globe*, 3 August 1881; *Graphic* (London, England), 1881, 261. NAC, MG 27
(1B4), Lord Lorne Papers. Ogista wore a scarlet beaded vest, black beaded
leggings, and a skunkskin headdress with eagle feathers.

34 NAC, RG 10, vol. 2092, file 15434, 31337, 'Petition, 1881.' The 345 acres in
question at this time were considered part of the reserve in the 1870s, but this
had changed by 1880. The matter had been slated to go to a board of arbitrators, but the issue seems to have been waylaid *en route* owing to problems in
making claims against the old Province of Canada for the period prior to
1867. Rankin argued that he had paid for, and thus owned, the 345 acres.
NAC, RG 10, vol. 2048, file 9266, 'Rankin to the Honorable Thomas White,' 9
February 1888. See also, NAC, RG 10, vol. 2092, files 15,434, 15,811-2, 'Memorial to His Excellency Lord Lorne, 1879'; NAC, RG 10, vol. 2092, file 15,009,
'Van Abbott to John A. Macdonald,' 15 June 1880; NAC, RG 10, vol. 2092, file
15,434, 'Van Abbott to the Minister of the Interior,' 3 October 1879.

35 AO, Irving Papers, MU 1465, 27/31/1 (1), 'Simon J. Dawson to Colonel C.
Stewart,' 7 October 1881.

36 NAC, RG 10, vol. 2185, file 37,479, pt 0, 'George F. Austin, acting on behalf of
the chiefs and warriors of the Goulais Bay and Batchewana Bands of Indians,'
31 May 1882.

37 NAC, RG 10, vol. 2185, file 37,479, pt 0, 'Edward Langevin regarding Austin's correspondence,' 31 July 1882.

38 NAC, RG 10, vol. 2211, file 42,451, 'Van Abbott to the Superintendent of the Indian Department, 2 April 1883, and reply.'

39 NAC, RG 10, vol. 3251, file 70,622, '8th Grand Council, Cape Croker Reserve, 10 to 15 September 1884, 5. Minutes, Discussion of the Indian Advancement Act of 1884.' The Grand Council discussion sessions focused on an act which provided for annual elections of councillors, regular council meetings, collection of taxes, enforcement of by-laws, possession of land by location ticket, and annual property assessment.

40 Ibid., 5–22.

41 NAC, RG 10, vol. 1954, file 4472, 'Extract of a meeting with the Treasury Board held on the 26 June 1886.'

42 Van Abbott continually maligned Waubmama and interfered with Waubmama's ability to rent a house, exercise trusteeship over his grandson, and communicate his grievances to Ottawa. NAC, RG 10, vol. 1982, file 6230 and NAC, RG 10, vol. 2191, file 38,593.

43 NAC, RG 10, vol. 2296, file 59,090, pt 0, 'Van Abbott to the Indian Department,' 17 April 1885.

44 NAC, RG 10, vol. 2354, file 71,687, pt 0, 'Reply to Van Abbott's letter of the 17th Inst.,' 30 April 1885; NAC, RG 10, vol. 2354, file 71,687, pt 0, 'Nebenagoching to Simon J. Dawson,' 21 December 1886.

45 NAC, RG 10, vol. 2296, file 59,090, pt 0, 'Regarding powers of chief and council. Van Abbott to the Indian Department,' 30 January 1891. With a population of 437 in 1891, the band was permitted to have 'two head chiefs and four second chiefs.' The band chose to have only one head chief and four councillors.

46 Ogista personally offered to pay relief from his own annuity payments to assist 'old blind ... Shebakezick,' but would allow no money to be taken from the band funds for the same purpose. NAC, RG 10, vol. 2067, file 10,307, pt 1, 'Van Abbott to the Indian Department regarding the Council Meeting of 8 April 1890.'

47 *Algoma Pioneer and District General Advertiser,* 12 January 1881.

48 NAC, RG 10, vol. 2067, file 10,307, pt 1, 'Buhkwujjenene to Van Abbott,' 1887; 'Van Abbott to the Indian Department,' 26 August 1887.

49 NAC, RG 10, vol. 2067, file 10,307, pt 1, 'Van Abbott to the Indian Department,' 3 September 1887.

50 NAC, RG 10, vol. 2067, file 10,307, pt 1, 'Messrs. Scott and Scott, Barristers, to L. Vankoughnet,' 23 February 1890.

51 Ibid.

52 Ibid.

53 *Sault Express*, 31 January 1891.

54 'To the Editor, Garden River, January 9, 1882,' *Algoma Missionary News and Shingwauk Journal*, 5, no. 3 (1 March 1883).

55 *Algoma Missionary News and Shingwauk Journal*, 6, no. 10 (1 October 1883): 55–8.

56 'Letter to the Editor,' *Algoma Missionary News and Shingwauk Journal*, 5, no. 12 (16 December 1893): 86.

57 'Shall We Keep On?' *Algoma Missionary News and Shingwauk Journal*, 6, no. 10 (1 October 1883).

58 Ibid.

59 David Nock traces this development in Wilson. Nock argues that Wilson, because of his upper-class British background, was able to act to a degree independently of the Native church policy of Henry Venn and his evangelical colleagues. After studying events in Red River and visiting Cherokee settlements in Oklahoma, Wilson came to see the value of encouraging self-government among the Native peoples. Nock, *A Victorian Missionary and Canadian Indian Policy*.

60 Borron had been mine manager at Bruce Mines before entering Algoma politics. His views on Shingwaukonse's role in the mine takeover of 1849 were incorrect. There can be no doubt that the chief's policy had been an exclusive one. Oral testimonies at Garden River, as well as documentary evidence, strongly suggest that Shingwaukonse was not in any way allied in 1850 with head chiefs east of Thessalon and Mississauga. When asked in 1850 whether Yellowhead of Rama had any claims on lands west of Moose Deer Point, Shingwaukonse denied the validity of Yellowhead's assertions. Morris, ed., *Indian Treaties and Surrenders*, 1:20. In March of 1851 Ironside had noted that the names of the interior Indians in 1850 had never been mentioned in the Robinson Treaties, this 'being quite intentional on the part of the chiefs of the main land.' NAC, RG 10, vol. 188, 199548, 'Ironside to Indian Department,' 13 March 1851. Yet, oddly, Lawrence Vankoughnet contended in 1884 that 'the omission to include their names was unintentional on the part of the mainland chiefs.' Ontario, *Sessional Papers*, No. 45, 1885: 25, 'Vankoughnet to J.M. Courtney,' 17 September 1884. Borron considered Shingwaukonse to have acted indiscriminately on behalf of all Indian and Métis people north of Lakes Huron and Superior. AO, Irving Papers, MU 1465, 27/32/10, 'John Driver to E.B. Borron,' 5 June 1893; AO, Irving Papers, MU 1465, 27/32/09, 'Robinson Treaty Annuities, Revision of Pay Lists for 1890–91 by Mr. Borron'; 'Report by E.B. Borron Relative to Annuities Payable to Indians in terms of the Robinson Treaties, 31st December 1892'; 'Report on the Robinson Trea-

ties and claims of the Indians Under the Same'; 'Supplementary Report by
E.B. Borron on the Right of Half Breeds to participate in the benefits of the
Robinson Treaties, 27th October, 1894.' John Driver interviewed Buhkwujjenene, Nebenagoching, Black Potato of Sucker Creek – a member of Abatossaway's band – and Peter Ahbahjigance – a son-in-law of Chief Gagiosh of
Whitefish Island who was a brother of Apequash and Mishkeash. Frank Daigle
was another son-in-law of Gagiosh and a well-known figure in Sault Ste Marie
society. Driver himself joined the Garden River band by exercising kin ties
through his brother, William, who was Ogista's son-in-law.

61 NAC, RG 10, vol. 2552, file 112,279, 'Van Abbott to Indian Department,'
9 January 1891.

62 NAC, RG 10, vol. 2580, file 117,364, 'Petition,' 3 July 1891.

63 NAC, RG 10, vol. 2631, file 128,145; NAC, RG 10, vol. 2647, file 129,029, pt 0.

64 NAC, RG 10, vol. 2544, file 111,470; NAC, RG 10, vol. 2580, file 117,364; NAC,
RG 10, vol. 2192, file 38,590, pt 0.

65 Records of the Church of the Immaculate Heart of Mary, Garden River,
Priest's Diary, 'Council Meeting and Election,' 28 August 1897. Recorded in
French by Father G. Artus.

66 NAC, RG 10, vol. 2631, file 128,145, 'Vankoughnet to the Honorable P. Daly,
Superintendent of Indian Affairs,' 16 January 1893.

67 NAC, RG 10, vol. 2631, file 128,145, 'Document, Exhibit "A," dated 8 December 1848'; NAC, RG 10, vol. 1954, file 4472, 'Petition signed by Nebenagoching,' 7 November 1896; NAC, RG 10, vol. 1954, file 4472, 'To His Excellency
the Governor General in Council,' 27 May 1896.

68 NAC, RG 10, vol. 2631, file 128,145, pt 0, 'Correspondence regarding the
Tegoosh claim,' 1892; NAC, RG 10, vol. 2649, file 131,221, 'A. Dingman's
Report,' 1 November 1892; NAC, vol. 2832, file 170,073-1.

69 In 1900, Jacob Wagimah and William J. Pine were constables. NAC, RG 10, vol.
2662, file 133,095-2. NAC, RG 10, vol. 2940, file 197,341; NAC, RG 10, vol.
2945, file 198,776.

70 NAC, RG 10, vol. 2878, file 177,991-1, pt 0, 'Correspondence regarding
boundary dispute and subdivision of the reserve, 1896–1921.' Includes a list of
lands sold on the Garden River reserve.

71 NAC, RG 10, vol. 2878, file 177,991-1, pt 0, 'Memoranda for the Superintendent General of Indian Affairs,' 17 October 1896. Revenue accruing to the
Band under the 1859 Pennefather Treaties came to be placed in an 'Indian
Land Management Fund' – apparently a borrowing or unilateral extension of
the system already established in other parts of the province by 1846. Monies
from this fund were used for colonization officials' salaries, as well as for the
maintenance of the reserve system. No indications that the fund would be
employed in this manner were given in the Pennefather Treaties. NAC, RG 10,

vol. 2498, file 102,986-1, 'Memorandum to the Honorable the Superintendent of Indian Affairs,' 25 February 1892.

72 NAC, RG 10, vol. 2878, file 177,991-1, pt 0, 'Council of 8 February, 1897.'

73 NAC, RG 10, vol. 2878, file 177,991-1, pt 0, 'Frank Pedley to chiefs,' 20 December 1907; NAC, RG 10, vol. 2572, file 116,426, pt 0, 'Van Abbott to Indian Affairs,' 19 October 1891; 'Reply,' 24 October 1891.

74 NAC, RG 10, vol. 2824, file 168,291-1, 'Correspondence regarding the cession of Whitefish Island.' Whitefish Island contained a Native burying ground. Nevertheless, in March of 1899 four railway companies, the Algoma Central Railway, the Pacific and Atlantic Railroad Company, the Hudson's Bay and Western Railway, and the Ontario and Lake Superior Railroad, became involved in proceedings which led to the expropriation of the island under the Railway Act. Gagiosh's band were relocated in 1905 to Gros Cap, fifteen miles northwest of Sault Ste Marie, where Apequash had previously purchased land.

75 NAC, RG 10, vol. 2572, file 116,426, 'Van Abbott to L. Vankoughnet,' 4 October 1891.

76 NAC, RG 10, vol. 2572, file 116,426, pt 0, 'Chief and Councillors to Wilfrid Laurier,' 20 October 1896.

77 Ibid.

78 NAC, RG 10, vol. 2572, file 116,426, pt 0, 'Hayter Reed to Van Abbott,'   21 November 1896; 'Van Abbott to Reed,' 23 November 1896; 'Petition of Band,' 25 November 1896; 'Reed to Van Abbott,' 2 December 1896. NAC, RG 10, vol. 2572, file 116,426. 'Jarvis Pine to Indian Affairs,' 10 May 1897. Jarvis indicated that goods from merchants were 'exceedingly dear.'

79 NAC, RG 10, vol. 2903, file 185,154, 'Acting Secretary of Indian Affairs to Gervais [Jarvis] Pine,' 30 April 1897.

80 NAC, RG 10, vol. 2903, file 185,154, 'Father Artus on behalf of Jarvis, 1897.'

81 NAC, RG 10, vol. 2903, file 185,154.

82 NAC, RG 10, vol. 1954, file 4472.

83 NAC RG 10, vol. 2572, file 116,426, 'Jarvis Pine to Indian Affairs,' 10 May 1897, and 'Van Abbott to the Deputy Superintendent General of Indian Affairs,' 12 May 1897; Buhkwujjenene, meanwhile, petitioned Ottawa for assistance so that the band could purchase horses and oxen. NAC, RG 10, 2903, file 185,154, 'Buhkwujjenene to Indian Affairs,' 25 February 1897. Merchants refused to supply provisions to the Ojibwa without a government guarantee. NAC, RG 10, vol. 2572, file 116,426, 'Van Abbott to Indian Affairs,' 3 December 1900.

84 NAC, RG 10, vol. 2572, file 116,426, 'Band Council Resolution,' 25 January 1902.

85 NAC, RG 10, vol. 2572, file 116,426, 'J.D. Maclean to Nichols,' 28 January 1902.

86 Ibid.

87 NAC, RG 10, vol. 2572, file 116,426, 'Band Council Minutes,' 8 February 1902; 'Nichols to Indian Affairs,' 4 February 1902; 'Contract with the Harris Tie and Timber Company,' 13 January 1902; 'Chief George [Menissino] Shingwauk and sub chiefs. Regarding Contracts with Burton Brothers. Agreements of 17 September and 14 September 1902'; 'George Chitty to J.D. Maclean [nd]'; 'Contract of the 5th October 1903'; 'Frank Pedley to George Shingwauk, 19 September 1902.'

88 L.O. Lawrence was a colonization officer for the CPR. The Hiawatha play was taken on tour to many centres in Ontario and Michigan (Leslie Monkman, *A Native Heritage*, 127). In 1905, under the auspices of F.W. Burton and 'Mr. Gordon, a musical director of the Hiawatha company,' the players travelled to England and the continent of Europe. Stranded in London, England, for lack of funds, the small group appealed to Ottawa for assistance to return home. Ottawa, even as late as 1905, responded angrily at the thought of Native people being absent from their reserves. To this Nichols replied, 'As to leaving the reserve, they frequently have to do so for a great part of the year to obtain a living and I do not believe that their [exposures with] ... the outside world will be any more detrimental to them than they do [would be] with the outside element nearer home.' NAC, RG 10, vol. 3092, file 285,050, 'Nichols to Indian Affairs,' 23 August 1905. Rights to the Hiawatha play were transferred to the Grand Rapids and Indiana Railway, which staged productions at Round Lake, near Petosky, Michigan. See Lockwood, *Hiawatha: A Play*. George Kabaosa continued to maintain relations with playwrights, scholars, and other visitors to Garden River. In November of 1937 a photograph of him, taken in 1923, appeared in an issue of the *National Geographic*. Stirling, 'America's First Settlers, The Indians.' Sara Stafford meanwhile presented a number of legends which she learned from Buhkwujjenene concerning contests between men and the spirit guardians of the copper and silver deposits near Fort William. Stafford, *The Keeper of the Gate*, 1–20.

89 NAC, RG 10, vol. 2878, file 177,991-1, pt 0, 'Petition of chiefs and sub chiefs,' 27 November 1907.

90 NAC, RG 10, vol. 2878, file 177,991-1, pt 0, 'James W. Curran to Sir Wilfrid Laurier,' 26 October 1906; 'J.D. Maclean to P. Rowland,' 23 June 1910.

91 Regardless of these conditions, a dispute arose concerning whether or not the band would contribute to the rebuilding of a bridge which had washed out on the reserve in 1910. The province argued that the band should be charged at least half the cost of renewing the structure, since the bridge lay on the line of an older road running between Bruce Mines and Sault Ste Marie. Ottawa opposed the province's claim, since the allowance for the older road, known

as the Great North Road, had never been surrendered. NAC, RG 10, vol. 2579, file 177,991-2, pt 0, Reports and correspondence pertaining to the construction of the highway.

CHAPTER 8   Preserving a Distinct Community

1 Jean Friesen and Laura Peers discuss the goals of western Ojibwa negotiators during these years: Friesen, 'Grant Me Wherewith to Make My Living'; Peers, *The Ojibwa of Western Canada, 1780 to 1870*, 203–6.

2 Miller, *Skyscrapers Hide the Heavens*, ch. 11.

3 The term pertains particularly to the administration of Duncan Campbell Scott, deputy superintendent general of Indian Affairs from 1913 to 1932, but would not be out of place in describing the department's policies at least twenty years earlier. Titley, *A Narrow Vision. Duncan Campbell Scott and the Administration of Indian Affairs in Canada*.

4 During the spring *sahsahguhwejegawin*, or spring feast of thanksgiving, a small animal, such as a small dog, might be sacrificed. Flannery, 'The Cultural Position of the Spanish River Indians'; O'Meara, 'Report of a Mission to the Ottawahs and Ojibwas on Lake Huron,' 14. I am indebted to members of the Pine family for their discussions of the relationship between the sun and the 'made tree' or *natig.kan*, used in the *sahsahguhwejegawin* ritual.

5 Numerous reassignments of locations occurred after 1888. See, for example, NAC, RG 10, vol. 2000, file 7320; NAC, RG 10, vol. 2847, file 179,899; NAC, RG 10, vol. 2389, file 79,921; NAC, RG 10, vol. 2000, file 8669; NAC, RG 10, vol. 2892, files 181,609–127, 128, 129, pt 0. These involved members of the Sayer, Jourdain, Nolin, Nootsai, Jones, and Robinson families. William Erskine [Askin] Pine, John Askin, and George Shingwauk [Menissino] all held mining locations in Duncan township.

6 Interview with Fred Pine, Sr, and George Agawa, 20 June 1984.

7 Interview with Bertha Sayers, 20 November 1982.

8 One seminal study investigates the value placed by the Ojibwa on individual initiative and creativity, especially as translated into action in the sphere of women's activities: Buffalohead, 'Farmers, Warriors, Traders: A Fresh Look at Ojibway Women.'

9 Adrian Tanner, *Bringing Home Animals*, 6–13.

10 Interview with Fred Pine, Sr, 20 June 1984.

11 This gravel allegedly was the best grade of stone available between Sault Ste Marie and Sudbury, and was used for building the 'Soo to Sudbury Trunk Road.' NAC, RG 10, vol. 2068, file 10,307, pt 2, 'M. McLennan to J.D. MacLean,' 25 March 1912.

310 Notes to pages 227–30

12 NAC, RG 10, vol. 2068, file 10,307, pt 2, 'George Kabaosa to the Superintendent General of Indian Affairs,' 11 April 1897; 'Band Council Resolutions,' 15 April 1911 and 21 August 1911; 'Thomas G. Wigg to the Superintendent of Indian Affairs,' 21 August 1911.

13 NAC, RG 10, vol. 2068, file 10,307, pt 2, 'A.M. Goodman and D. Galbraith to J.D. MacLean,' 11 December 1911; 'J.D. MacLean to E.W. Beatty, General Solicitor of the C.P.R.,' 20 January 1912; 'Affidavit citing gravel prices from the Stone Lumber Company, St Joseph's Island,' 14 September 1911; 'George Kabaosa to the Superintendent of Indian Affairs,' 15 November 1911.

14 NAC, RG 10, vol. 2068, file 10,307, pt 2, 'J.D. MacLean to E.W. Beatty,' 21 September 1911.

15 The land was expropriated under Section 199 of the Railway Act of 1879. The award, from which there was no appeal, arose from the arbitrators' decision to place a value of $100 per acre on twenty-seven acres and $400 on five acres. This news shook the Garden River band, who thought the matter of trespass would be dealt with exclusively. NAC, RG 10, vol. 2068, file 10,307, pt 2, 'Moses McFadden to Indian Affairs,' 1 October 1913. The Indian Affairs Department, the Garden River band, the CPR, and the Province of Ontario each were represented on the arbitration board. Ramsden was not selected to represent the band, however. While not a leading participant, the Province of Ontario was present since, by the decision arising in 1889 from the case known as the 'St. Catherine's Milling and Lumber Company *vs* the Queen,' the province held proprietary interest in land and resources even on unsurrendered Indian territory. NAC, RG 1, Indian Lands Papers, A-1-7, vols 7 and 8.

16 NAC, RG 10, vol. 3169, file 405,123, pt 0. A complaint was lodged by Alex Wabanosa. AO, Sault Agency Records, Department of Indian Affairs, MS 216. The band was annoyed since a sixty-six-foot land allowance around Echo Bay for landing purposes had been overlooked in future land sales. The last of these allowances, on the Hartman mining location, was eliminated in 1936. NAC, RG 10, vol. 2208, file 42,033. By March 1914, the Garden River band also was well aware of the great amount of unsold or forfeited land existing on both the Garden River and the Batchewana tracts. For lists of such lands, see NAC, RG 10, vol. 2434, file 89,600, pt 16. There were attempts after 1914 to sell these lands at public auction, although many lots still remained unsold.

17 NAC, RG 10, vol. 3053, file 243,190, 'White to Indian Affairs,' 1914; AO, MS 216 (4), Sault Ste Marie Agency Records, Department of Indian Affairs, 28 February 1914.

18 AO, MS 216 (8), Sault Ste Marie Agency Records, Department of Indian Affairs, 1924. *Sault Star*, 23 November 1928.

19 Interview with Norman Jones, 22 September 1982.

20 A.D. McNabb ignored speeches which contravened the policy he was expected to promote. On 9 December 1913, for instance, he wrote, 'All our time was taken up with speeches that amounted to nothing by the usual Orators all about surrenders etc.' When faced with a complaint that Partridge Point had been alienated without a surrender taking place, McNabb retorted on 12 June 1916 that the matter already had been settled 'once and for all.' AO, MS 216 (4) and (5), Sault Ste Marie Agency Records, Department of Indian Affairs, 9 December 1913, and 12 June 1916. Partridge Point had been subdivided into allotments by 1902. MNR, Map 34329/02, 'Plans of Water Lots in the Township of Rankin adjoining the town of Sault Ste Marie. Signed Joseph Cozens, P.L.S., 29 November 1902.'

21 Undeterred by the government's opposition to his protests, George Kabaosa continued to press for the return of the Indian Strip to band control. Kabaosa's struggle on this issue was taken up by Chief Amable Boissoneau in the 1930s. NAC, RG 10, vol. 2463, file 95,805–7, pt 2.

22 NAC, RG 10, vol. 2903, file 185,154, 'Van Abbott to Deputy Superintendent of Indian Affairs,' 12 May 1897. Financing for heavy horses to draw ploughs and timber was arranged on 3 December 1915.

23 The years immediately following the onset of the First World War were ones of extreme hardship for the band. The decline of the Canadian economy, injured by loss of export markets, particularly affected market gardeners and employees of the local veneer mills. Vegetable gardens on the reserve were reduced in size and often became weed infested as families sought alternative livelihoods, including a greater emphasis than previously on hunting, fishing, and snaring rabbits for subsistence. By 1916, however, economic prospects at Garden River had improved owing to the shift in the Canadian economy towards specialized war demands. Canada, *Sessional Papers*, Department of Indian Affairs, No. 27. 7 George V, A 1917, 'Report of A.D. McNabb, Indian Agent for the Ojibbewas of Lake Superior, Eastern Division, Ontario.'

24 AO, MS 216 (6), Sault Ste Marie Agency Records, Department of Indian Affairs.

25 AO, MS 216 (6), Sault Ste Marie Agency Records, 3 May 1917.

26 Canada, Department of Energy, Mines and Resources, Surveys and Mapping Branch, 1916 Plan of Subdivision of Garden River Reserve, Plan 1590. Copy in Garden River Band Office, Garden River. The shifts of property lines on the Garden River reserve may be traced quite easily, since elders remember the positioning of allotments and their respective 'owners' back to 1880. Today, individuals may 'own' lands on which they do not reside. There has been a gravitation away from the waterfront to residence along the highway. Origi-

nally the village lay on the east side of the Garden River, with the missionary establishments and graveyards situated on the west bank. Point St Charles, farther to the west, could flood on occasion, prior to the regulation of the water level in the St Mary's channel by the modern lock system. Around the time of the signing of the Robinson Treaties the only other landmark besides the Garden River village was John Bell's trading establishment at Bell's Point, west of Point St Charles. Then, after 1858, farms belonging principally to members of the Batchewana band arose along the coast of 'French Bay' (so named because many of this band were Métis), lying between Partridge Point and Point St Charles. Members of the Pine family, on the other hand, seasonally resided along the Echo River, on the eastern boundary of the reserve. A list of families living along the Echo River is provided for the year 1914 in NAC, RG 10, vol. 3175, file 437,632.

27 NAC, RG 10, vol. 2366, file 73,850, pt 2, 'A.D. McNabb to Indian Affairs,' 18 December 1913.

28 NAC, RG 10, vol. 2463, file 95,808–7, pt 2.

29 NAC, RG 10, vol. 2367, file 73, 850–2; AO, MS 216 (6), 59, Letterbook, Sault Ste Marie Agency Records, 'Report on Garden River and Batchewana Bands.'

30 Frederick W. Abbott, an American who visited Garden River in 1914, found that 'nearly all these Indians have tuberculosis and do not present a hopeful appearance, though they all live in fairly good houses.' At this time the chief drew an annual salary of $100 from band funds. The Indian agent earned $1,200 a year and had an assistant. Abbott also estimated that about $500 a year accrued to the band from licences on timber sold. Abbott, *The Administration of Indian Affairs in Canada*, 1878.

31 The election for chief took place on 4 March 1916. AO, MS 216 (5), Sault Ste Marie Agency Records.

32 AO, MS 216 (5), Sault Ste Marie Agency Records, 20 December 1916.

33 The term 'clean up' was used by elders in discussions regarding the lack of control the Band had over group membership. External officials would 'clean up' the reserve and in so doing 'hurt everybody.' Author's field notes, 10 August 1982.

34 'Batchewana and Garden River Indians Differ on Who Was Last High Chief,' *Sault Star*, 23 November 1939. Interview with Abe Lesage, 10 August 1982; interview with Bertha Sayers, 20 November 1982.

35 NAC, RG 10, vol. 2068, file 10,307, pt 2, 'A.D. McNabb to J.D. Maclean,' 17 December 1912.

36 AO, MS 216 (5), Sault Ste Marie Agency Records, 4 March 1916.

37 NAC, RG 10, vol. 3175, file 437,632. On 8 June 1915 the Garden River band

awarded John Askin a monthly stipend of five dollars for as long as he lived for 'services he has given the Band for a great number of years.' AO, MS 216 (5), Sault Ste Marie Agency Records.

38 NAC, RG 10, vol. 2406, file 84,041, pt 2, 'Re Proposed Stated Test Case of the Validity of the Robinson Treaties,' 18 December 1916.

CHAPTER 9   A Unifying Vision

1 George Agawa, on being asked in August of 1982 whether the Ojibwa ever felt themselves to be self-sufficient, spoke about what happens where a rival power has severed the link with the source of supply: 'Indians were never self-suffi-cient ... and years ago they nearly killed one another. I'm sorry to say this but my dad's uncle and my dad, they got mad at each other. We pretty near starved. He couldn't catch anything. Fished out in the lake with a line. Nothing. With traps, nothing. They try to catch rabbit ... Nothing. Nothing.'

2 Bishop, 'The Question of Ojibwa Clans.'

3 Service, *Primitive Social Organization.*

4 Cooper, 'Is the Algonquian Family Hunting-ground System Pre-Columbian?'

5 Ibid., 90.

6 Steward, 'The Economic and Social Basis of Primitive Bands.'

7 Jenness, *The Indians of Canada,* 124–5; Leacock, 'The Montagnais "Hunting Territory" and the Fur Trade'; Rogers, 'The Hunting Group–Hunting Terri-tory Complex among the Mistassini Indians.'

8 Speck and Eiseley, 'The Significance of the Hunting Territory Systems of the Algonkian in Social Theory.'

9 Leacock, 'The Montagnais "Hunting Territory" and the Fur Trade'; Murphy and Steward, 'Tappers and Trappers: Parallel Processes in Acculturation.'

10 Rogers, 'Natural-Environmental-Social Organization – Witchcraft: Cree versus Ojibwa – A Test Case.'

11 Hickerson, 'Some Implications of the Theory of Particularity, or "Atomism," of Northern Algonkians'; Dunning, 'Comment on Harold Hickerson's article, "Some Implications of the Theory of Particularity, or 'Atomism,' of Northern Algonkians."'

12 Preston, 'When Leadership Fails: The Basis of a Community Crisis.'

13 Adrian Tanner, *Bringing Home Animals.*

14 Feit, 'The Future of Hunters within Nation States: Anthropology and the James Bay Cree.'

15 Black-Rogers, 'Dan Raincloud: "Keeping Our Indian Way"'; Hedican, *Applied Anthropology in Canada.*

16 J.G.E. Smith, *Leadership among the Southwestern Ojibwa*; J.G.E. Smith, 'Kindred, Clan and Conflict.'

17 Black[-Rogers], 'The Ojibwa Power Belief System.'

18 AO, Irving Papers, MU 1465, 27/31/1 (1), 'Simon J. Dawson to Colonel C. Stewart,' 7 October 1881.

19 NAC, RG 10, vol. 2000, file 8669.

20 NAC, RG 10, vol. 2544, file 111,470.

21 Oquaio was the ancestor of the Agawa family at Goulais Bay. NAC, RG 10, vol. 331, 'Census for 1865 of the Indians belonging to Batchewahnah Band.' Oquaio's sons and daughters were to follow the Roman Catholic faith.

22 AO. Harry D. Blanchard Collection, M Section Papers, 1766–1932, MU 275, 'Information and complaint of Edward Pawyawbedeussung of Garden River vs Kechenebaunewbeu of Thessalon.' Edward Piabetassung was the ancestor of the Edwards family of Sugar Island. Interview with Fred Pine, Sr, 10 August 1982.

23 Berkhofer, Jr, *Salvation and the Savage*, 135.

24 See, for example, Peterson, 'Many Roads to Red River.' In one important cartographical source on Aboriginal communities in the Great Lakes region, Garden River is mentioned as having two distinct villages in its immediate environs, rather than just one, as was the actual case. Helen Hornbeck Tanner, ed., *Atlas of the Great Lakes Indian History*, 132. This mention of two villages, however, may refer to the fact that, after 1859–60, the Batchewana group lived in an enclave just west of the original Garden River village. The Batchewana band's cluster of dwellings, however, was an artificially created community, developed by government fiat, and not a natural one, and it broke down as soon as the Batchewana band could purchase and remove to another land base.

25 Landau, *The Realm of the World*, 59.

26 This desire of the Batchewana band for a land base led to a campaign, launched by the Batchewana chief and council, to have a number of articles published in the *Sault Star* which contended that Nebenagoching's claim to the position of head chief was as good as or better than Shingwaukonse's. In the past, such an argument would have proved redundant, since each chief had been leader of his own distinct band, although Shingwaukonse acted as a spokesman for many bands in the 1840s. These articles reflected tensions prevailing in the 1930s over land rather than a long-standing conflict. Shingwaukonse and Nebenagoching had always worked together. Moreover, Nebenagoching was much younger than Shingwaukonse, being born in 1801, and he followed a Métis lifestyle in owning his own plot at the rapids, whereas Shingwaukonse adhered to an Ojibwa lifestyle. A good example of the kind of

article referred to in the above paragraph is 'Document of 1819 May Reveal Ojibway Chief,' *Sault Star,* 24 December 1934.

27 For an instance in northern Ontario where Ojibwa bands still conform some-what to the stated model, see Sieciechowicz, 'Northern Ojibwa Land Tenure.'

28 Occasionally, individuals at Garden River who included their names or marks on petitions to the government were residents of the community but not regarded by law as status Indians.

29 Field notes, 10 August 1983.

30 This is Shingwaukonse's reputation among some modern-day Ojibwa cultural and political organizations. See, for example, 'From the Anishinabek (The Ojibway, Ottawa, Potowatomi and Algonquian Nations) to the Parliament of the Dominion of Canada,' *Ontario Indian* (December 1982): 25; Sallot and Peltier, *Bearwalk,* 182–4. The Ojibwe Cultural Foundation on Manitoulin in 1995 began a project on the life of Daniel Erskine Pine, Sr (1836–1993), Shingwaukonse's grandson, who, like his father, John Askin, was regarded as a noted leader and healer.

31 Interview with Fred Pine, Sr, 20 June 1983.

32 McCay, 'The Ocean Commons and Community.'

33 AO, Department of Indian Affairs, MS 216 (8), Sault Ste Marie Agency Records, 1924. 'Garden River Trap Rock Deposit to Be Operated – $1,000,000 Plant Assured,' *Sault Star,* 23 November 1928.

34 Interview with ex-councillor Fred Erskine Pine, Sr, 5 January 1984.

Bibliography

Primary Sources

Archival Sources

Anglican Church Archives, Wellington Street, Sault Ste Marie
  Anglican registers from Little Current, Thessalon, and Garden River
Anglican General Synod Archives, Toronto
  Annual Reports of the Society for Converting and Civilizing the Indians and
    Propagating the Gospel among the Destitute
  Canadian Church Magazine 1890
  Journal of the Canadian Church Historical Society 2, no. 2 (1953)
  Reports of the Colonial Church and School Society
  Reports of the Upper Canadian Clergy Society
Anglican Heritage Collection Archives, Bishophurst, Sault Ste Marie
  Church Records and Registers, Algoma District, Ontario (*c.* 1870–1914)
  Reverend Canon Colloton Papers
  Edward F. Wilson, Letterbooks
Archives of Ontario, Toronto (AO)
  Manuscript Groups
    Thomas Gummersall Anderson Papers
    John Askin Papers
    Harry D. Blanchard Collection
    George Brown Papers
    Buell Family Papers
    Claus Family Papers
    Dawson Family Papers
    Frederick Fauquier Papers

Howland Papers

Aemilius Irving Papers

Alexander Macdonell Estate Papers

Anne Macdonell Papers

John ('Spanish John' or John Le Pretre) Macdonell Papers

William MacTavish, Letterbooks, Hudson's Bay Company

F.L. Osler Papers

Jarvis-Powell Papers

John Prince Diaries

Peter Russell Papers

Father Joseph Specht, SJ, Indian Genealogical Records. Status Animarum (Ancien et nouveau) for La Cloche, Coborn and Cockburn Islands, Mississaugi, Wikwemikong, Michipicoten, and Grand Portage

John Strachan Papers

Edward F. Wilson, Autobiography and Family History and Letterbooks

Record Groups

   Canada. District of Algoma. Census, 1861, 1871, 1881

   Canada. Minutes of the Executive Council, State Books (micro.)

   Crown Lands Records (RG1, Series A-1–6)

   Sault Ste Marie Indian Agency Records, Department of Indian Affairs

   Upper Canada Land Petitions (micro.)

Assinins Roman Catholic Mission

   Status Animarum Missionis Sanctissimi Nominis Jesus, Assinins

Bayliss Library, Sault Ste Marie, Michigan

   American Fur Company Records

   Gabriel Franchère Papers

   George Johnston Papers

   John R. Livingston Papers Pertaining to the Treaty of 1836: Testimony of Charlie Shawano Regarding Treaty, and Records of Chieftancy, Sault Ste Marie

   Manuscripts and Record Collection of Steere Special Collections

Bruce Mines Museum Archives

   Indian File (including diverse copies of documents from NAC, RG 10)

Burton Historical Collection, Detroit Public Library, Detroit

   John Askin Papers

   Jean Baptiste Barthe Papers

   Dennison Genealogical collection

   George Johnston Papers, including Census of the Village of Wikwemikong, 20 December 1869

Catholic Archdiocesan Centre Archives, Toronto
  Bishop Alexander Macdonell Papers
  Bishop Michael Power Papers
Church of the Immaculate Heart of Mary, Garden River
  Diarium Missionis S.S. Cordis Jesu, Garden River Church, Residence of the
    Immaculate Heart of Mary, vol. 1, 1868–92
  Early registers
Church of Our Lady of the Sorrows, Goulais Bay
  Early registers
Church of St Isaac Joques, Batchewana Bay
  Early registers
Clarke Library, Central Michigan University, Mount Pleasant, Michigan
  Ancien Régistre des Baptêmes administrés dans la Parroine de Michilimakinac
    commancé le 20 d'avril 1695 (micro. copy)
  Thomas G. Anderson Papers
  Abel Bingham Papers
E.J. Pratt Library, Victoria College, University of Toronto
  Diary of the Reverend James Evans
Great Britain, Colonial Office (CO 42 – micro. at AO)
Hudson's Bay Company Archives, Winnipeg (HBCA). (Hudson's Bay Company
    Records [originals]. Copies on microfilm MG 20, at the National Archives of
    Canada, Ottawa)
  Batchewana Post, Account Book, 1868–9
  La Cloche Post, 1825–63
    a) Post Journals, 1827–36 (HBCA 1M69 and HBCA 1M70)
    b) Correspondence Books, 1827–36 (HBCA 1M183)
    c) Correspondence Inward, 1829–36 (HBCA 217)
    d) Reports on Districts, 1827–35 (HBCA 1M779)
    e) Miscellaneous Items, 1825–54 (HBCA 1M879)
  Michipicoten Post, 1797–1877
    a) Post Journals (HBCA 1M79 and HBCA 1M80)
  Nipigon House, 1792–1876
    a) Post Journals, 1792–1876 (HBCA 1M102 and HBCA 1M103)
    b) Correspondence Inward, 1827 (HBCA 1M377)
  Sault Ste Marie Post, 1818–64
    a) Post Journals, 1825–36 (HBCA 1M131)
    b) Correspondence Books, 1824–53 (HBCA 1M224 and HBCA 1M225)
    c) Correspondence Inward, 1824–61 (HBCA 1M381)
    d) Reports on Districts, 1825–35 (HBCA 1M782)

e) Miscellaneous Items, 1818–64 (HBCA 1M894)
L'Anse, Michigan, Courthouse Records
    Vital Statistics and Land Records
Metropolitan Toronto Public Library, Baldwin Room (MTPL)
    James Givens Papers
    Thomas Gummersall Anderson Papers
    Montreal Mining Company Reports
    Peter Grant, Journal. The Sauteux Indians
    Quebec and Lake Superior Mining Association Reports
    Summons served by Angus Macdonell on George Ironside et al.
Michigan State University, East Lansing, Michigan
    Indian Affairs Records (RG 75 [micro. copies])
    Schoolcraft Papers (micro. copies)
National Archives, Washington, D.C. (NA)
    Henry Rowe Schoolcraft Papers (micro. copies at Michigan State University,
        East Lansing, and the Clarke Library, Michigan Central University, Mount
        Pleasant, Michigan)
National Archives of Canada, Ottawa (NAC)
    Manuscript Groups
        Askin Family Papers
        Church Missionary Society
        Claus Family Papers
        S.P. Hall (drawings and sketches)
        Hargrave Correspondence
        Hudson's Bay Company Records (MG 20 – micro.)
        John Douglas Sutherland Campbell, Marquis of Lorne, Papers
        Macdonell of Collachie Papers
        North West Company Records
        Allan Salt Diaries
    Record Groups
        British Military and Naval Records (RG 8)
        Governor General's Office (RG 7)
        Indian Affairs (RG 10)
        Land Petitions (RG 1 L3)
        Minutes of the Executive Council, 1841–67 (RG 1 E1)
        Orders-in-Council (RG 1 E8)
        Submissions to the Executive Council (RG 1 E5)
Regional Collections, University of Western Ontario, London
    1973 Sarnia Indian Reserve History and a Study of Family Connections
    Plain, (Chief) Alymer

Alexander Vidal Papers
Wawanosh Family Correspondence
Regis College Archives, Catholic Archdiocese, Toronto
  Paquin, Julien. 'Modern Jesuit Missions in Ontario.' Typescript, nd
St John's Anglican Church, Garden River
  Early registers
St Mary's Pro-Cathedral, Sault Ste Marie, Michigan
  Early registers
St Peter's Cathedral Archives, Marquette
  Copy of Guide to the Baptismal Records of La Pointe and L'Anse (copied by
    Fr Bertrand Kotnick from the State Archives of Wisconsin)
Sault Ste Marie, Ontario, Library, Canadiana Section
  Aileen Collins, Chronicle of Francis Roussain, Mamainse, 1805–90
  Garden River File, Scrapbook
  Mrs Dave Bussineau's Journal, 18 May 1910–15 September 1929
  Sault Ste Marie, Ontario, Public Archives
United Church Archives, Victoria University, Toronto
  Annual Reports of the Missionary Society of the Wesleyan Methodist Church,
    1851–88
  The Cyclopedia of Methodism in Canada, vol. 1
  Diaries of Rev. Allan Salt
Zeba Methodist Church, L'Anse
  Methodist Church Society Records

Government Documents and Publications

British Parliamentary Papers. House of Commons, *Sessional Papers*, No. 34. Copies
  or Extracts of Correspondence since 1 April 1835. Correspondence between
  the Secretary of State for the Colonies and the Governors of the British North
  American Provinces Respecting the Indians in Those Provinces. 1839
– House of Commons, *Sessional Papers*, No. 44. Reports from
  Governors of British Possessions in North America, on the Present State of the
  Aboriginal Tribes. 1834.
– Reports from the Select Committee on the Hudson's Bay Company, Together
  with the Proceedings of the Committee, Minutes of the Evidence, Appendix
  and Evidence. London 1857.
Canada (Province of). *Journals of the Legislative Assembly of the United Province of
  Canada*, App. EEE, 'Report on the Affairs of the Indians in Canada.' 1844–5.
– *Journals of the Legislative Assembly of the United Province of Canada*, App. T, 'Report
  on the Affairs of the Indians in Canada.' 1847.

– *Sessional Papers*, No. 63, 'Report No. 18.' 1863.
– *Sessional Papers*, App. 21, 'Report of the Special Commissioners to Investigate Indian Affairs in Canada.' 1858.
Canada. Department of Energy, Mines and Resources, Surveys and Mapping Branch (Toronto Office). 1874 Plan of Garden River Reserve from 1866 Report by George Kirkpatrick.
– 1878 Plan, Report, Fieldnotes and Diary of Check Survey of Mining Locations on Reserve. By J.B. Aubrey.
– 1897 Plan of Duncan Township. By Thomas Byrne.
– 1913 Plan of Trap Rock Location on St. Mary's River. By W.R. White.
– 1916 Plan of Subdivision of Garden River Reserve. By Messrs Lang and Ross.
Canada. *Sessional Papers*, Department of Indian Affairs, 'Report.' A 1907.
– *Sessional Papers*, Department of Indian Affairs, No. 85. 'A Pioneer's Mining Experience on Lake Huron and Lake Superior,' by Walter William Palmer. A 1893.
– *Sessional Papers*, Department of Indian Affairs, No. 27, 7 George V, 'Report of A.D. McNabb, Indian Agent for the Ojibbewas of Lake Superior, Eastern Division, Ontario.' A 1917.
Garden River First Nation. 'Submission to the Royal Commission on the Northern Environment, by Chief Ronald Boissoneau.' Ontario Ministry of Natural Resources 24 November 1977.
Grand Council of Ontario Indians. 'Reports of the Grand Council' (NAC), RG 10). Ontario Ministry of Natural Resources 1869–1885.
'Local History of Garden River.' Report on a student project. Ontario Ministry of Natural Resources 1977.
Ontario. Ministry of Natural Resources, Surveys and Mapping Branch, Peterborough (MNR). 1846 Plan of Town Lots, Sault Ste. Marie, Canada West. By Alexander Vidal.
– 1848 Diary, Notebook and Report. By Alexander Vidal, P.L.S.
– 1848 Map of Mining Locations of River St. Mary and Echo Lake. By Alexander Vidal.
– 1848 Mining Locations on River St. Mary and Echo Lake. Townships of Kehoe and Tarentorus, and the Garden River Indian Reserve. By Alexander Vidal.
– 1851 Instructions to Land Surveyors, Book No. 5.
– 1853 Garden River Indian Reserve No. 14. By J.S. Dennis. 14 May 1853.
– 1853 Report and Diary Covering Various Reserves. Report Dated 14 May 1853. By John Stoughton Dennis. Diary kept from 16 July to 7 November.
– 1854 Current Plans of Indian Reserves. Batcheewaunaung Reserve. By J.W. Bridgland. May 1854.
– 1864 Plan of Shinguiconce Township. By A. Russell, Commissioner. 19 June 1864.

- 1864 Instructions to Land Surveyors. By G.B. Kirkpatrick, P.L.S. Ontario – Crown Surveyors, Book No. 7.
- 1864 Fieldnotes, Book 823, Part 1. By G.B. Kirkpatrick.
- 1866 Plan of Shinguiconse Township. By Messrs Wilson and MacGhee, P.L.S. December 1866.
- 1883 Garden River Indian Reserve No. 14. By J. Cozens. 21 May 1883.
- 1902 Plan of Subdivision of Water Lots, Rankin Township.
- 1921 Garden River Indian Reserve No. 14. By W.R. White. 18 July 1921.

Robinson, Patricia J. 'Research Report on Squirrel Island Indian Land Claim and Garden River Indian Reserve No. 14.' Toronto: Office of Indian Resource Policy, Ontario Ministry of Natural Resources 31 December 1980.

Union of Ontario Indians. 'Lake Superior Claim.' Document chronology sheets, prepared by Mari Naumovski. Ontario Ministry of Natural Resources 1985.

United States. Government Records, National Archives, Washington, D.C. 1801–69 Documents Relating to Negotiations – Ratified and Unratified Treaties with Various Indian Tribes (FM-140 [micro.]).
- 1806–24 Letters Received by the Office of the Secretary of War Relating to Indian Affairs (FM-16 [micro.]).
- 1828 Claims at the Saulte de Ste Marie, within the County of Michilimackinac. House of Representatives, 20th Congress, 1st Session. Committee on Public Lands, 451–87. 2 January 1828.
- 1836 Treaty between the United States of America and the Chiefs and Delegates of the Ottawa and Chippewa Nations of Indians. Concluded 11 March 1836; ratified 27 May 1836.
- 1855 Proceedings of a Council with the Chippeways and Ottawas of Michigan Held at the City of Detroit, by the Hon. George W. Manypenny and Henry C. Gilbert, Commissioners of the United States. 25 July 1855.
- 1870 Annuity Roll of Chippewas and Ottawa of Michigan (FM-2 [micro.]).
- Records of the Bureau of Indian Affairs, Annual Reports (micro. copies at Mills Library, McMaster University).

Washington, D.C. *Treaties between the United States of America and the Several Indian Tribes from 1778 to 1837.* Washington: Langtree and O'sullivan, 1837

Published Primary Sources

Baraga, Frederick. *Answers to the Inquiries Respecting the History, Present Conditions and Future Prospects of the Indian Tribes, by the Revd. Frederick Baraga, Catholic Missionary at the Ance, Michigan, Lake Superior.* 1847.

Blair, E.H., ed. *The Indian Tribes of the Upper Mississippi Valley and Region of the Great Lakes.* 2 vols. Cleveland: Arthur H. Clark 1911.

Boutwell, William. 'Boutwell's Journal.' In Philip Mason, ed., *Schoolcraft's Expedition to Lake Itasca: The Discovery of the Source of the Mississippi*, ix–xxiii. East Lansing: Michigan State University Press 1958.

Bryant, W.C. 'Sketches of Travel.' In *The Prose Writings of W.C. Bryant*, edited by Parke Godwin. Vol. 2. New York: D. Appleton and Co. 1884. Repr. as 'New York and Elsewhere,' ch. 7, letters 587–91, in *The Letters of William Cullen Bryant*, ed. W.C. Bryant II and Thomas G. Voss. Vol. 2 (1836–49), 448–64. New York: Fordham University Press 1977.

Burpee, L.T., ed. *Journals and Letters of Pierre Gaultier de Varennes de La Vérendrye and His Sons*. Toronto: Champlain Society 1927.

Cameron, Duncan. 'A Sketch of the Customs, Manners and Way of Living of the Natives in the Barren Country about Nipigon.' In Masson, ed., *Les bourgeois de la compagnie du Nord-Ouest*, 2:239–65.

Cass, Lewis. *Inquiries Respecting the History, Traditions, Languages, Customs, Religion, etc. of the Indians Living within the United States*. Detroit: Sheldon and Reed 1823.

Coues, E., ed. *New Light on the Early History of the Greater Northwest: The Manuscript Journals of Alexander Henry, Fur Trader of the Northwest Company, and of David Thompson, Official Geographer and Explorer of the Same Company*. Minneapolis: Ross and Haines 1965.

Doughty, A.G., ed. *The Elgin-Grey Papers, 1846–1852*. 4 vols. Ottawa: Patenaude 1937.

Franchère, Gabriel. *Franchère's Journal*. Toronto: Champlain Society 1969.

Glazebrooke, G.P. de T., ed. *The Hargrave Correspondence, 1821–1843*. Toronto: Champlain Society 1947.

Grant, Peter. 'The Saulteux Indians about 1804.' In Masson, ed., *Les bourgeois de la compagnie du Nord-Ouest*, 2:303–66.

Johnston, George. 'Reminiscences.' *Michigan Pioneer and Historical Collections* 12 (1888): 605–8. Original MS in the Bayliss Library, Sault Ste Marie, Michigan.

Johnston, John. 'Autobiographical Letters.' *Michigan Pioneer and Historical Collections* 36 (1902): 53–90.

– 'Memoir of John Johnston.' *Michigan Pioneer and Historical Collections* 36 (1908): 59–60.

– 'An Account of Lake Superior.' In Masson, ed., *Les bourgeois de la compagnie du Nord-Ouest*, 2:135–74.

Landon, Frederick. 'Letters of the Rev. James Evans, Methodist Missionary, Written during His Journey to and Residence in the Lake Superior Region, 1838–39.' *Ontario Historical Society Papers and Records* 28 (1932).

Malhiot, François. 'A Wisconsin Fur Trader's Journal, 1804–1805.' *Wisconsin Historical Society Collections* 19 (1910): 163–233.

Masson, Louis R., ed. *Les bourgeois de la compagnie du Nord-Ouest, 1889–1890*. 2 vols. Quebec: A Coté et Cie 1890. Repr. New York: Antiquarian Press 1960.

Morris, Alexander, ed. *Indian Treaties and Surrenders, from 1680 to 1890*. 3 vols. Ottawa: Brown Chamberlain, Queen's Printer 1891.

Morse, Jedidiah. *Report to the Secretary of War of the U.S. on Indian Affairs, Comprising a Narrative of a Tour in the Summer of 1820*. New Haven: Davis and Force 1822.

Neill, Edward Duffield. 'Memoir of William T. Boutwell, the First Christian Minister Resident among the Indians of Minnesota.' Macalester College Contributions: Department of History, Literature and Political Science, No. 1. St Paul, Minn. 1891.

Nute, Grace Lee, ed. *Documents Relating to the Northwest Missions, 1815–1827*. Published for the Walworth Alvord Memorial Commission, Wisconsin Historical Society. St Paul, Minn. 1942.

Perrault, Jean Baptiste. 'Narrative of the Travels and Adventures of a Merchant Voyageur in the Savage Territories of Northern America Leaving Montreal the 28th of May, 1783 (to 1820).' *Michigan Pioneer and Historical Collections* 37 (1910): 508–619.

Quaife, Milo M., ed. *John Askin Papers*. 2 vols. Detroit: Detroit Public Library, Burton Historical Collection 1928.

Thwaites, R.G., ed. *The Jesuit Relations and Allied Documents*. 73 vols. Cleveland: Burrows Brothers 1896–1901.

– *Baron de Lahontan, Some New Voyages to North America*. 2 vols. Chicago: A.C. McLeary 1905.

Trowbridge, Charles C. 'Journal of Expedition of 1820.' *Michigan History* 23 (1942): 126–48.

Wood, W.C.H., ed. *Select British Documents of the Canadian War of 1812*. 3 vols. Toronto: Champlain Society 1920–8.

Secondary Sources

Abbott, Frederick H. *The Administration of Indian Affairs in Canada*. Washington, D.C.: U.S. Board of Indian Commissioners 1915.

Abel, Kerry, and Jean Friesen, eds. *Aboriginal Resource Use in Canada: Historical and Legal Aspects*. Winnipeg: University of Manitoba Press 1991.

Armstrong, Benjamin G. *Early Life among the Indians*. Ashland, Wis.: Thomas P. Wentworth 1892.

Arthur, M. Elizabeth. 'General Dickson and the Indian Liberating Army in the North.' *Ontario History* 62, no. 3 (1970): 151–62.

Arthur, Elizabeth, ed. *The Thunder Bay District*. Toronto: Champlain Society 1973

Audry, Frances. *By Lake and Forest: The Story of Algoma.* London 1915.

Axtell, James. *The European and the Indian: Essays in the Ethnohistory of Colonial North America.* Toronto: Oxford 1981.

Bald, F.C. *The Seigniory at Sault Ste. Marie.* Sault Ste Marie, Mich. 1937.

Barry, James. *Georgian Bay: The Sixth Great Lake.* Toronto: Clarke, Irwin 1978.

Bayliss, Joseph E., and Estelle Bayliss. *River of Destiny.* Detroit: Wayne State University Press 1955.

Beaven, James. *Recreations of a Long Vacation; Or a Visit to the Indian Missions in Upper Canada.* Toronto: Hand and W. Rousell 1896.

Berkhofer, Robert F., Jr. *Salvation and the Savage: An Analysis of Protestant Missions and American Indians' Response, 1787–1862.* New York: Atheneum [1965] 1976.

Bigsby, J. *The Shoe and the Canoe: Pictures of Travel in the Canadas.* London: Chapman and Hall 1850.

Bishop, Charles A. 'The Question of Ojibwa Clans.' In Cowan, ed., *Actes du vingtième congrès des algonquinistes,* 43–62.

Black[-Rogers], Mary. 'An Ethnoscience Investigation of Ojibwa Ontology and World View.' PhD diss., Stanford University 1967.

– 'The Ojibwa Power Belief System.' In R.D. Fogelson and R.N. Adams, eds, *The Anthropology of Power,* 141–51. New York: Academic Press 1977.

Black-Rogers, Mary. 'Varieties of "Starving": Semantics and Survival in the Sub-Arctic Fur Trade, 1750–1850.' *Ethnohistory* 33, no. 4 (1986): 353–83.

– 'Dan Raincloud: "Keeping Our Indian Way."' In Clifton, ed., *Being and Becoming Indian,* 226–48.

Blackbird, Andrew J. *History of the Ottawa and Chippewa Indians of Michigan.* Harbor Springs, Mich.: Babcock and Darling 1897.

Bleasdale, Ruth. 'Manitowaning: An Experiment in Indian Settlement.' *Ontario Historical Society Papers and Records* 66, no. 3 (1964): 147–57.

Bolt, Clarence. *Thomas Crosby and the Tsimshian: Small Shoes for Feet Too Large.* Vancouver: UBC Press 1992.

Bowden, Henry Warner. *American Indians and Christian Missions: Studies in Cultural Conflict.* Chicago: University of Chicago Press 1981.

Brazier, Marjorie Cahn. *Harps upon the Willows: The Johnston Family of the Old Northwest.* Ann Arbor: Historical Society of Michigan 1993.

Bremer, Richard G. *Indian Agent and Wilderness Scholar: Life of Henry Rowe Schoolcraft.* Mount Pleasant, Mich.: Clarke Historical Library, Central Michigan University Press 1987.

Brown, Jennifer S.H., and Robert Brightman. *'The Orders of the Dreamed': George Nelson on Cree and Northern Ojibwa Religion and Myth, 1823.* Winnipeg: University of Manitoba Press 1988.

Brown, Jennifer S.H., and Laura Peers. 'The Chippewa and Their Neighbours: A

Critical Review.' In Harold Hickerson, *The Chippewa and Their Neighbours: A Study in Ethnohistory*. Rev. ed. Prospect Heights, Ill.: Waveland Press 1988.

Buffalohead, Priscilla. 'Farmers, Warriors, Traders: A Fresh Look at Ojibway Women.' *Minnesota History* 48 (1983): 236–44.

Burden, M.N. *Manitoulin, or Five Years of Church Work among the Ojibway and Lumbermen*. London, Ont.: Simpkin, Marshall, Hamilton, Kent and Co. 1895.

Cadieux, Lorenzo, SJ. *Lettres des nouvelles missions du Canada, 1843–1852*. Montreal: Les éditions Bellarmin 1973.

Capp, Edward H. *The Story of Baw-a-ting, Being the Annals of Sault Ste. Marie, Ontario*. Sault Ste Marie, Ont.: Sault Star Press 1904.

Careless, J.M.S. *Brown of the Globe: The Voice of Upper Canada, 1818–1859*, vol. 1. Toronto: Macmillan 1959.

Carstens, Peter. 'Coercion and Change.' In Richard Ossenberg, ed., *Canadian Society*. Scarborough, Ont.: Prentice-Hall 1971.

Carver, J. *Travels through the Interior Parts of North America, in the Years 1766, 1767, and 1768*. First published 1778. Repr. Toronto: Coles Publishing 1974.

Catlin, George. *Letters and Notes on Manners, Customs, and Condition of the North American Indians*. 2 vols. First published 1844. Repr. New York: Dover Publications 1973.

Cave, Alfred A. 'The Failure of the Shawnee Prophet's Witch-Hunt.' *Ethnohistory* 42, no. 3 (1995): 445–75.

Chance, Mrs James. *In Memoriam: Reminiscence of Our Work among the Indians*. London, Ont.: Holland and Fleming *c.* 1898.

Chapman, Charles H. 'The Historic Johnston Family of the Soo.' *Michigan Pioneer and Historical Collections* 36 (1908): 305–28.

Chaput, Donald. 'Michipicoten Island Ghosts, Copper, and Bad Luck.' *Ontario History* 61, no. 4 (1969): 217–23.

Chute, Janet E. 'A Century of Native Leadership: Shingwaukonse and His Heirs.' PhD diss., McMaster University 1986.

– 'Ojibwa Leadership during the Fur Trade Era at Sault Ste. Marie.' *Papers of the Seventh North American Fur Trade Conference*. East Lansing: University of Michigan Press 1997.

– 'Preservation of Ethnic Diversity at Garden River: A Key to Ojibwa Strength.' In Pentland, ed., *Papers of the Twenty eighth Algonquian Conference*. In press.

– 'Pursuing the Great Spirit's Power: Ojibwa Ways of Revitalizing the Failing World System.' In Pentland, ed., *Papers of the Twenty-sixth Algonquian Conference*, 1996.

Clapp, Alice. 'George Johnston, Indian Interpreter.' *Michigan History* 23 (1939): 350–66.

Clifton, James A. *A Place of Refuge for All Time: Migration of the American Potawatomi into Upper Canada, 1830–1850*. National Museum of Man, Mercury Series No. 28. Ottawa 1975.

- 'Wisconsin Death March: Explaining the Extremes of Old Northwest Indian Removal.' *Transactions of the Wisconsin Academy of Sciences, Arts and Letters* 75 (1987): 1–39.

Clifton, James A., ed. *Being and Becoming Indian: Biographical Sketches of North American Indians.* Chicago: Dorsey Press 1989.

Conway, Thor. *A Remarkable Archaeological Site at Sault Ste. Marie.* Toronto: Ontario Ministry of Culture and Recreation 1975.

Cooper, John M. 'Is the Algonquian Family Hunting-Ground System Pre-Columbian?' *American Anthropologist* 41 (1939): 66–90.

Copway, George. *The Life History and Travels of Kah-ge-ga-gah-bowh (George Copway).* Albany: Wood and Parsons 1847.

- *The Traditional History and Characteristic Sketches of the Ojibway Nation.* London: Charles Gilpin 1850.

Cowan, William, ed. *Actes du huitième congrès des algonquinistes.* Ottawa: Carleton University 1978.

- *Actes du vint-cinquième congrès des algonquinistes.* Ottawa: Carleton University 1994.
- *Papers of the Seventh Algonquian Conference.* Ottawa: Carleton University 1975.
- *Papers of the Eleventh Algonquian Conference.* Ottawa: Carleton University 1980.
- *Papers of the Twenty-third Algonquian Conference.* Ottawa: Carleton University 1992.

Cumberland, F. Barlow. *Catalogue and Notes of the Oronhyatekha Historical Collection.* Toronto: Supreme Court and Independent Order of Foresters *c.* 1910.

Danziger, Edmund. *Chippewa of Lake Superior.* Norman: University of Oklahoma Press 1978.

Densmore, Frances. 'Chippewa Customs.' *Bulletin of the Bureau of American Ethnology* 85 (1929): 1–204.

Devens, Carol. *Countering Colonization: Native American Women and the Great Lakes Missions, 1630–1900.* Berkeley and Los Angeles: University of California Press 1992.

Dewdney, S. *The Sacred Scrolls of the Southern Ojibway.* Toronto and Buffalo: University of Toronto Press 1975.

Dickason, Olive Patricia. *Canada's First Nations: A History of Founding Peoples from Earliest Times.* Toronto: McClelland and Stewart 1993.

Dunning, R.W. 'Comment on Harold Hickerson's Article, "Some Implications of the Theory of Particularity, or 'Atomism,' of Northern Algonkians."' *Current Anthropology* 69 (1967): 331.

Eby, Cecil. *That Disgraceful Affair: The Black Hawk War.* New York: W.W. Norton 1973.

Edmunds, David R. *The Shawnee Prophet.* Lincoln and London: University of Nebraska Press 1983.

Elliot, Charles. *Indian Missionary Reminiscences.* New York: Mason 1837.

Emerson, Angela. 'Research Report on Forfeited Surrendered Lands, Garden River Reserve No. 14.' Toronto: Office of Indian Resource Policy, Ministry of Natural Resources, 1 July 1979.

Feit, Harvey. 'The Future of Hunters within Nation States: Anthropology and the James Bay Cree.' In Eleanor Leacock and Richard Lee, eds, *Politics and History in Band Societies,* 373–412. Cambridge: Cambridge University Press 1982.

Ferri, Camille Pisani. *Prince Bonaparte in America, 1861. Letters from His Aide-de-Camp.* Translated by Georges J. Joyaux. First printed 1861. New York and London: Kennikat Press 1973.

Firth, Raymond. *Symbols, Public and Private.* Ithaca, N.Y.: Cornell University Press 1973.

Flannery, Regina. 'The Cultural Position of the Spanish River Indians.' *Primitive Man* 13 (1940): 1–25.

Fox, George R. 'Isle Royale Expedition.' *Michigan History Magazine* 13 (1929): 309–23.

Fox, John Sharpless, ed. 'Narrative of the Travels and Adventures of a Merchant Voyageur in the Savage Territories of Northern America Leaving Montreal the 28th of May 1783 (to 1820), by Jean Baptiste Perrault.' *Michigan Pioneer and Historical Collections* 37 (1910): 506–619.

Friesen, Jean. 'Grant Me Wherewith to Make My Living.' In Abel and Friesen, eds, *Aboriginal Resource Use in Canada,* 141–55.

'From the Anishinibek (The Ojibway, Ottawa, Potowatomi and Algonquian Nations) to the Parliament of the Dominion of Canada.' *Ontario Indian* (December 1982): 25.

Frost, Frederick. *Sketches of Indian Life.* Toronto: William Briggs 1904.

Fulford, George. 'The Pictographic Account of an Ojibwa Fur Trader.' In Cowan, ed., *Papers of the Twenty-third Algonquian Conference,* 190–233.

Graham, Elizabeth. *Medicine Man to Missionary.* Toronto: Peter Martin Associates 1975.

Grand Portage Chippewa Band. *Kitchi Onigaming.* The Minnesota Chippewa Tribe, Cass Lake, Minn. 1983.

Grant, John W. *Moon of Wintertime: Missionaries and the Indians of Canada in Encounter since 1534.* Toronto: University of Toronto Press 1984.

Griffin, J.B. ed. *Lake Superior Copper and the Indians.* Ann Arbor: University of Michigan Press 1961.

Hall, Anthony. *1784–1984 Celebrating Together? Native People and Bicentennial.* Manitoulin Island: Plowshare Press 1984.

– 'The Red Man's Burden: Land, Law and the Lord in the Indian Affairs of Upper Canada, 1791–1858.' PhD diss., University of Toronto 1984.

Hall, P.J. *Clifford Sifton*, Vol. 1. *The Young Napoleon, 1861–1900*. Vancouver and London: University of British Columbia Press 1981.

Hallowell, A. Irving. 'The Backwash of the Frontier: The Impact of the Indian on American Culture.' In Paul Bohannan and Fred Plog, eds, *Beyond the Frontier*, 317–45. Garden City, N.Y.: Natural History Press 1967.

– 'Ojibwa Ontology, Behaviour and World View.' In Stanley Diamond, ed., *Culture in History*, 19–52. London: Oxford University Press 1960.

– *The Role of Conjuring in Saulteaux Society*. Philadelphia: University of Pennsylvania Press 1942.

Hanson, L.C. 'Chiefs and Principal Men: A Question of Leadership in Treaty Negotiations.' *Anthropologica* 29, no. 1 (1987): 39–60.

Harper, J. Russell. *Krieghoff*. Toronto: University of Toronto Press 1979.

Harper, J. Russell, ed. *Paul Kane: Paul Kane's Frontier, Including Wanderings of an Artist among the Indians of North America*. Published for the Amon Carter Museum, Fort Worth, and the National Gallery of Canada, Ottawa. Toronto: University of Toronto Press 1971.

Harrington, Carolyn Joanne. 'The Influence of Location on the Development of an Indian Community at the Rapids of the St. Mary's River.' MA thesis, University of Western Ontario 1979.

Hedican, Edward. *Applied Anthropology in Canada: Understanding Aboriginal Issues*. Toronto: University of Toronto Press 1995.

– *The Ogoki River Guides: Emergent Leadership among the Northern Ojibwa*. Waterloo, Ont.: Wilfrid Laurier University Press 1986.

Henry, Alexander (the Elder). *Travels and Adventures in Canada and the Indian Territories between the Years 1760 and 1766*. Edited by James Bain. Edmonton: Hurtig 1965.

Hickerson, H. *The Southwestern Chippewa: An Ethnohistorical Study*. American Anthropological Association Memoir 92. Menasha, Wis. 1962.

– *The Chippewa and Their Neighbours: A Study in Ethnohistory*. New York: Holt, Rinehart and Winston 1970.

– 'Some Implications of the Theory of Particularity, or "Atomism," of Northern Algonkians.' *Current Anthropology* 69 (1967): 362–3.

Hodgetts, J.E. 'Indian Affairs: The White Man's Albatross.' Chapter 13 in his *Pioneer Public Service: An Administrative History of the United Canadas, 1841–1867*, 205–25. Toronto: University of Toronto Press 1955.

Hoffman, W.J. 'The Midéwiwin or "Grand Medicine Society" of the Ojibwa.' Washington, D.C., Bureau of American Ethnology, *Seventh Annual Report* (1891): 145–300.

– 'Pictography and Shamanistic Rites of the Ojibwa.' *American Anthropologist* 1 (1888): 209–29.

Hornick, G.L., ed. *The Call of Copper.* Bruce Mines, Ont.: North Shore Printing 1969.

James, Edwin, ed. *A Narrative of the Captivity and Adventures of John Tanner.* First published 1830. Minneapolis: Ross and Haines 1956.

Jameson, Anna. *Winter Studies and Summer Rambles in Canada,* Vol. 3. London: Saunders and Otley 1835.

Jenness, Diamond. *The Indians of Canada.* National Museum of Canada Bulletin 65. Ottawa 1932.

– *The Ojibwa Indians of Parry Island: Their Social and Religious Life.* National Museum of Canada Bulletin 78. Ottawa 1935.

Johnston, Charles M., ed. *The Valley of the Six Nations.* Toronto: Champlain Society 1964.

Jones, Peter. *History of the Ojibway Indians.* London: A.W. Bennett 1861.

– *Life and Journals of Kah-ke-wa-quo-na-by (the Reverend Peter Jones) Wesleyan Missionary.* Toronto: Anson Green 1860.

Jones, W. 'Ojibwa Tales from the North Shore of Lake Superior.' *Journal of American Folklore* 29 (1916): 360–91.

Kellogg, Louis Phelps. *The French Regime in Wisconsin and the Northwest.* Madison: Historical Society of Wisconsin 1924.

Kingsmill, J. *Ojibwa Indians of Lake Huron: Missions and Missionaries.* London: Brown, Green and Longmans 1853.

Kinietz, W. Vernon. *Chippewa Village: The Story of Katikitegon.* Cranbrook Institute of Science Bulletin No. 25. Bloomfield, Mich. 1947.

– *Indians of the Western Great Lakes 1650–1760.* Occasional Contributions of the Museum of Anthropology, University of Michigan, No. 10. First published 1940. Ann Arbor 1965.

Knight, Alan. 'Allan Macdonell and the Pointe au Mines-Mica Bay Affair.' Research Paper for York University. Toronto 1982.

– '"A Charge to Keep I Have." Mission to the Ojibwe at Sault Ste. Marie. St. John's, Garden River 1983.' Typescript.

Kohl, J.G. *Kitchi-Gami: Wanderings around Lake Superior.* First published 1860. Repr. Minneapolis: Ross and Haines 1956.

Krugel, Rebecca. 'Religion Mixed with Politics: The 1836 Conversion of Mang'osid of Fond du Lac.' *Ethnohistory* 37, no. 2 (1990): 126–57.

Lambert, Bernard J. *Shepherd of the Wilderness: A Biography of Bishop Frederic Baraga.* Chicago: Franciscan Herald Press 1974.

Lambert, Richard S., and Paul Pross. *Renewing Nature's Wealth.* Toronto: Hunter Rose/Ontario Department of Lands and Forests 1967.

Landau, Paul Stuart. *The Realm of the World: Language, Gender and Christianity in a Southern African Kingdom.* Social History of Africa Series. Portsmouth, London, and Cape Town: Heinemann, James Currey Ltd, and David Philip Publishers 1995.

Landes, Ruth. 'The Ojibwa of Canada.' In Margaret Mead, ed., *Cooperation and Competition among Primitive Peoples*, 87–127. New York: McGraw-Hill 1937.

– *Ojibwa Religion and the Midéwiwin*. Madison, Milwaukee, and London: University of Wisconsin Press 1968.

– *Ojibwa Sociology*. New York: Columbia University Press 1937.

– 'The Personality of the Ojibwa.' *Character and Personality* 6 (1937): 51–60.

Lanman, Charles. *A Summer in the Wilderness*. New York: Appleton 1847.

Leacock, Eleanor. 'The Montagnais "Hunting Territory" and the Fur Trade.' American Anthropological Association Memoir 78. Menasha, Wis. 1954.

Leighton, Douglas. 'The Compact Tory as Bureaucrat: Samuel Peters Jarvis and the Indian Department, 1837–1845.' *Ontario History* 73 (1981): 40–53.

– 'The Development of Federal Indian Policy in Canada, 1840–1890.' 2 vols. PhD diss., University of Western Ontario 1975.

– 'The Historical Significance of the Robinson Treaties of 1850.' Paper presented at the Canadian Historical Association Conference, University of Ottawa 9 June 1981.

– 'The Manitoulin Incident of 1863: An Indian-White Confrontation in the Province of Canada.' *Ontario Historical Society Papers and Records* (1977): 113–24.

Leslie, John F. 'The Bagot Commission: Developing a Corporate Memory for the Indian Department.' Canadian Historical Association, *Historical Papers* (1982): 31–52.

Lewis, Randall M. 'The Manitoulin Letters of the Rev. Charles Crosbie Brough.' *Ontario Historical Society Papers and Records* 48 (1956): 63–80.

Lockwood, C.I. *Hiawatha: A Play*. Held at Wayagamug or Round Lake, near Petosky, Mich. Issued by General Passenger Department, Grand Rapids and Indiana Railway, Grand Rapids, Mich. 1912.

Long, John. *Voyages and Travels of an Indian Interpreter and Trader*. First published 1791. Repr. Toronto: Coles Canadiana Collection 1979.

McCay, Bonnie J. 'The Ocean Commons and Community.' *Dalhousie Review* (Fall/ Winter 1994–5): 310–39.

MacDonald, Graham Alexander. 'The Saulteur-Ojibwa Fishery at Sault Ste. Marie, 1640–1920.' MA thesis, University of Waterloo 1977.

McElroy, Robert, and Thomas Riggs, eds. *The Unfortified Boundary: A Diary of the First Survey of the Canadian Boundary Line from St. Regis to Lake of the Woods by Major Joseph Delafield*. New York 1943.

McKenney, Thomas L. *Sketches of a Tour to the Lakes*. First printed 1827. Minneapolis: Ross and Haines 1972.

McKenney, Thomas L., and James Hall, eds. *History of the Indian Tribes of North America*. Philadelphia: Rice and Co. 1844.

Maclean, Hugh D. 'An Irish Apostle and Archdeacon in Canada.' *Journal of the Canadian Church Historical Society* 15, no. 3 (1973): 50–67.

McNab, David. 'Herman Merivale and Colonial Office Indian Policy in the Mid-Nineteenth Century.' Toronto: Ministry of Natural Resources 1981.

Marano, Lou. 'Windigo Psychosis: The Anatomy of an Emic-Etic Confusion.' *Current Anthropology* 23, no. 4 (1982): 385–97.

Mason, Philip, ed. *Schoolcraft's Expedition to Lake Itasca.* East Lansing: Michigan State University Press 1953.

Miller, J.R. *Shingwauk's Vision: A History of Native Residential Schools.* Toronto: University of Toronto Press 1996.

– *Skyscrapers Hide the Heavens: A History of Indian-White Relations in Canada.* Toronto: University of Toronto Press 1989.

Millman, Thomas R. 'Frederick Augustus O'Meara.' *Dictionary of Canadian Biography,* vol. 11, 552–4. Toronto: University of Toronto Press 1982.

Monkman, Leslie. *A Native Heritage: Images of the Indian in English-Canadian Literature.* Toronto: University of Toronto Press 1981.

Morantz, Toby. 'The Fur Trade in the Eighteenth Century.' In Daniel Francis and Toby Morantz, eds, *Partners in Furs: A History of the Fur Trade in Eastern James Bay, 1600–1870.* Montreal and Kingston: McGill-Queen's University Press 1983.

– 'James Bay Trading Captains of the Eighteenth Century: New Perspectives on Algonquian Social Organization.' In Cowan, ed., *Actes du huitième congrès des algonquinistes,* 77–89.

Morgan, Lewis Henry. *The American Beaver and His Works.* Philadelphia: J.B. Lippincott and Co. 1868.

– *Ancient Society.* Chicago: Charles H. Kerr 1877.

Murphy, Robert, and Julian H. Steward. 'Tappers and Trappers: Parallel Processes in Acculturation.' *Economic Development and Cultural Change* 4 (1956): 335–55.

Nelles, H.V. *The Politics of Development: Forests, Mines and Hydro-electric Power in Ontario, 1849–1914.* Toronto: Macmillan of Canada 1972.

Nock, David Allan. *A Victorian Missionary and Canadian Indian Policy: Cultural Synthesis vs Cultural Replacement.* Waterloo, Ont.: Wilfrid Laurier University Press 1988.

– 'The White Man's Burden: A Portrait of E.F. Wilson, Missionary in Ontario, 1868–1885.' 2 vols. MA thesis, Carleton University 1972.

Noel, Dyck. *What Is the Indian 'Problem'? Tutelage and Resistance in Canadian Indian Administration.* St John's: Institute of Social and Economic Research, Memorial University of Newfoundland 1991.

Nute, Grace Lee. 'The American Fur Company's Fishing Enterprises on Lake Superior.' *Mississippi Valley Historical Review* 12, no. 4 (1926): 483.

- *Lake Superior.* Indianapolis: Bobbs Merrill 1944.
O'Meara, F.A. 'Report of a Mission to the Ottawahs and Ojibwas on Lake Huron.' In *Missions to the Heathen,* No. VI. London: Society for the Propagation of the Gospel 1846.
- 'Second Report of a Mission to the Ottawahs and Ojibwas on Lake Huron.' *Missions to the Heathen,* No. XIII. London: Society for the Propagation of the Gospel 1848.
Osborn, A.C. 'The Migration of Voyageurs from Drummond Island to Penetanguishene in 1828.' *Ontario Historical Society Papers and Records* 3 (1907): 123–66.
Osborn, Chase, and Stellanova Osborn. *Schoolcraft, Longfellow and Hiawatha.* Lancaster, Pa.: Jacques Cattel Press 1942.
Owram, Douglas. *Promise of Eden: The Canadian Expansionist Movement and the Idea of the West, 1856–1900.* Toronto: University of Toronto Press 1980.
Pannekoek, Frits. 'Some Comments on the Social Origins of the Riel Protest of 1869.' In A.L. Lussier, ed., *Riel and the Métis,* 66–83. Winnipeg: University of Winnipeg Press 1979.
Peers, Laura. *The Ojibwa of Western Canada, 1780 to 1870.* Winnipeg: University of Manitoba Press 1994.
Pentland, David, ed. *Papers of the Twenty-sixth Algonquian Conference.* Winnipeg: University of Winnipeg 1995.
- *Papers of the Twenty-eighth Algonquian Conference.* Winnipeg: University of Winnipeg 1996.
Peterson, Jacqueline. 'Many Roads to Red River: Métis Genesis in the Great Lakes Region, 1680–1815.' In Peterson and Brown, eds, *New Peoples,* 37–71.
- 'Prelude to Red River: A Social Portrait of the Great Lakes Métis.' *Ethnohistory* 25, no. 1 (1978): 41–67.
Peterson, Jacqueline, and Jennifer S. Brown, eds. *The New Peoples: Being and Becoming Métis in North America.* Winnipeg: University of Manitoba Press 1985.
Petoskey, Ella. 'Chief Petoskey: A Brief Sketch by His Grand-Daughter, Ella Petoskey.' *Michigan Historical Magazine* 13 (1929): 442–8.
Pitezal, John. *Life of Peter Marksman.* Cincinnati: Western Book Concern 1901.
- *Lights and Shades of Missionary Life.* Cincinnati: Western Book Concern 1862.
Preston, Richard. 'Reticence and Self-expression: A Study of Style in Social Relationships.' In Cowan, ed., *Papers of the Seventh Algonquian Conference,* 450–94.
- 'When Leadership Fails: The Basis of a Community Crisis.' *The Northland* 24, no. 3 (1968): 7–9.
Prucha, Francis P. *Lewis Cass and American Indian Policy.* Detroit: Detroit Historical Society 1966.
Radin, Paul. 'An Introductive Inquiry in the Study of Ojibwa Religion.' *Ontario Historical Society Papers and Records* 12 (1914): 210–18.

Rajnovich, Grace. *Reading Rock Art: Interpreting the Indian Rock Paintings of the Canadian Shield.* Toronto: National Heritage / Natural History Inc. 1994.

Ray, Arthur J. *Indians in the Fur Trade: Their Role as Hunters, Trappers and Middlemen in the Lands South of Hudson Bay, 1660–1870.* Toronto: University of Toronto Press 1974.

Ray, Arthur J., and Donald Freeman. *'Give Us Good Measure': An Economic Analysis of Relations between the Indians and the Hudson's Bay Company before 1763.* Toronto: University of Toronto Press 1978.

Rea, J.E. *Bishop Alexander Macdonell and the Politics of Upper Canada.* Ontario Historical Society, Research Paper No. 4. Ottawa 1974.

Read, Colin Frederick. 'John Stoughton Dennis.' *Dictionary of Canadian Biography,* vol. 11, 244–6. Toronto: University of Toronto Press 1982.

Redsky, James. *Great Leader of the Ojibway: Mis-quona-queb.* Toronto: McClelland and Stewart 1972.

Reid, C.S. *Mansion in the Wilderness: The Archaeology of the Ermatinger House.* Sault Ste Marie, Ont.: Ministry of Culture and Recreation 1977.

Rezek, Antoine I. *History of the Diocese of Sault Ste. Marie and Marquette.* 2 vols. Houghton, Mich. 1906.

Richardson, Boyce. 'Kind Hearts or Forked Tongues?' *The Beaver,* Outfit 67, no. 1 (1987): 16–41.

Richardson, Sir John. *Journal of a Boat Voyage through Rupert's Land to the Arctic Sea.* New York: Harper Brothers 1854.

Ritzenthaler, R., and O. Ritzenthaler. *Woodland Indians of the Western Great Lakes.* Garden City, N.Y.: Natural History Press 1970.

Rogers, Edward S. 'The Algonquian Farmers of Southern Ontario.' In Rogers and Smith, eds, *Aboriginal Ontario,* 122–66.

– *The Hunting Group-Hunting Territory Complex among the Mistassini Indians.* National Museums of Canada Bulletin 195. Ottawa 1963.

– 'Leadership among the Indians of Eastern Subarctic Canada.' *Anthropologica* 7 (1965): 263–84.

– 'Natural-Environmental Social Organization – Witchcraft: Cree versus Ojibwa – A Test Case.' In David Damas, ed., *Contributions to Anthropology: Ecological Essays,* 24–39. National Museums of Canada Bulletin 230. Ottawa 1969.

Rogers, Edward S., and Mary Black-Rogers. 'Adoption of Patrilineal Surname System by Bilateral Northern Ojibwa: Mapping the Learning of an Alien System.' In Cowan, ed., *Papers of the Eleventh Algonquian Conference,* 198–230.

– 'Who Were the Cranes? Groups and Group Identity Names in Northern Ontario.' In Margaret Hanna, ed., *Approaches in Algonquian Archaeology,* 147–88. Proceedings of the Thirteenth Annual Conference of the University of Calgary Archaeological Association. Calgary: University of Calgary Press 1982.

Rogers, Edward S., and Donald B. Smith, eds. *Aboriginal Ontario: Historical Perspectives on the First Nations.* Toronto: Dundurn Press 1994.

Rogers, Edward S., and James G.E. Smith. 'Cultural Ecology in the Canadian Shield Sub-arctic.' Paper presented at the IXth International Congress of Anthropological and Ethnological Sciences. Chicago 1973.

Rogers, Edward S., and Flora Tobobondung. *Parry Island Farmers: A Period of Change in the Way of Life of the Algonkians of Southern Ontario.* In *Contributions to Canadian Ethnology.* National Museum of Man, Mercury Series No. 31. Ottawa 1975.

Rowe, Sophia. 'Anderson Record from 1699–1896.' *Ontario Historical Society Papers and Records* 6 (1905): 109–35.

Salisbury, Richard. 'Transactions or Transactors? An Economic Anthropologist's View.' In B. Kapferer, ed., *Transaction and Meaning: Directions in the Anthropology of Exchange and Symbolic Behavior,* 41–59. Philadelphia: Institute for the Study of Human Issues 1976.

Sallot, Lynne, and Tom Peltier. *Bearwalk.* Markham, Ont.: Musson Book Co. 1977.

Schoolcraft, Henry Rowe. *Algic Researches, Comprising Inquiries Respecting the Mental Characteristics of the North American Indians.* New York: Harper and Brothers 1839.

– *Historical and Statistical Information Respecting the History, Condition and Prospects of the Indian Tribes of the United States.* 6 vols. Philadelphia: J.B. Lippincott and Grambo 1851–7.

– *The Indian in His Wigwam, Or Characteristics of the Red Race in America.* Buffalo: Derby and Hudson 1848.

– *The Literary Voyageur, or Muzzeniegan.* Edited by Philip Mason. Detroit: Wayne State University Press 1962.

– *The Myth of Hiawatha.* Philadelphia: J.B. Lippincott and Co. 1856.

– *Narrative Journal through the Northwestern Region of the United States, Extending from Detroit, through the Great Chain of American Lakes to the Sources of the Mississippi River.* Albany: E. and E. Hosford 1821.

– *Personal Memoirs of a Residence of Thirty Years with the Indian Tribes on the American Frontier A.D. 1812 to A.D. 1842.* Philadelphia: Lippincott, Grambo and Co. 1851. Repr. New York: Arno Press 1975.

– *The Red Race in America.* New York: W.H. Graham 1848.

– *Summary Narrative.* Edited by Mentor L. Williams. East Lansing: Michigan State University Press 1953; repr. New York: Kraus 1973.

Schull, Joseph. *Edward Blake: Leader in Exile, 1881–1912.* Toronto Macmillan of Canada 1976.

Schenck, Theresa. 'Identifying the Ojibwa.' In Cowan, ed., *Actes du vingt-cinquième congrès des algonquinistes,* 395–405.

Service, Elman R. *Primitive Social Organization: An Evolutionary Perspective.* New York: Random House 1971.

Sheriden, Warrick W. 'Henry Rowe Schoolcraft and the Administration of Indian Affairs in Michigan, 1822–41.' PhD diss., University of Chicago 1955.

Shingwauk, Augustine. *Little Pine's Journal: The Appeal of a Christian Chippeway Chief on Behalf of His People.* First published Toronto 1872. Facsimile edition, Sault Ste Marie, Ont., Shingwauk Reunion Committee 1991.

Shingwauk Project. 'From Teaching Wigwam to Shingwauk University.' Algoma University College Founders' Day, 1992. Sault Ste Marie, Ont: Algoma University College 1992.

Sieciechowicz, Krystyna. 'Northern Ojibwa Land Tenure.' *Anthropologica* 28, nos 1–2 (1986): 187–200.

Simpson, Sir George. *Narrative of a Journey Round the World during the Years 1841 and 1842.* Vol. 1. London: George Colborn 1847.

Slight, Benjamin. *Indian Researches; Or Facts Concerning the North American Indians; Including Notices of Their Present State of Improvement in Their Social, Civil and Religious Condition, with Hints for Their Future Advancement.* Montreal: J.E.L. Miller 1844.

Smith, Donald B. 'The Mississauga, Peter Jones and the White Man: The Algonkians' Adjustment to the Europeans on the North Shore of Lake Ontario to 1860.' PhD diss., University of Toronto 1975.

– *Sacred Feathers: The Reverend Peter Jones (Kahkewaquonaby) and the Mississauga Indians.* Toronto: University of Toronto Press 1987.

Smith, J.G.E. 'Kindred, Clan and Conflict: Continuity and Change among the Southwestern Ojibwa.' Unpublished MS *c.* 1974.

– 'Leadership among the Indians of the Northern Woodlands.' In Robert Hinshaw, ed., *Currents in Anthropology: Essays in Honor of Sol Tax,* 306–24. The Hague: Mouton 1979.

– *Leadership among the Southwestern Ojibwa.* National Museum of Canada, Publication in Ethnology No. 7. Ottawa 1973.

Speck, Frank. 'The Family Hunting Territory as the Basis of Algonkian Society.' *American Anthropologist* 17 (1915): 289–305.

Speck, Frank G., and Loren C. Eiseley. 'The Significance of the Hunting Territory Systems of the Algonkian in Social Theory.' *American Anthropologist* 41 (1939): 269–80.

Stafford, Sara. *The Keeper of the Gate; or the Sleeping Giant of Lake Superior.* Buffalo: The White-Evans-Penfold Co. 1903.

Stanley, George F.C. *The War of 1812: Land Operations.* Canadian War Museum Historical Publication No. 18. Toronto and Ottawa: Macmillan of Canada / National Museum of Man 1983.

Steward, Julian H. 'The Economic and Social Basis of Primitive Bands.' In R.H. Lowie, ed., *Essays in Honor of A.L. Kroeber,* 331–50. Berkeley: University of California Press 1936.

Stirling, Matthew. 'America's First Settlers, the Indians.' *National Geographic* (November 1937): 549.

Strachan, John. *Journal of a Visitation to the Western Portion of His Diocese.* London: Society for the Propagation of the Gospel 1846.

Surtees, Robert J. 'Land Cessions, 1763–1830.' In Rogers and Smith, eds, *Aboriginal Ontario,* 92–121.

Swainson, Donald. 'Allan Macdonell.' *Dictionary of Canadian Biography,* vol. 11, 552–4. Toronto: University of Toronto Press 1982.

Tanner, Adrian. *Bringing Home Animals: Religious Ideology and Mode of Production of the Mistassini Cree Hunters.* Institute of Social and Economic Research, Social and Economic Study No. 23. St John's, Nfld 1979.

Tanner, Helen Hornbeck, ed. *Atlas of Great Lakes Indian History.* Cartography by Miklos Pinther. Norman and London: University of Oklahoma Press 1987.

Telford, Rhonda. '"The Sound of the Rustling of the Gold Is under My Feet Where I Stand; We Have a Rich Country": A History of Aboriginal Mineral Resources in Ontario.' PhD diss., University of Toronto 1996.

Thomas, Nathan G. 'The Second Coming in the Third New England: The Millennial Impulse in Michigan, 1830–1860.' PhD diss., Michigan State University 1965.

Thomas, Robert K. 'Afterword.' In Peterson and Brown, eds, *The New Peoples,* 243–51.

Titley, E. Brian. *A Narrow Vision: Duncan Campbell Scott and the Administration of Indian Affairs in Canada.* Vancouver: UBC Press 1986.

Unger, Robert. 'Lewis Cass: Indian Superintendent of the Michigan Territory, 1813–1831. A Survey of Public Opinion as Reported by the Newspapers of the Old Northwest Territory.' PhD diss., Ball State University, Ind. 1967.

Van Dusen, C. (Enemikeese), ed. *The Indian Chief: An Account of the Labours, Losses, Sufferings, and Oppression of Ke-zig.ko.e.ne-ne (David Sawyer).* First published 1867. Repr. Toronto: Coles Publishing 1974.

Van Gennep, Arnold. *The Rites of Passage.* Translated by M.B. Vizedom and G.L. Caffee. London: Routledge and Kegan Paul 1909.

Verwyst, P. Chrysostom. *Life and Labors of the Rt. Rev. Frederic Baraga.* Milwaukee: M.H. Wiltzius and Co. 1900.

Waddilove, William. *The Stewart Missions.* London: J. Hatchard and Son 1838.

Waisberg, Leo. 'The Ottawa: Traders of the Upper Great Lakes.' MA thesis, McMaster University 1977.

Warren, William. 'History of the Ojibwa Indians.' *Minnesota Historical Collections* 5 (1885): 21–294.

– *History of the Ojibway Nation.* Minneapolis: Ross and Haines Inc. 1970.

Washburn, W.W., ed. *The American Indian and the United States: A Documentary History.* New York: Random House 1973.

Weiler, John M. 'Michipicoten: Hudson's Bay Company Post, 1821–1904.' In David Skene Melvin, ed., *Three Heritage Studies.* Toronto: Ontario Ministry of Culture and Recreation, Historical Planning and Research Branch 1980.

White, Bruce M. *The Regional Context of the Removal Order of 1850: A Report Prepared for the Mille Lacs Band of Ojibwe, Mille Lacs, Minnesota.* December 1993.

White, Richard. *The Middle Ground: Indians, Empires and Republics in the Great Lakes Region, 1650–1815.* Cambridge: Cambridge University Press 1991.

Williams, Mentor L., ed. *Schoolcraft's Indian Legends.* East Lansing: Michigan State University Press 1956.

Wilson, Edward F. *Missionary Work among the Ojibway Indians.* London: Society for Promoting Christian Knowledge 1886.

Winchell, N.H. *The Aborigines of Minnesota.* St Paul, Minn.: Minnesota Historical Society 1911.

Wightman, Nancy M., and W. Robert Wightman. 'The Mica Bay Affair: Conflict on the Upper-Lakes Mining Frontier, 1840–1850.' *Ontario History* 83 (1991): 193–208.

Wise, S.F. 'The American Revolution and Indian History.' In John S. Moir, ed., *Character and Circumstance,* 182–200. Toronto: Macmillan Co. 1970.

– 'The Indian Diplomacy of John Graves Simcoe.' *Canadian Historical Association Report,* 36–44. 1953.

Zaslow, Morris. 'Edward Barnes Borron, 1820–1915: Northern Pioneer and Public Servant Extraordinaire.' In F.A. Armstrong et al. eds, *Aspects of Nineteenth-Century Ontario: Essays Presented to James J. Talman,* 297–311. Toronto: University of Toronto Press 1974.

Illustration Credits

Algoma Art Gallery: Garden River water-colour, photograph by Michael Burtch

Archives of Ontario: Vidal and Anderson's map, Aemilius Irving Papers, MU 1465; Métis near Sault rapids; John Driver's affidavit, Irving Papers; St John's Anglican Church, Acc. 9538 s. 15506; Longfellow window, Acc. 9538 s. 15505; Hiawatha pageant, Acc. 10748 s. 16351; George Kabaosa, Acc. 10748 s. 16361

Centre for Northern Studies, Lakehead University: map showing Garden River and mining locations, from Janet Chute, 'Pursuing the Great Spirit's Plan,' in *Social Relations in Resource Hinterlands*, Papers of the 27th Annual Meeting of the Western Association of Sociology and Anthropology, vol. 1, ed. Thomas W. Dunk (Thunder Bay, 1991), 184

Clarke Historical Library, Central Michigan University: Shingabaw'osin

D.B. Weldon Library, University of Western Ontario: 1847 affidavit, Alexander Vidal Papers, J.J. Talman Regional Collection

Dover Publications, Inc.: Kaygayosh, line drawing by George Catlin. George Catlin, *Letters and Notes on Manners, Customs and Condition of the North American Indians* (New York, 1973)

National Archives of Canada: *dodemic* marks, RG 10, vol. 184; Ojibwa petition, RG 10, vol. 198, pt 1:1162989; Lord Lorne, C-012836; western boundary of Garden River Reserve, RG 10, vol. 2048, file 9266

Royal Ontario Museum: war club, 69 ETH 270 HD 5826; tomahawk pipe 76 ETH 507 HD 5854; Buhkwujjenene, courtesy of the National Portrait Gallery

Sault Ste Marie Public Library: Garden River gravehouse

Shingwauk Project, Algoma University: Shingwaukonse, circa 1849; first Anglican Church, from James Beaven, *Recreations of a Long Vacation, or a Visit to the Indian Missions in Upper Canada* (Toronto, 1896), 128; Robinson, Shingwaukonse, and Nebenagoching; Ogista; John Askin

Index

Mishiquongai (French River and, later,
    Manitoulin Island chief), 134, 140
Mishkeash (Goulais Bay subchief;
    brother to Apequash and Gagiosh),
    164–6, 173–4, 205
Misquabenokay (Shingwaukonse's
    son-in-law), 15, 72
Missegan family, 72
missionary role, 116
Mississauga Ojibwa, 26
Mississauga, place on the north shore
    of Lake Huron, 202
Mistassini Cree, 225, 240
Mitchell, Andrew, 66
Mocomanish (Ottawa chief), 77, 146
modes of interaction, Ojibwa, 6–7,
    17–18
Moffatt, Hon. Peter, 111
Montagnais of Quebec (Innu), 239
Montreal Mining Company, 111
Montreal River, 224
Morgan, Lewis Henry, 291n2
Morpeth, Lord, 98
Muckedayoquot (Black Cloud; father
    of John Kabaosa and Waubmama),
    68, 191, 258n4
Muckedaypenasse (Blackbird; La
    Pointe chief), 101–2, 153
Munising, Michigan, 15
Munsey, 26
Murphy, Robert, 240
Murray, Alexander, 115
Murray, Sir George, 44
Muskoka Ojibwa bands, 177
Muskoka region, 202

Nahwahquashkum (Shingwaukonse's
    son), 87–8
Nanabush (Great Hare, culture hero),
    19

narrows, of Lake Simcoe, 45, 47
'national policy,' 198
Nawgichigomee (Centre of the Lake;
    grandson of Great Crane), 50,
    258n4
Ne.ban.a.aw.bay, 266n83. *See also*
    Nebenagoching
Nebenagoching (Joseph Sayers; Sault
    Ste Marie and Batchewana chief),
    30, 64–8, 72–3, 111–12, 123, 127,
    132, 136, 144, 153–4, 161, 164–6,
    173–6, 178–9, 183–6, 195, 199,
    204–5, 211, 232, 249, 251, 266n83,
    266n84; demands William Van
    Abbott's resignation from office,
    214; obituary notice, 262–3n40
Nebish (or Neebish) rapids, 41
Neokema, 101
New Ontario, 230
Newton, John, 291n92
Nezhepenasse (or Single Bird; Kee-
    wenaw chief), 48
Niagara-on-the-Lake, 149, 192
Niagara region, 28, 149
Nichols, William, 218–19, 220, 226–7
Nipigon, 141
Nipissing, 202
nodal core group (concept), 13, 241
Nolin, Jean Baptiste, 292n62
Nolin family, Garden River, 195,
    224
North West Company, 61, 111, 134,
    163–5n63
Northwest Rebellion (1885), 105
Nourse, William, 53, 60
Nowquagabow (Nahwahquakahbo,
    Standing in the Centre), 111, 115,
    123, 133, 135
Nowquagezick (Noon Day), Joseph,
    213–14